Writing Real Programs in DCL

Digital Press Editorial Board

Thomas F. Gannon, Acting Chair
Scott E. Cutler
Donald Z. Harbert
William Laing
Richard F. Lary
Alan G. Nemeth
Robert M. Supnik

Writing Real Programs in DCL

Paul C. Anagnostopoulos
Windfall Software

Steve Hoffman
Compaq Computer Corporation

dp
Digital Press

Boston Oxford Johannesburg Melbourne New Delhi Singapore

Copyright © 1999 by Butterworth-Heinemann

℞ A member of the Reed Elsevier group

All rights reserved.

Digital Press™ is an imprint of Butterworth-Heinemann.

All trademarks found herein are the property of their respective owners.

Credits appear on page 467.

No part of this publication may be reproduced, stored in a retrieval system, or transmitted in any form or by any means, electronic, mechanical, photocopying, recording, or otherwise, without the prior written permission of the publisher.

Recognizing the importance of preserving what has been written, Butterworth-Heinemann prints its books on acid-free paper whenever possible.

Butterworth-Heinemann supports the efforts of American Forests and the Global ReLeaf program in its campaign for the betterment of trees, forests, and our environment.

Library of Congress Cataloging-in-Publication Data

Anagnostopoulos, Paul C., 1953–
    Writing real programs in DCL / Paul C. Anagnostopoulos and Steve Hoffman, — 2nd ed.
       p. cm.
    Rev. ed. of: VAX/VMS—writing real programs in DCL. Bedford, Mass. Digital Press, ©1989.
    Includes index.
    ISBN 1-55558-191-9 (alk. paper)
    1. VAX/VMS. 2. DCL (Computer program language) I. Hoffman, Steve (Stephen Richard), 1962– . II. Anagnostopoulos, Paul C., 1953– VAX/VMS—writing real programs in DCL. III. Title.
QA76.76.063A48   1998
005.4′449—dc21   98-44308
                                                  CIP

British Library Cataloguing-in-Publication Data

A catalogue record for this book is available from the British Library.

The publisher offers special discounts on bulk orders of this book.
For information, please contact:

Manager of Special Sales
Butterworth-Heinemann
225 Wildwood Avenue
Woburn, MA 01801-2041
Tel: 781 904-2500
Fax: 781 904-2620

For information on all Butterworth-Heinemann publications available, contact our World Wide Web home page at: http://www.bh.com

10 9 8 7 6 5 4 3 2

Printed in the United States of America

PCA   To *my mother*
          We love you now and always

SH   To Kelly Hoffman,
          and to the Honorable Marie Hoffman

I don't want to be another victim of fashion
I don't want to see my name in the paper each day
Leave that to the young Turks
They're more handsome and dashing
Posing for paparazzi down Laguna way

Down in the metro I feel the world start to multiply
Bastille, rubber wheels, spiked heels, subterranean lullaby
Met an African prancer, a hemisphere dancer
Spied the ghost of Brassens
We smiled at the secret we shared
And I hid it like contraband

Quietly making noise, making noise
Starts with kindergarten toys
Not too soft, not too loud
Just enough to draw a crowd
Quietly, quietly, quietly making noise

—Jimmy Buffett
Michael Tschudin

Contents

List of Tables	xv
Preface to the First Edition	xvii
Acknowledgments for the First Edition	xix
Preface to the Second Edition	xxi
Acknowledgments for the Second Edition	xxiii

1 Introduction   1

    1.1   Choosing to Use DCL   2
    1.2   The Application Domain for DCL   3
    1.3   A Word of Caution   6
    1.4   How to Use This Book   6

2 A Review of OpenVMS Concepts   11

    2.1   An Interactive Session   11
    2.2   The DCL Command Interpreter   12
    2.3   DCL Commands   12
    2.4   Files and Directories   14
    2.5   Logical Names   16
    2.6   User Identification Codes   16
    2.7   Privileges   17
    2.8   DCL Procedures   18

2.9   Procedure Verification   21
2.10 The Login Procedure   21

3 Symbols, Data, and Expressions — 23

3.1   Symbols   23
3.2   Types of Data   24
3.3   Assignment Commands   27
3.4   Expressions   33
3.5   Lexical Functions   38
3.6   Substring Assignment   43
3.7   Bit-Field Assignment   45
3.8   Summary of Assignment Commands   48
3.9   Deleting Symbols   48

4 Flow of Control — 49

4.1   Sequential Execution   49
4.2   The GOTO Command   50
4.3   The IF Command   51
4.4   Loops   55
4.5   Invoking a Command Procedure   58
4.6   The CALL Command   61
4.7   The GOSUB Command   62
4.8   The PIPE Command   64

5 Substitution — 65

5.1   Apostrophe Substitution   65
5.2   Implicit Substitution   69
5.3   Ampersand Substitution   72

6 Displaying Output — 75

6.1   Displaying Text   75
6.2   Terminal Control Sequences   76
6.3   Formatting Output   78
6.4   Redirecting Program Output   80
6.5   Displaying a File   81
6.6   Displaying a Web Page   81

7 The DCL Environment   83
    7.1   Aspects of the Environment   84
    7.2   Putting It All Together   89

8 Error Handling   91
    8.1   Status Codes   91
    8.2   The Default Error Handler   95
    8.3   Changing Error-Handling Behavior   95
    8.4   Checking a Status Code Explicitly   96
    8.5   Handling Errors When Cleanup Is Required   97
    8.6   Procedure Call Unwinding   99
    8.7   Ignoring an Error   101
    8.8   Obtaining the Message for a Status Code   101
    8.9   Obtaining the Complete Error Text for a Status Code   103

9 Interrupt Handling   105
    9.1   Interrupt Situations   105
    9.2   The Default Interrupt Handler   106
    9.3   Changing Interrupt Handler Behavior   107
    9.4   Using Interrupts for Other Purposes   110
    9.5   Tying It All Together   111

10 Application Structure   113
    10.1   Naming Conventions   113
    10.2   Invoking the Application   114
    10.3   The Main Procedure   116
    10.4   A Subprocedure   118
    10.5   The Subroutine Library   121
    10.6   The SIGNAL Subroutine   123

11 Obtaining User Input   125
    11.1   The INQUIRE Command   126
    11.2   The READ Command   127
    11.3   Default Answers   128
    11.4   Editing Input   129
    11.5   Checking the Validity of Input   130

11.6 Main Procedure Arguments 132
11.7 A Sophisticated Input Subroutine 133
11.8 Redirecting Program Input 135
11.9 Reading Input from a Pipe 136
11.10 Displaying Large Amounts of Text 136

12 Debugging 139

12.1 Verification 139
12.2 Temporary Debugging Output 143
12.3 Permanent Debugging Output 143
12.4 Capturing Procedure Output 145

13 Files and Directories 147

13.1 File Specifications 147
13.2 Parsing 152
13.3 Searching Directories 155
13.4 File Protection 160
13.5 File Attributes 160
13.6 File Operations 161

14 Logical Names 165

14.1 Defining and Using Logical Names 166
14.2 Complete File Spec Parsing Algorithm 169
14.3 Displaying Logical Names 170
14.4 Access Modes 172
14.5 Standard Logical Names 173
14.6 MOUNT Logical Names 173
14.7 Other Uses for Logical Names 174
14.8 Obtaining Logical Name Information 178
14.9 Deleting Logical Names 181
14.10 Overview of OpenVMS System Directory Organization 181
14.11 Overview of Logical Name Tables 184

15 Sequential File Operations 189

15.1 Reading an Existing File 190
15.2 Creating and Writing a New File 193
15.3 Appending to an Existing File 195

  15.4 Temporary Files 195
  15.5 Displaying a File 198
  15.6 Searching Files 199

16 Data Manipulation   201

  16.1 Arithmetic Techniques 201
  16.2 Lists 203
  16.3 Keywords 206
  16.4 Dates and Times 207
  16.5 Record Structures 210

17 Indexed File Operations   215

  17.1 Sample File 216
  17.2 Reading an Existing File 217
  17.3 Creating a File 221
  17.4 Writing a File 223
  17.5 Updating a File 224
  17.6 Deleting Records 225
  17.7 File Sharing 226

18 File Protection   229

  18.1 UIC-Based Protection 230
  18.2 Access Control Lists 234
  18.3 Default File Protection 241
  18.4 The Access Algorithm 242
  18.5 Mandatory Access Controls 244

19 Devices   245

  19.1 Device Names 245
  19.2 Device Information 246
  19.3 Obtaining a List of the Devices on a System 248
  19.4 Terminal Characteristics 250
  19.5 Device Allocation 251
  19.6 Volume Initialization 253
  19.7 Volume Mounting 254

20 Processes — 257

- 20.1 Information about the Current Process 258
- 20.2 Information about Other Processes 261
- 20.3 Setting Process Information 263
- 20.4 Subprocesses 264
- 20.5 Process-Permanent Files 269
- 20.6 Jobs 270
- 20.7 An Example with SPAWN 271
- 20.8 PIPE 273

21 Batch Jobs — 277

- 21.1 The Batch Environment 277
- 21.2 Submitting a Batch Job 278
- 21.3 Sending Mail about Job Status 281
- 21.4 Restartable Batch Jobs 283
- 21.5 Periodic Batch Jobs 286
- 21.6 Preventing Duplicate Jobs 288

22 Arrays — 291

- 22.1 Arrays with Integer Indexes 291
- 22.2 Arrays with String Indexes 295
- 22.3 The DCL Symbol Table 297

23 DECnet Communications — 299

- 23.1 Clients and Servers 300
- 23.2 Task-to-Task Communications 301
- 23.3 DECnet Networking 301
- 23.4 Advanced Considerations 303
- 23.5 DECnet Access Controls 305
- 23.6 DECnet Object Specifications 307
- 23.7 Troubleshooting Task-to-Task Problems 307
- 23.8 Advanced Networking Applications 308

24 Security — 311

- 24.1 Captive and Restricted Logins 312
- 24.2 Controlled Access via DECnet 314
- 24.3 Automatic Logins 316

24.4 System Resources 316
24.5 Guidelines for Maintaining Security 317

25 The World Wide Web   319

25.1 HTML 320
25.2 HTML Tags 321
25.3 Common Gateway Interface (CGI) 321
25.4 CGI Symbols 324
25.5 CGI File Types 324
25.6 Advanced CGI Processing 326
25.7 CGI Subprocesses 327
25.8 URLs 327
25.9 Input 328
25.10 HTML Page Design Considerations 332

App. A Hexadecimal Notation   333

App. B Character Sets   335

App. C Dates and the Year 2000   339

C.1 OpenVMS and the Year 2000 341
C.2 Code Review and Testing 341
C.3 Code Changes 342

App. D Hypertext Markup Language   345

App. E Subroutine Library   347

App. F Sample Application   355

F.1 Using MODL 356
F.2 MODL Commands 357
F.3 File Layout 362
F.4 Listings 364

Glossary   403
Index   423
About this Book   467

List of Tables

3.1	DCL's interpretation of data as Boolean values	27
3.2	Integer operators	34
3.3	Character string operators	35
3.4	Boolean operators	35
3.5	Operator precedence	36
3.6	Summary of assignment commands	48
4.1	Summary of subroutine facilities	63
6.1	F$FAO directives	79
8.1	Status code fields	92
8.2	Status code severity levels	93
8.3	OpenVMS message files	103
13.1	F$FILE_ATTRIBUTES items	160
13.2	OpenVMS file utilities	162
13.3	File selection qualifiers	163
14.1	Defining logical names in different modes	173
14.2	Standard process and job logical names	174
14.3	F$TRNLNM items	180
14.4	System logical names	183
15.1	How /MATCH affects searching	200
16.1	Fields in a record structure	211
17.1	Fields in the sample indexed file	217
18.1	Access needed for directory operations	232

18.2	Access needed for file operations	232
18.3	SET SECURITY command qualifiers	239
19.1	F$GETDVI items	247
19.2	MOUNT command qualifiers	255
20.1	F$GETJPI items	259
20.2	F$ENVIRONMENT items	261
20.3	Commands to set process environment	264
20.4	SPAWN command qualifiers	265
20.5	Standard PPFs: Interactive procedure	270
20.6	Standard PPFs: Batch procedure	271
20.7	PIPE separators	275
21.1	SUBMIT command qualifiers	279
23.1	Network service commands	300
24.1	Prohibitions for CAPTIVE users	312
25.1	HTML tags	322
25.2	CGI symbols	324
25.3	CGI file types	325
F.1	MODL file: Header record	363
F.2	MODL file: Keyword record	363
F.3	MODL file: User record	363

Preface to the First Edition

During 1983, while working in the VMS Development Group at Digital Equipment Corporation, I was given the task of developing a new software installation procedure for VMS. The purpose of this procedure was to provide a uniform environment and methodology for installing software products on a VMS system. There were no preconceived notions about how this procedure should be structured, other than its required name: VMSINSTAL. I was annoyed by the missing "L" in the name, but I nevertheless accepted the task with enthusiasm. After giving the problem some careful thought, I decided to implement the required software in the Digital Command Language, DCL.

My decision raised a few eyebrows. Some people said, "It's too big and complicated, DCL will just get in your way." Others said, "DCL isn't a programming language!" I was convinced it was the correct decision, however, given the requirements of the project. Most of the actions taken by an installation procedure involve the manipulation of files: restoring from backup, copying, renaming, and so on. DCL is certainly a language that makes file manipulation easy. VMSINSTAL has to interact with a program written by the developers of the product being installed. The product's program drives the installation process in conjunction with VMSINSTAL. DCL makes this kind of interaction simple: one procedure simply invokes the other, and vice versa. One need not worry about compiling or linking the programs. Finally, I felt that the user interface to VMSINSTAL would be simple and not require any fancy programming.

After a couple of months' work I had written a 1,300-line DCL procedure that performed software installation in a consistent and extensible fashion. In the process, I was forced to develop stylistic and organizational guidelines for programming in DCL.

Since that time I have developed many complex DCL procedures and lent a hand to other people who were developing them. I have also read many procedures and remain overwhelmed by their lack of style and organization. I have three goals in writing this book. The first is to help people make and intelligent choice between DCL and more conventional programming languages. You will only be comfortable with the decision to write an application in DCL if you understand DCL's capabilities and limitations.

My second goal is to offer a programming language to computer users who are not conversant with conventional languages. Secretaries, administrative assistants, word processing folks, database administrators, system managers: all will be more challenged and productive if they can create new programs and solve problems on their own. Never forget what Commander Grace Hopper said: It's easier to apologize later than it is to get permission.

My final goal is to make the DCL programming process enjoyable for everyone. Programming is satisfying when you understand the features of the language, know how to apply them, and have the ability to build upon previous work to meet new situations. The entire software development process is more rewarding when the resulting software is correct and the programs are easy to understand.

If you find any errors in this book, or descriptions that could be made clearer, please send me e-mail: paul@windfall.com.

If you are going to write an application in DCL, you might as well take is seriously. Then you can have fun.

Paul C. Anagnostopoulos
March 1989

Acknowledgments for the First Edition

VERY SPECIAL APPRECIATION goes to my wife, Cynthia L. Sorn, for her constant support and patience during the past year. She read all the chapters and gave me suggestions and criticisms that directed the book toward a broad audience with a wide range of background knowledge. The project was a lot more fun with her participation. She spurred me on when my enthusiasm was lagging and gave me encouragement when I grumped about some difficult section. I wonder what she'll think if I start another book?

I particularly appreciate the help of the folks at UIS, Inc. in Lexington, Massachusetts. They let me use their VMS Version 5 system to develop all the examples in this book. Samir Bhatia and Charles Struass reviewed some chapters for me.

Lots of friends at Digital Equipment Corporation reviewed part of all of the book: Ruth Goldenberg, Joel Magid, Brian Mahoney, Rich Robbins, Rachel Ross, Hal Shubin. Thanks to all of them. Extra thanks to Rich and Hal, who read the entire book twice. As Rich said when he reviewed the chapter on debugging: "Debugging can be avoided if programmers refrain from making errors."

I appreciate my friend Bill Rothman spending time on some of the introductory chapters. He was not a VMS user back then, so his comments were invaluable for clarifying fundamental concepts.

The official technical reviewers from among the VMS user community were helpful and supportive: Ted Maryan of LTV Missiles and Electronics, James F. Peters of Kansas State University; Ronald Sawey of Southwest Texas State University; Joy Veronneau of Cornell University.

Particular recognition goes to Donald E. Knuth and Leslie Lamport. This book was composed with the TeX typesetting system running the LaTeX macro package. It was sure fun to typeset the whole thing myself!

Additional recognition goes to everyone who helped produce the book: Howard Burrows, Sandra Calef, Alice Cheyer, Stephani Colby, Chase Duffy, Timothy Evans, Hartley Ferguson, Amy Hendrickson, John Mann, Mike Meehan, Marilyn Rash, Rosemary Simpson, Joe Snowden.

A final thank you to Jimmy Buffett, an artist whose homemade music kept me going through all those long hours staring at the terminal screen.

> Miss the beat if you close your eyes
> Every night wears a new disguise
> And I live when a new surprise surrenders
> Feel it all with a willing heart
> Every stop is a place to start
> If you know how to play the part with feeling
> I play with feeling
>
> That's why I wander and follow *la vie dansante* . . .
>
> —Jimmy Buffett
> Will Jennings
> Michael Utley

Preface to the Second Edition

I WAS SURPRISED AND PLEASED when Digital Press, now an imprint of Butterworth-Heinemann, asked me to do a second edition. A lot had happened in the OpenVMS world since 1989, and it really made sense to update the book with information related to these changes.

Unfortunately, I had not used VMS since 1992, so I knew nothing about enhancements to DCL since then. This is where Steve Hoffman came in. He is a Digital employee who uses OpenVMS every day. He provided all the new information, wrote the new chapters, and updated the appendices.

If you find any errors, descriptions that can be made clearer, or important information that is missing, please send me e-mail at paul@windfall.com.

If you are going to write an application in DCL, you might as well take it relatively seriously. Then you can still have fun. Keep chewing up the cycles with those big DCL applications!

Paul C. Anagnostopoulos
October 1998

Acknowledgments for the Second Edition

PAUL C. ANAGNOSTOPOULOS

Again, special thanks goes to my wife, Cynthia L. Sorn, for support, patience, and a critical eye during the course of this project. And this time thanks also go to our children, Lucas and Rose, for putting up with a little less Dad time. My love to all of you.

Realistically speaking, however, they didn't need as much patience as with the first edition, because my illustrious coauthor, Steve Hoffman, did all the work. What do I know about DCL's evolution since 1992? Nothing. If it wasn't for Steve, there would be no second edition.

Kudos to Cheryl Debankah, who rekeyboarded the entire book after both archival copies were discovered to be corrupted. After 661,000 keystrokes, more or less, we found few typos. Better her than me. After Cheryl was finished, Sarah Lemaire entered all the indexing commands to reproduce the superb first edition index. Then Kristin Landon copyedited the book from beginning to end.

I just love the cover. Great job, Dick Hannus.

Hurrahs for the smart folks at Butterworth-Heinemann who decided a second edition was in order: Pam Chester, Elizabeth McCarthy, and Susan Prusak.

STEVE HOFFMAN

"You can't do that in DCL!" my friend Brian Cuttler once told me. DCL could not be used for DECnet task-to-task network communications, he assured me. The code that resulted from that conversation became the basis for

xxiii

the material you will see in Chapter 23 in this book, and resulted in a newfound appreciation for the capabilities of DCL. It also resulted in Brian's subsequent and entirely understandable hesitation to use that phrasing again. Thanks, Brian.

Thanks also to the folks here in OpenVMS Engineering that reviewed chapters, that contributed suggestions, that contributed DCL code, or that simply supported the project. A partial list would have to include Linda Benson, Richard Bishop, Don Jones, Karen Marion, Vittorio Mezzano, Atlant Schmidt, and Hein van den Heuvel. And to Liz McCarthy, Pam Chester and the other folks at Digital Press. Also to Ruth Goldenberg for her help connecting the various folks involved in creating this book together, to get this whole project going.

Paul Anagnostopoulos is the wizard that handled the page design, the TeX formatting, and the multitude of necessary tasks involved with the production of the second edition of this book—writing a book taught me how much I don't know about writing a book. I owe thanks to Paul for the lessons learned.

And thanks to Kelly, for putting up with me while I wrote this. And yes, I'll fix that pesky laptop before I write another book.

Writing Real Programs in DCL

CHAPTER 1

Introduction

THE DIGITAL COMMAND LANGUAGE, DCL, is the vehicle by which the interactive user communicates with the OpenVMS operating system. The user enters commands, which are analyzed and executed by the DCL command language interpreter to perform actions or display information. Commands can have dozens or hundreds of variations, many of which the user must understand intimately. A command language layer is present on all interactive operating systems, manifested as the Shell on Unix or REXX on IBM VM/SP. There are other command language interpreters for OpenVMS, including the Monitor Console Routine (MCR) command interpreter for PDP-11 RSX-11 compatibility, and the DEC/shell and the POSIX shell, both of which create an environment similar to the Unix command shell.

OpenVMS users soon find that they want to capture a series of DCL commands in a file so they can use the same series of commands quickly and accurately in the future. In this way, the file acts as a script, specifying actions to be taken automatically when the script is called up. Often the script can be significantly more useful if its commands can be varied from one use to the next. Therefore, most command languages inevitably evolve into programming languages. In the case of OpenVMS, DCL is the name given to both the interactive command language and the command programming language, which are really one and the same thing. A file containing a DCL program is called a *command procedure*.

The goal of this book is to help you write better DCL procedures. The book assumes a familiarity with OpenVMS; it does not attempt to teach the operating system from the ground up. However, even if you have written only a few rudimentary procedures, you can become skilled in the art of DCL programming by the time the last chapter is read.

1.1 Choosing to Use DCL

DCL is by no means the solution to all programming problems. However, there are programming tasks for which it is perfectly suited, and there are even some aspects of DCL that are refreshing when compared to conventional languages. The following is a list of DCL's strong points:

- DCL is available on every OpenVMS system.
- DCL procedures can be developed rapidly. The programmer is freed from the edit/compile/link/test cycle because DCL is an interpreted language.
- DCL procedures can be modified quickly when requirements change or expand.
- DCL procedures can employ OpenVMS utilities and other software products in a simple and natural manner.
- Some tricky aspects of OpenVMS programming, such as error and interrupt processing, are significantly simplified by DCL (as long as the necessary processing is straightforward).
- Unsophisticated programmers can use DCL procedures as building blocks to create sophisticated programs. So, for that matter, can sophisticated programmers.

If one or more of these points stand out as important to the application being planned, then DCL may be the programming language of choice. Nevertheless, DCL's weak points must also be considered:

- A DCL procedure runs slower than a program written in a conventional language because the procedure is executed by an interpreter. This is particularly true if the procedure is computationally intensive (i.e., if it performs many arithmetic calculations), less true if the procedure spends most of its time doing file manipulations.
- DCL is missing some important arithmetic facilities such as floating-point numbers.
- Data-structuring capabilities, important to many software algorithms, are virtually nonexistent in DCL.

- DCL is missing some of the modern structured programming constructs such as `WHILE` and `FOR` loops.
- Only the simplest user interface can be programmed in DCL. DCL has no windowing or graphics capabilities.
- A program can be invoked directly from DCL procedures only if it has a command interface. In particular, shareable images cannot be called directly from DCL procedures.
- The flexibility of DCL can make it particularly difficult to create a *captive command procedure*, a procedure that permits an untrusted user to perform specific tasks not directly authorized. For example, commands such as `INQUIRE` not only accept input, they can be used to execute lexical functions.

DCL is a programming language that allows rapid development of OpenVMS utilities and software products. DCL is also a language whose original design did not foresee the side range of applications for which it would be used, so parts of DCL are not as well structured as other modern programming languages.

1.2 The Application Domain for DCL

In light of these pros and cons, DCL is an appropriate choice of implementation language for some applications and not for others. The following sections describe a few of the application domains for which it is well suited. This is in no way an exhaustive list.

1.2.1 Environment Extension

One of the most common uses for DCL is to extend a user's personal OpenVMS environment. Any sequence of commands that is frequently needed can be embodied in a DCL procedure. Such a procedure reduces the amount of typing required and, if properly written, can make decisions and alter its actions based upon the current state of the environment.

Simple procedures can be used to submit batch and print jobs. It is often helpful to use a procedure to run an application consisting of two or three programs executed in sequence. A procedure can be written to replace the `LOGOUT` command: Before logging out it can delete scratch files and purge the user's directories in order to save disk space.

A moderately sophisticated but extremely handy procedure can be written to enhance the `SET DEFAULT` command, which is the OpenVMS way of establishing the current working directory. This procedure can accept commands (e.g., `UP`, `DOWN`, `SIDEWAYS`) that reset the working directory by moving around in the directory tree. An additional feature can allow the user to record the working directory, switch to a new working directory, and then pop back to the original one.

Extremely complex procedure libraries have been written to add a layer of features "on top of" DCL. These procedures provide an extended set of facilities, including a calendar and a telephone directory. The calendar interacts with the OpenVMS batch facility to submit and run batch jobs at predetermined times. The telephone directory interacts with OpenVMS electronic mail to provide powerful distribution list capabilities. These procedure libraries even allow users to write their own procedures, assign them command names, and integrate them into the library.

1.2.2 System Management

DCL is perfect for extending the system management facilities included in OpenVMS, particularly since many of these facilities are missing essential features. A procedure can tie together the many different system management tools, allowing complex tasks to be performed easily. Such a procedure also reduces the chance of doing things in the wrong order or of leaving out a critical step (a mistake made in system management can leave the system unusable).

A simple procedure can be used to run the `AUTHORIZE` utility, the OpenVMS program that is used to authorize new system users. Because `AUTHORIZE` has no corresponding DCL command, and because it must locate the system authorization database, the utility must be invoked in a special way. This is easily accomplished by a short procedure, whose only real purpose is to save typing.

A moderately complex procedure can be written to perform daily disk backups. It would use the `BACKUP` utility to create incremental backups on tape. It might also include a simple tape library facility, which would automatically label the tapes and keep track of backup cycles. This backup procedure could be extended to deal with weekly backups, monthly backups, disk restoration, and so on.

A more complex procedure can be used to add new OpenVMS Cluster satellite systems to an OpenVMS Cluster. This procedure is useful in an OpenVMS Cluster environment, where each node has its own system-specific root and where multiple nodes can share a common system root. A procedure to perform just this task is included with OpenVMS. It is provided in the file `CLUSTER_CONFIG.COM` residing in the `SYS$MANAGER` directory.

1.2.3 Complex File Manipulation

Many applications require relatively complicated file manipulation. Files must be created, copied, backed up, and reorganized. OpenVMS provides a host of utilities to help with such operations, but many of them cannot be called from conventional programs; they have no callable interface. DCL procedures are one way to sequence the utilities and control their subtler aspects.

In a simple application, a frequently updated file may need to be archived periodically. A batch job would run every 4 hours and make a copy of the file, purging all but the last five versions.

A distributed application might require that certain files be copied over a network every evening. A batch job is run that copies the files form the remote node to the local node. Relatively sophisticated error handling is necessary in case the network link is lost during a file transfer. It is essential to inform the application manager of the problem and to ensure that a consistent set of files is maintained on the local node.

The OpenVMS software installation procedure, `VMSINSTAL`, is an example of a complex DCL procedure that essentially solves a file manipulation problem. The files making up a software product are distributed on CD-ROM or magnetic tape. These files, along with additional files created at the customer's site, must be placed in the appropriate OpenVMS and product-specific directories. Some files, such as command definitions and help text files, must be placed in specific libraries. All of these file operations must be performed in such a way as to minimize the confusion caused by a system failure during the installation.

1.2.4 Software Development

The software development process often requires complex procedures to create, maintain, and assemble the components of the software system. Many of the common procedures are addressed by products already on the market. For example, DEC/CMS is a source code management system that keeps track of program modules and prevents two developers from altering a module in an inconsistent fashion. It is always best to consider available products before embarking on a project to create one from scratch. However, developmental methodologies are constantly changing and a new idea may necessitate the development of in-house tools.

DCL procedures can tie together existing developmental tools to improve communication between members of a developmental group. For example, when a developer replaces a module after modification, electronic mail can be sent to other members of the group so that they know the module is available.

Most software systems must be "built" before they can be tested. Building a system from its myriad components is a time-consuming process that must take into account the many interdependencies between the components. A set of DCL procedures, perhaps constructed around a system-building product such as DEC/MMS, can drive the building process from start to finish. The procedures can maintain and use a description file that lists all the software components and their relations. The procedure can make use of multiple nodes in an OpenVMS Cluster or network to perform the build in parallel.

DCL procedures can act as the backbone of an automated regression test system. The purpose of a regression test system is to verify a software product from one release to the next, to ensure that everything that worked in the previous release works in the new release. A critical aspect of such systems is the maintenance of a test case library and the execution of the tests within it. The results of the tests must be carefully recorded and compared with known correct results. Either or both of these requirements can be met with a set of DCL procedures.

1.3 A Word of Caution

A DCL procedure often runs with a high level of system privilege, particularly if the procedure performs system management functions. Beware of accepting "black box" procedures from people you do not know, or from a public bulletin board. There have been instances of "viruses" and "worms"—procedures that have deleted system files or destroyed the system in some other fashion.

1.4 How to Use This Book

This book can teach you how to write DCL procedures even if you have never written one before. However, the authors assume that you have a basic knowledge of OpenVMS concepts and facilities. Do not attempt to learn about OpenVMS by reading this book; choose an introductory OpenVMS text, such as *OpenVMS User's Manual* in the OpenVMS Documentation Set, to read instead. Chapter 2 is a review of the OpenVMS concepts required to understand the rest of the book. If you are a novice OpenVMS user, read it carefully; otherwise, a quick review is all that is necessary. Chapters 3 through 5 provide a detailed description of the facilities DCL provides for data manipulation and decision making. The authors recommend that everyone read these chapters, because even experienced DCL programmers will discover new features and ideas.

The remaining chapters of the book address various DCL topics in detail. They have been arranged to allow each chapter to rely almost exclusively on features introduced in previous chapters. The goal of this book is to teach you a set of techniques for building applications in DCL. This is by no means a DCL reference manual; not every command and option is described in full. When you want to the complete description of a particular feature, consult the OpenVMS Documentation Set. References to the appropriate documents are given throughout the text. A list of the most important documents is presented in Section 1.4.2.

This book presents features of OpenVMS that may not be available on the version running on your system. Whenever there is an important difference among the Version 7, Version 6, or Version 5 systems, the difference is explicitly noted.

Program examples are best presented within the context of a particular application. Throughout the book, examples are written as if they were part of a fictitious DCL application called "Example DCL Application," or XDA. The XDA application does not really exist, but you can pretend it does while reading the examples. This lends some coherence and consistency to the many DCL examples illustrated in the book. In order to tie together all the information presented in the book, the procedures for a real application are presented in Appendix F.

A glossary of the terms introduced in this book is provided following the appendixes.

1.4.1 Typographic Conventions

The following typographic conventions are used throughout this book:

Emphasize a word   A word is emphasized in italics.

Introduce a ***term***   A new term is introduced in bold italic.

Document Name   The name of a volume in the OpenVMS Documentation Set is specified in italics.

OpenVMS `KEYWORD` or `NAME`   A keyword or name that is provided by OpenVMS and entered as shown is specified in an uppercase "typewriter" typeface, as in `SHOW TIME`. This command is composed of two words, which must be spelled and punctuated as shown.

RETURN key   The name of a key on the terminal keyboard is specified in small capitals.

Metalinguistic *symbol*   A metalinguistic symbol is shown in italics. A ***metalinguistic symbol*** is a symbolic name that stands for some information to be included in a DCL command. For example: DELETE *file-spec*. The metalinguistic symbol *file-spec* stands for a file specification, which must be included in the command in place of the symbol.

DCL programs and examples of the interaction between the user and OpenVMS are illustrated as follows:

```
$!   This is a DCL procedure
$
$    show time
         .
         :  do other things
         .
$    exit
```

The program is set off from the text, uses the same typewriter typeface, but is shown in lowercase letters. A program example may include metalinguistic symbols or ellipses to indicate portions of the program that are missing from the example.

> Sec. 1.4.1, p. 7

When a complicated or tricky DCL feature is being used, a reference to the chapter or section in which it is described may be called out in the margin so you can easily refresh your memory.

1.4.2   OpenVMS Documentation Set

The definitive description of the Digital Command Language is provided in the OpenVMS Documentation Set. Three of the manuals in the set are particularly important for the DCL programmer.

OpenVMS User's Manual   An introduction to OpenVMS for the novice user, including information on commonly used utilities and on DCL programming.

OpenVMS DCL Dictionary   A two-volume set containing detailed descriptions of the DCL commands and facilities. This manual defers to other manuals to describe some of the more complicated commands, such as BACKUP.

Guide to Creating OpenVMS Modular Procedures   A summary of the OpenVMS naming standards, which allow various DIGITAL products and user applications to coexist on a OpenVMS system.

Additional information and pointers are available in the OpenVMS Frequently Asked Questions (FAQ) document. The OpenVMS FAQ is available via the OpenVMS World Wide Web site at www.openvms.digital.com, and via the comp.os.vms Internet newsgroup.

This book does not describe every feature of DCL, nor does it list every option of every DCL command. You must consult the *OpenVMS DCL Dictionary* when you need the full details of any particular DCL feature. This book is not a replacement for the *OpenVMS DCL Dictionary*.

So you want to learn a new programming language? There are only four things you need to find out:

- What does a semicolon do?
- Are vector indexes based at zero or one?
- How is a compound statement formed?
- Does it have macros?

If the answer to the last question is no, forget it.

—Technical Folklore

CHAPTER 2
A Review of OpenVMS Concepts

THIS CHAPTER REVIEWS SOME BASIC OpenVMS concepts, which any user of OpenVMS must understand in order to use the operating system effectively. You may already understand all the concepts presented here, but a review is certainly helpful. If you find yourself stumbling over these ideas, it is best to study them in more detail by reading the volume *OpenVMS User's Manual* in the OpenVMS Documentation Set. All the concepts presented in this chapter are described in greater detail in subsequent chapters of this book.

2.1 An Interactive Session

An interactive OpenVMS session is initiated by logging in to OpenVMS from a terminal. OpenVMS creates an *interactive process*, which can perform work on your behalf. The process executes the programs making up the applications that you choose to run on the VAX or Alpha system. These programs may be supplied by DIGITAL, purchased from third-party software vendors, or written at your own site.

A OpenVMS process has many items of information associated with it. Here are of the more interesting items:

- The *user name* with which you logged in to OpenVMS. This may be your actual name or some other identifier for your account.

- The name of the OpenVMS process. For your first interactive session, the process name is the same as your user name.

- The name of the terminal at which you logged in. You use this terminal to tell OpenVMS what to do, and OpenVMS uses it to display information.

2.2 The DCL Command Interpreter

Once you have established an interactive session, there must be some way to tell OpenVMS what you want to do. To instruct OpenVMS to perform an action, you issue a *command* at the terminal. This command is carried out by a special program called a *command language interpreter*. The standard command language interpreter for OpenVMS is called DCL, which stands for Digital Command Language. DCL accepts commands from the keyboard, analyzes them, and them performs them.

DCL has control of your terminal during an interactive session. It signals that it is ready to accept a command by displaying the *DCL prompt*, which is a dollar sign ($) unless you explicitly change it. A command is entered by typing it at the dollar sign prompt and pressing the RETURN key.

Most commands cause DCL to run a program in your process. The program is then responsible for further analyzing the command and eventually carrying it out. Once the program has finished, DCL prompts for another command from the keyboard. A few commands do not run any program but are instead carried out directly by the DCL interpreter. These are simple commands that do not warrant their own complete program.

The DCL command repertoire is extremely rich in features, as the size of the *OpenVMS DCL Dictionary* attests. The *OpenVMS DCL Dictionary* is the two-volume manual in the OpenVMS Documentation Set that describes most of the commands and other features of DCL. Whenever you are in doubt about the features of a command, consult the *Dictionary*.

2.3 DCL Commands

Every DCL command adheres to the same basic format. The first item in a command is called the *command verb*. The command verb is a single English word, or combination of words, that identifies the command and summarizes what it does. For example, the command LOGOUT is used to terminate an interactive session. Command verbs may be entered in an abbreviated form as long as the abbreviation is unambiguous. The LOGOUT command may be abbreviated to LOG but to L, because there is also a LINK command. A verb is guaranteed to be unique if four or more letters are specified.

Many commands accept one or more *parameters* following the verb. A parameter is an item of information used by the command to further refine the action it will take. Often a parameter names some entity upon which the command will operate, such is a data file to be copied. The command verb specifies the action, while the parameter specifies an object to be acted upon.

Some command parameters are *required parameters*; they must always be specified. Others are *optional parameters* and are specified only when needed. Each command description points out which parameters are required and which are optional.

The following command deletes all the files called NAMES.DAT:

```
$ delete names.dat;*
```

The command verb is DELETE and the first parameter is file specification NAMES.DAT;*. The format for the file specifications is described in a later section.

The operation of DCL commands is modified and augmented by the presence of command *qualifiers*. Almost all qualifiers are optional. When specified, they alter certain aspects of the operation performed by the command. A qualifier consists of the slash character (/) followed by a word that describes the qualifier's effect on the command. In addition, some qualifiers accept values that further determine the operation. As with the command verb, qualifiers may be abbreviated as long as the abbreviation is unique (four letters guarantee uniqueness).

Here is the DELETE command with two qualifiers:

```
$ delete /confirm /log names.dat;*
```

The /CONFIRM qualifier specifies that the DELETE command should ask the user to confirm each file deletion before it is performed. The /LOG qualifier requests that a message be displayed naming each file after it is deleted. Without the qualifiers the command neither confirms nor displays messages about files as it deletes them. The particular action taken when a qualifier is omitted is called the default action. The default action for the /CONFIRM qualifier is to not confirm; the default for the /LOG qualifier is to not display log information.

When a qualifier requires a value, the qualifier name is followed by an equal sign (=) and then the value. For example:

```
$ delete /before=1-jan-1998 names.dat;*
```

The /BEFORE qualifier specifies that only files created before 1 January 1998 are to be deleted.

The overall format of DCL commands and the rules that govern their format are together called *command syntax*. The complete syntax rules are

2.3 DCL Commands

given in the OpenVMS manual entitled *OpenVMS User's Manual*. You will learn about many DCL commands and their syntax as this book proceeds. Here is a summary of the syntax rules:

- A command begins with a verb, which may be preceded by one or more spaces. The verb may be abbreviated as long as the abbreviation is unambiguous. Verbs are guaranteed unique if at least four letters are specified. When used in a command procedure, a verb should not be abbreviated.

- A command may take parameters, some of which are required and some optional. The verb and parameters are separated from one another by one or more spaces.
    - When a parameter contains non-alphanumeric characters such as spaces, commas, slashes, or when it contains lowercase letters, it must be enclosed in double quotes (").
    - Some parameters may include a list of items. The items in the list are separated by commas (,).

- Most commands allow qualifiers, which consist of a slash (/) followed by a name. The name may be abbreviated as long as the abbreviation is unambiguous. As with verbs, qualifiers are guaranteed unique if at least four letters are specified. And qualifiers should not be abbreviated when used in command procedures.
    - Some qualifiers require a value; others accept an optional one. The value is separated from the qualifier name by an equal sign (=).
    - When a qualifier value contains spaces, commas, slashes, or lowercase letters, it must be enclosed in double quotes (").
    - Some qualifiers may include lists of values. The items in the list are enclosed in parentheses [( )] and separated by commas (,).

- A command can be continued on additional lines by ending each line (except the last) with a hyphen (−). The command can be split at any point where a space or a comma appears.

2.4 Files and Directories

A *file* is a collection of data stored on a parameter medium such as disk or magnetic tape. The information in a file is organized into *records*, each one containing a portion of the total collection of data. One of the primary purposes of any operating system is to support the creation and manipulation of data files. On OpenVMS, a file is designated by a sequence of characters called a *file specification*, or *file spec* for short. The complete format for a file spec is given here, and each component of the file spec is summarized:

node::*device*:[*directory*]*name*.*type*;*version*

Node The node component identifies a particular node in the DECnet network. The name of the node is included in the specification, followed by a double colon to distinguish it from a device name. If the node is omitted, the local node is assumed.

Device The device component specifies the disk or tape on which the file resides. If it is omitted, the device containing the working directory is assumed (see below for a description of the working directory).

Directory The directory component specifies a file catalog on the device, the catalog containing the desired file. Multiple catalogs are allowed on some devices. If the directory component is omitted, the working directory is assumed.

Name The name component, taken together with the type component, identifies a particular file in the chosen directory. The purpose of the file name is to assign a meaningful identifier to the file.

Type The type component is used with the file name to uniquely identify a file in a directory. This two-level name/type scheme allows the file name to identify a family of related files, while the file type identifies particular kinds of files within the family.

Version The version component allows multiple generations of the same file to exist simultaneously. More than one generation can exist in the same directory. If the version component is omitted, the latest version is assumed.

Certain classes of storage media, most notably disks, can contain hundreds or thousands of catalogs and data files. The concept of a *directory* is introduced to allow a collection of files to be cataloged together under one name, while another collection is cataloged under a different name. A directory can catalog not only data files, but other directories as well. This permits a hierarchy of directories to be formed, with data files cataloged at all levels of the hierarchy.

Two directories are of notable importance to the OpenVMS user. When a user logs in to OpenVMS, one particular directory is established as the user's *login directory*, or *home directory*. This directory acts as the repository for the user's files, and the user can create subdirectories for additional files. At any time during a OpenVMS session, one directory, not necessarily the login directory, is chosen as the *default directory*. When a file is accessed using a file spec that does not include a device and directory, the file is assumed to reside in the default directory. Thus, if the directory in which you are currently working is established as the default directory, most file specs need not include an explicit device or directory. When you log in, the login directory is automatically established as the default directory. You can change the default directory with the SET DEFAULT command.

Files and directories are discussed in detail in Chapters 13 through 18.

2.5 Logical Names

A *logical name* is a names entity that stands for part or all of a file specification. The primary purposes of a logical name are to relieve the OpenVMS user from having to remember the disk and directory location of a file, and to avoid the problems that typically arise when explicitly coded device, directory, or file specifications must be changed. To this end, OpenVMS defines many logical names such as SYS$HELP, which you can use to locate system files and system directories.

A logical name is created and assigned a value with the DEFINE command. The DEFINE command requires a logical name and its corresponding value:

```
$ define data_files user_disk:[smith.data]
```

Once the logical name DATA_FILES is defined, a file in Smith's data directory can be referred to without having to explicitly specify the disk or the directory:

```
$ type data_files:october.dat
```

This command will display the contents of the OCTOBER.DAT file in the data directory. Logical names defined in the manner of DATA_FILES are only available to your process. Other logical names defined by OpenVMS or the system manager can be made available to all processes.

Chapter 14 describes logical names in detail.

2.6 User Identification Codes

The *user identification code* (UIC) is a number assigned to certain objects to identify the *owner* of the object. Files and disk volumes are two kinds of objects that have an owner. A file is assigned an owner when it is created, a disk volume when it is initialized. A UIC is also assigned to each authorized user of a OpenVMS system. When you log on to OpenVMS, your UIC is located and becomes associated with the interactive process OpenVMS creates for you. Every OpenVMS process has a UIC associated with it.

OpenVMS uses the UIC as part of its object protection scheme. An object can be protected so that only certain users can read or modify it. For example, a file can be protected so than many users can read it, fewer users can modify it, and only one user can delete it. File protection is described in detail in Chapter 18. The protection scheme is based upon comparing the UIC of the process accessing the object with the owner UIC of the object itself.

A UIC is an integer that is divided into two parts. The first part is called the *group number* and the second part the *member number*. The system manager determines how the group/member hierarchy is used when assigning UIC numbers to users. A typical scheme is that all the users in one department are assigned the same group number, with separate member numbers assigned to each person in the group.

A numeric UIC is displayed in the format [123,456], where 123 is the group number and 456 is the member number. The group and member number are specified and displayed in the octal radix numbering system, which means that their digits must range from 0 through 7 (8 and 9 are not allowed). As a convenience to users, OpenVMS typically displays the numeric values in alphanumeric form, not as numeric values. The numeric values are mapped to alphanumeric form using *rights identifiers*. Each group is assigned a mnemonic identifier, such as DEVELOPMENT, and each group member is also assigned an identifier, such as ROBERTSON. If the development group is group 123 and Robertson is member 456, then Robertson's UIC is displayed as [DEVELOPMENT,ROBERTSON] instead of [123,456]. This identifier format conveys much more information than the numeric format. A member identifier is almost always identical to the member's user name.

Sec. 18.2, p. 234

Certain group numbers are reserved for *system groups*. A user in a system group can generally access system files that are not available to regular users. The system group numbers usually range from 1 through 10 octal (1 through 8 decimal), although the system manager can alter the range using a system parameter. A UIC in the system group implicitly grants system privilege, often refered to by the explicit mnemonic privilege name SYSPRV.

Sec. 18.1, p. 230

2.7 Privileges

The OpenVMS privilege scheme is the means by which OpenVMS restricts the use of those system functions and resources that can have a negative impact on the system when used indiscriminately. For example, the capability to terminate another user's interactive sessions has the potential to be misused. Another example is the ability to delete files that normally cannot be deleted: only a few authorized users should be able to do so.

Every critical system function has one or more privileges associated with it. Each privilege has a name, so that it can be specified in DCL commands. The OPER privilege, for example, is required to perform various operator activities, such as broadcasting a message to all system users. Only users with OPER privilege can broadcast messages to all users.

There are four sets of privileges associated with each OpenVMS process, two of which are important to DCL. The first set is the *authorized privileges*, which are assigned to a user by the system manager. The authorized privileges are those the user is allowed to enable. As long as OPER privilege is authorized, a user can enable it and then broadcast a message to all system users. The second privilege set is the *process privileges*. These are the privileges the user has in fact enabled. Again, the system manager determines which privileges will be enabled when a user logs in, but the user can change the enabled privileges at any time with the SET PROCESS/PRIVILEGES command. A user cannot enable privileges that are not in the authorized set unless the user has SETPRV privilege. The SETPRV privilege allows a user to enable any privileges whatsoever, and therefore it should be authorized with extreme caution.

Some DCL commands can only be performed when you have certain privileges enabled. Such restrictions will be stated in this book whenever they apply.

2.8 DCL Procedures

After using OpenVMS for a while, you may find yourself entering the same sequence of DCL commands over and over. This quickly becomes tedious, so users look for a way to capture the command sequence, assign it a name, and request the command sequence by name. A command sequence can be stored in a text file using an editor, and the text file can be "played back" later by DCL, just as if the commands were reentered at the terminal. The command test file is called a *DCL command procedure*. Command procedures are what this book is all about.

A command procedure is a file of text that you can create with your favorite editor. In its simplest form, a procedure file consists of a sequence of DCL commands, one per line:

```
$    show default
$    show process
$    show quota
```

Each command in the procedure must begin with a dollar sign, which tells DCL that the line contains a command for it to interpret. One or more spaces can follow the dollar sign. Then the DCL command is specified exactly as it would be typed at the DCL prompt.

By convention, a DCL command procedure file is given the file type COM, for "command." Assume that the previous procedure is contained in a file named SIMPLE.COM. Once a procedure file is created with an editor, the commands in the procedure can be played back using the at-sign (@) command:

```
$ @simple.com
```

The at-sign tells DCL that the file spec for a command procedure follows. DCL looks for the file SIMPLE.COM and interprets the commands contained in it, one at a time, until it runs out of commands. When the commands have all been interpreted, DCL requests another command from the terminal. The at-sign command is said to *invoke* or *call* the procedure, and DCL subsequently *executes* the commands contained within it. The commands in a DCL procedure are sometimes called *DCL code*.

DCL assumes that the file type of a procedure is .COM, so it can be omitted from the preceding command:

```
$ @simple
```

The procedure displays the following information at the terminal:

```
SYS$SYSDEVICE:[HOFFMAN.BOOK]
11-MAR-1998 16:41:44.30  User: HOFFMAN   Process ID:    000000C2
                         Node: WILTON    Process Name: "HOFFMAN_0042"
Terminal:           FTA17:
User Identifier:    [VMSENG,HOFFMAN]
Base Priority:      4
Default File Spec:  SYS$SYSDEVICE:[HOFFMAN.BOOK]
Number of Kthreads: 1

Devices allocated:  WILTON$DKA100:
                    WILTON$FTA17:

Devices mounted: WILTON$DKA100:
```

  User [VMSENG,HOFFMAN] has 303195 blocks used, 696805 available,
  of 1000000 authorized and permitted overdraft of 1000 blocks
  on DKA100

If a procedure line contains nothing but a dollar sign, DCL ignores it and moves on to the next line. Such a line can be used for visual separation of commands:

```
$    show default
$    show process
$
$    show quota
```

2.8.1 Comments

A *comment* in a command procedure is a phrase or sentence that describes the procedure to the human reader. Comments are completely ignored by DCL; they have absolutely no effect on the execution of the procedure, the actions it takes, or the output it displays. The beginning of a comment is marked with an exclamation point (!) and the rest of the line contains the comment. DCL ignores the exclamation point and all other characters to the end of the line.

```
$!   This is the procedure SIMPLE.COM
$!   It displays information about the current process.
$
$    show default
$    show process ! The process name and other info.
$    show quota   ! Disk space used by this user.
```

This procedure contains four kinds of lines:

- Lines beginning with $!, which contain only comments.
- Separator lines containing only the dollar sign.
- Command lines with no comments.
- Command lines that also include a comment at the end.

Comments allow a complex procedure to be annotated so that future readers and maintainers of the procedure can better understand how the procedure works.

2.8.2 Abbreviation

DCL allows command verbs and qualifiers to be abbreviated. In a command procedure, however, it is best to avoid abbreviation. Abbreviations are harder to read, and searching for particular command verbs or qualifiers is difficult when spellings are inconsistent. If you insist on abbreviating a verb or qualifier, *never* abbreviate to fewer than four letters. The names of verbs and qualifiers are guaranteed to be unique within the first four letters, but not in the three or fewer.

Take the SET PROTECTION command, for example. In OpenVMS Version 2, you could include the following line in a procedure:

```
$ set pro=(o:rwed) *.dat;*   ! Abbreviate "protection".
```

However, the SET PROMPT command was added in a later version of OpenVMS. Suddenly the abbreviation PRO was not unique, because it matched both PROTECTION and PROMPT.

2.9 Procedure Verification

The following command will cause DCL to *verify* the lines in a command procedure as it performs them:

```
$ set verify
```

As DCL reads the command procedure and interprets its commands, each command line is displayed at your terminal. In this way you can trace the procedure and see what it is doing. The SET VERIFY command can be useful as you read this book and try out examples.

Procedure verification is described in Chapter 12.

2.10 The Login Procedure

As you log in to an OpenVMS system, most command interpreters check for a login command procedure. When you are using the DCL command interpreter, DCL checks for a file named LOGIN.COM. If such a file exists, it is automatically invoked as if specified with an at-sign command. All the commands in this login procedure are executed before DCL issues the first command prompt. The login procedure can be used to establish a personal working environment: it can define logical names, enable privileges, or change the DCL prompt.

As you read further, you may discover interesting things to put in your login procedure. You will also discover a few things you should not include.

CHAPTER 3
Symbols, Data, and Expressions

CHAPTER 2 INTRODUCED BASIC concepts that are important for all OpenVMS DCL users. This chapter begins an examination of DCL facilities that make it useful as a general-purpose programming language. The focus of this chapter is on data and the manipulation of data.

3.1 Symbols

A *symbol* is the DCL equivalent of what most programming languages call a variable. A symbol is a named entity with which you can associate an item of data. Later on, the data can be retrieved and manipulated by using the name to refer to it. The item of data is called the symbol's *value*. The same symbol may have different values at different points in the program. It is the ability of a symbol to take on different values that makes it such a powerful programming tool. A DCL symbol has three items of information associated with it:

Name Each symbol has a name that is used to refer to it. The name of a symbol, together with its level, uniquely distinguishes if from all other existing symbols.

Level Each symbol has a level, which is determined by the context in which the symbol was originally created. The various symbol contexts are described in Section 3.3. A symbol with the same name may exist in two different contexts, but duplicate names may not exist in the same context.

Therefore, a symbol's name and level uniquely distinguish it from all other symbols.

Value   Each symbol has a value associated with it. The value is an item of data that can be manipulated by referring to it by way of the symbol's name. In other words, the symbol name acts as a "handle" for the data item.

A symbol name is composed of letters, digits, dollar sign ($), and underscore (_), but its first character cannot be a digit. Use of the dollar sign is reserved to DIGITAL. You may type a symbol name in lowercase or uppercase letters; DCL converts the name to uppercase before doing anything with it. A symbol name is limited to 255 characters in length. The symbol value is an item of data, associated with the symbol, that can be accessed using the symbol name. In DCL, data items can be integers or character strings.

Here is a simple example to illustrate the creation of a symbol:

```
$     sym1 = 42
```

This is an *assignment command*, which creates a new symbol. The symbol has the four-character name SYM1, a level determined by the context of the assignment command, and the value 42, which is an integer. Once a symbol is created, its value can be replaced with a new value by performing another assignment command:

```
$     sym1 = "I'd rather be sailing"
```

This command does not create a new symbol but rather replaces the existing symbol's value with the character string `"I'd rather be sailing"`. An assignment command creates the symbol if it does not already exist and then sets it to the value specified on the right-hand side of the command.

It is difficult to fully appreciate the power of symbols without some further background. The rest of this chapter describes symbols, data items, and assignment commands in detail.

3.2   Types of Data

The ultimate purpose of every program is to create and manipulate data. The collective term *data* refers to all the information available to, or generated by, a program. This data is composed of individual *data items*, each of which can be manipulated separately from the rest. In DCL, a data item has an associated *data type*, which signifies what kind of data it is. Strictly speaking, DCL supports two types of data: integers and character strings. However, a particularly useful third type of data, Boolean data, can be implemented with the first two. The following sections discuss these data types.

Every data item has two representations, an internal one and an external one. The internal representation is determined by the host computer, which for DCL is the OpenVMS VAX or Alpha system. Almost all computers operate in binary, representing data items as numbers in base 2. Each binary digit is called a *bit*, so we speak in terms of data occupying a certain number of bits of computer memory.

Computer users are much happier when data can be represented in natural forms such as decimal numbers or letters of the alphabet. These familiar forms are the external representations of the data, and all programming languages provide for them. When the external representation of a data item appears in a program, it is called a *literal*. The following DCL command contains two literals:

```
$    write sys$output "The answer is ", 13
```

The first literal is the character string "The answer is" and the second is the decimal integer 13.

3.2.1 Integers

An integer is a whole number, which can be negative, zero, or positive. DCL supports signed integers that occupy 32 bits of memory, thus restricting them to the range from -2,147,483,648 to +2,147,483,647. In the VAX and Alpha architectures, a 32-bit quantity is referred to as a *longword*. Although the internal representation of an integer is in binary, the external representation is made up of digits and other characters, which allows a "natural" specification of the number.

Integer literals can be represented in base 10 (decimal), base 16 (hexadecimal), or base 8 (octal). Decimal integers are discussed in this section, and hexadecimal integers in Appendix A. Octal integers are rarely used and will not be discussed in this book. A decimal integer is composed of the ten decimal digits 0–9, optionally preceded by a plus sign (+) or minus (−). Punctuation marks such as commas are not allowed in integers. The following are examples of decimal integers:

```
0    7    07    42    +3286    1    -39840938
```

3.2.2 Character Strings

A character string is a sequence of individual characters. A character can be an actual glyph, such as an uppercase A or a plus sign (+). Glyphs are usually called *printable characters*. A character can also be a *control character*, which does not represent a glyph but rather a formatting operation, such as tab or line feed. Each distinct character is assigned a code number, and the complete collection of characters and their code numbers is called a *character set*. The VAX and Alpha architectures employ the *ASCII character set* (ASCII stands for American Standard Code for Information Interchange) subset of the *ISO Latin 1 character set*. In both ISO Latin 1 and in ASCII, the characters occupy eight bits and the code numbers range from 0 to 255. Procedures to generate character set tables are provided in Appendix B.

The number of individual characters in a character string is called its *length*. A character string can be composed of any number of characters from 1 to approximately 900. The upper limit depends on the context in which the string is used. A character string can also contain no characters at all, in which case it is called the *null string*.

A character string literal is represented by enclosing its constituent characters in a set of double quotes ("). Here are a few examples:

```
""    "x"    "X"    "*"    "a short string"
"This is a sentence complete with punctuation."
```

The first example is the null string. You can represent any printable character in a string literal, but there is no way to represent control characters. A special case is made of the double quote character: you must represent each double quote character in the literal with an adjacent pair of double quotes:

```
"This string contains ""a quoted phrase""."
```

The string literal shown here consists of six words, the last three of which are inside double quotes. Each double quote that is part of the literal, but not the ones that enclose the literal, must be paired. It is a common mistake to forget to pair the double quotes inside a string:

```
"This string contains "a quoted phrase"."
```

It appears to DCL that the string literal ends with the space following the word contains and that the final three words are not part of the string literal.

3.2.3 Booleans

The Boolean data type encompasses the two logic values true and false. Logical values are important in programming because true/false, yes/no decisions are constantly being made by a program in order to guide its flow of execution. Many conventional programming languages distinguish the Boolean data type from other data types, but DCL does not. However, the Boolean data type can

Table 3.1 DCL's interpretation of data as Boolean values

Boolean value	Data so interpreted
TRUE	Odd integers; character strings beginning with t, T, y or Y; character strings representing odd integers (e.g.,"381")
FALSE	Even integers; all other character strings

be simulated using the integer and character string data types. Whenever DCL needs a true/false value to use with a logical operation, it accepts an integer or character string and interprets it as true or false depending on its value. Table 3.1 specifies how this interpretation is made.

The following data items are considered true:

```
1    3    "True"    "Y"    "Yes"    "yupsters"
```

The following are considered false:

```
0    2    "False"    "N"    "No"    "nope"
"random!nonsense"    "380"
```

Symbolic literals for the two Boolean values true and false round out the simulation of the Boolean data type. DCL provides no such literals, so the authors choose the symbols TRUE and FALSE to represent them. Thses symbols can be established with the assignment command described in the next section.

3.3 Assignment Commands

The assignment command is the means by which DCL symbols are created and assigned values. Because most languages refer to their commands as *statements*, the assignment command is often called assignment statement. The assignment statement has the following general format:

```
$    symbol = expression
```

The symbol named on the left-hand side of the equal sign is assigned the value determined by the *expression* on the right-hand side. For example:

```
$    my_name = "Brian Cuttler"
```

Here the symbol MY_NAME is assigned the character string "Brian Cuttler". We read the assignment statement as "MY_NAME gets "Brian Cuttler"" and say that the symbol MY_NAME is set to the value of the expression "Brian Cuttler". The word *equals* is not used when discussing the action of an assignment statement because it is too easily confused with the idea of equality for comparison purposes, as in "1 does not equal 2." Integer and string literals are examples of simple expressions; a literal can appear by itself on the right-hand side of an assignment statement. Section 3.4 describes expressions in detail.

A symbol is created the first time a command is used to assign it a value. Subsequent assignments to the same symbol discard the current value and replace it with the new value. A symbol can have an integer value at one point in the program and a character string value at another point. The data type is associated with the value, not with the symbol, as it is in many languages such as Pascal. Because the data type is associated with the value and not with the symbol, a symbol can be set to any type of data. The following assignment statements illustrate these rules:

```
$    days_per_year = 366
$    days_per_leap_year = days_per_year
$    days_per_year = 365
$    days_per_leap_year = "three hundred sixty-six"
```

In the second assignment statement, the symbol DAYS_PER_LEAP_YEAR is set to the value of the previously created symbol DAYS_PER_YEAR. A symbol by itself is another example of a simple expression on the right-hand side of an assignment command. Note that DAYS_PER_LEAP_YEAR is assigned both types of data at different times.

In addition to its name and value, each symbol has a level. The name and the level together uniquely identify the symbol from among all existing symbols. A symbol's level is determined by the context in which it is created and by the kind of assignment statement used to create it. The following sections describe the different levels: prompt level, procedure level, and global level.

3.3.1 DCL Prompt Level

Symbols created at the DCL prompt are associated with the DCL prompt level. You might create such a symbol to remember something to do later:

```
$ note = "Remember to call Jim before leaving."
```

This symbol is at the prompt level because it was created with an assignment statement at the DCL prompt. You can display the value of the symbol with the SHOW SYMBOL command (you type the first line, and OpenVMS responds with the second line):

```
$ show symbol note
```

```
NOTE = "Remember to call Jim before leaving."
```

The symbol can be used to create another symbol at the prompt level:

```
$ old_note = note
$ note = "Don't forget to pick up the video tape"
```

Now two prompt-level symbols exist, NOTE and OLD_NOTE.

Symbols at the prompt level remain in existence during your entire login period unless explicitly deleted. Section 3.9 describes how to delete symbols.

3.3.2 Procedure Level

Each DCL command procedure has its own symbol level. When you invoke a procedure with the at-sign (@) command, a new level is established. Any symbols created by the procedure are associated with the procedure's level. If the procedure invokes another procedure, the second procedure has its own level and its symbols are associated with its level. In this way, each procedure has a set of symbols that "belong" to it.

Here is a simple procedure named SIMPLE-PROC:

```
$    name = "OpenVMS is VMS"
$    show symbol name
```

When invoked, this procedure creates the procedure-level symbol NAME and assigns a character string to it. The procedure then displays the value of the symbol:

```
$ @simple-proc
    NAME = "OpenVMS is VMS"
```

When a procedure terminates, all the symbols created at its level are deleted. Since the symbols are associated with the procedure's level, it makes no sense for them to exist once the procedure has terminated. Should the procedure be invoked again, its symbols will be recreated from scratch by DCL; they will have lost their old values.

A procedure can refer to a symbol at the prompt level as long as the symbol does not have the same name as a symbol created by the procedure. If symbols with the same name are created at the prompt and procedure levels, the one at procedure level "shadows" or "hides" the one at prompt level. Similarly, a subprocedure invoked from a main procedure can refer to symbols created by the main procedure. For example, if procedure A invokes procedure B, B can refer to the symbols created by A. The ability to use symbols created at an outer level allows you to write a procedure that displays the NOTE symbol created at the prompt level:

3.3 Assignment Commands

```
$!     Procedure to display the note.
$
$      write sys$output "Your note is:"
$      show symbol note
```

> Chap. 6, p. 75

The WRITE command displays the text in double quotes. The SHOW SYMBOL command refers to the NOTE symbol created at the prompt level. Because this little procedure does not create its own symbol named NOTE, the reference to NOTE gets the symbol at prompt level. The display produced by this procedure is shown here:

```
Your note is:
Note = "Don't forget to pick up the video tape."
```

When DCL is executing a procedure and needs the value of a symbol, it performs a simple search process. As soon as it finds a symbol with the given name, it terminates the search and uses the value of the symbol. Here is the process as described so far:

1. DCL looks for the symbol among the symbols created by the currently executing procedure.
2. If the procedure was invoked by another procedure, DCL looks for the symbol among the invoking procedure's symbols.
3. Step 2 is repeated for each additional level of command procedure
4. DCL looks for the symbol among the symbols created at DCL prompt level.

Although a procedure can use the values of symbols at outer levels, it cannot create or change symbols at outer levels. This is somewhat restrictive, so a special global level exists to solve the problem.

3.3.3 Global Level

Sophisticated DCL applications are composed of multiple procedures, which invoke one another in various combinations. Sometimes it is necessary for a procedure B to calculate a value and pass it back to another procedure A, which invoked it. With what you know so far, there is no way to accomplish this. If B stores the value in a symbol at its own level, that symbol will be deleted when B terminates. The alternative is for B to store the value in a symbol at A's level, but DCL provides no means of doing so. The global symbol level exists to solve this dilemma.

Symbols created at the global level are called *global symbols*. You must explicitly request that a global symbol be created by using a variant of the assignment statement:

```
$     xda_answer == 42
```

Note that two equal signs are used in the example. The double equal sign requests that the symbol XDA_ANSWER be created at the global level and assigned the value 42. Global symbols are only created when you use the double equal sign form of the assignment command.

Sec. 10.1, p. 113

By convention, global symbol names begin with the application facility code and a single underscore. In the preceding example, the facility code is XDA.

Global symbols can always be created, whether you are at the DCL prompt or executing a command procedure. This capability is what distinguishes global symbols from prompt-level symbols and is the only major difference between the two kinds of symbols. The double equal sign forces a global symbol to be created regardless of the level at which the assignment statement is executed. Subsequent global assignment to the same symbol changes the global symbol's value. The value of a global symbol can be obtained at any level as long as there are no symbols of the same name at a procedure level or prompt level. To accommodate global symbols, the symbol search process is extended to its final form:

1. DCL looks for the symbol among the symbols created by the currently executing procedure.
2. If the procedure was invoked by another procedure, DCL looks for the symbol among the invoking procedure's symbols.
3. Step 2 is repeated for each additional level of command procedure.
4. DCL looks for the symbol among the symbols created at prompt level.
5. DCL looks for the symbol among the global symbols.

The following simple example illustrates a subprocedure that creates a global symbol in order to pass a value back to its calling procedure:

```
$!    This is procedure A
$
$     @b ! B will set global symbol XDA_ANSWER

$!    This is procedure B
$
$     xda_answer == 42
$     exit
```

3.3 Assignment Commands

Procedure A invokes procedure B to establish the global value. Procedure B creates the global symbol XDA_ANSWER using a double equal sign assignment statement. It then exits, allowing procedure A to continue. Procedure A displays the value of the global symbol. Because XDA_ANSWER is global, it is not deleted when procedure B exits, thus allowing A to obtain its value.

It is quite easy to omit the second equal sign when you mean to perform a global assignment. Look at the following code:

```
$    xda_answer == 42
     .
     .
     .
$    xda_answer = 43          ! Meant to use ==
$    show symbol xda_answer
```

The first assignment command creates the global symbol XDA_ANSWER and assigns it the value 42. The second assignment command was intended to change the value of the global symbol, but only one equal sign is present. Therefore, the assignment command creates a *procedure-level* symbol with the same name, XDA_ANSWER. This procedure-level symbol hides the global symbol. The SHOW command displays 43 quite nicely, but the global symbol still has the value 42. Be careful always to use two equal signs when performing global assignments.

Global symbols remain in existence during your entire login period, unless explicitly deleted.

Section 3.9 describes how to delete symbols.

3.3.4 Symbol Scope

Symbol scoping allows a cautiously written, modular command procedure to avoid unintended and undesirable interactions involving symbols. Scoping does not delete any existing symbols; it controls the visibility of symbols in the current procedure level.

You can control symbol scoping using the SET SCOPE command. When SET SCOPE is called at a procedure level, it can hide the global symbols, the local symbols created at any outer procedure levels, or both, from the current procedure scope. SET SCOPE can also be used avoid problems where one or more symbols might conflict with DCL command verbs.

When the procedure level that called SET SCOPE exits, the scoping rules for the outer level are restored.

3.4 Expressions

Sec. 4.3, p. 51

An assignment statement assigns a value to a symbol. The value is determined by an expression on the right-hand side of the equal sign. Expressions are also used in other DCL commands, such as the IF command. Literals and symbols have already been used as simple expressions. When used in an expression, a literal stands for itself and a symbol stands for its current value. These simple expressions are useful but not powerful enough to compute new values, such as the sum of two integers.

New values are computed using expressions composed of *operators* and *operands.* An operator is a character or sequence of characters that stands for some mathematical operation, such as multiplication, or for a string operation, such as concatenation. The operands associated with an operator determine the values that are to participate in the operation. Here is a simple expression:

```
a * b
```

This denotes that the value of the symbol A is to be multiplied by the value of the symbol B to produce a new value. The gate of the new value is determined by the context in which the expression appears. So far, the only context in which an expression can appear is the assignment statement:

```
$    product = a * b
```

Here, the product of the values of A and B is assigned to the symbol PRODUCT. When DCL encounters an expression, it applies the operators to their operands in a certain predetermined order, producing a final result that is assigned to a symbol or used for some other purpose. When DCL processes an expression in this manner, we say that DCL *evaluates* the expression.

In order to completely understand expressions, you must become familiar with the available operators, the operands they expect, and the order in which the operators are applied to their operands. Tables 3.2, 3.3, and 3.4 describe the operators provided by DCL for use with integer, character string and Boolean values, respectively. Table 3.5 illustrates the order in which operators are applied.

Not all operators require two operands as multiplication does. Some require only one operand. (In the C language there is an operator that requires three operands.) The number of operands required by an operator is called its *arity*.

Operators with arity of 2 are called *binary operators.* Those with an arity of 1 are called *unary operators.* A few examples:

Table 3.2 Integer operators

Operator	Arity	Result type	Result value
+	Unary	Integer	Integer operand unchanged.
-	Unary	Integer	Negative of integer operand.
+	Binary	Integer	Sum of integer operands.
-	Binary	Integer	Difference of integer operands.
*	Binary	Integer	Product of integer operands.
/	Binary	Integer	Quotient of integer operands, truncated toward zero.
.EQ.	Binary	Boolean	True if integer operands are equal, false otherwise.
.NE.	Binary	Boolean	True if integer operands are unequal, false otherwise.
.GT.	Binary	Boolean	True if first integer operand is greater than second, false otherwise.
.GE.	Binary	Boolean	True if first integer operand is greater than or equal to second, false otherwise.
.LT.	Binary	Boolean	True if first integer operand is less than second, false otherwise.
.LE.	Binary	Boolean	True if first integer operand is less than or equal to second, false otherwise.
.NOT.	Unary	Integer	Bitwise Boolean NOT of integer operand. A bit in the result is 1 if the corresponding bit in the operand is zero, and vice versa.
.AND.	Binary	Integer	Bitwise Boolean AND of integer operands. A bit in the result is 1 if both of the corresponding bits in the operands are 1.
.OR.	Binary	Integer	Bitwise Boolean inclusive OR of integer operands. A bit in the result of 1 if either or both of the corresponding bits in the operands are 1.

```
$    sum = a + b - c
$    sum = -sum
$    positive = sum .gt. 0
$    negative = not. Positive
```

The first example contains an expression composed of two binary operators. The operands for the plus operator are A and B; the operands for the minus operator are the resulting sum and C. The second example uses the unary minus operator to negate its operand. Notice how the hyphen character us

Table 3.3
Character string operators

Operator	Arity	Result type	Result value
*	Binary	String	A copy of the first string operand with a copy of the second one concatenated to it (e.g., "Hello-" + "there." produces "Hello-there.").
-	Binary	String	A copy of the first string operand with the leftmost occurence of the second one removed from it (e.g., "oh-why-oh-why" - "why" produces "oh--oh-why").
.EQS.	Binary	Boolean	True if string operands contain the same character sequence, false otherwise.
.NES.	Binary	Boolean	True if string operands contain different character sequences, false otherwise.
.GTS.	Binary	Boolean	True if first string operand is alphabetically greater than second, false otherwise. The collating sequence is based on the ASCII character set.
.GES.	Binary	Boolean	True if first string operand is greater than or equal to second, false otherwise.
.LTS.	Binary	Boolean	True if first string operand is less than second, false otherswise.
.LES.	Binary	Boolean	True if first string operand is less than or equal to second, false otherwise.

Table 3.4
Boolean operators

Operator	Arity	Result type	Result value
.NOT.	Unary	Boolean	True if Boolean operands is false, false if it is true.
.AND.	Binary	Boolean	True if both Boolean operands are true, false otherwise. There is no guarantee about which operand is evaluated first.
.OR.	Binary	Boolean	True if either or both Boolean operands are true, false otherwise. There is no guarantee about which operand is evaluated first.

used as two different operators with different arities, its meaning determined by context. The third example uses the binary "greater than" operator to compare two numbers. The final example uses the unary "not" operator to invert its Boolean operand. The operator tables specify the arity and meaning of every DCL operator.

3.4 Expressions

Table 3.5 Operator precedence

Precedence	Operator
8 (highest)	( )
7	unary + −
6	* /
5	binary + −
4	.EQ. .NE. .GT. .GE. .LT. .LT. .EQS. .NES. .GTS. .GES. .LTS.
3	.NOT.
2	.AND.
1 (lowest)	.OR.

The order in which operators are applied to operands is determined by operator *precedence*. Table 3.5 lists the precedence of the DCL operators. An operator with a high precedence is applied before an operator with a lower precedence, regardless of the order of their appearance in the expression. Every operator is assigned a precedence so that the order of application can be determined without ambiguity. Here are a few expressions to illustrate operator precedence:

```
$     value = a * b + c
$     value = c + a * b
$     value = a * b - c * d
$     value = -x + y
```

Because multiplication has a higher precedence than addition, the first two examples both multiply by A by B before adding C. This is true even though, in the second example, the multiply operator appears after the add operator. The order of evaluation is determined by operator precedence, not merely by order of appearance. The third example calculates the product of A and B, and then the product of C and D, and finally subtracts one product from the other. The fourth example negates X and then adds Y; the precedence of unary minus is higher than that of addition. If there are two or more operators of equal precedence in an expression, such as the multiply operators in the third example above, the operators are evaluated from left to right. In the third example, A * B is evaluated before C * D.

Sometimes the order of evaluation determined by operator precedence is not what you want. Parentheses are used to force operators to be evaluated in a certain order regardless of their precedence. When parentheses surround a portion of an expression, that portion is evaluated before the surrounding expression, regardless of precedence. Here are the preceding examples with parentheses added:

```
$    value = a * (b + c)
$    value = (c + a) * b
$    value = a * (b - c) * d
$    value = -(x + y)
```

The first example now calculates the sum of B and C and then multiplies it by A. The sum appears in parentheses, so it is evaluated first, even though the precedence of multiplication is higher. The second one adds C and A and then multiplies the sum of B. The third example subtracts C from B, multiplies the difference by A, and then multiplies that result by D. The final example adds X and Y and negates the resulting sum. In each case, the final value is different when parentheses are used.

As DCL evaluates an expression, it must decide whether each operand represents an integer, string, or Boolean value. In some cases, the type of the operands actually affects the meaning of the operator. Such a case is the plus (+) operator, which performs addition when its operands are integers, but performs string concatenation when its operands are character strings. DCL uses the following rules to match operators and operand types:

- If the operator accepts only integer operands (e.g., * for multiply), then any string operands are first converted to integers.

- If the operator accepts only string operands (e.g., .EQS. for string compare equal), then any integer operands are first converted to strings.

- If the operator accepts either integers or strings (e.g., + for add or concatenate) and its operands are of different types, then integers win over strings and the string operand is first converted to an integer. For example, if you attempt to add an integer and a string, the string is first converted to an integer.

- If the operator is a Boolean operator (e.g., .AND. for logical and), then the operands are interpreted as Boolean values according to the rules given in Table 3.1.

A string can be converted to an integer as long as it contains a valid external representation of an integer (e.g., "-372" can be converted to -372). If it does not, it is converted to the integer 0. An integer can always be converted to a string by simply creating a string containing its external representation.

Because these operator/operand matching rules are complicated, it is best to avoid using operators with mixed operand types. You can explicitly request that a string be converted to an integer, or vice versa, using the lexical functions F$INTEGER and F$STRING presented in the next section.

3.4 Expressions

3.5 Lexical Functions

So far, we have worked with operands that can be integer literals, character string literals, symbols, or expressions. There is another form of operand called the *lexical function*. A lexical function, or simply function, is a built-in DCL subroutine that can perform complex operations related to character strings, files, processes, and other OpenVMS entities. A lexical function may be used in an expression wherever an operand is allowed. The general format of a lexical function is as follows:

    f$*name*(*argument1*, *argument2*, ...)

Each lexical function has a name beginning with F$ and includes a meaningful word or phrase that describes what the function does. Following the name is a pair of parentheses enclosing the *arguments* to the function. Each argument is itself an expression whose value is needed by the function in order to perform its intended operation. A lexical function may require one or more arguments, each of which is separated from the others by a comma. A few lexical functions require no arguments, but the parentheses must be included anyway.

A lexical function uses its argument values to perform its intended operation. The operation always results in a new value, which is returned by the function. The *return value* is used *in place of* the lexical function as DCL continues to evaluate the expression in which the function appears. Lexical functions are similar to symbols in this regard: The value of the symbol or lexical function is used in place of the symbol or lexical function itself.

A simple lexical function is F$LENGTH. It requires one argument, which must be a character string. The function determines the length of the string and returns it as an integer value. Assume that the symbol NAME contains a character string:

```
$    name_length = f$length(name)
$    name_too_long + f$length(name) .gt. 31
```

In the first example, F$LENGTH is used by itself to determine the length of the name and assign it to the symbol NAME_LENGTH. In the second example, the name length is compared to 31 to decide whether it is too long. The symbol NAME_TOO_LONG is set to true if the length is greater than 31, false otherwise. Lexical functions may be used by themselves or in combination with operators and other operands.

A lexical function that requires no arguments is F$TIME. It returns the current system time as a character string:

```
$    current_time = f$time()
```

Note that the parentheses are required even though they enclose no arguments. In this example, the system time is assigned to the symbol `CURRENT_TIME`.

Each argument to a lexical function is an expression. This means that an argument to a lexical function can be another lexical function, as in this example:

```
$     time_length = f$length(f$time())
```

The argument to the `F$LENGTH` function is the `F$TIME` function. The `F$TIME` function returns the current system time, which is then passed to `F$LENGTH` to determine its length. The `F$LENGTH` function returns to the length, which is assigned to `TIME_LENGTH`.

Some lexical functions accept *optional arguments.* An optional argument may be included or omitted according to the requirements of each use of the lexical function. If an optional argument is omitted, the function provides a *default value* that is commonly needed. The `F$GETSYI` lexical function is one that takes an optional argument. The function obtains information about a OpenVMS system ("get system information"). Its first argument is required and specifies the desired item of information. The second argument is optional and specifies the OpenVMS Cluster node from which the information is to be obtained. If the second argument is omitted, the information is obtained from the local node, the one on which you are running. This default represents the most common use of the function, particularly since the local node is the only available node on a system that is not a member of a cluster. Here are some examples:

```
$     OpenVMS_version = f$getsyi("NODE_SWVERS")
$     node_version = f$getsyi("NODE_SWVERS", node)
```

The first example obtains the OpenVMS version for the local node and assigns it to the symbol `OpenVMS_VERSION`. Note how the second argument is not specified, so the local node is assumed. The second example obtains the OpenVMS version for the node whose name is the value of the symbol `NODE`. The symbol can contain the name of any node in the OpenVMS Cluster, including the local one.

When the lexical function accepts three or more arguments, and some of the arguments in the middle are not included, you must still specify the correct number of commas preceding the arguments you include. For example, the `F$PARSE` function accepts up to five arguments. If only the first and fourth arguments are desired, three consecutive commas are required to signify that the second and third arguments are missing:

Sec. 13.2, p. 152

```
$     file_name = f$parse(file_spec,,,"NAME")
```

The `F$GETSYI` lexical function is one of many functions that accept *keyword* arguments. A keyword argument is a character string selected from a fixed set of strings, each of which specifies an item of information or a particular operation to be performed by the function. The first argument to `F$GETSYI` is a keyword that names the item of system information to be returned. The keyword cannot be arbitrary character string but must be chosen from a predetermined repertoire of strings, each of which denotes a particular item. Keyword strings can be specified in uppercase or lowercase letters. In this book, all keywords appear in uppercase to emphasize that they are keywords and not arbitrary strings.

The following sections describe lexical functions that determine the type of a data item and convert between the integer and string types.

3.5.1 A Type-Checking Function

The `F$TYPE` lexical function provides a type-checking capability for DCL. The `F$TYPE` function requires a single argument, which must be a symbol name; an arbitrary expression is not allowed. The function inspects the value of the symbol and returns one of three strings:

"INTEGER" This string is returned if the value of the symbol is an integer or a string whose value is the external representation of an integer (e.g., `"0"`, `"42"`, `"-4872"`.

"STRING" This string is returned if the value of the symbol is a string (unless the string represents a valid integer).

"" The null string is returned if the symbol has not been created.

So `F$TYPE` is useful not only to determine the type of a symbol's value, but also to determine whether the symbol exists at all. If the symbol has not been created, the null string is returned. Here are a few examples:

```
$ number = 42
$ type = f$type(number)
$ show symbol type
    TYPE = "INTEGER"
```

—or—

```
$ string = "Margaritaville!"
$ type = f$type(string)
$ show symbol type
    TYPE = "STRING"
```

—or—

```
$ string = "  -987"
$ type = f$type(string)
$ show symbol type
    TYPE = "INTEGER"
```

–or–

```
$ type = f$type(nonexistent_symbol)
$ show symbol type
    TYPE = ""
```

3.5.2 Conversion Functions

DCL provides two lexical functions to perform data conversions: F$INTEGER and F$STRING. The F$INTEGER function requires a single argument, which can be any expression producing a character string result. The string is converted to an integer, and the integer is returned. If the string does not contain the external representation of an integer, zero is returned. The F$STRING function requires a single argument, which can be any expression producing an integer result. As you might expect, the integer is converted to a string, and the string is returned. If the argument to one of these functions is already of the correct type, it is simply returned by the function.

Here are a few examples:

```
$ string = "108"
$ integer = f$integer("-" + string)
$ show symbol integer
    INTEGER -108   Hex = FFFFFF94   Octal = 37777777624
```

–or–

```
$ string = "gobble-dee-gook"
$ integer = f$integer(string)
$ show symbol integer
    INTEGER + 0   Hex = 00000000   Octal = 00000000000
```

–or–

```
$ integer = 384726
$ string = f$string(integer/2)
$ show symbol string
    STRING = "192363"
```

3.5.3 Character String Manipulation

The F$LENGTH lexical function allows you to determine the length of a character string. There are two more lexical functions that are fundamental to the manipulation of strings: F$LOCATE and F$EXTRACT.

The F$LOCATE function searches one string (the target) for an occurrence of another string (the pattern). It returns the *index* in the target of the first (leftmost) occurrence of the pattern. The index of the first character in a string is zero, the second character is 1, and so forth. If the pattern does not occur in the target, the length of the target is returned. The pattern is the first argument to the function, the target the second. For the following examples, assume that the symbol PHRASE contains an English phrase and the symbol WORD contains a single word:

```
$!    Find the position of a question mark in the phrase.
$
$     qm_index = f$locate("?", phrase)
$
$!    Determine whether the phrase contains the word "who"
$
$     who_index = f$locate("who", phrase)
$
$!    Find the position of the word in the phrase.
$
$     word_index = f$locate(word, phrase)
```

The F$EXTRACT lexical function makes a copy of a portion of a character string and returns a new string containing the copy. The portion of the string to be copied is called the *substring*. A substring can be any part of a string: perhaps the first few characters, a section in the middle, the final few characters, or even the entire string. The F$EXTRACT function requires three arguments: the starting index of the substring, the length of the substring, and the string from which the substring is to be extracted. The portion of the string beginning at the starting index and continuing for the length is copied and returned by the function. The following examples expand upon the previous ones:

```
$!    Chop off the phrase at the end of the question mark.
$
$     phrase = f$extract(0, qm_index, phrase)
$
$!    Eliminate the word "who" from the phrase.
$!    (Note that the hyphen is a continuation character.)
$
$     wo_who = f$extract(0, who_index, phrase) + -
              f$extract(who_index+3, 9999, phrase)
```

```
$
$!      Get a copy of the word plus its surrounding characters.
$
$       context = f$extract(word_index-1, f$length(word)+2, -
                              phrase)
```

Assume that the value of PHRASE is "So who is the winner?" and the value of WORD is "the". After the above commands are executed, the values of the resulting symbol are as follows:

```
QM_INDEX: 20
WHO_INDEX: 3
WORD_INDEX: 10
PHRASE: "So who is the winner"
WO_WHO: "So  is the winner"
CONTEXT: " the "
```

When working with character strings and the lexical functions that manipulate them, there are a few things to keep in mind:

- The characters in a string are indexed beginning with zero.
- Therefore, the index of the last character in a string is 1 less than the length of the string.
- The F$LOCATE function returns the length of the target if the pattern does not occur in it.
- The first argument to the F$EXTRACT function is an index, but the second argument is a length.
- If the starting index for an F$EXTRACT function is past the end of the string, the null string is returned. If the length extends past the end of the string, only the existing characters are returned.
- Therefore, to extract a substring beginning at a certain point and extending for the rest of the string, specify a length greater than the longest possible string (e.g., 9999).

3.6 Substring Assignment

DCL provides a facility that lets you alter a substring of an existing character string. When a substring assignment is specified, you choose the portion of the string to be replaced.

The general form of a substring assignment is as follows:

```
$    symbol[index,length] := "replacement"
```

The *symbol* is the name of a symbol containing the character string to be altered; *index* and *length* specify the boundaries of the substring. The substring begins with the character specified by the index. The length determines the number of characters in the substring; it must be zero or positive. The assignment statement will replace the characters beginning at the index and extending for the length. Both the index and length can be arbitrary expressions. The replacement text is specified as a string literal following the substring assignment indicator (:=). The characters in the substring are replaced by the characters in the replacement string.

If the replacement string is shorter than the substring, it is padded on the right with spaces to make it the required length. If it is longer than the substring, it is truncated to the require length.

Here are a few examples:

```
$    string = ".This is a string."
$    string[0,1] := "("
$    string[f$length(string)-1,1] := ")"
$
$    string[0,9] := " "
$
$    i = 10
$    string[i,3] := "---"
```

The goal of the first example is to replace the first and last characters of the string with parentheses. Replacing the first character is easy: the index is zero and the length is 1. The index of the last character is determined by obtaining the length of the string and subtracting 1. This index, coupled with a length of 1, is used to replace the last character. Note that the length of a string is 1 greater than the index of its final character because the indexes begin at zero. The result of the first example is "`(This is the string)`".

The second example replaces the first nine characters of the string with a single space. Because the replacement string is shorter than the substring, it is padded on the right with spaces to the length of the substring being replaced. This results in a string of nine spaces that overlays the substring. It would work just as well to specify the null string ("") as the replacement value, but the single space emphasizes that the substring is being blanked. The result of the second example is "` a string)`".

The third example replaces three characters of the string with dashes. The starting index is specified by the symbol I, which in this case has the value 10. Therefore, the characters within the indexes 10 through 12 are replaced with dashes. The result of the third example is "` a---ring)`".

If the starting index of the substring is beyond the end of the existing string, the string is padded with spaces to extend it to the required length. After the padding is performed, the substring is replaced. For example:

```
$    buffer = ""
$    buffer[4,4] := "abcd"
```

The BUFFER symbol is first initialized to the null string. The starting index of the substring assignment is 4, so the buffer is padded with four spaces, and then the fourth through seventh characters are set to "abcd". The resulting string is "   abcd".

The substring assignment indicator := specifies that the assignment is done to a symbol at the current procedure level. The indicator :== specifies that the assignment is done to a global symbol.

You must be wary of a few idiosyncrasies exhibited by the substring assignment:

- No space can appear between the symbol and the left square bracket [.

- The length of the symbol name plus the length of the replacement string cannot exceed 1,024 characters.

- The maximum index value is 768. The sum of the index and length cannot exceed 769.

- In an obsolete variation of substring assignment, the replacement text need not be enclosed in double quotes. In this case, all the characters following the := operator are taken as the replacement text. The behavior of this form of assignment is confusing, because you expect an expression on the right-hand side of the assignment operator.

- The previous point makes it clear that the replacement text cannot be an expression or even a simple symbol. However, there is a way to replace a substring with the value of a symbol using a substitution operation.

Sec. 5.3, p. 72

3.7 Bit-Field Assignment

The bit-field assignment facility allows you to alter the sequence of bits that make up the value of a symbol. Bits can be altered in both integer and character string values. The general form of a bit-field assignment is as follows:

$ *symbol[position, size]* = *expression*

The use of bit-field assignment to alter bits in an integer value is rare and will not be described in detail in this book. It is more common to create or alter character strings. In order to effectively use bit-field assignment on character strings, you must first illustrate how the bits in a character string are numbered. The following picture illustrates the numbering scheme for the bits in the character string "ABC":

```
index 0    [    A    ]
           7         0

index 1    [    B    ]
           15        8

index 2    [    C    ]
           23       16
```

Every character is composed of eight bits. The first character has bits numbered 0–7, the second has bits numbered 8–15, and so on. In other words, the position of the least significant bit of each character is equal to the character's index in the string times eight. The bit-field assignment specifies both the *position* of the least significant bit and the *size* of the field to be altered. The position is limited to 6,151 and the size to 32 bits.

The assignment indicator = specifies that the bit assignment is done to a symbol at the current procedure level. The indicator == specifies that the assignment is done to a global symbol.

The *replacement* expression must be an integer expression. When the *symbol* specified in a bit-field assignment does not exist, DCL creates a new symbol with a character string value. The characters in the string are derived from the integer value of the replacement expression. Each bit in the integer value becomes the corresponding bit in the character string value. So bits 0–7 of the integer become the first character, bits 8–15 become the second character, and so on. A character string of up to four characters can be created in this manner. For example, here is an assignment statement that creates a character string containing a form feed:

```
$    formfeed[0,8] = %x0C
```

Assuming the symbol FORMFEED does not exist, this assignment creates the symbol and assigns it a character string value. The bit position is 0 and the size 8, so the symbol's value will be a 1-character string derived from the replacement expression. The replacement expression has the hexadecimal value 0C, which is the ASCII code for a form feed.

There is a trick to creating a string with more than one character. The following assignment statement creates a string containing a carriage return/line feed pair:

```
$       crlf[0,16] = %x0A0D
$!                    ^^--- first character
$!                  ^^----- second character
```

The bit position is 0 and the size 16, so a two-character string is created. The hexadecimal literal contains two characters, a carriage return (%x0D) and a line feed (%x0A). They appear to be backwards, but remember that the first character is in bits 0–7 and the second in bits 8–15. So the carriage return will be deposited as the first character in the string, and the line feed as the second one.

Bit-field assignment is the best way to create character strings containing control characters. Do not include a control character directly in a DCL procedure, because strange things can happen when you display the procedure at a terminal or if you print it.

If the symbol in a bit-field assignment already exists and has a character string value, then the assignment replaces characters in the string with new ones. As always, the bit position and size specify the particular characters that are replaced, and the replacement expression gives the ASCII value of the new characters. If the position specifies bits beyond the end of the string, it is extended with zero bits to the required length. Here is an example of replacing a character in a string.

```
$       message = "Hello there.XXGood-bye."
$       message[12*8,16] = %x0A0D
```

The symbol MESSAGE is assigned a character string. The bit-field assignment then replaces the XX sequence with the carriage return/line feed combination. The bit position of the first X is specified as the product of 12, the character index of the X and 8, the number of bits per character.

The above assignment will work, but it is certainly not perspicuous. It is better to create the message with simple concatenation:

```
$       message = "Hello there." + crlf + "Good-bye."
```

This method of creating the message does not use bit-field assignment at all. However, it does the value of the CRLF symbol created above to obtain the carriage return/line feed characters.

If the symbol in a bit-field assignment exists and has an integer value, then the assignment alters bits in the integer value. This form of bit-field assignment is rarely used and will not be described in this book.

Table 3.6
Summary of assignment commands

Command	Operation
A = *expression*	Set procedure-level symbol to value of expression.
A == *expression*	Set global symbol to value of expression.
A[*i,l*] := "*text*"	Replace substring of procedure-level symbol with new text.
A[*i,l*] :== "*text*"	Replace substring of global symbol with new text.
A[*p,s*] = *expression*	Replace bit field of procedure-level symbol with value of expression.
A[*p,s*] == *expression*	Replace bit field of global symbol with value of expression.

3.8 Summary of Assignment Commands

Table 3.6 summarizes the various forms of the DCL assignment command.

3.9 Deleting Symbols

Symbols at the prompt and global levels are never deleted automatically by DCL; they remain in existence as long as your process does. All the symbols created at a procedure level are deleted when the procedure exits. You can explicitly request that a symbol be deleted using the DELETE/SYMBOL command. There are two variations of the command, the first being used to delete prompt- or procedure-level symbols:

```
$ delete/symbol note
```

When used at the DCL prompt, the command will delete the prompt-level symbol named NOTE. When used in a procedure, the command will delete the procedure-level symbol NOTE.

The second variation of the command is used to delete global symbols. A global symbol can be deleted at the DCL prompt or in a procedure, as follows:

```
$    delete/symbol/global xda_answer
```

The /GLOBAL qualifier specifies that a global symbol is to be deleted.

There is rarely any reason to delete procedure-level symbols. Because they are deleted automatically when the procedure exits, you don't have to worry about lots of symbols cluttering up procedure levels or conflicting with other procedures.

CHAPTER 4

Flow of Control

THE PREVIOUS CHAPTER PRESENTED SYMBOLS and expressions, the tools DCL provides for creating and manipulating data. Without some means for making decisions about data, however, there is not much a procedure can do with data other than display it. This chapter presents DCL commands that allow a procedure to make decisions and take different actions based on those decisions. These commands are called *flow-of-control commands* because they are used to control and alter the flow of execution through the procedure. Each time the procedure is run, DCL can execute distinct portions of the procedure based on data obtained or calculated by it.

4.1 Sequential Execution

When you run a DCL procedure with the at-sign (@) command, DCL executes the commands in the procedure one at a time, in order, from top to bottom. This is called *sequential execution* of commands. Simple procedures can be written using only sequential execution:

```
$!   A procedure named SIMPLE-PROC
$
$    show time
$    directory
$    show users
```

This procedure first displays the current date and time. It then displays a listing of the files in the working directory. Finally it displays a list of the users logged in to the system.

In order to run this procedure, you use the at-sign command. The name of the procedure file is specified following the at-sign, and DCL runs the procedure:

```
$ @simple-proc
18-MAR-1988 17:54:39:17

Directory LISPW$: [GREEK]

ARCHREQ.TXT;10    BACK-UP-VAXSTATION.COM;1    BASE-DEVO,DIS;3
BASE-DEVOS.DIS;2  BINDECLIB.DIS;4  CHECKSZ.COM;1   CLCS.DIR;1
 .
 .
 .
$
```

We say that the at-sign *runs* or *executes* a procedure. When DCL reaches the end of a procedure file, the procedure is terminated and the DCL prompt appears again. DCL is ready for the next command.

4.2 The GOTO Command

Simple procedures can be written using only sequential execution, but flow-of-control commands are needed to construct the majority of useful procedures. The GOTO command is a fundamental flow-of-control command that allows a procedure to alter the normal sequential execution of commands. A GOTO command breaks sequential execution and redirects DCL to another part of the procedure.

Here is a procedure containing a GOTO command:

```
$    show time
$    directory
$    goto another_place
$    show users
$
$another_place:
$    show memory
```

This procedure begins by displaying the time and directory listing. Then DCL encounters the GOTO command, which specifies ANOTHER_PLACE as its destination. The name of the destination of a GOTO command is called a *label* because it labels a particular point in the procedure. When DCL encounters a `GOTO`, it ceases sequential execution, ignoring the commands immediately following the `GOTO`, and takes up execution at the line containing the label. Sequential execution is resumed at the line containing the label. In this example, DCL continues execution at the line labeled `ANOTHER_PLACE` after displaying information about system memory and finally terminates the procedure. The `SHOW USERS` command is *never* executed.

A `GOTO` command can specify a label preceding it in the procedure as well as one following it. Here is an example:

```
$    show time
$again:
$    show users
$    goto again
$    show memory
```

After displaying the time, DCL encounters the label `AGAIN`. DCL executes the `SHOW USERS` command. It then comes to the `GOTO` command, which specifies the label that appeared earlier in the procedure. DCL suspends sequential execution, locates the label, and resumes execution at the line containing the label. This causes the `SHOW USERS` command to be executed once more, followed by the `GOTO`, followed again by `SHOW USERS`, and so on indefinitely. The procedure stuck in an *infinite loop* and never terminates. The `SHOW MEMORY` command is never executed.

A procedure should not contain duplicate labels. When a duplicate label appears in a procedure, it "replaces" the previous label of the same name. DCL remembers the position of the second label and forgets the first one without issuing a warning message. Your procedure may then behave in a strange manner, because `GOTO` commands might not alter the flow of execution to the expected point in the procedure.

The `GOTO` command is of little use by itself. All you can do with it is skip commands or cause infinite loops. Some kinds of decision-making commands are needed to vary the action of the `GOTO` command.

4.3 The IF Command

The `IF` command is the means by which procedures can make decisions. Once a decision is made, a procedure can choose one of two alternative actions. The actions are disjoint; DCL executes one or the other but not both. The ability to make decisions, coupled with the `GOTO` command's ability to alter the sequential flow of execution, provides all the power you need to solve arbitrarily complex problems with a computer.

In all recent OpenVMS versions, there are two forms of the IF command: simple and compound.

The first form of the IF command, the simple form, consists of an expression and a command, as follows:

```
$    if expression then command
```

Sec. 3.2.3, p. 26

The expression must result in a Boolean value. If the value is true, the command following the word THEN is executed. If the value is false, the command is ignored. Nothing else is done with the expression value; its sole purpose is to determine whether or not the command is executed. The expression is called the *condition*, because its true/false condition determines whether the command is executed.

Here is a simple example:

```
$    if f$getsyi("PAGEFILE_FREE") .lt. 50000 then -
        write sys$output "WARNING: paging space is low."
$    show time
```

The expression in this IF command uses the F$GETSYI lexical function to determine whether the amount of free paging file space is less than 50,000 blocks. The expression's value is true if there are fewer than 50,000 blocks, false if there are 50,000 or more. When the value is true, the WRITE command is executed to display the message. When the value is false, the WRITE command is ignored. In either case, sequential execution continues and the time is displayed.

The real power of the IF command emerges when it is used in conjunction with the GOTO command. The following code uses the IF command to skip a group of commands in the event they should not be excuted.

```
$    if f$getsyi("PAGEFILE_FREE") .ge. 50000 then goto skip
$       write sys$output "WARNING: paging space is low."
$       show memory
$skip:
$    show time
```

The expression in the IF command tests the number of free paging file blocks, just as in the previous example. However, instead of testing whether the number is less than 50,000, the condition is inverted to test whether the number is greater than or equal to 50,000. If so, the GOTO command redirects execution to the SKIP label. If not, the GOTO command is ignored and *both* the WRITE and SHOW MEMORY commands are executed. This is how a group of commands can be executed or skipped based on an IF test. In either case, sequential execution continues at the SKIP label and the SHOW TIME command is executed.

Now that you understand how to use IF and GOTO to conditionally execute a group of commands, it is time to learn how the GOTO can be avoided. Modern programming practice dictates that commands such as `GOTO`, which allow arbitrary changes to a program's control flow, should be shunned because a program with a lot of GOTOs can easily deteriorate into a complex "bowl of spaghetti," which is difficult to follow. The `GOTO` command also requires that you constantly devise labels that serve no purpose other than to group statements together. The compound form of the `IF` command allows a group of commands to be executed when the condition expression is true, without the use of the `GOTO` command. The previous example can be rewritten as follows:

```
$	if f$getsyi("PAGEFILE_FREE") .lt. 50000
$	then
$	  write sys$output "WARNING: paging space is low."
$	  show memory
$	endif
$	show time
```

When the condition in the `IF` command is true, all the commands between the `THEN` and the `ENDIF` are executed. When the condition is false, the commands are skipped. In either case, execution continues with the command following the `ENDIF`. Notice how the `IF` command has reverted to testing for free blocks less than 50,000, a more natural test because the critical condition is "less than 50,000 blocks," not "greater than or equal to 50,000 blocks." Notice also that there are no `GOTO` commands with their clutter of command labels.

The first command in the group (`WRITE`) can appear on the same line as the `THEN` keyword, although the authors feel it is better style to use a separate line for the first command. The `ENDIF` keyword must appear on a line by itself. Note also that the commands between the `THEN` and the `ENDIF` are indented two columns to emphasize that they are grouped together. This is not required, but it helps a reader of the procedure to see where the group begins and ends.

It is often the case that one group of commands is to be executed when a condition is true and an alternative group is to be executed when it is false. The second form of the `IF` command accommodates this requirement with the `ELSE` keyword:

```
$	if f$getsyi("PAGEFILE_FREE") .lt. 50000
$	then
$	  write sys$output "WARNING: paging space is low."
$	  show memory
$	else
$	  write sys$output "Paging space is fine."
$	endif
$	show time
```

4.3 The IF Command

The block of commands between the ELSE and ENDIF keywords is only executed if the condition is false. So if the condition is true, the WRITE and SHOW MEMORY commands are executed, and if it is false, the single WRITE command is executed to display "Paging space is fine.". As usual, regardless of whether the condition is true or false, execution continues with the SHOW TIME command following the ENDIF.

The two forms if the IF command provide the capability to conditionally execute single commands or groups without the need for any GOTO commands.

4.3.1 The IF Command Prior to OpenVMS Version 5.0

The compound form of the IF command, which allows groups of commands to be executed as one unit, is not available prior to OpenVMS Version 5.0. If a version prior to Version 5.0 is being used, the compound IF command must be constructed with simple IF and GOTO commands. Here is the example of an IF with a group of commands to be executed when the Boolean expression is true:

```
$     if f$getsyi("PAGEFILE_FREE") .ge. 50000 then goto 19
$        write sys$output "WARNING: paging space is low."
$        show memory
$19:
$     show time
```

The WRITE and SHOW MEMORY commands are to be executed when there are fewer than 50,000 free paging file blocks. The IF expression is arranged so that the GOTO will skip the command when there are enough blocks. The label 19 marks the end of the commands that are conditionally executed, and it serves as the target of the GOTO.

Here is the example with one group of commands to be executed when the condition is true, another when it is false:

```
$     if f$getsyi("PAGEFILE_FREE") .lt. 50000 then goto 15
$        write sys$output "WARNING: paging space is low."
$        show memory
$        goto 19
$15:
$        write sys$output  "Paging space is fine."
$19:
$     show time
```

In the previous example, the GOTO command specified label 19, the end of the entire IF construct. In this example, it specifies label 15, which marks the beginning of the commands to be executed when the IF expression is false. In addition, a new GOTO command is required after the SHOW MEMORY command in order to skip around the second WRITE command. Here is the overall flow of control depending upon the number of free paging file blocks:

Less than 50,000 The condition is false, so the GOTO is ignored. The WRITE and SHOW MEMORY commands are executed. The GOTO 19 command skips to the end of the IF construct.

Greater than or equal to 50,000 The condition is true, so the GOTO is performed. Execution continues at label 15 and the "Paging space is fine." message is displayed. Execution falls through to the end of the construct.

The authors use the following labeling convention for an IF construct prior to OpenVMS Version 5.0: the end of the construct is marked with a numeric label equal to a multiple of ten plus nine. If the construct has an "else" alternative, it is assigned a label equal to the same multiple of ten plus five. The example uses 15 and 19. This labeling scheme is consistent with the one presented for loops.

4.4 Loops

A *loop* is a sequence of commands that is repeatedly executed until some termination condition arises. Section 4.2 described how to set up an infinite loop, one that never terminates. This is rarely useful because the command procedure executes forever. A loop that eventually terminates must check for a termination condition and stop looping when the condition is met. Each execution of the commands in a loop is called an *iteration*.

Here is a loop that iterates exactly ten times:

```
$       count = 0
$10:    count = count + 1
$       if count .gt. 10 then goto 19
$       show users
$       goto 10
$19:
```

The symbol COUNT is used to maintain a count of the number of iterations. It is initialized to zero and incremented at the beginning of each iteration. The loop is terminated when the counter exceeds ten. The SHOW USERS command is therefore executed exactly ten times. Here is what happens on the first iteration:

1. The value of COUNT is incremented from 0 to 1.

2. The value of COUNT is compared to 10. Since it is less, the condition is false and the GOTO 19 command is ignored.

3. The SHOW USERS command is executed.

4. The GOTO 10 command redirects execution back to the beginning of the loop.

In contrast, this is what happens on the 11th iteration:

1. The value of COUNT is incremented from 10 to 11.

2. The value of COUNT is compared to 10. Since it is greater, the condition is true and the GOTO 19 command is executed. It redirects execution to the line labeled 19, thus terminating the loop.

The authors use the following labeling convention for a loop: The beginning of the loop has a numeric label that is a multiple of ten. The line following the loop has a numeric label equal to the beginning label plus nine. The example use 10 and 19. In addition to the labeling convention, the commands within the loop are indented two columns. These commands are called the *loop body*.

There are many ways to control loop termination other than with a simple counter. Assume we have a character string in the symbol LINE and we want to remove all the spaces from the string. The following loop accomplishes this task:

```
$10:    if f$locate(" ",line) .eq. f$length(line) then goto 19
$         line = line - " "
$         goto 10
$19:
```

Sec. 3.5.3, p. 42

The F$LOCATE lexical function takes two arguments, a pattern string and a target string. It scans the target string for an occurrence of the pattern and returns the index of the pattern in the target. If the pattern does not occur in the target, the length of the target string is returned. In this example, the F$LOCATE function is used to determine whether the line contains any spaces. If not, the loop is terminated. If so, the leftmost space is removed from the line with the string reduction operator (−) and the loop is repeated. Eventually, all spaces will be removed and the loop will terminate.

Sec. 3.5.3, p. 42

The preceding loop could also be written as follows:

```
$10:    line = line - " "
$         if f$locate(" ",line) .eq. f$length(line) then goto 19
$         goto 10
$19:
```

It is perfectly fine to write the loop this way, because the string reduction operator is harmless if there is no space in the line. The loop removes a space if there is one and then checks the line to see if it is free of spaces. If not, the loop is repeated. By reorganizing the loop this way, we push the termination test to the bottom of the loop. This allows us to combine the terminating IF command with the final GOTO command:

```
$10:    line = line - " "
$       if f$locate(" ",line) .ne. f$length(line) then goto 10
$19:
```

In this case, the IF command determines whether there are any more spaces in the line and redirects execution to the beginning of the loop if there are. When all spaces have been removed, the IF command "falls through" to the label following the loop and the loop is terminated. The label 19 is no longer the target of any GOTO commands and is therefore technically unnecessary, but it is left as a visual indicator of the end of the loop.

A loop may require more than one termination test. The following loop finds the first parenthesis in a string:

```
$       i = -1
$10:    i = i + 1
$       if i .ge. f$length(line) then goto 19
$       if f$extract(i,1,line) .eqs. "(" .or. -
            f$extract(i,1,line) .eqs. ")" then goto 19
$       goto 10
$19:
```

The symbol I is used as an index into the string. It is initialized to 1 and incremented each time through the loop. Remember that the characters in a string are indexed beginning with zero. Two termination tests are required. The first one checks to see if I has become too large to index the string. If the first check does not terminate the loop, then I can be used as a string index. The second IF checks to see if the character indexed by I is an open or a close parenthesis and terminates the loop if so. If neither test terminates the loop, another iteration is started.

Sec. 3.5.3, p. 42

The condition of the second IF command in the preceding example is more complicated than in previous IF commands. The Boolean expression contains the .OR. operator. Because of the relative precedence of the .EQS. and .OR. operators, the string comparisons are performed first. The first comparison produces a true value if the character is an open parenthesis, false if not. The second comparison produces a true value if the if the character is a close parenthesis, false if not. The result of the .OR. operation is true if either comparison was true, false if both were false. In other words, the final result is true if the character is a parenthesis, false if not.

4.4 Loops

4.5 Invoking a Command Procedure

Chapter 2 presented a cursory overview of the at-sign command and how it is used to run a command procedure. This section describes the at-sign command in greater detail. When you enter a command at the DCL prompt, DCL reads the command form the keyboard and executes it. If the command is an at-sign command, DCL stops reading commands from the keyboard and instead reads them from the command procedure file specified following the at-sign. Once it has read all the commands from the procedure, DCL resumes reading commands from the keyboard. At first, this may seem like a trivial concept, but it is really quite a powerful one.

We use the *level* to refer to DCL's source of commands. The DCL prompt is at *prompt level*, and a procedure invoked from prompt level is said to run at *procedure level* 1. It is perfectly permissible for a procedure running at level 1 to invoke another procedure, which would then be running at procedure level 2. Here is an example:

```
$!    This is procedure A
$
$     show time
$     @b
$     show time


$!    This is procedure B
$
$     show users
```

If you invoke procedure A from the DCL prompt, it runs at procedure level 1. After displaying the current time, it invokes procedure B with the at-sign command. Procedure B then runs at procedure level 2, displays a list of the current users, and terminates. When B terminates, execution continues in procedure A with the line following the at-sign command (the second SHOW TIME). The time is displayed again, A terminates, and the DCL prompt reappears. The important point is that DCL remembers the line in procedure A where execution must continue after B terminates. This place is called the *return point*. DCL can keep track of the return points for up to 32 procedure levels, more than most applications ever require.

In the jargon of programming languages, a procedure invoked by another procedure is called a *subprocedure* or *subroutine*. The at-sign command provides the DCL programmer with a straightforward subroutine capability.

4.5.1 Parameters

In order to create a procedure that can vary its actions from one use to the next, there must be a way for the user of the procedure to provide it with data and control information. For example, a procedure that deletes or purges all the files with the file type TMP must be told whether it should delete or purge. There are many ways to provide a procedure with information; one of the most common is called the procedure *parameter*. A procedure parameter is an item of information passed to the procedure when it is invoked with the at-sign command. You can pass as many as eight parameters to a procedure.

Here is a procedure that can delete or purge all of the TMP files in the working directory:

```
$!      Procedure CLEAN-UP
$!      First parameter is the word DELETE or PURGE.
$
$       if p1 .eqs. "DELETE" then delete *.tmp;*
$       if p1 .eqs. "PURGE"  then purge  *.tmp
```

When this procedure is invoked, it is provided with a parameter that specifies whether temporary files should be deleted or purged. There are two ways to invoke it:

```
$ @clean-up delete
```

—or—

```
$ @clean-up purge
```

The parameter is specified after the procedure name and must be separated from it by one or more spaces. Before DCL begins to execute the procedure, it creates a special procedure-level symbol named P1 whose value is the specified parameter. The parameter is converted to uppercase letters unless it is enclosed in double quotes. The value of the P1 symbol is always a character string, even if the parameter is an integer. When CLEAN-UP is invoked with the first command, P1 has the value "DELETE". When it is invoked with the second command, P1 has the value "PURGE". The IF commands in the procedure compare the value of P1 against two literal strings to decide which function to perform.

You can specify up to eight parameters to a procedure. They are stored in the symbols P1, P2, and so on, up through P8. There are always eight symbols regardless of the number of parameters specified. Those symbols that have no corresponding parameter are set to the null string. Do not use these special symbols for any purpose other than to access the parameters. The symbols are procedure-level symbols and so are deleted when the procedure exits.

Spaces are used to separate the parameters in an at-sign command. If a single parameter contains spaces or slashes (/), it must be enclosed in quotation marks. The quotation marks group all the enclosed characters into one parameter. Here is a procedure that accepts two messages, displays them, and remembers them in two global symbols:

```
$!    Procedure REMEMBER
$!    The first parameter is one message
$!    The second parameter is another message
$
$     write sys$output p1
$     write sys$output p2
$     save_message1 == p1
$     save_message2 == p2
```

The two messages are passed as parameters 1 and 2 and so are obtained by the procedure using symbols P1 and P2. Both messages are displayed and then saved in the symbols SAVE_MESSAGE1 and SAVE_MESSAGE2. The procedure is invoked with a command such as

```
$ @remember "go to the grocery store" "get a video tape"
```

Because the messages contain spaces, they must be enclosed in quotation marks. This makes it clear that the first message is "go to the grocery store" and the second one is "get a video tape". If the procedure is invoked without the quotation marks:

```
$ @remember go to the grocery store get a video tape
```

then each word appears to be a separate parameter, because parameters are separated by spaces. In this case, there would be nine parameters, more than are allowed by DCL.

A procedure parameter must be enclosed in quotation marks in the following circumstances:

- When the parameter contains spaces or slash characters.

- When the parameter contains lowercase letters that must not be converted to uppercase.

4.5.2 The EXIT Command

When DCL runs out of commands in a procedure file, it automatically terminates the procedure. If the procedure was invoked from the DCL prompt, the prompt reappears and you can enter another command. If the procedure was invoked form another procedure, the original procedure resumes execution with the command following the at-sign command. The termination of a procedure is called *procedure exit*. The EXIT command can be used to cause procedure exit before DCL gets to the bottom of the procedure.

Here is the CLEAN-UP procedure with an EXIT command:

```
$!    Procedure CLEAN-UP
$!    First parameter is the word DELETE or PURGE.
$
$     if p1 .nes. "DELETE" .and. p1 .nes. "PURGE"
$     then
$       write sys$output "Parameter must be DELETE or PURGE."
$       exit
$     endif
$
$     if p1 .eqs. "DELETE" then delete *.tmp;*
$     if p1 .eqs. "PURGE"  then purge  *.tmp
```

The new IF command checks the parameter to make sure it is either "DELETE" of "PURGE". If not, an error message is displayed and an EXIT command is executed: the procedure terminates immediately. If the parameter is valid, the procedure continues with its task.

The preceding example illustrates a common use for the EXIT command. Procedure parameters are checked at the beginning of the procedure to ensure that they are valid. If not, the EXIT command is employed to terminate the procedure before it begins its real work. Be careful not to overuse the EXIT command; a person reading your procedure has to be particularly aware of each EXIT command because it stops the natural flow of execution from top to bottom.

4.6 The CALL Command

The CALL command provides a subroutine capability similar to the at-sign command, except that the subroutine resides in the same procedure file as the command that invokes it. The CALL command was introduced in OpenVMS Version 5.0 Here is a procedure that uses the CALL command:

```
$     call show_disks "Before the program:"
$     run sys$system:application-pgm
$     call show_disks "After the program:"
$     exit
$
$show_disks:
$     subroutine
$     write sys$output p1
$     show time
```

```
$   show device/mounted
$   exit
$   endsubroutine
```

The CALL commands are used to invoke a subroutine named SHOW_DISKS. Parameters can be passed to the subroutine just as if it were a separate procedure invoked with the at-sign command. In this example, the subroutine is called twice, the first time with the parameter "Before the program:" and the second time with the parameter "After the program:".

The subroutine begins with a label specifying its name, followed by the DCL command SUBROUTINE. This command marks the start of the subroutine, which includes all the commands down through the corresponding ENDSUBROUTINE command. When the subroutine is invoked with CALL, a new procedure level is established, new procedure-level symbols P1-P8 are defined, and the commands in the subroutine are executed. When the ENDSUBROUTINE is reached, the subroutine is terminated and execution continues after the CALL command. As with procedures, an EXIT command can be used to terminate the subroutine at any point during its execution.

If DCL runs into a SUBROUTINE command as it executes a procedure sequentially, all the subroutine's commands are skipped and execution continues after the ENDSUBROUTINE. The only way to execute the commands in a subroutine is to call it. Therefore, the first EXIT command in the preceding procedure is technically unnecessary. DCL would skip over the subroutine as it executed the main portion of the procedure file, and terminate the procedure. However, the use of the EXIT command in this circumstance makes the procedure easier to read and follows our convention that an explicit EXIT command is used at the end of every procedure.

Table 4.1 summarizes the similarities and differences between the at-sign and CALL commands.

A disclaimer: When the term *subroutine* is used in this book, it does not necessarily refer to a subroutine invoke with the CALL command. The term is used in a general way to signify any sequence of commands invoked by a DCL procedure, whether they are in the same procedure file or another one, and regardless of how they are invoked. Subroutines therefore encompass procedures invoked with the at-sign command, subroutines invoked with CALL, and those invoked with GOSUB.

4.7   The GOSUB Command

The GOSUB command is similar to the CALL command. It invokes a subroutine that resides in the same procedure as the caller. However, there are some

Table 4.1 Summary of subroutine facilities

Feature	At-sign	CALL	GOSUB
Location of subroutine	Separate procedure	Same procedure	Same procedure
Creates new procedure level	Yes	Yes	No
Pass P1–P8 parameters?	Yes	Yes	No
Implicit termination	End of procedure	ENDSUBROUTINE	End of procedure
Explicit termination	EXIT	EXIT	RETURN
Can alter caller's local symbols?	No	No	Yes
Can return values in global symbols?	Yes	Yes	Yes

important differences, summarized in Table 4.1. In particular, GOSUB does not create a new procedure level and there is no way to pass the P1–P8 parameters to the subroutine. The subroutine is limited to performing relatively simple operations and must receive its input data in symbols created by the caller. Here is the CALL example modified to use GOSUB:

```
$   heading = "Before the program:"
$   gosub show_disks
$   run sys$system:application-pgm
$   heading = "After the program:"
$   gosub show_disks
$   exit
$
$show_disks:
$   write sys$output heading
$   show time
$   show devices/mounted
$   return
```

The GOSUB command requires one parameter, the label of the subroutine to be invoked. The subroutine itself contains no special surrounding commands like SUBROUTINE and ENDSUBROUTINE. It performs a series of commands and then terminates with the RETURN command. Because there is not a way to pass parameters to the subroutine, it must receive the heading string in the symbol HEADING. The symbol acts as a parameter for the subroutine. The EXIT command is required in the main procedure to prevent DCL from falling through and executing the subroutine's commands. Because the subroutine is

4.7 The GOSUB Command

not delineated by commands such as SUBROUTINE and ENDSUBROUTINE, DCL does not know to skip the subroutine when it is encountered during sequential execution.

In effect, a subroutine invoked with GOSUB is executed exactly as if it appeared in its entirety in the place of the GOSUB command. A subroutine invoked with GOSUB can itself invoke another subroutine with GOSUB. For each procedure level, DCL can remember the return points for up to 16 GOSUB levels.

4.8 The PIPE Command

The PIPE command provides a construct within which several standard DCL commands can be executed, or can be conditionally executed. The particular behavior of the PIPE command is determined by the DCL commands specified, and by the command separators used.

Using specific separators, PIPE can execute a series of commands, can pass the output from one command into the input of the next command, can execute a series of commands, and can conditionally execute DCL commands based on the results of preceding DCL commands. Examples of separators include ";", "|", and "||".

The following example PIPE transfers the output of the DIRECTORY command into the SORT command, sorting the resulting directory listing into descending order, writing the results into the file REVERSE.TXT:

```
$ pipe -
_$ directory/column=1/noheader/notrailer | -
_$ sort sys$input: /key=(position=1,size=255,descending) -
_$ reverse.txt
```

Although the above example could also be implemented using a temporary file, the PIPE command avoids the need for the temporary file between the DIRECTORY and SORT commands.

The PIPE command is described in full detail in Section 20.8; it was introduced in OpenVMS V7.1.

CHAPTER 5
Substitution

Up to this point, the book has focused on DCL language features that are similar to those found in conventional languages. The similarity fades, however, with the introduction of a powerful feature called *substitution*. The substitution facility is akin to macros in assembly language or preprocessor definitions in the C language. However, substitution in DCL is unrelated to the syntax of commands: it is purely textual replacement. Any part of a command, from a single character to a portion of a file specification to an entire command line, can be created on the fly by the appropriate use of substitution. This is an extremely potent feature, which allows you to create DCL commands "customized" for particular circumstances. It also grants you the power to create malformed or completely garbled commands.

DCL provides three kinds of substitution: apostrophe substitution, implicit substitution, and ampersand substitution. The principle underlying all three kinds is that a symbol or lexical function appearing in a command is removed and replaced with its value. The differences among the three kinds of substitution lie in how they are specified and when they occur.

5.1 Apostrophe Substitution

This section describes *apostrophe substitution*, which is one form of explicit substitution. Using an apostrophe ('), you explicitly request that DCL perform a substitution where it would not otherwise do so. (In contrast, the next section describes substitution that DCL performs automatically.) Apostrophe substitution occurs after a command is read but before it is analyzed and executed. Therefore, DCL performs simple textual replacement, independent of the format of the command. Once a substitution has been performed, DCL rescans the entire command, including the new portion, for additional substitutions of any type.

An apostrophe substitution is requested by enclosing a symbol or lexical function in apostrophes, as follows:

```
$    type 'file_spec'
```

If the value of FILE_SPEC is the string "FOO.BAR;1", the following command results:

```
$    TYPE FOO.BAR;1
```

The apostrophes and the symbols they enclose have been removed and replaced with the value of the symbol. Here is an example with a lexical function:

```
$    type 'f$environment("PROCEDURE")'
```

The F$ENVIRONMENT lexical function returns the file specification of the current command procedure. If the procedure is named TEST.COM;1 and resides in directory $DISK1:[ROBBINS], the following command results:

```
$    TYPE $DISK1:[ROBBINS]TEST.COM;1
```

The apostrophe was chosen as the substitution indicator because it serves no other purpose in DCL. However, apostrophes are common inside string literals, particularly in contractions or quotations. For this reason, *two* apostrophes are required to perform substitution inside a string literal:

```
$    @log_line "The file ''file_spec' was typed."
```

After substitution:

```
$    @LOG_LINE "The file $DISK1:[ROBBINS]TEST.COM;1 was typed."
```

Notice that substitution requires only a single trailing apostrophe regardless of whether it is specified outside or inside a string. This trailing apostrophe is quite interesting. The "official" syntax for substitution calls for one trailing apostrophe; however, it is unnecessary in many cases. In fact, it is only required in the following situations:

- When the character following the symbol could be construed as part of the symbol (i.e., the character is alphanumeric, a dollar sign, or an underscore). This situation does not arise with the substitution of lexical functions, because the lexical function ends with a close parenthesis.

- When another apostrophe substitution immediately follows. If the trailing apostrophe were not present, the leading apostrophe of the second substitution would be mistaken for the missing trailing one.
- When the substitution is specified as the last thing in a string literal. In this situation, a trailing apostrophe is required for both symbol and lexical function substitution.
- When the character following the symbol is a grave accent (`` ` ``), tilde (~), percent sign (%), ampersand (&), curly brace ({ }), backslash (\), or vertical bar (|). This is because DCL "accidentally" treats these characters as part of the symbol (the authors believe this was unintentional).
- When the character following the symbol is a space, and the next character is a sharp sign (#), circumflex (^), close parenthesis [ )], plus sign (+), equal sign (=), close square bracket (]), comma (,), question mark (?), slash (/), or greater than sign (>). The authors do not know the reason for this behavior. These last two situations do not arise in practice very frequently.

Here is an example of each of the situations:

```
$    type 'prefix'_table.dat
```

—or—

```
$    type 'file_name''file_type;
```

—or—

```
$    @log_line "Done with file ''f$parse(file_spec)'"
```

—or—

```
$    @log_line "It took ''cpu_pc'% of the CPU."
```

—or—

```
$    @log_line "Number of ''what' = ''count."
```

Trailing apostrophes will be used in this book only when necessary, because the authors believe this convention improves the readability of command procedures, even though it means that the programmer must remember the foregoing rules. If you find the rules confusing, by all means specify a trailing apostrophe for all substitutions.

5.1.1 Substituting Expression Values

With the apostrophe, it is easy to substitute the value of a symbol or lexical function. It is a little trickier to substitute the value of an arbitrary expression.

This is accomplished with two lexical functions. The `F$INTEGER` function takes an arbitrary expression and returns its value, converted to an integer if necessary. The `F$STRING` function takes an arbitrary expression and returns its value, converted to a string if necessary. These functions allow the value of an arbitrary expression to be inserted in a command.

Assume the symbol `COUNT` is set to the number of people attending a future meeting. This command prints two copies of the agenda for each person:

```
$    print/copies='f$integer(count*2) agenda.txt
```

When `COUNT` is 3, the following command is executed by DCL:

```
$    print/copies=6 agenda.txt
```

If you did not use the lexical function and instead just wrote `'COUNT*2`, the multiplication would not occur and the following command would result:

```
$    print/copies=3*2 agenda.txt
```

Unfortunately, an expression is not a legal value for the `/COPIES` qualifier (or any other qualifier, for that matter).

5.1.2 Common Mistakes

Programmers are often confused about the context in which apostrophe substitution is required, and this results in overuse of the construct. Substitution is difficult to comprehend and debug, particularly when used in string literals, and therefore should be avoided when not necessary. The primary point to keep in mind is this: when DCL allows an *expression* in a given context, explicit substitution is normally unnecessary because DCL evaluates all symbols and lexical functions as part of evaluating the expression. DCL allows expressions in the following contexts:

- On the right-hand side of an assignment statement (using = or ==, but not := or :==).
- In the square brackets on the left side of an assignment statement that performs substring or bit-field replacement.
- In the `DEPOSIT`, `EXAMINE`, `EXIT`, `IF`, `RETURN`, and `WRITE` statements.
- As an argument to a lexical function, regardless of where the function itself is used.

The following pairs of lines show commands as they might be entered with unnecessary substitution and the same commands without the substitution:

```
$   string1 = "''string2'"
$   string1 = string2
```

—or—

```
$   buffer['index,1] := " "
$   buffer[index,1] := " "
```

—or—

```
$   if 'count + 1 .gt. 10 then goto 19
$   if count + 1 .gt. 10 then goto 19
```

—or—

```
$   delete 'f$parse("''spec'", ".tmp;*")
$   delete 'f$parse(spec,". tmp;*")
```

5.2 Implicit Substitution

After DCL performs all the explicit substitutions specified by apostrophes, it performs a single implicit substitution. This substitution is often called *automatic substitution* or *personal command substitution*. DCL analyzes the beginning of the command line and determines whether the first item is a symbol. If so, it replaces the symbol with its value. Implicit substitution is done at the beginning of the command analysis phase and thus occurs after apostrophe substitution.

All the following conditions must be met for DCL to carry out an implicit substitution:

- The command must not be an assignment statement. Implicit substitution is never performed in assignment commands, because it would render the assignment command useless.
- The first item in the command must be a symbol.
- The symbol must not be a label.
- The symbol must have a value.
- The value cannot be hidden with the SET SYMBOL/SCOPE command.

Once an implicit substitution is performed, DCL does *not* rescan the new portion of the command. This prevents recursive substitutions, as we shall see.

5.2.1 Personal Commands

One of the most common uses for implicit substitution is in the definition of *personal commands*. A personal command is a synonym for a command verb or a contraction for all or part of a complete command. Using personal commands, you can build up a collection of customized DCL verbs tailored to your working environment. When a personal command is defined in the login command procedure, it is available for use immediately.

The following personal commands illustrate some of the possibilities:

```
$    backup     == "backup/log"
$    deletedir  == "@sys$login:deletedir"
$    notices    == "type sys$system:notice.txt"
$    send       == "mail"
$    sp         == "set process/privilege="
```

Assume these commands were defined in the login procedure. The following pairs of lines show a command as it might be entered and the resulting command executed by DCL.

```
$    backup *.*; msa0:save.bck/saveset/rewind
$    BACKUP/LOG *.*; MSA0:SAVE.BCK/SAVESET/REWIND
```

—or—

```
$    deletedir work
$    @SYS$LOGIN:DELETEDIR WORK
```

—or—

```
$    notices
$    TYPE SYS$SYSTEM:NOTICE.TXT
```

—or—

```
$    send agenda.txt sally_smith/subject="Tomorrow's agenda."
$    MAIL AGENDA.TXT SALLY_SMITH/SUBJECT="TOMORROW'S AGENDA."
```

—or—

```
$    sp (oper,sysprv)
$    SET PROCESS/PRIVILEGE=(OPER,SYSPRV)
```

The first example illustrates why DCL does not rescan the new portion of a command after implicit substitution. If it did rescan, the substitution process would never terminate, because the personal command BACKUP is again present in the command line after each substitution.

5.2.2 Personal Commands in Procedures

Personal commands and DCL procedures interact in two important ways. Command combinations that are frequently used in the procedure can be assigned synonyms during procedure initialization. This assists in making the procedure more readable. On the other hand, personal commands that were defined outside of the procedure can wreak havoc, on the procedure's execution. Predefined personal commands must be disabled while the procedure is running.

There are a few commands that are so common that synonyms are useful in virtually every command procedure of any complexity. The examples in the rest of this book rely on the following personal command definitions, which are assumed to be defined in every main procedure. Additional personal commands can be defined according to the requirements of the application. Do not abbreviate commands used in procedures; this will just confuse the future reader.

```
$       define   = "define/nolog"
$       inquire  = "inquire/nopunctuation"
$       display  = "write sys$output"
$       undefine = "deassign"
```

When you invoke a procedure from the DCL prompt, all the personal commands defined outside the procedure are available to the procedure. Rather than being a help, this feature is extremely dangerous. Imagine what would happen if personal commands like the following were defined and then mistakenly employed by an "unsuspecting" procedure.

```
$       backup = "backup/rewind"    ! Rewind tape before using.
$       delete = "delete/confirm"   ! Ask user before deleting.
$       mount  = "mount/assign"     ! Do operator-assisted mounts.
$       rename = "rename/log"       ! Log renames to terminal.
```

The first definition, for example, would cause a backup saveset to be placed at the beginning of the tape volume, overwriting any data previously recorded. This is not the default behavior of the BACKUP utility, and it is extremely dangerous. One of the first things you should do in a main procedure is to prevent DCL from considering personal commands defined outside of the procedure. Unfortunately, there is no straightforward way to accomplish this. You must define a personal command for each DCL command used in the procedure, thus "hiding" any personal commands defined outside the procedure.

Chap. 7, p. 83

5.3 Ampersand Substitution

A second form of explicit substitution is called *ampersand substitution.* Using an ampersand (&) you can request that DCL perform a limited kind of substitution, one that replaces a symbol with its value. Ampersand substitution takes place after apostrophe and implicit substitution but before the command is executed. This second form of explicit substitution was intended to be used in concert with apostrophe substitution in certain rare instances where double replacement is necessary.

📌 Chap. 22, p. 291

Double replacement is most often useful when simulating arrays with symbols. A simple example is presented here. Imagine a procedure that accepts multiple parameters, each one a file specification. The procedure displays the contents of the files at the terminal:

```
$     i = 0
$10:  i = i + 1
$     if i .gt. 8 then goto 19
$     if p'i .eqs. "" then goto 19
$     type &p'i        ! Uses both forms of substitution.
$     goto 10
$19:
```

The interesting line is the one invoking the TYPE utility. Assume the value of I is 3 and the third parameter is NAMES.TXT. After apostrophe substitution, the command becomes TYPE &P3. After ampersand substitution, the final command is TYPE NAMES.TXT. The loop types all the files, terminating after the eighth one or as soon as a null parameter is encountered.

A command containing an ampersand substitution can always be replaced by two commands with an apostrophe substitution in each one. For example, the critical line in the preceding example can be replaced by

```
$     file = p'i
$     type 'file
```

Ampersand substitution should be avoided, for two reasons. First, its use results in rather inscrutable code, particularly for the majority of people who are unfamiliar with it. Second, ampersand substitution is subject to the following restrictions and idiosyncrasies:

- An ampersand may only be used with a symbol, not with a lexical function.
- Because there is no trailing delimiter, the character following the symbol must not be a symbol character (i.e., alphanumeric, dollar sign, underscore).

- The ampersand is ignored in the at-sign (`@`) and `CALL` commands.
- The ampersand is ignored in string literals, even if doubled.
- The ampersand character has an additional use within the `PIPE` command.

  Sec. 20.8, p. 273
- Ampersand substitution is performed after the command is converted to uppercase letters. This can have startling results. For example, if the value of the symbol being substituted is another symbol name that happens to be in lowercase letters, DCL will not recognize the second symbol.
- If verification has been enabled with `SET VERIFY`, the command line is traced before ampersand substitution is performed.

CHAPTER 6
Displaying Output

THIS CHAPTER DISCUSSES METHODS for displaying output during the execution of a procedure. The word *display* is used because today most interactive users have access to graphics displays or video display terminals rather than hardcopy terminals. DCL provides facilities for displaying text and simple graphics on video terminals and web pages. Such facilities are used in procedures to present results, status information, and error messages.

Chap. 25, p. 319

The user's terminal or web browser has both an input and an output capability. DCL treats these two functions of a terminal as separate devices: an input device, which receives keystrokes from the keyboard, and an output device, which displays characters on the video screen. When a user logs in, OpenVMS creates a process to execute programs on behalf of the user. Associated with this process is a *process-permanent file*, which can be used to write to the video screen. This output file is assigned the logical name SYS$OUTPUT and is always available. Text is displayed on the terminal by writing to SYS$OUTPUT.

Sec. 20.5, p. 269

6.1 Displaying Text

Text is displayed with the WRITE command. This command takes two arguments. The first is a logical name referring to the file that is to receive the output (note that it is a logical name, not a symbol). The second is an expression or list of expressions whose values are to be written. When you want to display text on the terminal, use the logical name SYS$OUTPUT:

```
    $   write sys$output "Greetings from procedure land."
```
—or—
```
    $   write sys$output "The value of X is: ", x
```
—or—
```
    $   write sys$output "Your name is ", name, -
                " and your age is ", age, "."
```
—or—
```
    $   write sys$output "The average is: ", (v1+v2)/2
```

The last example shows that the values can be complex expressions, not just string literals or symbols. Because the WRITE command accepts expressions, apostrophe substitution is not usually required to produce the values to write.

Procedures often write to the terminal, so it is handy to set up a short personal command that can be used in place of WRITE SYS$OUTPUT. This is done during procedure initialization:

```
    $   display = "write sys$output"
```

This leaves more space on the line to include lengthy expressions:

```
    $   display "Your name is ", name, " and your age is ", -
            age, "."
```

6.2 Terminal Control Sequences

All modern video terminals accept *control sequences*, which specify video operations above and beyond the display of simple text. Control sequences can be used to clear the screen, change the video rendition to boldface or reverse video, draw lines, and so forth. Using the WRITE command, you can send control sequences to the terminal.

A control sequence is a series of ASCII characters beginning with a control sequence initiator. On terminals capable of eight-bit characters, such as the VT500 and DECterm series, the initiator is the CSI character (hexadecimal 9B). On seven-bit terminals, such as the VT100 series, the initiator is two characters, an ESC character (hexadecimal 1B) followed by the open square bracket ([ ). Because older terminals use seven-bit characters and thus initiate a control sequence with an escape character, control sequences are often called *escape sequences*.

In this book, seven-bit control sequences are illustrated because they work on both seven- and eight-bit terminals. Furthermore, control sequences acceptable to the VT100, VT200, VT300, VT400, VT500, and DECterm families of terminals are used. To set up the control sequence initiator for such a terminal, it is best to use a bit-field assignment command to create a character string containing the ESC character. Do not place an actual ESC character in the procedure file, as this can cause unpredictable behavior if the procedure is typed to the terminal or printed on a printer. Here is how to set up the control sequence initiator:

    Sec. 3.7,
    p. 45

```
$    esc[0,8] = %x1B   ! Prepare a 7-bit CSI string:
$    csi = esc + "["   ! an ESC followed by an open bracket.
```

Once this is done, control sequences are sent to the terminal by writing the initiator followed by the appropriate additional characters. The complete repertoire of control sequences is described in the user's guide for your particular terminal.

```
$    display csi,"2J"           ! Clear the entire screen.
$    display csi,"1;1H"          ! Position cursor to 1,1.
$    display csi,"0;1m", -       ! Select bold rendition,
             "A Bold Heading", - ! display a heading,
             csi,"0m"            ! and reset rendition.
```

All control sequences follow a predefined format, allowing a terminal to correctly locate the end of the control sequence, even if the sequence is not supported by that particular terminal. Because of this, standard ANSI-compliant terminals will correctly and silently ignore any unrecognized control sequences. Once you check for the ANSI compliance, this behavior permits you to avoid conditionally coding newer or terminal-specific control sequences when working with terminals that do not support the sequences, but it also makes debugging an application that uses control sequences somewhat more difficult. For information on the format of control sequences, see the *OpenVMS I/O User's Reference Manual*.

Some control sequences are used frequently, such as the one that clears the entire screen. Using some additional symbols, you can assign a symbolic name to a complete sequence. This helps avoid errors in the repeated specification of identical control sequences.

```
$    bold   = csi + "0;1m"
$    clear  = csi + "2J"
$    home   = csi + "1;1H"
$    normal = csi + "0m"
```

6.2 Terminal Control Sequences

With these symbols, the DISPLAY commands in the preceding example are simplified and become more readable:

```
$    display clear
$    display home
$    display bold, "A Bold Heading", normal
```

You can find information on the available control sequences in the DECterm documentation and in the programming documentation available for most terminals. You can also find the most common control sequences listed in the screen management library (SMG) source file SYS$SYSTEM:SMGTERMS.TXT.

6.3 Formatting Output

It is often desirable to perform some fancy formatting of text before displaying it on a terminal. For example, if you are displaying a table containing integers, the integers look best when shown in columns with the low-order digits lined up, that is, right-justified. This is easily accomplished if every integer occupies the same number of columns. DCL provides a lexical function, F$FAO, which is used to format text.

The F$FAO lexical function provides a moderately powerful facility for text formatting. The acronym FAO stands for "formatted ASCII output." The function accepts multiple arguments, the first being the *control string* and the remainder being expressions whose values are to be formatted according to the control string. In other words, the control string argument acts as a template for the formatted text, while the remaining arguments are the values to be inserted in the template. The F$FAO function returns a character string containing the formatted text (it does not actually display the text).

The control string contains fixed text plus directives. The fixed text is placed in the resulting string exactly as it appears. A directive is not placed in the resulting string, but instead is replaced with the corresponding argument value, formatted in accordance with the directive. A directive consists of an exclamation point (!) followed by a one- or two-character code indicating the formatting to be performed. The code, by convention, is specified in uppercase letters. An integer may be included between the exclamation point and the code to specify the width of the formatted field. Table 6.1 describes some basic directives; the complete set is described in the *OpenVMS DCL Dictionary*.

An example is now in order. Assume that a procedure has calculated statistics for a set of numbers. The symbols COUNT, MINIMUM, MAXIMUM, and

Table 6.1 F$FAO directives

Directive	Description	Argument
!AS	Insert a character string.	String expression
!SL	Insert an integer in decimal.	Integer expression
!/	Begin a new line.	None
!*x	Repeat a character (denoted by x) the number of times specified by the field width.	None
!%S	Used to construct plurals. Inserts the letter "s", using the same case as the preceding character, if the preceding directive formatted a numeric value other than 1.	None
!%T	Insert the current time in OpenVMS format.	The integer 0 (any other value causes an error)
!%D	Insert the current date and time in OpenVMS format.	The integer 0.

MEAN contain the statistical results. The goal is to clear the screen and format the statistics as pictured here:

```
Statistics on   3-Apr-1998
------------------------


Count:         73
Minimum:        3
Maximum:      485
Mean:         119

73 records evaluated.
```

This is accomplished with the following code:

```
$    display clear, home
$    display f$fao("Statistics on !11%D", 0)
$    display f$fao("!25*-!/")
$    display f$fao("Count:   !7SL", count)
$    display f$fao("Minimum:!7SL", minimum)
$    display f$fao("Maximum:!7SL", maximum)
$    display f$fao("Mean:    !7SL", mean)
$    display f$fao("!/!SL record!%S evaluated.", count)
```

Notice that the !SL directive right-justifies the integer in the specified field width.

6.4 Redirecting Program Output

Many OpenVMS utilities and other programs display output under the assumption that they are being used interactively, that is, directly by the user. This assumption fails when the programs are used by procedures as tools to accomplish some part of the application at hand. In this case, the output may be misleading to the user who does not know how the procedure operates internally. Another possibility is that the output must be directed to a file and then processed by a later step of the procedure. In these cases, it is necessary to redirect the displayed output so that it does not appear on the terminal.

Most OpenVMS utilities support the /OUTPUT qualifier on their command line, as do all command procedures invoked with the @ command. With this qualifier you can specify the destination for output that would, by default, be displayed on the terminal. In the following example, the output from the DIRECTORY command is redirected to a scratch file:

```
$   directory/output=sys$scratch:dirout.tmp sys$manager:*.com
```

Sec. 15.4, p. 195

Rather than appearing on the terminal, the list of command procedures in the system manager's directory is placed in the file DIROUT.TMP in the system scratch directory. The procedure can then process the file as required.

Some commands do not accept the /OUTPUT qualifier, and many programs are not invoked with a DCL command at all. In these cases, the program's output can be redirected using the PIPE command, or with the DEFINE command:

Sec. 20.8, p. 273

```
$   define/user_mode sys$output sys$scratch:pgmout.tmp
$   run sys$system:pgm
```

The DEFINE command redefines the SYS$OUTPUT logical name to refer to the desired scratch file. The /USER_MODE qualifier makes this redefinition temporary, lasting only for the *next* image execution. Therefore, all output from the PGM program is redirected to the PGMOUT.TMP file, and then SYS$OUTPUT reverts to the terminal for subsequent programs.

Sec. 14.4, p. 172

Redefining SYS$OUTPUT redirects output but does not redirect error messages resulting from errors signaled by the program. This is because error messages are written to both SYS$OUTPUT and SYS$ERROR. The process-permanent file SYS$ERROR is directed to the terminal, so error messages appear there even if normal output does not. If you know that a program is going to produce error messages that the user should not see, you must suppress them. Use a second DEFINE command to do this:

```
$   define/user_mode sys$output sys$scratch:pgmout.tmp
$   define/user_mode sys$error nl:
$   run sys$system:pgm
```

The second DEFINE command redirects the SYS$ERROR logical name to the null device (NL:). All output to the null device is discarded.

The null device is useful when you want to discard all output and error messages produced by a program. In this case, both SYS$OUTPUT and SYS$ERROR are redirected to the null device:

```
$    define/user_mode sys$output nl:
$    define/user_mode sys$error  nl:
$    run sys$system:pgm
```

All output produced by the PGM program is discarded.

6.5 Displaying a File

This chapter does not describe how to display the contents of a data file, because files have not yet been discussed in detail. Chapter 17 addresses the issues surrounding the display of data files.

6.6 Displaying a Web Page

Another common display target for applications is a *web page* on the World Wide Web (WWW). Web pages can be served from a wide variety of hosts, including OpenVMS, can be displayed from a wide variety of hosts, and can be accessed from the local host or from other hosts elsewhere on the same network. For additional information, see Chapter 25.

CHAPTER 7

The DCL Environment

THE REVIEW OF BASIC DCL CONCEPTS and facilities was completed in the previous chapter. The remainder of the book describes how to use these facilities to create real programs: programs that are useful, correct, and robust. The proposed techniques are directed toward the development of complex procedures, applications composed of multiple procedures, or applications to be used by many people. If you are just writing a 20-line procedure for personal use, don't worry about following every guideline to the letter. Pick and choose the ones that are pertinent to your task.

The term *DCL environment* refers to a collection of information that guides the actions and responses of the DCL command interpreter. The environment information affects the operation of DCL commands, the content of messages displayed by DCL, and the behavior of command procedures. Commands are available for setting and displaying the various items of information making up the environment. This chapter describes the most important aspects of the environment:

- Verifying command procedures.
- Hiding predefined personal commands.
- Setting message components.
- Setting process privileges.
- Setting the user identification code (UIC).
- Changing the default directory.

7.1 Aspects of the Environment

The following sections describe some important aspects of the DCL environment. These environment features will be important in the remainder of this book.

7.1.1 Procedure Verification

As an aid to debugging command procedures, the execution of a procedure can be traced. A procedure trace shows each line as it is executed by DCL, after apostrophe and personal command substitution is performed. The act of tracing a procedure is called *verifying* the procedure. The SET VERIFY command is used to enable and disable verification as needed. Some texts suggest the use of this command to disable verification upon entry to a large procedure. The rationale for this suggestion is that no user could possibly want to see the trace of such a procedure. The authors believe it is generally best not to change the state of verification in a procedure; do not enable or disable it. The user may be pursuing a suspected bug in the procedure, in which case the trace is invaluable.

The SET VERIFY command is discussed in detail in Chapter 12.

7.1.2 Predefined Personal Commands

Chapter 5 discussed the danger inherent in allowing predefined personal commands to affect the execution of a command procedure. For example, if the symbol BACKUP is defined as "BACKUP/REWIND", savesets will be placed at the beginning of a tape volume (overwriting any existing data), even though this is not the default behavior of the utility. There is no simple way to prevent a procedure from using personal commands defined outside it. In the procedure, you must define a new personal command for each command used by the procedure. This new personal command, because it is a procedure-level symbol, will hide any prompt- or global-level symbols of the same name:

```
$    backup = "backup"
$    copy   = "copy"
$    delete = "delete"
```

Each personal command is defined as the command verb, by itself, with no qualifiers. In other words, each command is defined as itself. When DCL makes a personal command substitution for BACKUP, the result will simply be BACKUP, with no extra qualifiers or parameters to affect its operations. Any definitions of BACKUP outside the procedure are effectively hidden.

It is tedious to define a personal command for every DCL command used in the procedure. What you will probably end up doing is defining a personal command for potentially "dangerous" commands, such as `BACKUP`, `COPY`, `DELETE`, and `MOUNT`. Once a new procedure is near completion, give some thought to which commands need to be safe from interference from personal commands.

DCL does make an attempt to solve the personal command problem with the `SET SYMBOL` command. This command allows a procedure to circumvent the normal rules of symbol lookup and hide *all* of the prompt- and global-level symbols. Unfortunately, the command also prevents the procedure from creating any new global symbols, something which many large procedures need to do. Any attempt to create a new global symbol results in an error. If you are developing a procedure that does not create any global symbols, you can use the following command near the top of the procedure to hide all existing personal commands:

```
$    set symbol/scope=(nolocal,noglobal)
```

The `NOLOCAL` keyword specifies that all existing prompt-level symbols and outer procedure-level symbols are ignored by DCL. It is as if they are hidden from the current procedure level. The `NOGLOBAL` keyword specifies that all existing global symbols are ignored by DCL and that *no new ones can be created*.

The examples in this book assume that all the procedures need to create global symbols; therefore they do *not* use the `SET SYMBOL` command.

7.1.3 Messages

Messages are an important aspect of the OpenVMS style of user communication. An OpenVMS message consists of four components:

Facility The name of the utility or application that generated the message.

Severity The severity level of the message: success, informational, warning, error, or fatal error.

Identification An identifier for the message, unique among all the identifiers for this facility. The message identifier is used to index the message in documentation.

Text The actual text of the message, which conveys the information or describes the error.

When OpenVMS displays a message, it normally includes all four components in order:

```
%DCL-I-IVVERB, unrecognized command verb-check validity and spelling
```

The facility is `DCL`, the severity `I` (informational), the identifier `IVVERB`, and the text everything following the comma.

OpenVMS provides a command that allows you to customize the format of the message, omitting components of no interest. A well-written procedure does not produce arbitrary error messages during normal operation, so any abnormal circumstances that do occur can result in unexpected error messages that are out of context (after all, the user did not type the command that produced the error). It is best, then, to display all message components so that the user has the greatest chance of understanding the problem in context and correcting it.

Because you cannot be sure which message components are enabled when the procedure is invoked, it is necessary to enable all of them as part of procedure initialization. Sound modular design also demands that the user's original message settings be restored when the procedure exits. The following two commands will record the current message settings and then enable all components:

```
$    saved_msg = f$environment("MESSAGE")
$    set message/facility/severity/identification/text
```

The first command uses the `F$ENVIRONMENT` lexical function to obtain the current message settings and store them in the `SAVED_MSG` symbol. They are automatically stored in the form required by the `SET MESSAGE` command, which will ultimately reset them. For example, if all components are disabled except the text, the following string will be stored in the symbol:

```
"/NOFACILITY/NOSEVERITY/NOIDENTIFICATION/TEXT"
```

The second command enables all message components.

Upon exit from the main procedure, the original message settings in effect when the procedure was invoked must be restored. This is accomplished with the following command, which reestablishes the saved message settings using the `SAVED_MSG` symbol:

```
$    set message 'saved_msg
```

7.1.4   Privileges

Some procedures, particularly those that perform system management functions, may require that specific privileges be enabled for proper execution. Because you cannot be sure which privileges are enabled when the procedure is invoked, it is necessary to enable the required ones as part of procedure initialization. Again, accepted modular design practice requires that the user's original privilege settings be restored when the procedure exits.

The `F$SETPRV` lexical function is used to enable and disable privileges in a command procedure. This function takes one argument, a list of privilege settings. The user's process privileges are enabled or disabled according to the list (assuming the user is authorized for such privileges), and the *previous* settings of the specified privileges are returned in a similar list. For example:

```
$!     Enable OPER.
$      prev_privs = f$setprv("OPER")
```

—or—

```
$!     Enable SYSPRV, disable BYPASS.
$      prev_privs = f$setprv("SYSPRV,NOBYPASS")
```

—or—

```
$!     Enable every privilege.
$      prev_privs = f$setprv("ALL")
```

—or—

```
$!     Enable WORLD (uses last setting).
$      prev_privs = f$setprv("NOWORLD,WORLD")
```

The following two commands will record all privilege settings in the symbol SAVED_PRIVS and then enable some required ones:

```
$      saved_privs = f$setprv("ALL")
$      junk = f$setprv(saved_privs+",OPER,PRMMBX,WORLD")
```

The first line enables *all* privileges and then sets the symbol SAVED_PRIVS to their previous state. The user's original privilege settings are therefore recorded in the symbol. The second line creates a new list of privileges, which is identical to the original list but with the addition of OPER, PRMMBX, and WORLD. Privileges are enabled and disabled according to the new list, thus reestablishing the original privilege state except for the required privileges, all three of which are enabled. The value returned by the second F$SETPRV is superfluous, so it is stored in the symbol JUNK.

There is a good reason to record the state of all privileges and not just the ones being changed. Doing so ensures that all privileges will be reset to their original state, even if some are changed during the execution of the main procedure and its subprocedures. Upon exit from the main procedure, all original privilege settings in effect when the procedure was invoked must be restored. This is accomplished with the following command, which resets the privileges to their saved state:

```
$      junk = f$setprv(saved_privs)
```

7.1.5 User Identification Code

Every OpenVMS process has a user identification code (UIC) associated with it. This UIC determines which objects the process can access and which operations it can perform on those objects. The UIC also determines the owner of a file created by the process: the file will be owned by the UIC of the process unless the owner is otherwise specified. On most systems, the system manager has assigned each user a unique UIC value. The ways in which the UIC affects file operations are described in detail in Chapter 13.

The SET UIC command can be used to change the process UIC. This command is considered obsolete in OpenVMS V6.0 and later releases, because of the problems that often result from the use of the command, and because of the availability of security mechanisms such as access control lists (ACLs). You should avoid changing the process UIC, particularly in a command procedure. Changing the UIC requires the CMKRNL (Change Mode to Kernel) privilege, a privilege which most users do not and should not have. Once the UIC is changed, the process may be able to access files it normally could not, and may not be able to access others. And if the target user has identifiers granted, these identifiers are not granted using SET UIC and the new process may not be able to access specific files or objects that the user associated with the UIC would normally be able to. Further, any files or subprocesses created by the process will be owned by the new UIC, not the UIC normally assigned to the user of the procedure. Always try to design procedures so that they do not need to change the process UIC.

In most cases, identifiers and access control lists (ACLs) can be used to avoid the need to change the UIC. The uses of identifiers and ACLs are discussed in detail in Chapter 18.

7.1.6 Default Directory

The *default directory* is the directory in which OpenVMS locates and creates file when no other directory is explicitly included in a file spec. Because the word *default* is overused in OpenVMS, this book uses the term *working directory* or *current directory*. The working directory exists as a convenience to the interactive user, so that an explicit directory need not be included in every file spec. The SET DEFAULT command is used to establish a new working directory.

Do *not* change the working directory in a command procedure. Include a device and directory in every file specification unless it is one entered by the user. Leaving the working directory as is and being explicit about directories has the following benefits:

- The user can reasonably expect that file specs entered without a directory refer to the working directory that was current when the procedure was invoked. Many procedures prompt the user for a file; it is disconcerting to the user if the procedure does not operate on the file in the working directory that was current when the procedure was invoked.

- You are forced to consider every file reference and determine where the file will be or where it should be created. For example, scratch files should be created in SYS$SCRATCH, not in the working directory.

There are, of course, exceptions to every rule. If the primary purpose of a procedure is to operate on files in a particular directory, and if that procedure always prompts the user for files in that directory, then it may be appropriate for the procedure to change the working directory. An example is a procedure that builds a software system in a specific "build" directory. Any procedure that changes the working directory should reset it to the original directory before it exits, regardless of the correct or incorrect termination of the procedure.

7.2 Putting It All Together

Now that the important environment items have been described, it is time to illustrate the beginning and end of a main procedure. The items that must be set during the procedure (e.g., privileges) are saved and established by initialization code and reestablished by termination code. The items to be left alone (e.g., working directory) are simply not mentioned.

```
$       backup = "backup"     ! Hide dangerous personal commands.
$       copy   = "copy"
$       delete = "delete"
$
$       saved_msg = f$environment("MESSAGE")
$       set message/facility/severity/identification/text
$       saved_privs = f$setprv("ALL")
$       junk = f$setprv(saved_privs+",OPER,PRMMBX,WORLD")
            .
            .
            .
$exit:
$       junk = f$setprv(saved_privs)
$       set message 'saved_msg
$       exit
```

The order of initialization is important. Predefined personal commands are hidden first, so that the entire procedure is unaffected by them. The message components are enabled next in order to ensure that all messages, even ones occurring during the remainder of procedure initialization, are displayed in full. Privileges are set last. Termination activities are carried out in reverse order, unfolding the "protective cover" wrapped around the procedure by its initialization.

These code sequences do not take into account the difficulties that arise when the user presses CTRL/Y during initialization. This topic will be addressed in Chapter 10, after we have discussed interrupt handling.

CHAPTER 8

Error Handling

ERROR HANDLING IS A CRITICAL ASPECT of every software application. It is sheer folly to assume that everything will go as planned, that no unusual or unforeseen events will occur. Error handling is no less important for DCL applications, particularly since they are often interactive and operate in the highly variable OpenVMS environment. It is impossible to predict every variation in the environment when you write the application.

Error handling is a weak point in many DCL applications. Error-handling logic is either missing entirely or suffers from a lack of overall organization. In other words, there is no error-handling scheme to deal with all errors in a consistent and predictable fashion. This chapter presents an overview of the OpenVMS error mechanism and describes how this mechanism is employed by DCL. It then goes on to present an error-handling scheme for DCL applications.

8.1 Status Codes

The *status code* is the means by which an OpenVMS program returns an indication of the success or failure of a requested operation. All programs, be they system services, run-time library routines, utilities, or entire applications, return a status code upon completion. The user or program that requested the operation can determine from the status whether the request succeeded or failed. The status may also indicate the reason for the success or failure.

Table 8.1
Status code fields

Bits	Field	Description
0–2	Severity	Severity of the status code (see Table 8.2).
3–14	Message number	Identifies a specific status code for the facility. A facility is limited to 4,096 status codes.
15	Facility specific	This bit is on for a status code that is specific to a facility. It is off for a status code that is shared by multiple facilities.
16–26	Facility number	Identifies the software facility that defines the status code.
27	Customer facility	This bit is on for software facilities produced by third-party vendors or by customers. It is off for facilities produced by DIGITAL, and third-party facilities registered with DIGITAL.
28	Inhibit display	This bit is set on to inhibit the `EXIT` command or `$EXIT` system service from displaying the message corresponding to the status.
29–31	(reserved)	Reserved for future use by DIGITAL.

8.1.1 Format

A status code is a 32-bit (longword) value that is divided into several bit fields. Table 8.1 describes the fields. Bits 16–27 identify a particular software facility, supplied either by DIGITAL or another source. Bits 3–15 identify a particular status code produced by the facility. Therefore, bits 3–27 uniquely identify every status code defined by every facility. Because a status code contains so many bit fields, it is usually specified in hexadecimal.

App. A, p. 333

The severity of a status code designates whether it represents successful or unsuccessful completion of the facility. There are five severity levels, each described in Table 8.2. The severity levels indicating a successful completion have odd values, while those indicating an unsuccessful completion have even values. This allows a procedure to treat a status code as a Boolean value: true if odd (successful), false if even (unsuccessful).

8.1.2 Command Status

Like all programs, OpenVMS commands and utilities return a status code. DCL sets the reserved symbol `$STATUS` to the status code and sets the reserved symbol `$SEVERITY` to its severity. A well-written procedure needs an efficient way to check the status code after every command and must take corrective action if the code indicates an error. There are three methods you can employ to check the status code:

Table 8.2
Status code severity levels

Level	Name	Description
0	Warning	A noncritical error or unusual condition occurred.
1	Success	The program completed normally.
2	Error	The program completed unsuccessfully because of some error.
3	Informational	The program completed normally but with an alternative condition.
4	Severe error	A fatal error terminated the program prematurely.
5–7	(reserved)	Reserved for future use by DIGITAL.

- Rely on a DCL feature that checks the status code automatically and supplies a default error handler.
- Rely on DCL's automatic status checking, but provide your own error handler.
- Disable DCL's automatic status checking, and check the status code explicitly.

These three methods will be described in the following sections.

There are a few DCL commands, such as IF and GOTO, that do not return a status code when they complete *successfully* and therefore do not always cause the $STATUS and $SEVERITY symbols to be set. The list of such commands is difficult to remember, so the authors recommend that you not rely on this "interesting" but inconsistent behavior. Write the error-handling code in procedures as if every command always returns a status code and sets the reserved symbols.

8.1.3 Procedure Status

DCL provides a feature whereby a command procedure can return a status code. The EXIT command accepts an expression parameter whose value is the status code to be returned. When an EXIT command is encountered, DCL ceases execution of the current command procedure, evaluates the expression, and returns control to the calling procedure with the status code specified by the expression. When the *main* procedure exits, control is returned to the DCL command level and the dollar sign ($) prompt appears.

You should use the EXIT command to return a status code from every procedure, both main ones and subprocedures. This allows the methods of status checking described in the rest of this chapter to be used when a procedure is invoked, treating it exactly like a command in that regard. Consistency among commands, utilities, and procedures makes an overall error-handling scheme significantly simpler.

A DCL program requires some application-specific status codes to use with the EXIT command. These codes are returned from procedures to indicate various success or error conditions peculiar to the application. In particular, every application needs a success status code to return from procedures when they complete normally. Status codes are usually defined with the MES-SAGE utility, but it was designed to be used with conventional programming languages that are compiled and linked. For DCL procedures, symbols whose values are the status codes must be established during procedure initialization.

Before you can establish status codes, you must choose a customer facility number for your application. For personal applications, you may as well choose the number zero. For other applications, it is best to have a "facility registrar," who keeps track of all the facilities in your organization and assigns facility numbers. The XDA example application is assigned the facility number 66. During procedure initialization, a basic status code is established from which all others are derived:

```
$    xda__status = %x18428000
```

This status code has a severity and message number of zero. The facility-specific bit is set to indicate that the status code is specific to this application. The facility number is 66 (42 in hexadecimal). The customer facility bit is set to indicate that this is a customer application. The inhibit-display bit is set to prevent the EXIT command from displaying the status.

By convention, the name of a customer facility status code begins with the facility code and two underscores.

Sec. 10.1, p. 113

With XDA__STATUS established, additional status codes are defined by adding the appropriate message number and severity to it. For example, a success status code is always needed. It is assigned message number 0 with severity 1:

```
$    xda__success = xda__status + %x0001
```

The hexadecimal number 0001 includes the severity in bits 0–2 and the message number in bits 3–14, as required by the status code format. The value of XDA__SUCCESS is %x18428001. Now it is possible for a subprocedure to exit with a success status code using the following command:

```
$    exit xda__success
```

8.2 The Default Error Handler

After the completion of each command, utility, or procedure, DCL normally checks the returned status code. When the severity indicates an error or a severe error, DCL executes its default *error handler* if no other error handler has been established. The default error handler terminates the current procedure and returns the error status code. Before exiting, the code is modified by setting the inhibit-display bit so that the message associated with the status code is not displayed as part of the procedure exit. This is done under the assumption that the message was already displayed when the command or utility terminated. The default error handler is not executed if the status code contains a success, informational, or warning severity.

The default error handler was designed with typical utilities and applications in mind. Errors and severe errors indicate that some disastrous problem has occurred and that the program has terminated prematurely. Warnings, on the other hand, supposedly indicate a minor problem that did not affect the outcome in any harmful way.

A significant problem with DCL's default error handler is that syntax errors in DCL flow-of-control commands (e.g., IF, GOTO) result in *warning* messages. When such a warning occurs, the error handler is not invoked and the procedure continues to execute with indeterminable results. There is an exception to this rule in the case of the GOTO command. If the specified label does not exist, a warning is issued *but* the procedure exits as if the severity had been error or severe error. For some reason, the original designers of DCL felt that this particular syntax error, unlike others, was drastic enough to warrant terminating the procedure.

A procedure should detect syntax errors during its execution; such errors indicate significant bugs in the procedure. The default error handler does not do so, and therefore you should replace it with one that does. The following section describes how this is done.

8.3 Changing Error-Handling Behavior

In order to modify DCL's behavior so that it invokes the error handler for warnings in addition to errors and severe errors, you must establish your own error handler. An error handler is established with the ON command, which specifies how status codes are to be checked and what action is to be taken when an unsuccessful status is detected. The ON command is placed near the top of a command procedure:

```
$    on warning then exit $status .or. %x10000000
```

The use of the keyword `WARNING` specifies that warnings, errors, and severe errors are to be detected. The command following the keyword `THEN` is the error handler itself; this command is executed when the specified severities are detected. In this case it is an `EXIT` command, which causes the procedure to exit and return the status code specified by the expression `$STATUS .OR. %X10000000`. This expression takes the status that caused the handler to be invoked (stored in `$STATUS`) and turns on the inhibit-display bit (`.OR. %X10000000`) so that the status message will not be displayed as the procedure exits. The `ON` command sets up an error-handling environment identical to the default one, except that warnings are also detected.

📌 Table 3.2, p. 34

📌 Table 8.1, p. 92

The examples in the remainder of this book assume that every procedure contains this `ON` command unless otherwise stated. The error-handling environment established with this command is a simple and robust one: every procedure detects unsuccessful status codes and immediately exits, returning the status to its caller. However, there are variations of the `ON` command that are also useful. The error-handling statement, rather than simply exiting, can perform a `GOTO` to a more complex error handler requiring multiple lines of code. An example of this kind of error handler is presented in Section 8.5.

8.4 Checking a Status Code Explicitly

There are times when a procedure must check a status code explicitly and act on it in special ways, rather than relying on the automatic error-handling mechanism. For example, the `DIFFERENCE` command returns a success status code if two files are identical or an informational code if the files are different. Differentiating the two cases is quite simple, since neither status code will trigger the error handler. You can simply test the `$SEVERITY` symbol after the command completes:

```
$    difference old_file.txt new_file.txt
$    if $severity .eq. 3 then action when different
```

Things become more complicated when a command returns a warning or error status code. Assume you want to copy a file from a remote node and need to handle the failure of the copy in a special fashion. In other words, the error handler should not gain control when `COPY` returns an error status code, but rather the procedure should continue executing in order to check the code explicitly. The following procedure will not work:

```
$    copy remote-file.dat local-file.dat
$    if .not. $status then action upon failure
```

The error status code from `COPY` will trigger the error handler, which will cause the procedure to exit immediately. It is necessary to disable DCL's automatic checking of status codes, thus allowing the procedure to continue and execute the `IF` command. This is accomplished with the `SET NOON` ("set no on") command and its complement, the `SET ON` command:

```
$    set noon    ! Not SET 12:00 o'clock noon, but SET NO ON.
$    copy remote-file.dat local-file.dat
$    status = $status
$    set on
$    if .not. status then  action upon failure
```

The `SET` commands are wrapped around the sequence of commands that must execute without automatic status checking. It is necessary to save the status code from the copy in another symbol *before* executing the `SET ON`; otherwise, the value of `$STATUS` will be replaced by the status code from the `SET ON` itself. After status checking is reenabled, the status code from the copy can be checked explicitly.

Automatic status checking should be disabled in the shortest possible sequences of commands. Leaving it disabled across many commands can result in undetected errors. Note carefully that the `SET NOON` does not prevent error messages from being displayed; it only disables automatic status checking.

8.5 Handling Errors When Cleanup Is Required

It is often the case in complex procedures that some *cleanup* must be performed before the procedure exits. For example, a procedure that opens a file should close it before exiting. The cleanup presents no problem when the procedure exits normally; it is simply performed just before the `EXIT` statement. However, if an error occurs during procedure execution, the error handler must also arrange to perform the cleanup. This is not possible if the error handler simply exits, as illustrated in Sections 8.2 and 8.3. The error handler must instead perform a `GOTO` to some code, which eventually executes the cleanup logic.

The following procedure illustrates the technique for establishing an error handler that includes cleanup. The procedure opens a sequential file, which must be closed before exiting:

Sec. 15.1, p. 190

```
$    xda__status = %x18428000
$    xda__success = xda__status + %x0001
$    status = xda__success
$    on warning then goto error
```

```
            :
            :
    $    open/read file 'p1
            .
            : process the file
            .
    $    goto exit
    $
    $error:
    $    status = $status
    $    goto exit
    $
    $exit:
    $    set noon
    $    close file
    $    exit status .or. %x10000000
```

Examine this procedure starting at the bottom. Cleanup and exit are performed at the label EXIT. A SET NOON command is executed to disable automatic checking of status codes. This allows the remainder of the procedure to execute completely regardless of any error that may occur during cleanup. The CLOSE command ensures that the file is closed regardless of whether the procedure exits normally or because of an error. The procedure finally exits with the status code contained in the symbol STATUS. Every possible path to the cleanup code must set STATUS to a meaningful exit status.

To initialize the procedure, the symbol STATUS is set to a facility-specific success status code. This is the code that will be returned by default if no other code is appropriate. The ON statement establishes an error handler that detects all errors and jumps to the label ERROR.

The procedure opens a file, processes it, and ultimately exits.

If a warning or other error is detected while the procedure is executing, the error handler jumps to the ERROR label. This causes the error status code to be placed in the STATUS symbol, so that it will be returned by the procedure. The error logic then jumps to EXIT, which performs the cleanup and exits with the error status code.

This organization, although a bit complicated, accomplishes the following important goals:

- The cleanup code is executed regardless of the cause of procedure exit. The file is always closed.

- The status code returned by the procedure is either a success code (default) or an error code detected and handled by the error handler. The status code returned by the procedure gives a true indication of what happened.

8.6 Procedure Call Unwinding

A DCL application is often large enough to require more than one command procedure. One of the procedures is the main procedure; it invokes other procedures as subroutines, which in turn may invoke still more procedures. With such nested flow of control, an overall error-handling scheme must be devised to deal with errors at all levels in the procedure hierarchy. The simplest such scheme is called *procedure call unwinding*. The idea is simple: when an error occurs in a subprocedure, exit the subprocedure and all intervening subprocedures until the main procedure is reached. The main procedure's error handler will then deal with the error.

This scheme is straightforward to implement. If you follow the rules set forth in the preceding sections, procedure call unwinding will occur automatically. The rules are as follows:

- Every procedure must return a success or informational status code when it completes normally.

- Every procedure must have an error handler that exits the procedure. It might have to perform some cleanup first.

- The error handler must return the error status code that caused it to be invoked, thus propagating the error status up one procedure level to the caller.

Procedure call unwinding is illustrated by three cooperating procedures, MAIN, SUB1, and SUB2:

```
$!      Procedure MAIN.
$
$       xda__status = %x18428000
$       xda__success = xda__status + %x0001
$       status = xda__success
$       on warning then goto error
         .
         .
         .
$       @sub1 'p1
         .
         .
         .
$error:
         .    error handling for MAIN procedure
         .
```

```
$!     Subprocedure SUB1.
$
$      status = xda__success
$      on warning then goto error    ! Cleanup required.
          .
          .
$      open/read file 'p1
$      @sub2
          .
          .
$      goto exit
$
$error:
$      status = $status
$      goto exit
$
$exit:
$      set noon
$      close file
$      exit status .or. %x10000000


$!     Subprocedure SUB2.
$
$      on warning then exit $status .or. %x10000000
          .
          .  an error occurs here!
          .
```

When an error is detected in procedure SUB2, the following sequence of events occurs:

1. Its error handler exits with the error status code. The inhibit-display bit prevents DCL from displaying the status message.

2. The flow of control returns to procedure SUB1. DCL checks the status code from the invocation of SUB2, and because it is an error code, the error handler in SUB1 is invoked. It jumps to the ERROR label.

3. The error logic saves the error status code, closes the file, and exits with the error code.

4. The flow of control returns to procedure MAIN. Again DCL checks the status code and invokes the error handler in MAIN. It jumps to the ERROR label.

5. The code at the ERROR label performs the error handling for the main procedure.

The error in procedure SUB2 causes the procedure calls to be unwound, and each procedure's error handler gets a chance to run. This technique works regardless of the depth of procedure call.

8.7 Ignoring an Error

Sometimes it is necessary for a procedure to ignore an error caused by a subprocedure. Imagine a main procedure that allows the user to enter the name of another procedure to execute. The main procedure might want to ignore any errors in the user's subprocedure and continue execution rather than invoking its error handler. Assume that the user entered a procedure name and it was stored in the symbol XDA_PROC:

```
    .
    .
    .
$   set noon
$   @'xda_proc
$   set on
    .
    .
    .
```

The SET NOON command causes DCL to ignore any error status that may be returned when the subprocedure exits. Thus, the main procedure's error handler is not invoked. The SET ON command reestablishes automatic error checking.

8.8 Obtaining the Message for a Status Code

An OpenVMS status code is an integer. OpenVMS provides a service to translate a status code into message text so it can be displayed in a meaningful format. This service makes use of *message files*, which are tables that map each status code into its facility name, identification, and message text. The translation service is available to the DCL programmer through the F$MESSAGE lexical function.

The F$MESSAGE function requires one argument, a status code. It looks up the code in certain message files and returns a character string composed of the code's facility, severity, identification, and message text in the standard display format. If the status code cannot be located in the message files, the following string is returned:

```
%NONAME-s-NOMSG, Message number xxxxxxxx
```

In this string, the *s* represents the severity, and *xxxxxxxx* represents the hexadecimal value of the status code.

OpenVMS includes several message files in the SYS$MESSAGE directory, but not all of them are searched by the F$MESSAGE function. The SYSMSG.EXE file is always searched, because it contains common messages pertaining to OpenVMS system services, the RMS record management system, and file operations performed by many utilities. No other message file is searched unless you explicitly request one with the SET MESSAGE command.

As an example, assume you are implementing a DCL application that uses the BACKUP command and needs to report problems that arise during backup operations. Many of the status codes returned by BACKUP are specific to the utility and thus are not stored in the common SYSMSG.EXE message file. Because F$MESSAGE searches only the common message file, the following procedure will *not* work:

```
$     set noon
$     backup ...                ! Perform the backup operation.
$     backup_status = $status
$     set on
$     if .not. backup_status
$     then
$       message = f$message(backup_status)
            .
            .  perhaps write the message to a log file
            .
$     endif
```

The F$MESSAGE function is not able to return the message string for those BACKUP status codes that are specific to the BACKUP utility. If presented with a facility-specific BACKUP status, it returns the NOMSG status. In order to ensure that the function can return the message string for BACKUP statuses, you must request that OpenVMS search an additional message file, namely the system management message file SYSMGTMSG.EXE. This is accomplished with the SET MESSAGE command:

```
$     set message sys$message:sysmgtmsg.exe
$     set noon
$     backup ...                ! Perform the backup operation.
$     backup_status = $status
$     set on
$     if .not. backup_status
$     then
$       message = f$message(backup_status)
```

Table 8.3 OpenVMS message files

File	Commands
CLIUTLMSG.EXE	ANALYZE/MEDIA, MAIL, PHONE, PRINT, SUBMIT, RUN, SET, SHOW, SEARCH
FILMNTMSG.EXE	ANALYZE/OBJECT, ANALYZE/IMAGE, EDIT/FDL, ANALYZE/DISK
LMF_MESSAGE.EXE	License Management Facility
PRGDEVMSG.EXE	SET COMMAND, DIFFERENCES, LIBRARIAN, LINK, MESSAGE
SYSMGTMSG.EXE	ACCOUNTING, BACKUP, INSTALL, MONITOR, AUTHORIZE, SYSMAN
SYSMSG.EXE	Common system messages
TPUMSG.EXE	TPU

   perhaps write the message to a log file
```
$    endif
```

Now the F$MESSAGE function will search the system management message file, followed by the common system message file. The status codes specific to BACKUP are found in the system management file, while other status codes are found in the common system file.

Unfortunately, the SET MESSAGE command only allows one additional message file to be searched at any given time. If an application gets status codes from two or more facilities whose messages are in different files, the SET MESSAGE command must be used repeatedly to establish the appropriate message file for each status as it is looked up.

Table 8.3 lists the message files you are most likely to need, along with some of the OpenVMS commands whose messages reside in those files. A complete list is included in the *OpenVMS Programming Concepts Manual*.

8.9 Obtaining the Complete Error Text for a Status Code

You may find it useful to display the complete error message and user action text associated with a particular error status. This text is more substantial than the text returned by the F$MESSAGE lexical function. This text is available using the DCL command HELP/MESSAGE.

An interactive user can display the text for a status using its facility and identification code:

```
$ help/message/facility=rms fnf
FNF, file not found

Facility: RMS, OpenVMS Record Management Services

Explanation: The specified file does not exist.

User Action: Check the file specification and verify that
    the device, directory, file name, and file type are all
    specified correctly. If a logical name is specified,
    verify the current equivalence assigned to the logical
    name. If the equivalence is correct, verify that the
    correct volume is mounted on the specified device and
    that the file was not inadvertently deleted.
```

In a procedure, however, a second form of the HELP/MESSAGE command is more useful. It accepts the status code itself and displays the complete text for that status.

```
$    set noon
$    a command that fails
$    status = $status
$    set on
$    if user wants complete text then -
        help/message /status='status
```

Note that the /STATUS qualifier without a value displays the text for the status code currently in $STATUS. This is not particularly useful because a procedure almost always executes other commands between the one that failed and the HELP/MESSAGE command. The HELP command also accepts the /OUTPUT qualifier so you can redirect the text to a file and then display it in some other format.

CHAPTER 9

Interrupt Handling

AN *INTERRUPT* IS CAUSED BY AN EVENT requiring immediate attention when it occurs. If a program is executing when an interrupt takes place, program execution must be suspended so that the event can be handled as soon as possible. Once interrupt handling is complete, program execution is resumed at the point of suspension. DCL procedures need only deal with one kind of interrupt, that which occurs when the CTRL/Y key is pressed. The CTRL/Y key is the means by which the OpenVMS user signals that program execution is to be temporarily suspended or permanently canceled.

9.1 Interrupt Situations

There are two situations in which a CTRL/Y interrupt can occur during procedure execution. The first is while DCL is interpreting the command lines in the procedure. In this situation, both the CTRL/Y and the CTRL/C keys generate an interrupt: the two keys are equivalent. The second situation is during the execution of a program image invoked by a command in the procedure (e.g., the COPY command invokes the COPY.EXE image). In this situation, the CTRL/Y key generates an interrupt. Whether the CTRL/C key is equivalent to CTRL/Y depends on how the program image handles CTRL/C. If the image explicitly requests special handling of CTRL/C, then that key will not generate a CTRL/Y interrupt.

Regardless of the circumstance under which a CTRL/Y interrupt occurs, it is handled in a consistent fashion by DCL. The remainder of this chapter presents the various methods of handling interrupts.

9.2 The Default Interrupt Handler

DCL has a default interrupt handler, which it uses if you do not specify any other handler. Upon the occurrence of a CTRL/Y interrupt, DCL suspends execution of the current procedure and invokes its default interrupt handler. The action taken by the default handler depends upon the current procedure level.

When a main procedure is executing, DCL creates a *temporary command level* and issues the dollar sign ($) prompt. At this point you can enter DCL commands to display information about the executing procedure. For example, you can use the SHOW SYMBOL command to display the value of symbols used by the procedure. However, care must be taken to enter only commands interpreted directly by DCL. If you should enter a command that invokes an image, the temporary command level is canceled, the DCL procedure is canceled, and the image is executed back at the DCL prompt level. This feature reduces the usefulness of temporary command levels. To resume execution of the main procedure once the temporary command level is no longer needed, enter the CONTINUE command. To cancel the procedure altogether, enter the STOP command.

Sec. 20.4, p. 264

One command that can safely be entered at the temporary command level is SPAWN. With the SPAWN command you can create a new OpenVMS process with its own environment and DCL interpreter. In this new process you can issue any OpenVMS command whatsoever. However, since the process has its own environment, independent from the original process, you cannot alter the state of the interrupted command procedure. (To terminate the subprocess and continue in the temporary command level, enter the LOGOUT command.)

Another command that can be entered at the temporary command level is SHOW SYMBOL. This command can be used to inspect the value of symbols created by the procedure.

When a subprocedure is executing, default interrupt handling is somewhat different. If neither the subprocedure's caller nor any of its caller's callers have established their own interrupt handlers, then the interrupt handler behaves as described above. In other words, if all procedures use the default interrupt handler, then the default interrupt handler establishes a temporary command level. However, as soon as a procedure establishes its own interrupt handler, then any subprocedures it calls will acquire a different default handler. Rather than establishing a temporary command level, this default handler simply causes the subprocedure to exit with a status of %X10000001. The status has a success severity with the inhibit-display bit set so that no message is displayed as the subprocedure exits. Once the subprocedure exits, its caller continues normal execution, ignoring the interrupt because the status has a success severity. The caller's interrupt handler is *not* invoked. The interrupt is forgotten!

To summarize the default interrupt handler:

- The default interrupt handler for a procedure creates a temporary command level, unless
- A caller of the procedure had established its own interrupt handler, in which case the default handler causes the procedure to exit.

The default interrupt behavior is relatively complex. The value of temporary command levels is minimal, and the appearance of one in a production application would surely confuse the naive user. The default behavior is not modular, since the action taken by a handler depends upon the handlers of its calling procedures. Finally, the default interrupt handler does not always guarantee that cleanup code in procedures is executed. All in all, the default interrupt behavior is unsatisfactory; sophisticated procedures require their own interrupt handlers.

9.3   Changing Interrupt Handler Behavior

The easiest way to manage sophisticated interrupt handling for a DCL application is to integrate its interrupt handling with its error handling. The underlying premise is that a CTRL/Y interrupt is an error, a fatal error that should result in controlled termination of the procedure. (There are some situations in which an interrupt should not terminate the entire procedure. See Section 9.4.) The integration of interrupt handling with error handling requires that you establish your own interrupt handler in each procedure, which is accomplished with the ON CONTROL_Y command. The place to begin is with a main procedure. The following example takes the error-handling code from Chapter 8 and adds CTRL/Y interrupt handling:

```
$    xda__status  = %x18428000
$    xda__success = xda__status + %x0001
$    xda__ctrly   = xda__status + %x000C  ! A CTRL/Y status.
$    status = xda__success
$    on control_y then goto control_y    ! Establish handler.
$    on warning then goto error
        .
        .
$    open/read file 'p1
        . process the file
```

```
$       goto exit
$
$control_y:                             ! Handle the interrupt.
$       status = xda__ctrly
$       goto exit
$
$error:
$       status = $status
$       goto exit
$
$exit:
$       set noon
$       close file
$       exit status .or. %x10000000
```

The additional commands required for interrupt handling are marked with comments. A status is created for CTRL/Y interrupts so that the procedure, when canceled because of an interrupt, can exit with a distinct status. The status has a fatal error severity and a message number of 1. The ON CONTROL_Y command establishes an interrupt action for the procedure, which jumps to the interrupt handler at the CONTROL_Y label. This interrupt handler sets the STATUS symbol to the special CTRL/Y status and then joins the procedure cleanup code at the EXIT label. Note the similarity between the interrupt handling and the error handling. Both set the STATUS symbol to reflect the reason for procedure termination, and both ensure that the cleanup code is executed.

The interrupt handler should be established with the ON command as close to the beginning of the procedure as possible. However, you must be careful not to establish the handler until all initialization required by the handler has been performed. Imagine that the ON command appeared first in the preceding example. If the user pressed CTRL/Y after the ON command was executed but before the XDA__CTRLY symbol was established, then the interrupt handler would fail when trying to set the STATUS symbol to XDA__CTRLY.

When the interrupt handler cannot be established immediately, what happens if the user *does* press CTRL/Y before it is established? The default interrupt handler creates a temporary command level and presents it to the user. The naive user, not realizing this, simply continues typing DCL commands. These are executed at the temporary level until one of them invokes an image. The temporary level and the procedure are then canceled and the user's environment is returned to normal. Other than a slight delay as the procedure is canceled, the user does not see any confusing behavior!

To complete the interrupt handling for a complex application, you must deal with subprocedures. If a subprocedure has cleanup code, then the interrupt handling is performed precisely as it is in the main procedure. Once the cleanup code is completed, the subprocedure exits with the XDA__CTRLY status. Because this is a fatal status, the error handler in the subprocedure's caller will be invoked, the entire procedure stack will be unwound, and the application will terminate. This illustrates the advantage of fashioning an interrupt to behave like an error: no matter how deep the procedure calls are, an interrupt causes the application to terminate.

If a subprocedure has no cleanup code, then its interrupt handler can be simplified. Instead of branching to a CONTROL_Y label, it can simply exit with the appropriate status:

```
$    on control_y then exit xda__ctrly
```

If you study the preceding main procedure example, imagining that it has no cleanup code, you will see that it simply exits with the XDA__CTRLY status after an interrupt. So the ON CONTROL_Y command can specify the interrupt handler directly when cleanup code is not needed.

One problem remains with subprocedure interrupt handling. If some initialization is required before the ON CONTROL_Y command is executed, the user has a chance to press CTRL/Y before the interrupt handler is established. In this case DCL's default interrupt handler will cause the subprocedure to exit, because the main procedure has already established its own handler. Unfortunately, the exit status has a success severity, so the subprocedure's caller will blithely continue to execute as if the subprocedure had completed successfully. There are two choices in this situation. The first is to ignore the problem. After all, the probability of its occurrence is low. The second is to use the SET NOCONTROL command to block CTRL/Y interrupts during initialization:

```
$    set nocontrol=y
     .
     . initialization
     .
$    set control=y
$    on control_y then ...
```

The SET NOCONTROL command disables CTRL/Y interrupts. If the user presses CTRL/Y during the initialization sequence, the interrupt is ignored. The SET CONTROL command reenables interrupts. This may appear to do the trick, but the problem is still not solved and a new problem is introduced:

- A CTRL/Y interrupt just before the SET NOCONTROL command (i.e., as the subprocedure is being invoked but before the first line is executed) still causes the subprocedure to exit with a success status.
- If the initialization code goes awry and begins to loop or takes a bad branch, CTRL/Y interrupts will remain disabled. The only way to cancel the procedure may be to stop the OpenVMS process from another terminal.

The authors recommend ignoring the interrupt "window" at the beginning of a subprocedure. There is no general way to completely eliminate the window. There is one specific case, the captive login command procedure, where this window can be kept closed.

Sec. 24.1, p. 312

9.4 Using Interrupts for Other Purposes

There may be times when you want to use CTRL/Y for something other than canceling the entire application. For example, a procedure may display a long list of items for the user to peruse. If the user is not required to inspect the entire list, CTRL/Y can be used to cancel the list and go on to the next step of the procedure. The procedure must temporarily override normal interrupt handling while the list is being displayed. The following example illustrates a subprocedure in which a list is displayed:

```
$       on control_y then goto control_y
$       on warning then goto error
        .
        .
        .
$       on control_y then goto cancel_display
        .
        : display the list
        .
$cancel_display:
$       on control_y then goto control_y
```

The subprocedure establishes the standard interrupt handler when it starts up. At the point where the list is to be displayed, it establishes a new interrupt handler, which jumps to the CANCEL_DISPLAY label, thereby canceling the display. This interrupt handler is in effect during the entire process of displaying the list. After the display completes or is canceled, the standard interrupt handler is reestablished for the remainder of the procedure. The standard handler must be explicitly reestablished, because it was superseded by the special handler for the list display. Special interrupt handlers can be established whenever needed, but do not forget to reestablish the standard one.

9.5 Tying It All Together

Chapters 7, 8, and 9 have presented significant complex material. The DCL environment and error and interrupt handling not only are deeply intertwined but are also the most frequently neglected aspects of DCL programming. The next chapter ties all this material together by discussing the overall structure of DCL applications.

CHAPTER 10

Application Structure

THE PREVIOUS CHAPTERS have addressed the DCL programming environment, error handling, and CTRL/Y interrupt handling. These three aspects of DCL application design are by far the most complicated. You have gotten through the most difficult part of this book. With the knowledge gained so far, you can structure an entire DCL application, large or small, and feel confident that the application will behave in a consistent and reliable fashion.

This chapter brings together all the information presented so far in order to demonstrate one method of structuring an entire application. It also describes some conventions that should be followed when developing an application so that the application will be compatible with other OpenVMS applications and can coexist with them.

10.1 Naming Conventions

A wide variety of software products can be simultaneously installed and running on a OpenVMS system. Such products may be provided by DIGITAL, by third-party software vendors, or by your own development staff. In order to prevent these products from interfering with one another, a series of guidelines must be followed by each and every product. These guidelines are presented in the OpenVMS document entitled *Guide to Creating OpenVMS Modular Procedures*. The majority of guidelines do not pertain to DCL, but a few important ones do. These are the naming conventions for various system objects, such as logical names and files. If you adhere to the naming conventions carefully, your DCL application will not interfere with other applications written in DCL or any other language. The following paragraphs describe the naming conventions relevant to DCL applications:

Facility name Each software package should have a facility name, a unique mnemonic string that is associated with the package. This string is also sometimes referred to as a facility code.

Directories The name of the top-level directory containing the application files must be the same as the facility code or begin with the facility code and an underscore (e.g., XDA or XDA_ROOT).

Files The names of all the component files of the application must consist solely of the facility code or begin with the facility code and an underscore (e.g., XDA.COM, or XDA_CONFIG.DAT).

Global symbols The names of all global symbols created by the application must begin with the facility code and an underscore (e.g., XDA_MODE). This is particularly important because DCL applications usually leave global symbols around after they exit. These global symbols remain in existence until the process terminates, so they must not conflict with global symbols created by other applications.

Logical names All logical names defined by the application must begin with the facility code and an underscore (e.g., XDA_SYSTEM).

Status codes The status code symbols created by the application should begin with the facility code and two underscores (e.g., XDA__SUCCESS). Because status symbols are not global, this convention is only a suggestions.

The examples in this book follow these naming conventions.

10.2 Invoking the Application

A complex DCL application can consist of many procedures and data files. When the application is installed on an OpenVMS system, the files must be placed in appropriate directories, so that they can be accessed when the application is run. The simplest directory organization involves creating a single directory to contain all of the application's files. A system logical name is defined to refer to the directory, so that users can locate the application files.

The following discussion assumes that the example application, XDA, has been installed in a single directory. The logical name XDA_SYSTEM is defined to refer to that directory. To run the application, a user must invoke its main procedure, which establishes the application environment and directs its execution. The main procedure for the sample application is named XDA.COM. The following personal command is established in each user's login procedure or in the system login procedure:

```
$    xda == "@xda_system:xda"
```

Once the command XDA is established, a user invokes the application by name in a fashion similar to other OpenVMS applications:

```
$ xda
```

10.2.1 Foreign Commands

A *foreign command* is a command that is invoked by name, but is not defined in the DCL command tables. A foreign command can be a command procedure or an executable image (the AUTHORIZE utility, for example, has no corresponding DCL command). A foreign command is invoked by name, but without the need for a personal command definition such as XDA in the preceding example.

There are two ways to establish a foreign command. The first method has been available since OpenVMS V1 and does involve a personal command and a dollar sign preceding the value of the symbol. This method is not described here because it has been replaced with a better method in OpenVMS V6.2. The new method is called *automatic foreign command definition,* and involves the logical name DCL$PATH. If you define this logical name as a directory or list of directories, DCL will automatically search the directories for command procedures or executable images.

Chap. 14, p. 165

```
$ define dcl$path xda_system:,sys$system:
```

When a command name is not defined as a verb in the DCL command tables, the automatic foreign command facility checks for a definition of the DCL$PATH logical name. If it finds the above definition, it then searches the XDA_SYSTEM directory, followed by the SYS$SYSTEM directory, for a command procedure or executable image whose name matches the command name.

When you define DCL$PATH as shown above, you can enter the XDA command without the need to define a personal command.

10.3 The Main Procedure

Every DCL application has a *main procedure*, the procedure that executes first when the application is run. The main procedure is responsible for establishing the overall environment in which the application will execute. A small application may consist only of the main procedure, but most applications will include other procedures invoked by the main procedure, which execute in its established environment.

The techniques used to establish the application environment have been introduced in preceding chapters. These techniques are brought together in the following main procedure, which is the main procedure of the hypothetical application, XDA:

```
$!      The main procedure for the XDA application.
$
$!      1. Block the use of dangerous "external"
$!         personal commands.
$
$       backup = "backup"
$       copy   = "copy"
            .
            .
$
$!      2. Save the current message and privilege settings.
$
$       saved_message = f$environment("MESSAGE")
$       saved_privs   = f$setpriv("all")
$
$!      3. Define some simple status codes for the application.
$
$       xda__status  = %x10428000
$       xda__success = xda__status + %x0001
$       xda__ctrly   = xda__status + %x000C
$
$!      4. Establish the interrupt and error handlers. Make sure
$!         the summary status indicates success when we exit
$!         normally.
$
$       status = xda__success
$       on control_y then goto control_y
$       on warning then goto error
$
$!      5. Establish the message and privilege environment.
```

```
$
$       set message/facility/severity/identifier/text
$       junk = f$setprv(saved_privs+"PRMMBX,SYSPRV")
$
$!      6. Set up some useful symbols for the application.
$
$       ask     = "read sys$command /prompt="
$       define  = "define/nolog"
$       libcall = "@xda_system:subroutine-library"
$       false   = 0
$       display = "write sys$output"
$       true    = 1
$       undefine = "deassign"
$
        ⋮  the application
        ⋮
$       goto exit
$
$!      The interrupt handler sets the summary status to
$!      indicate that CTRL/y was pressed and then joins the
$!      cleanup code.
$
$control_y:
$       status = xda__ctrly
$       goto exit
$
$!      The error handler sets the summary status to the
$!      "offending" status and also joins the cleanup code.
$
$error:
$       status = $status
$       goto exit
$
$!      The exit routine first performs cleanup. Then it
$!      restore the original DCL environment. Finally, it
$!      exits with the summary status.
$
$exit:
$       set noon
        ⋮  cleanup code
        ⋮
$       set message 'saved_message
$       junk = f$setprv(saved_privs)
$       exit status .or. %x10000000
```

10.3 The Main Procedure

The application environment is initialized by performing the following steps in order (numbers refer to comments in the code):

1. Personal commands are defined for "dangerous" OpenVMS commands, so that any personal commands defined outside the procedure are effectively hidden and will not interfere with the application. Alternatively, if your procedure is completely self-contained, you can use the SET SYMBOL/SCOPE command.

2. The current settings of DCL environment items, such as the message format and privileges, are saved.

3. Basic status values needed by the error and interrupt handlers are defined.

4. The error and interrupt handlers are established. Up to this point, errors and interrupts will cancel the procedure harmlessly. From this point on, they will cause the appropriate handler to be invoked.

5. The settings of DCL environment items are altered as required by the application.

6. Various symbolic constants, personal commands, and other useful symbols are defined. These can be used by the rest of the application.

Once these steps are completed, the actual application can commence. The remainder of the main procedure, along with all subprocedures of the application, runs in the environment established by the initialization code.

The interrupt and error handlers are identical to those illustrated in previous chapters. They set the STATUS symbol to the appropriate status and join the cleanup code at the EXIT label. The cleanup code performs application-specific cleanup operations, such as closing open files or deleting temporary ones. It then reestablishes the DCL environment as it was prior to the application and exits with the summary status. Another procedure that invokes the XDA application can use this status to determine the success or failure of its request.

10.4 A Subprocedure

When a DCL application is complex, it is difficult to organize all the necessary code in one procedure. Just as large programs written in conventional languages are broken down into modules and subroutines, so are large DCL programs. One of the application procedures is the main procedure and the rest are *subprocedures*. The subprocedures are designed to run in the environment established by the main procedure. All the procedures must cooperate to allow error and interrupt handling to proceed smoothly.

The application procedures invoke one another using the logical name referring to the directory containing the procedures. For example, the main procedure in our application invokes subprocedure XDA_SEARCH as follows:

```
$       @xda_system:xda_search parameter ...
```

The skeletal structure of a subprocedure depends upon whether it requires any cleanup code. Cleanup code consists of commands that *must* be executed regardless of the manner in which the subprocedure exits. It might close open files, delete temporary files, or deassign logical names. A subprocedure without cleanup code is organized as follows:

```
$!      A subprocedure for the XDA application.
$
$       on control_y then exit xda__ctrly
$       on warning then exit $status .or. %x10000000
$
          .
          . initialization
          .
$
          .
          . body of subprocedure
          .
$       exit xda__success
```

The subprocedure establishes a CTRL/Y interrupt handler, which simply exits with the XDA__CTRLY status. This status has a fatal error severity, so the caller's error handler is invoked and the procedure stack is unwound. The subprocedure also establishes an error handler, which exits with the offending status (the inhibit-display bit is set to prevent display of the corresponding message). The error handler traps warnings, errors, and fatal errors, returning them to the caller, so that again its error handler is invoked. Both interrupts and errors cancel the subprocedure and allow its caller to determine subsequent actions. The initialization section and subprocedure body perform the actions attributed to the subprocedure. Once complete, the subprocedure exits with a success status and its caller continues execution.

The organization of a subprocedure with cleanup code is a bit more elaborate. The interrupt and error handlers must arrange to execute the cleanup code before the procedure exits. The normal paths through the subprocedure must do the same:

```
$!      A subprocedure for the XDA application.
$
$       status = xda__success
```

```
$       on control_y then goto control_y
$       on warning then goto error
$
          : initialization
          .
$
          : body of subprocedure
          .
$
$       goto exit
$
$control_y:
$       status = xda__ctrly
$       goto exit
$
$error:
$       status = $status
$       goto exit
$
$exit:
$       set noon
          : cleanup code
          .
$       exit status .or. %x10000000
```

A subprocedure with cleanup code is organized almost identically to the main procedure. The symbol STATUS must be set to the desired exit status before joining the cleanup code at the EXIT label. In the normal case, STATUS is set to the success status, the subprocedure executes, and eventually it branches to the EXIT label. If an interrupt or error occurs, the handler resets the STATUS symbol to the appropriate status and then branches to the EXIT label. In all cases, the cleanup code is executed and the status is returned to the caller with the inhibit-display bit set.

Variations on the preceding themes are certainly possible. In Chapter 9, for example, interrupt handling was modified to allow a display to be canceled in the middle without terminating the application. You may find that other variations are required by your application; do not hesitate to devise new procedure organizations to accept these variations. Just keep in mind the following requirements:

- Every procedure must exit with a success or error status that accurately reflects what happened in the procedure.

- Unintentional errors and interrupts must be detected and cause the procedure to exit with the appropriate error status.

- Cleanup code must be executed regardless of the reason for procedure exit.

If you are diligent in the application of these rules, your application will behave in a predictable manner through all execution paths and regardless of any errors or interrupts that might occur.

10.5 The Subroutine Library

Chap. 8, p. 91

A large DCL application often includes a handful of subprocedures that perform general operations needed by all parts of the application. A good example is the `SIGNAL` subroutine, which is called to display an informational or error message in the standard format used by all OpenVMS software. This operation is performed in quite a few places in the application, and many lines of code are necessary to implement it, so it is a perfect candidate for a subroutine. Section 10.6 describes the `SIGNAL` subroutine in detail. Rather than creating a separate procedure file for each of these general subroutines, it is easier to group them together into a single large procedure, which serves as the subroutine "library" for the application. The subroutine library is not an OpenVMS library in the technical sense, but it serves a similar purpose: to collect a set of useful subroutines in a single place for easy access and maintenance.

The library resides in a single procedure file with the name `SUBROUTINE-LIBRARY`. A subroutine is called by invoking the procedure with certain parameters. The first parameter is always the name of the desired subroutine. The remaining parameters act as "arguments" to the subroutine; they specify information the subroutine needs to perform its assigned function. Here is a skeletal procedure library that might be included in the XDA sample application:

```
$       on control_y then exit xda__ctrly
$       on warning then exit $status .or. %x10000000
$
$       goto 'p1
$
$ASK:   ! P1:ASK P2:symbol P3:prompt P4:data-type P5:default
$       !         P6:options
           ⋮
           perform ask function
           ⋮
$
$SIGNAL: ! P1:SIGNAL P2:severity P3:identifier P4:text ...
           ⋮
           perform signal function
           ⋮
$
```

```
$UNIQUE_NAME: ! P1:UNIQUE_NAME P2:symbol P3:pattern
```
   perform unique name function

After establishing the usual interrupt and error handlers, the procedure performs a GOTO to the label specified by P1, the first parameter. The apostrophe substitution causes the value of P1, the subroutine name, to be substituted in the GOTO command. The target of the branch thus becomes the name of the subroutine.

Each subroutine begins with the label that names the subroutine (e.g., SIGNAL) and acts as the target of the initial GOTO. A comment is provided to describe the subroutine's parameters. The subroutine is responsible for performing the requested function and finally exiting with a summary status: a success status if the operation succeeded, or some error status if it failed. The success status will cause the calling procedure to continue executing, but an error status will trigger its error handler. (The library illustrated here includes subroutines named ASK, SIGNAL, and UNIQUE_NAME.)

The easiest way to call subroutines in the library is to set up a personal command. Assuming that the logical name XDA_SYSTEM has been established before the application is invoked, the following personal command can be established in the main procedure's initialization code:

```
$    libcall = "@xda_system:subroutine-library"
```

Once this personal command is established, individual subroutines can be called as follows:

```
$    libcall ask xda_ans s "What is your name:"
```

—or—

```
$    libcall signal xda e baddev "Invalid device specified."
```

—or—

```
$    libcall unique_name xda_name xda_?.tmp
```

A general-purpose DCL subroutine library is presented in Appendix E. This subroutine library is not specific to any one application, but contains subroutines useful to all applications. The library procedure is self-initializing and thus does not rely on any symbols or logical names defined by the application. The authors hope that you will find the subroutine library useful for your own DCL programming.

10.6 The SIGNAL Subroutine

<small>☞ Chap. 8, p. 91</small>

The `SIGNAL` subroutine is the first subroutine introduced in this book, and it is perhaps the most important one. `SIGNAL` provides the means for a procedure to display a success or error message and then invoke its error handler if appropriate. The term *signal* is borrowed from the OpenVMS run-time library routine `LIB$SIGNAL`, which is the routine called by programs written in conventional languages to perform a similar function. The `SIGNAL` subroutine performs two major steps:

1. It displays one or more messages based upon its parameters. These messages are formatted according to the OpenVMS convention for informational and error messages.

2. It exits with a status whose severity depends upon one of its parameters. If the severity is an error or fatal error, the caller's error handler will be invoked.

The content of the messages and the severity of the exit status are determined by the subroutine's parameters. At least five parameters must be specified; more are allowed:

P1 As with all subroutines in the library, the first parameter is the name of the subroutine: `SIGNAL`.

P2 The second parameter is the facility code of the facility signaling the error.

P3 The third parameter is the severity of the signaled message. A single letter is used: `S` for success, `I` for informational, `W` for warning, `E` for error, `F` for fatal error.

P4 The fourth parameter is the identification code for the message. It is composed of letters, digits, and underscores (`_`).

P5 The fifth parameter is the text of the message. It must be enclosed in quotation marks.

P6–P8 If multiple messages are desired, additional text parameters can be specified. Each message is displayed on a separate line.

The following examples illustrate calls to the `SIGNAL` subroutine and the resulting messages.

```
    $    libcall signal xda i copydone -
                    "All files have been copied."
    %XDA-I-COPYDONE, All files have been copied.
```

—or—

```
    $    libcall signal xda i copydone "Copying is complete." -
                    "''file_count files were processed."
%XDA-I-COPYDONE, Copying is complete.
-XDA-I-COPYDONE, 37 files were processed.
```

—or—

```
    $    libcall signal xda e nodisk -
                    "The specified disk does not exist."
%XDA-E-NODISK, The specified disk does not exist.
```

—or—

```
    $    libcall signal xda f nosuchfil -
                    "The file ''file_spec does not exist."
%XDA-F-NOSUCHFIL, The file SPECIAL.DAT does not exist.
```

The SIGNAL subroutine treats warning messages in a special fashion. Instead of returning a warning status to correspond to the warning message, it returns an informational status. This prevents the caller's error handler from being invoked and allows messages to be issued as a matter of course.

The SIGNAL subroutine is fully documented in Appendix E.

CHAPTER 11

Obtaining User Input

OpenVMS is an interactive operating system, so it is not surprising that many of the programs written for it are also interactive. The dialog between a computer program and a user flows in two directions, from the program to the user and from the user to the program. Chapter 6 explained how to format and display output for the benefit of the user. This chapter discusses how to obtain input from the user.

A video terminal consists of an output device, the screen, and an input device, the keyboard. In addition to the process-permanent files SYS$OUTPUT and SYS$ERROR, which are used to write information to the screen, OpenVMS maintains two process-permanent files from which input can be obtained. These files are accessed via the logical names SYS$COMMAND and SYS$INPUT. Exactly which files are accessed depends upon the current environment, as follows:

Sec. 20.5, p. 269

At the DCL prompt Both SYS$COMMAND and SYS$INPUT refer to the terminal keyboard.

During execution of an interactive procedure SYS$COMMAND refers to the terminal keyboard; SYS$INPUT refers to the procedure file.

During execution of a batch procedure Both SYS$COMMAND and SYS$INPUT refer to the procedure file.

At the DCL prompt or during interactive procedure execution, keyboard input can be obtained by reading from SYS$COMMAND. During batch procedure execution, there is no keyboard from which to obtain input.

11.1 The INQUIRE Command

The INQUIRE command is the simplest method of obtaining input from the user. Unfortunately, the command has many quirks that diminish its usefulness. Because of these quirks, INQUIRE is explicitly not permitted in certain contexts. The command requires two parameters: a symbol and a prompt string. The prompt string cannot be an expression but must be a simple literal string enclosed in quotation marks. The prompt string is displayed, a line is read from SYS$COMMAND, and the symbol is set to a character string containing the text of the line. The character string does not include the carriage return at the end of the line. The following behavior should be noted:

- The prompt string is actually optional. The INQUIRE command uses the symbol name as the prompt if the string is omitted.
- A colon and a space are appended to the prompt string in an effort to make it pretty (this can be suppressed with the /NOPUNCTUATION qualifier, as described below).
- An apostrophe in the input causes substitution to take place before the symbol is set to the input line. This is potentially dangerous, because the user can "sneak in" the value of any symbol whose name is known.
- Leading and trailing whitespace is removed from the input, and each occurrence of embedded whitespace is collapsed to a single space. The term *whitespace* refers to a sequence of one or more spaces or tabs.
- The input is converted to uppercase letters.
- The previous two actions do not take place for portions of the input enclosed in quotation marks, but the quotation marks themselves are removed.
- The INQUIRE command is deliberately not permitted within captive command procedures, to maintain the security necessary for the captive command procedure.

This complex behavior makes the content of the input difficult to predict and control.

The format of the prompt can be controlled using the /NOPUNCTUATION qualifier. When this qualifier is present, the colon and space are not appended to the prompt; the prompt will be displayed exactly as it appears in the command. There are other qualifiers, which are described in the *OpenVMS DCL Dictionary*.

Because of the idiosyncratic nature of the INQUIRE command, it should only be used in personal command procedures that perform simple input operations.

11.2 The READ Command

The READ command is the preferred means of obtaining input from the user. The READ command can do everything that the INQUIRE command can, yet it has none of the latter's idiosyncracies. The READ command requires two parameters: a logical name identifying the file from which input is to be read, and a symbol that is set to the input. A line is read from the file and the symbol is set to a character string containing the text of the line. Terminal input is obtained by reading from the file SYS$COMMAND. In addition, the /PROMPT qualifier is necessary in order to specify a prompt string. Here are a few examples of the READ command, along with the resulting prompts:

```
$     read sys$command/prompt="Name: " line
Name:
```

—or—

```
$     read sys$command -
          /prompt="Do you want to delete the file? " answer
Do you want to delete the file?
```

—or—

```
$     prompt = f$fao("(!5%T) Command: ", 0)
$     read sys$command/prompt="''prompt'" command
( 9:28) Command:
```

The third example demonstrates how the F$FAO lexical function can be used to create a prompt string containing the current time, which is then substituted in the READ command line. Unlike the INQUIRE command, the READ command does not alter the prompt string or input text in any way. Unfortunately, there is no way to use the READ command to obtain single keystrokes, cursor control keys, or editing keys like those on the application keypad.

A personal command can be used to make READ commands more concise:

```
$     ask = "read sys$command/prompt="
          :
          :
$     ask "Name: " line
$     ask "Are you sure you want to delete the file? " answer
$     ask "''f$fao("(!5%T) Command: ", 0)'" command
```

It is a OpenVMS convention to use the CTRL/Z character to signify *end-of-file* when reading from a terminal. Of course, there is no physical end-of-file on a terminal; the user can always type more characters. However, it makes sense to rely on a logical end-of-file to terminate a series of related input lines. For example, most interactive OpenVMS programs will exit when the user enters CTRL/Z, because the CTRL/Z marks the end of the input related to the program. If you are creating a procedure to look like any other OpenVMS program, this behavior should be emulated.

The READ command accepts an /END_OF_FILE qualifier that specifies a label. If (and only if) CTRL/Z is pressed while the read is in progress, DCL transfers control to the command containing the label. This is an "arbitrary goto" and should be used with care so as not to adversely affect the readability of the program.

```
$     ask "Command: " command /end_of_file=15
      .
      . process command
      .
$     goto 19
$15:
      .
      . process end-of-file
      .
$19:
```

If some input is typed on the line before CTRL/Z is pressed, the symbol is set to the input typed so far, and then control is transferred to the end-of-file label. The code at that label may need to process the characters in the symbol before performing end-of-file cleanup.

11.3 Default Answers

It is common practice to associate a ***default answer*** with a question. The default answer is the answer the program will assume if the user presses RETURN without entering any information. The default answer should be the most likely answer to the question, unless that answer is potentially dangerous. For example, the default answer to the question "Do you want to delete all your files?" should be no. By convention, the prompt string for a question contains the default answer in square brackets at the end of the question, before the trailing punctuation character.

It is quite simple to implement default answers in DCL. If the user presses RETURN without entering any other characters, the symbol specified in the

READ command will be set to the null string. This condition can be determined and the symbol set to the default answer.

```
$       ask "Are you sure you want to delete the file [NO]? " -
            delete
$       if delete .eqs. "" then delete = false
```

–or–

```
$       ask "Which directory is to be listed [working]: " dir
$       if dir .eqs. "" then dir = f$environment("DEFAULT")
```

–or–

```
$       ask "Number of copies to print [1]: " copies
$       if copies .eqs. "" then copies = 1
```

In each case, a check is made to see if the input symbol is set to the null string. If so, it is reset to the default answer.

11.4 Editing Input

In some circumstances, it is necessary to edit the user's input before processing it. For example, if the input is a product name that is to be compared to a set of valid names, it is necessary to convert the name to uppercase letters so that it will compare correctly with the valid choices. The F$EDIT lexical function provides a set of editing capabilities that make it quite easy to perform most common input editing. The F$EDIT function takes two arguments: the string to be edited and a string containing a keyword or list of keywords, which determine the exact editing performed. The function returns the edited string.

Assume that some input has been read into the symbol LINE. The following are examples of some of the editing you can perform:

```
$!      Convert the line to uppercase.
$       line = f$edit(line,"UPCASE")
```

–or–

```
$!      Remove leading and trailing whitespace from the line.
$       line = f$edit(line,"TRIM")
```

–or–

```
$!      Remove leading and trailing whitespace, and compress
$!      occurrences of whitespace to a single space.
$       line = f$edit(line,"TRIM,COMPRESS")
```

–or–

```
$!     Remove leading and trailing whitespace, compress
$!     whitespace, and convert to uppercase.
$      line = f$edit(line,"TRIM,COMPRESS,UPCASE")
```

As the examples illustrate, the various editing operations can be performed singly or in any combination.

11.5 Checking the Validity of Input

Once a procedure accepts input from the user, it is often necessary to check the input for errors. For example, if the input is supposed to be an integer, the procedure must ensure that the characters entered form a valid integer and that the integer is in the desired range. It is a mark of a well-written procedure that all user input is checked as carefully as possible, as soon as possible. The longer a procedure waits to check its input, the more out-of-context the resulting error messages will be. The following sections discuss input checking for each type of data.

11.5.1 Integers

Whenever a procedure expects an integer value in response to a query, it must check the user's input to ensure that it represents a valid integer. Because the READ command always reads its input as a character string, the user's input will be represented as a string even though it is intended to be an integer. The F$TYPE lexical function is used to check the type of the input: if the input string contains the valid external representation of an integer, the function will return "INTEGER"; otherwise, it will return "STRING".

After it is determined that the input is a valid integer, the input is converted to an integer data type. Once this is done, any additional validation such as range checking, can be performed. If any of the tests fail, an appropriate message is issued and the question is asked again. The following loop illustrates a method for checking an integer that is intended to be a year number:

```
$      input_ok = false
$10:   ask "Which year do you want to report: " year_string
$      if f$type(year_string) .eqs. "INTEGER"
$      then
$         year = f$integer(year_string) ! Integerize year.
$         input_ok = year .ge. 1900 .and. year .le. 2100
```

```
$         if .not. input_ok then libcall signal xda w badyear-
$                   "The year must be in the range 1900--2100."
$         else
$           libcall signal xda w badint "Please enter an integer."
$         endif
$         if .not. input_ok then goto 10
```

The loop is controlled by the Boolean variable INPUT_OK, which is initialized to FALSE before the loop is entered and tested at the bottom of the loop to determine whether another iteration is necessary. On each iteration the user is prompted for a year. If the input is a valid integer *and* the integer is in the required range, then INPUT_OK is set true. Otherwise, an appropriate warning message is displayed and INPUT_OK remains false. The loop is continuously executed until valid input is received.

After the loop terminates, the symbol YEAR will be set to the desired year, stored as an integer. Note the use of the F$INTEGER lexical function to convert the year from a string to an integer.

11.5.2 Character Strings

Strings are generally the easiest kind of input to check. Sometimes no checking is required at all, because any string is valid. Often the length of the string must be checked to ensure that it is within a required range. At other times, the content of the string must be inspected because only certain characters are allowed. The following loop asks the user to enter a comment for a history file:

```
$10:    ask "History comment: " comment
$       input_ok = f$length(comment) .ge. 1 .and. -
                   f$length(comment) .le. 80
$       if .not. input_ok then libcall signal xda w commlen -
                   "The comment must contain 1--80 characters."
$       if .not. input_ok then goto 10
```

This loop uses the INPUT_OK variable in the same fashion as the previous example. No data type checking is required, because the input is guaranteed to be a string. The length of the input is checked to ensure that it is in the required range 1–80. The COMMENT symbol contains the comment string after the loop terminates.

The following example illustrates the situation where the input must be chosen from among a fixed set of valid strings:

```
$10:    ask "Print DETAIL or SUMMARY report [SUMMARY]: " -
            report_type
$       if report_type .eqs. "" then report_type = "SUMMARY"
$       report_type = f$edit(report_type,"UPCASE")
```

```
$          input_ok = report_type .eqs. "DETAIL" .or. -
                     report_type .eqs. "SUMMARY"
$          if .not. input_ok then libcall signal xda w badtype -
                                  "Please enter DETAIL or SUMMARY."
$          if .not. input_ok then goto 10
```

The checking methodology is similar to the one in the previous example, except that the input must be one of two particular strings. The input is converted to uppercase letters before it is checked against the two strings; this allows the user to enter input in uppercase or lowercase. The query also provides a default answer ("SUMMARY").

11.5.3 Booleans

Table 3.1, p. 27

Strictly speaking, validation of a Boolean response is unnecessary because any string is a valid Boolean value. In spite of this, you should do the user a favor and accept only the words YES or NO and their abbreviations. Otherwise, the user can accidentally enter TO when NO was meant, and DCL will interpret this as a true value because it begins with T.

The following loop asks a yes/no question and validates the answer:

```
$10:       ask "Do you want to clear the directory [NO]? " clear
$          if clear .eqs. "" then clear = "NO"
$          clear = f$edit(clear, "UPCASE")
$          input_ok = f$locate(clear,"YES") .eq. 0 .or. -
                     f$locate(clear,"NO")  .eq. 0
$          if .not. input_ok then libcall signal xda w badyesno -
                                  "Please enter YES or NO."
$          if .not. input_ok then goto 10
```

A default answer of NO is provided, and the input is converted to uppercase letters for comparison purposes. The F$LOCATE function is used to ensure that the input is YES, NO, or an abbreviation thereof. To test that the input is an abbreviation of YES, the input must match the string "YES" beginning at position zero. The only inputs that pass the test are "Y", "YE", and "YES". A similar test is used for NO, allowing only the inputs "N" and "NO". All other inputs are rejected.

11.6 Main Procedure Arguments

A procedure often requires input values before it can determine the exact operations to perform. These input values must be obtained before the procedure can begin its intended task. For example, a procedure that copies a file from the local network node to another node requires two input values: the file spec and the remote node name. One method of passing these values to the procedure is via procedure parameters. Unfortunately, this requires that the user remember both the order and the syntax of the parameters. Another method of obtaining the values is to prompt the user and read the values from the keyboard at the beginning of the procedure. This solves the first problem, but fails to work when the procedure is submitted to batch because there is no keyboard. A combination of both techniques offers the maximum flexibility.

Assume that the procedure expects two parameters: the file to be copied and the remote node name. The following code will check for the parameters, and if either one is missing, prompt for it and read it from the keyboard:

```
$!    This procedure accepts two parameters, as follows:
$!    P1: the file to be copied
$!    P2: the remote node to receive the copy
         .
         .
         .
$     if p1 .eqs. "" then ask "File: " p1
$     if p2 .eqs. "" then ask "Remote node: " p2
```

For each parameter in turn, the procedure determines whether the parameter was specified when the procedure was invoked by testing it for the null string. If the parameter is missing, an `ASK` command is used to prompt and obtain a value for it (remember that the personal command `ASK` is short for `READ SYS$COMMAND /PROMPT=`). The user can pass a required value as a parameter *or* choose to be questioned for the value. When the procedure is submitted to batch, the values must be supplied as parameters. If they are not, the `ASK` command fails and the procedure terminates with an error.

11.7 A Sophisticated Input Subroutine

As demonstrated in the previous sections, the operation of asking a question is both a common and a complex one. For this reason, it is useful to embody the techniques for asking questions in a subroutine that can be invoked whenever a question needs to be asked. This subroutine is included in the subroutine library listed in Appendix E, where it is fully documented. Only some of its features are described here.

Sec. 10.1, p. 113

The subroutine is called `ASK` and requires at least three parameters: a global symbol that will be set to the answer, a data type specifier, and a prompt string. There are optional parameters, the first of which is the default answer (if omitted, there is no default and the user must input a value). The procedure performs the following steps, shown here in simplified form:

1. Display the prompt, including the default answer if specified.
2. Read the answer from SYS$COMMAND.
3. If RETURN was pressed without entering any data:
   - Go back to step 1 if no default was specified.
   - Assume the default answer if one was specified.
4. Check the answer to ensure that it conforms to the data type specifier. If not, display a message and go back to step 1.
5. Set the global symbol to the answer.
6. Exit.

Once the subroutine exits, the answer is available in the global symbol provided as the first parameter.

The data type specifier is a single letter that restricts the type of data the user can enter: I for integer, S for string, B for Boolean (yes/no).

Here are a few examples:

```
$!      Ask for the user name of the person to whom the mail
$!      is sent.  The answer must be a string.
$
$       libcall ask xda_user s "User to receive mail:"
```

—or—

```
$!      Ask for the number of copies to be printed.  The answer
$!      must be an integer, the default being 1.
$
$       libcall ask xda_copies i "Number of copies to print:" 1
```

—or—

```
$!      Determine if the user really wants to delete the file.
$!      The answer must be a Boolean, the default being NO.
$
$       libcall ask xda_delete b -
                "Do you really want to delete the file?" no
```

—or—

```
$!      Wait for the user to press RETURN.
$
$       libcall ask xda_ s "Press RETURN when ready:" continue
```

Notice how the global symbols used in the ASK conform to the OpenVMS convention for naming global symbols. When the user's answer is just discarded, as in the last example, the "throw-away" symbol XDA_ is specified.

11.8 Redirecting Program Input

An interactive OpenVMS program normally obtains input from SYS$INPUT. This works fine when the program is run from the DCL prompt, but has an unexpected consequence when the program is run from a procedure. Because SYS$INPUT is directed to the procedure file while a procedure is executing, the program attempts to read its input from the procedure file. This is why the procedure examples in this chapter read from SYS$COMMAND: it is directed to the terminal keyboard during procedure execution. There is a way to force a program image to read from SYS$COMMAND.

Before tackling that problem, however, it is interesting to point out some uses for the standard behavior. If a procedure runs an interactive program but wants to provide "canned" answers to all the questions asked by the program, these answers can be placed directly in the procedure file. For example, assume you want to extract message number 1 from the mail folder named BOILERPLATES and place it in a temporary file:

```
$    mail
read boilerplates 1
extract/noheader sys$scratch:xda_boilerplate.tmp
exit
$
     .
     .  process the boilerplate file
     .
```

Because SYS$INPUT is directed to the procedure file, the MAIL utility will read its commands from the procedure. The three commands (READ, EXTRACT, EXIT) accomplish the task of extracting the message into a temporary file, just as if an interactive user had typed them in. The EXIT command is not strictly necessary, because the first line containing a dollar sign signals end-of-file to the program. Program input data included directly in a procedure is called *image data*. The technique of placing input in the procedure works only when the input is entirely static. Apostrophe substitution is not performed on the input lines, so they cannot be customized the way normal DCL commands can be.

When an interactive program needs to read its input from the terminal, it must be forced to read from SYS$COMMAND. This is accomplished with the

DEFINE command. Suppose, for example, you want to run the EDIT/EDT utility as part of a procedure and have it read from the terminal:

```
$    define/user_mode sys$input sys$command
$    edit/edt
```

The DEFINE command redefines the SYS$INPUT logical name so that it refers to the SYS$COMMAND logical, which in turn is directed at the terminal keyboard. The /USER_MODE qualifier makes this redefinition temporary, lasting only for the next image execution. Therefore, the EDIT/EDT utility will obtain its input from the terminal, even though it is invoked by a procedure.

> Sec. 14.4, p. 172

11.9 Reading Input from a Pipe

As mentioned earlier, a DCL command procedure reads its command input from SYS$INPUT, the command procedure file. And within the execution of the PIPE command, each stage of the pipe reads its input, passed from the previous stage, via SYS$INPUT. Because there would be a conflict with SYS$INPUT within a command procedure that would make it quite difficult to use a command procedure within a pipe, the PIPE command provides command procedures with an additional process permanent file: SYS$PIPE. A piped procedure can read the output from the previous stage using SYS$PIPE, without conflicting with the DCL commands read from SYS$INPUT.

You can read a single line of the output from the previous stage of the pipe using the following command:

```
$    read sys$pipe text
```

Section 20.8 describes pipes in more detail.

11.10 Displaying Large Amounts of Text

During the execution of a command procedure, SYS$INPUT refers to the procedure file. If a procedure displays large amounts of text whose content does not vary from one time to the next, it is easier to use a single TYPE command than multiple DISPLAY commands. In the following example, a lengthy help message is displayed:

```
$    type sys$input:
This is a lengthy help message.  It doesn't change from one
use to the next, so symbol values aren't used and
```

substitution is unnecessary. Because SYS$INPUT refers to
the procedure file, the TYPE command displays lines directly
from the file. The command will display lines until it
encounters the next procedure command (i.e., a line beginning
with a dollar sign).

We can even have blank lines for paragraph separation.

This is much easier than a series of DISPLAY commands with
strings in double quotes.
$
$ *next command*

11.10   Displaying Large Amounts of Text

CHAPTER 12
Debugging

THE TASK OF PROGRAM DEBUGGING is an integral part of developing DCL applications, just as it is with every programming project. Unfortunately, the comprehensive collection of OpenVMS debugging facilities is of no help to the DCL programmer. There is no symbolic debugger, no backtrace upon program failure, and no program analysis tools. You are forced to use "old-fashioned" debugging techniques, such as printing the values of variables at critical points in the program.

DCL does have one advantage over most other programming languages. Because it is strictly interpreted, the edit/compile/link/test cycle is simplified to an edit/test cycle. Making simple modifications to a procedure so it will display debugging information is not particularly painful, because you do not have to wait for a compile and link. The following sections describe the various techniques for debugging DCL procedures.

12.1 Verification

Procedure verification is the most powerful debugging tool available to the DCL programmer. There are two types of verification, each of which can be independently enabled or disabled:

Procedure verification   When this is enabled, DCL displays each command line in the procedure as it is executed. The command line is displayed *after* apostrophe and personal command substitution is performed.

Image verification   When this is enabled, DCL displays each image data line as it is read by an executing image. *Image data* is program input data that appears directly in a command procedure.

When verification is enabled, command and data lines are displayed at the terminal (specifically, to `SYS$OUTPUT`), intermixed with the normal output from the procedure.

12.1.1 Enabling Verification before Invoking the Procedure

The easiest way to verify a procedure is to enable verification before the procedure is invoked. This is accomplished with the SET VERIFY command:

```
$ set verify
```

This simple form of the command will enable both procedure and image verification. To enable only one type of verification, leaving the other type in its current state, use the following commands:

```
$ set verify=procedure
```

—or—

```
$ set verify=image
```

Once the SET VERIFY command is entered, all subsequent procedures and subprocedures will be verified. To disable verification when the debugging session is over, use the SET NOVERIFY command:

```
$ set noverify
```

12.1.2 Enabling Verification in a Procedure

When an entire procedure is verified, the volume of output may be so large that it becomes overwhelming. In this case, you can enable verification for a portion of the procedure, but this requires that you modify the procedure by inserting some temporary command lines. One line is inserted before the commands to be verified, and one after:

```
$     saved_verify = f$verify(true)      !!!
      .
      . commands to be verified
      .
$     junk = f$verify(saved_verify)      !!!
```

The F$VERIFY lexical function enables or disables both procedure and image verification according to its Boolean argument, enabling them if the argument is true, disabling if false. The function returns a Boolean value that reflects the state of procedure verification *before* the function was called. The `SAVED_VERIFY` symbol is therefore set to the prior state of procedure verification. Note that the function enables or disables both procedure and image verification, but returns the prior state of procedure verification only: an interesting inconsistency that is addressed in the next section. Once verification is enabled, the exiting commands are displayed at the terminal as they are executed. Finally, procedure verification is reset to its former state by using the `SAVED_VERIFY` symbol as an argument to the `F$VERIFY` function. In this case, the return value from the function is uninteresting, so it is discarded.

The former state of verification is saved and restored so that the verification of one sequence of command lines is independent of the verification of any other sequence. If, in a subprocedure, verification were enabled and then indiscriminately disabled, any verification in progress in a caller of the subprocedure would be thwarted. The minimal extra work to make each verification independent is well worth the effort.

The two temporary debugging commands are flagged with a triple exclamation point so they can be found and removed when debugging is complete. Triple exclamation points stand out when you read the procedure and are easily located by searching with an editor or the `SEARCH` utility. The authors recommend that all debugging lines be flagged with a unique marker of your own choosing.

Some experienced DCL programmers advocate using `SET NOVERIFY` or the `F$VERIFY` function at the beginning of main procedures to disable verification in case the "innocent" user accidentally has it enabled when the procedure is invoked. Explicitly disabling verification can sometimes be a mistake, because there are legitimate reasons to see the procedure verification.

12.1.3 Advanced Verification Features

As mentioned in the previous section, the `F$VERIFY` lexical function exhibits some inconsistent behavior. It sets both procedure and image verification according to its argument but only returns the prior state of procedure verification. In fact, `F$VERIFY` will accept two arguments, the first specifying the new setting for procedure verification and the second the new setting for image verification:

```
$    saved_verify = f$verify(true, false)        !!!
```

In this example, procedure verification is enabled, but image verification is disabled. If `F$VERIFY` is given one argument, the argument is used to set the state of both types of verification. If it is given two arguments, then the first is used for procedure verification and the second for image.

This additional feature still does not remove the inconsistency. Regardless of the number and value of its arguments, `F$VERIFY` returns only the prior state of procedure verification. If this single value is saved and used to reset verification after a sequence of commands, both procedure and image verification will be reset to the original state of *procedure* verification. The original state of image verification is lost. You can work around this inconsistency by employing the `F$ENVIRONMENT` lexical function in addition to `F$VERIFY`:

```
$    saved_image = f$environment("VERIFY_IMAGE")    !!!
$    saved_proc  = f$verify(true)                   !!!
       .
       . commands to be verified
       .
$    junk = f$verify(saved_proc, saved_image)       !!!
```

The additional first line uses the `F$ENVIRONMENT` function to obtain the current state of image verification and saves the state in `SAVED_IMAGE`. The second line enables both types of verification and saves the previous state of procedure verification. The final line correctly restores the state of both types of verification.

Nine times out of ten it is unnecessary to distinguish the two types of verification. The simpler method illustrated in the previous section will almost always suffice.

12.1.4 Annotating Verification Output

DCL allows you to include a prefix string on the output it produces while verifying a procedure. This prefix string can include information such as the name of the procedure being verified or the current system time.

```
$    set prefix= -
         "''f$parse(f$environment("PROCEDURE"),,,"NAME"): "
```

—or—

```
$    set prefix="(!11%T) "
```

Sec. 6.3, p. 78

The prefix string is a control string suitable for the `F$FAO` lexical function. DCL formats the prefix each time is displays verification output.

Displaying the procedure name is useful when you are debugging a group of related procedures, because it lets you easily identify the procedure that produces the verification output. Unfortunately, because there is no `F$FAO` directive to insert the current procedure name, such a prefix must be established at the beginning of each and every procedure you want to verify.

12.2 Temporary Debugging Output

There are circumstances in which procedure verification is overkill or does not display the necessary information. In particular, verification displays only command lines, not the values of symbols used in those command lines. In the case of assignment or IF commands, the values of symbols in the evaluated expression may be important. Such values are easy to display using temporary debugging lines:

```
$     show symbol count    !!! Count seems to be way off.
$     blocks = 50 + count*20
```

—or—

```
$     show symbol blocks     !!! Something is wrong
$     show symbol threshold  !!!
$     if blocks .lt. threshold then blocks = threshold
```

Any DCL commands that produce pertinent output can certainly be employed to display temporary debugging information. Just remember to remove such commands before installing the DCL application for public use. A marker such as the triple exclamation point is invaluable for finding and removing temporary debugging commands.

12.3 Permanent Debugging Output

Sometimes it is advantageous to leave debugging output commands in a procedure even when it is available for public use. This might be true, for example, during the "field test" of a new application. Under normal operation, the procedure must not display the debugging output. But there should be a way to enable debugging output when a problem is suspected. This can be accomplished using a global debug flag, or a logical name.

A global symbol is designated as the debug flag. The debug flag for the example application is XDA_DEBUG. If the symbol is undefined or set to false, debugging output is suppressed. If the symbol is set to true, debugging output is produced. The following initialization lines are needed in the main procedure to establish the debugging environment:

```
$     if f$type(xda_debug) .eqs. "" then xda_debug == false
$     if_debug = "if xda_debug"
```

The first line uses the F$TYPE lexical function to determine whether the global symbol XDA_DEBUG is defined. If not, it is defined but set false to prevent debugging output. The second line establishes the personal command IF_DEBUG, which is used to prefix debugging output lines.

As an alternative to using a global symbol to control the debugging output, you can use a logical name to set a local version of XDA_DEBUG:

```
$    xda_debug = f$trnlnm("xda_debug")
```

Although this does not appear to provide any immediate benefits over using a global symbol, you can use it to enable the debugging output from another process, by creating the logical name in a shared logical name table, such as LNMJOB, LNMGROUP, or LNM$SYSTEM. Using a logical name to enable debugging can be particularly useful when debugging detached processes and batch jobs.

When a command is prefixed with IF_DEBUG, it becomes conditional, executed only if debugging is enabled:

```
$    if_debug then display "This is debugging output."   !!!
```

After personal command substitution, the line becomes:

```
$    IF XDA_DEBUG THEN DISPLAY "This is debugging output."
```

Output is produced only if the XDA_DEBUG symbol is true. The symbol is true if it was explicitly set true by a knowledgeable person interested in tracking down a bug. If the symbol is undefined, it will be defined and set false by the first initialization line shown above. The personal command can also be used with a block IF command when multiple debugging lines are needed:

```
$    if_debug    !!!
$    then
$      display "This is debugging output."
$      display "This is more debugging output."
$    endif
```

Using the scheme presented here, debugging commands can be left in a procedure permanently. They are rendered harmless unless explicitly enabled by an informed user. Even when disabled, however, debugging commands use up some execution time. Procedure execution slows down in proportion to the number of command lines contained in the procedure.

This technique has various advantages. It can be useful when debugging large command procedures, because it can control the verification of specific sections of the procedure. It can also be used to disable verification around sections of the procedure that are not currently of interest and around "uninteresting" loops, particularly those that require large numbers of iterations to complete. And this technique obviously avoids the need to edit the command procedure file to enable verification.

12.4 Capturing Procedure Output

It is difficult to debug a procedure that displays a lot of information quickly. The information tends to flash by, scroll off the terminal screen, and disappear. The problem is exacerbated when a procedure is displaying significant amounts of debugging information intermixed with normal output.

There are three ways to capture the output of a procedure in a text file. The first is to use the /OUTPUT qualifier on the at-sign command that invokes the procedure. This qualifier specifies a file into which all the output of the procedure and its subprocedures is placed:

```
$ @xda_display/output=debug.lis
```

Any output written to SYS$OUTPUT is placed instead into the file DEBUG.LIS in the working directory. Note that it does not appear on the screen. Also note that the /OUTPUT qualifier must occur immedately after the procedure file specification, and before any parameters.

📌 Sec. 20.8, p. 273

The second method uses the PIPE command, and you can redirect all output to a file using the following command:

```
$    pipe @xda_display >debug.lis
```

Because the output does not appear on the screen, these two methods of capturing procedure output may be of little use in debugging an interactive DCL application. The third method of capturing output produces a log of the entire terminal session, while still allowing output to appear on the screen. This method requires the use of DECnet. Use various SET HOST commands to log in to your local node, creating a second interactive session:

```
$ set host 0 /log=debug.log
```

The SET HOST command usually creates a connection from the local DECnet node to a remote node, allowing you to log in at the remote node. In this case, however, the remote node is specified as 0. This node is always the local node, so the command creates a second terminal session on the same node. The /LOG qualifier specifies that a log file of the entire session is to be kept in the file DEBUG.LOG in the working directory.

Once the second terminal session is initiated, you can log in and test the application in a normal fashion. All output appears at the terminal; everything behaves as usual. When the second session is terminated, a complete log of keyboard input and screen output can be found in the log file.

CHAPTER 13
Files and Directories

This chapter begins the discussion of OpenVMS files. A *file* is a collection of information stored on some physical medium, such as magnetic disk or magnetic tape. All permanent information available to an OpenVMS system and its applications ultimately resides in files, so every OpenVMS programmer must understand files. This understanding is even more critical for DCL programmers because DCL applications are often centered on the manipulation of files and their contents.

13.1 File Specifications

A *file specification* is a character string that identifies an individual file or set of files on a OpenVMS system. A similar kind of specification can also be used to name a device or a disk directory, without reference to any particular files. In this book, the term *file spec* refers to all manner of device, directory, and file specifications, even though some do not identify individual files.

The format of a file spec was reviewed in Chapter 1, but it will be presented here in greater detail. A complete OpenVMS file spec has the following format:

node::*device*:[*directory*...]*name*.*type*;*version*

13.1.1 Node

The node component serves to specify a file on a particular DECnet or IP node. The name of the node is included in the spec, followed by a double colon to distinguish it from a device name. Multiple nodes can be included, each one followed by a double colon. In this case, the final node names the location of the file, with preceding nodes specifying the network path to be taken from the local node to the final node. For example, `BOSTON::STLOUS::WILTON::` results in a path from the local node through node `BOSTON`, through node `ST-LOUS`, and finally to the target node `WILTON`. In most cases, intermediate nodes should not be specified, because the DECnet and IP routing capabilities render the specification of intervening nodes unnecessary. Whether intermediate nodes can or must be specified depends upon the local network configuration. Talk to your system manager to find out.

Network nodes are actually identified by integers known as network addresses. The node names are a convenience to the user. Do not be surprised if you occasionally see file specs with numeric node components, such as the DECnet Phase IV compatible addresses `17::` and `12639::`. This usually occurs when information is sent from a remote node and the local node does not know its name. In order to determine the equivalence between names and addresses, you must again consult your system manager.

It is perfectly valid for a file spec to include the local node as its target DECnet or IP node. In this case, DECnet or IP simply makes a connection "to itself" to access the file. The node component is not ignored: a real connection is established, albeit to the local node. Therefore, specifying the local node on a file spec is not without network overhead. Instead of specifying the local node name, you can always refer to the local DECnet node via the number zero, as in `0::`. This still makes a DECnet connection; it is just easier to specify. With IP, one refers to the name `localhost::`.

The use of IP node specifications typically requires the use of DECnet-Plus operating over an IP transport, or an IP package and the TCP/IP integration provided in OpenVMS V6.2 and later.

13.1.2 Device

When a file is being accessed, the device component specifies the disk or tape on which the file resides. If the file spec refers to the device by itself and does not contain a directory or file name, then the device can also be a terminal, card reader, or any other device that is not file-structured (i.e., does not contain individual files). Device names have various formats depending upon the type of device, how many of them there are, whether the device is attached to the local OpenVMS Cluster node or another one, and so on. It is sheer folly to assume you know the format of a device name.

Sec. 19.1, p. 245

It is a common and well-advised practice to refer to devices with logical names. When a procedure refers to a device with a logical name, it is quite easy to substitute one device for another by simply redefining the logical name. If the procedure refers directly to the device, the procedure will have to be modified when a different device is substituted.

The logical name `SYS$DISK` always refers to the disk containing the working directory, as established with the `SET DEFAULT` command.

A handy device is the *null device*, referred to as `NLA0:`. Any output to this device is discarded. Reading from the device will result in an end-of-file condition, as if an empty file were being read.

13.1.3 Directory

The directory component specifies the directory containing the file. A directory is itself a file, but its purpose is to act as a catalog for a collection of files. Every file on a disk is cataloged in some directory (possibly more than one) so that it can be easily located.

Because a directory is a file, it can appear in another directory. This allows a "tree structure" of directories, with each directory containing some files and possibly some other directories, which are called *subdirectories* of the original directory. The original directory is called the parent directory, and the subdirectories are its child directories. The entire directory tree is rooted in a special directory called the *master file directory*. The master file directory has the name 000000 (six zeros). Here is a possible directory tree on a disk referred to by the logical name `DISK1`:

```
disk1:[000000]              ! The master file directory.
disk1:[jones]               ! The directory for user JONES.
disk1:[jones.project]       ! Jones' project directory,
disk1:[jones.project.data]  ! with a subdirectory for data.
disk1:[jones.personal]      ! Jones' personal directory.
disk1:[smith]               ! The directory for user SMITH.
   .
   .
```

The directory portion of a file spec is enclosed in square brackets. Each subdirectory is separated from its parent with a dot. It is not necessary to specify the master file directory except when referring precisely to that directory.

The empty directory specification `[ ]` stands for the working directory, as established with the `SET DEFAULT` command. When used with the `SYS$DISK` logical name, as in `SYS$DISK:[ ]`, a complete specification of the working disk and directory results. This specification allows you to be explicit in commands that manipulate files in the working directory.

Sec. 13.6, p. 161

The directory specification `[.DATA]` stands for the `DATA` subdirectory under the working directory. In general, any subdirectory of the working

13.1 File Specifications

directory can be accessed by beginning the directory portion of the file spec with a dot.

The directory specification [-] stands for the parent directory of the working directory. The dash can be followed by a subdirectory, as in [-.OTHER], which refers to the directory named OTHER under the parent directory of the working directory (i.e., OTHER is a directory parallel to the working directory).

A little-known fact about directory specifications is that they can also be enclosed in angle brackets, such as in DISK1:<JONES.PROJECT>. This is because angle brackets are international characters and appear on more terminal keyboards than do square brackets. Angle brackets must be taken into account when performing various manipulations of file specs, as illustrated in Section 13.2.1. Angle brackets are prohibited within the PIPE command.

13.1.4 Name

The name component, taken together with the file type, identifies a particular file in a directory. The purpose of the file name is to assign a meaningful identifier to the file. The name can be composed of letters, digits, and the dollar sign ($), underscore (_), and hyphen (-) characters. Its length is restricted to a maximum of 39 characters on typical file structures, but that allows plenty of room for meaningful names. Because a directory is just a file, directory names follow the same rules as file names.

OpenVMS Alpha V7.2 and later support both much longer file names, and a much wider variety of characters in file names, on specific file structures.

13.1.5 Type

The type component is used with the file name to uniquely identify a file in a directory. This two-level name/type scheme allows the file name to identify a family of related files, while the file type identifies particular kinds of files within the family. For example, a small application written in Fortran may include a set of files all having the name BUDGET, but with the following file types:

FOR The Fortran source file.

OBJ The object file produced by the Fortran compiler.

LIS The listing file produced by the compiler.

EXE The executable image produced by the linker.

MAP The image map produced by the linker.

The standard file types have been chosen over the years to be meaningful abbreviations for the contents of the file. The type `OBJ` stands for "object" and `EXE` for "executable." The restrictions on character set and length for file types parallel those for file names. Most of the standardized file types are three letters, because the file type was once limited to three characters in length.

13.1.6 Version

On many computer systems, the device/directory/name/type is sufficient to identify any individual file. Such systems do not allow multiple copies of the same file and thus run into trouble when a modified version of a file is created. The modified version replaces the original version, which cannot be recovered if an error or program bug corrupts the modified version. OpenVMS supports the concept of multiple file generations or versions. More than one version of the "same file" can exist in a given directory. The term *same file* is in quotes because each version is an autonomous file, entirely distinct from the other versions, but all the versions represent successive generations of the same information.

Every file is assigned a version number. When a file with a new name and type is created in a directory, it receives version number 1. When another file with the same name and type is created in that directory, it receives version number 2. The version 1 file is not deleted. Whenever a new generation of an existing file is created, it is assigned the first available version number that is higher than all of its ancestors in the directory. Version numbers range from 1 to 32767.

An existing version of a file is accessed by including its unique version number in the file spec. For example:

`$disk1:[smith]login.com;3`

This file spec accesses version 3 of the file `LOGIN.COM`. If version 3 does not exist, an error is signaled. It does not matter which other versions exist.

Because certain versions of a file, most notably the latest one, are accessed frequently, OpenVMS provides some special version number syntax. If an existing file is being accessed and the version number is missing or specified simply as a semicolon (e.g., `LOGIN.COM` or `LOGIN.COM;`) or as version number 0 (e.g., `LOGIN.COM;0`), the latest version of the file is accessed. This is the file with the highest version number. If the version number is specified as -1 (e.g., `LOGIN.COM;-1`), then the second-latest version of the file is accessed. This is the file with the next highest version number (not necessarily 1 less than the highest). Versions numbers -2, -3, and so on are also allowed, and access successively older versions of the file. The version number -0 can be used to access the file with the lowest version number (e.g., LOGIN.COM;-0). The lowest version number is not necessarily 1, because some of the original versions of the file may have been purged or deleted.

In addition to the semicolon (;), the period (.) can also be used to delimit a version number. The semicolon is used whenever the version number is retrieved from a parse operation; it is the prefered separator character.

13.2 Parsing

The process of preparing a file spec to access a directory or file is called *parsing* the file spec. The goal of parsing is to take a file spec that may have some missing components and flesh it out into a complete spec with all components included. OpenVMS parses a file spec whenever the spec is used to access a file for any kind of input, output, or control operation. The complete file spec returned by the parsing operation is called the ***resultant file spec***. The algorithm used to parse a spec is made available to the DCL programmer through the F$PARSE lexical function. *Do not attempt to parse a file spec by assuming knowledge of the character delimiters or even the character set used within a file spec.* Use F$PARSE when parsing is required.

The general form of the lexical function is shown here:

```
f$parse(base-spec, default-spec, related-spec, component, options)
```

The only required argument is the first one; the rest are optional. The *base-spec* is the file spec to be parsed and expanded into a complete file spec. It may be missing certain components, such as the directory or version number. Rarely does a user enter a complete file spec with all components specified explicitly. The function parses the base file spec, expands it into a resultant file spec with all components, and returns part or all of the resultant file spec. The parsing algorithm can make use of two additional file specs, the *default-spec* and the *related-spec*. These files specs may be complete, or, as with the base spec, they may include only some components. The parsing algorithm is as follows:

1. Examine the base spec. If any components are missing, use the components from the default spec (if it was specified).

2. If components are still missing, use the components from the related spec (if it was specified).

3. If any of the node, device, or directory components are still missing, use the components from the user's current working directory.

4. If any components are missing from this complete spec, do not fill them in.

5. If the *component* argument is not specified, return the complete resultant file spec. If it is specified, extract the specified component and return it by itself. The component argument is one of the following keywords: `"NODE"`, `"DEVICE"`, `"DIRECTORY"`, `"NAME"`, `"TYPE"`, `"VERSION"`.

To summarize, the base spec is completed using three levels of defaults: the default spec, the related spec, and the working directory. The lexical function then returns either the entire resultant spec or an individual component of it. (The complete algorithm used by the parse system service is actually more complicated because of logical names.)

_{Chap. 14, p. 165}

In the process of parsing the file spec, OpenVMS checks for the existence of the device and directory. If either does not exist, the parse fails and the lexical function returns the null string. You may wish to disable this checking, particularly when assembling a file spec that will be used to create a new directory. To disable the check, specify the keyword string `"SYNTAX_ONLY"` as the *options* argument to the lexical function. This option also results in a faster parse operation.

Here are examples of file spec parsing. The examples assume that a file spec has been obtained from the user and saved in the symbol USER_SPEC.

```
$!    Parse the file spec, filling in the device and directory
$!    from the user's working one.
$
$     parsed_spec = f$parse(user_spec)
```

—or—

```
$!    Parse the file spec, filling in unspecified components
$!    from the default spec SYS$SCRATCH:XDA_DATA.TMP
$
$     parsed_spec = f$parse(user_spec, -
                            "sys$scratch:xda_data.tmp")
```

—or—

```
$!    Create a spec for the new directory [XDA_WORK] on the
$!    working disk.  Make sure OpenVMS doesn't check for prior
$!    existence of the directory.
$
$     dir = f$parse("[xda_work]",,,,"SYNTAX_ONLY")
$     dir = f$parse(dir,,,"DEVICE") + -
              f$parse(dir,,,"DIRECTORY")
```

—or—

13.2 Parsing

```
$!      Obtain the file name and type from the spec.
$
$       name = f$parse(user_spec,,,"NAME")
$       type = f$parse(user_spec,,,"TYPE")
```

When you obtain an individual component from the resultant spec, as in the last example above, the resulting string contains the delimiting punctuation that accompanies the component. A node contains the double colon, a device the single colon, a directory the brackets, a file type the dot, and a version number the semicolon. The file name does not include any delimiting punctuation.

13.2.1 Parent and Child Directories

There are two file spec manipulations that cannot be performed by the F$PARSE lexical function. The first one takes a directory spec and a subdirectory name and produces the merged spec naming the subdirectory. Given an arbitrary file spec containing the directory [JONES.PROJECT] and the subdirectory name DATA, it must produce [JONES.PROJECT.DATA]. Assume that the symbol SPEC contains a directory spec and the symbol CHILD contains the name of the desired subdirectory. The merge is easily accomplished with the following commands:

```
$       parent = f$parse(spec,,,"DIRECTORY")
$       subdir = "[" + -
                (parent - "["-"]"-"<"-">"-"] ["-"><") + -
                "." + child + "]"
```

The first line extracts the directory portion of the file spec. The second line strips the brackets off the directory (be they square brackets or angle brackets) and builds a new directory spec identifying the desired subdirectory. The resulting directory spec uses square brackets regardless of the brackets present in the original spec.

Another file spec manipulation that you might be tempted to perform is that of determining the parent of a given arbitrary directory. This manipulation is virtually impossible and should be avoided at all costs. Almost insurmountable problems arise when the file spec includes a rooted directory.

Sec. 14.7.1, p. 175

13.2.2 Changing the File Type

The individual files in a related family of files often have the same name but different types. For example, a Fortran source file has the type FOR, while the object and listing files generated by the compiler have the types OBJ and LIS. The Fortran compiler must construct the object and listing file specs by replacing the file type of the source file with the new types `OBJ` and `LIS`. This "retyping" operation is common in sophisticated procedures.

The `F$PARSE` function does the work quite easily:

```
$    source_file = f$parse(source_file)
$    obj_file = f$parse(".OBJ",source_file)
$    lis_file = f$parse(".LIS",source_file)
```

The source file spec is parsed first in order to fill in missing components from the working directory. The resultant file spec is stored back in the same symbol. The related object file spec is created by parsing a base spec containing only the desired file type, using the source spec to fill in all other components. The listing file spec is created similarly. Note that the base specs `.OBJ` and `.LIS` include the dot punctuation for file types. If they did not, the strings `OBJ` and `LIS` would be mistaken for file *names*.

This same technique can be used to replace any other component of a file spec.

13.3 Searching Directories

An OpenVMS user frequently needs to locate an individual file or group of files in a directory. Sometimes the user is not sure how a file name is spelled or which directory the file is in. The *wildcard* facility allows the user to search a directory or directory tree for a set of files. The wildcard facility provides special characters, which can be inserted in a normal file spec at various points. A file spec containing wildcard characters is presented to OpenVMS and a *search operation* is requested. Instead of locating a single file, as it does when given a normal file spec, OpenVMS locates one or more files whose specs match the wildcard spec.

A file spec can include the following wildcard characters:

* An asterisk can be used in the directory name, file name, type, or version. It matches any number of characters, including none.

% A percent sign can be used in the directory name, file name, or type. It matches exactly one character.

... An ellipsis can be appended to a directory name in a directory spec. It matches the entire directory subtree below the named directory.

The simplest way to perform a search operation is with the `DIRECTORY` command. This command accepts a wildcard file spec and lists all of the files matching the spec:

```
$ directory *.dat
```

—or—

```
$ directory $disk1:[smith...]xda*.com
```

—or—

```
$ directory [project*...]*.%
```

The file spec in the first example matches all the files with type DAT in the working directory, regardless of name. The asterisk in the name position matches any characters and therefore any name.

The file spec in the second example searches the subdirectory tree under the [SMITH] directory of disk $DISK1. The ellipsis specifies that the subdirectory tree is to be searched. The spec matches any files in the subdirectory tree whose name begins with XDA and whose type is COM.

The file spec in the third example causes a search of the subdirectory trees under any directory beginning with PROJECT. The directory spec PROJECT* matches any directory beginning with PROJECT, and the ellipsis causes the subdirectories under those directories to be searched. The spec matches any file regardless of name, as long as the type is exactly one character in length.

As you can see, wildcards provide a powerful tool for searching directories and selecting files within them.

DCL provides a lexical function that a procedure can use to perform directory searches. The F$SEARCH lexical function requires one argument, which must be a file spec. The spec can name a single file or it can contain wildcards. When F$SEARCH is called with a file spec that does not contain wildcards, it determines whether or not the specified file exists. First it parses the file spec using the working device and directory as the default. It then checks to see whether the file exists, and if so, returns the resultant, fully expanded file spec. If the file spec is invalid or the file does not exist, F$SEARCH returns the null string.

Here is an example using F$SEARCH to check whether a specified file exists:

```
$10:    libcall ask xda_file s "Enter a file spec:"
$       if f$search(xda_file) .nes. "" then goto 19
$       libcall signal xda w filnotfnd -
                   "File ''xda_file does not exist."
$       goto 10
$19:
```

This procedure asks the user for a file spec. It then uses the F$SEARCH function to check for the existence of the file. If the function returns an expanded file spec, the file exists. If the function returns the null string, a message is displayed and the user is asked for another file spec. Note that this procedure does not distinguish the case of a nonexistent file from the case of an invalid file spec. If you want to distinguish these two cases, use the F$PARSE function in conjunction with F$SEARCH.

```
$10:    libcall ask xda_file s "Enter a file spec:"
$       if f$parse(xda_file,,,,"SYNTAX_ONLY") .nes. ""
$       then
$         if f$search(xda_file) .nes. "" then goto 19
$         libcall signal xda w filnotfnd -
                    "File ''xda_file does not exist."
$       else
$         libcall signal xda w invspec -
                    "File spec ''xda_file is invalid."
$       endif
$       goto 10
$19:
```

This procedure first checks the validity of the file spec with the F$PARSE function. If the spec is valid, it goes on to search for the file. If the spec is invalid, it displays a message and requests another spec.

When the F$SEARCH function is called with a wildcard file spec, it searches for the first file matching the spec and returns its resultant spec. If there are no files matching the spec, the null string is returned. An additional matching file spec is obtained by calling F$SEARCH again *with the same wildcard spec*. Each call returns the next matching file spec. When there are no more matching files, the null string is returned. The following code displays the name of every data file in the working directory, each on its own line:

```
$10:    file = f$search("*.dat;")
$       if file .eqs. "" then goto 19
$       display f$parse(file,,,"NAME")
$       goto 10
$19:
```

The F$SEARCH function is called with the wildcard spec "*.DAT;". The asterisk matches every file name. A semicolon is specified for the version number, so that only the latest version is located. If no version number is given, F$SEARCH locates all versions.

The following procedure asks the user for a file spec and counts the number of files matching the spec:

```
$       libcall ask xda_file s "Files to count:"
$       count = 0
```

13.3 Searching Directories

157

```
$10:    file = f$search(xda_file)
$       if file .eqs. "" then goto 19
$       count = count + 1
$       goto 10
$19:
$       display "Count of files found: ", count
```

There is a special precaution you must take when programming a search loop if you are not sure whether the file spec will contain wildcards. The preceding example loops forever if the user enters a file spec without wildcards, because the F$SEARCH function never returns the null string. It continually locates the single file and returns its resultant spec. To prevent an infinite loop, extra code is needed:

```
$       libcall ask xda_file s "Files to count:"
$       count = 0
$       last_file = ""
$10:    file = f$search(xda_file)
$       if file .eqs. "" .or. file .eqs. last_file then -
            goto 19
$       count = count + 1
$       last_file = file
$       goto 10
$19:
$       display "Count of files found: ", count
```

The procedure now checks to make sure F$SEARCH does not return the same file on two consecutive calls. If the same file is returned, the file spec must not contain any wildcards and the loop terminates. The loop is executed exactly once for file specs without wildcards, multiple times for file specs with wildcards.

13.3.1 Simultaneous Searches

The F$SEARCH function begins a new search whenever it is presented with a new wildcard file spec. In the previous examples, the same file spec was used on each call to F$SEARCH, so the function carried on the search from the previous call. Once there are no more matching files, the function returns the null string and resets its search context so that the next call will begin a new search regardless of the file spec. This is reasonable behavior that you can rely on whenever you are performing one search at a time. However, when multiple searches must be performed simultaneously, another feature of F$SEARCH is required.

The F$SEARCH function accepts a second argument, called the *stream ID*. The stream ID is an arbitrary integer that identifies a particular search context and distinguishes it from other search contexts that may be in progress simultaneously. Whenever the F$SEARCH function is used to perform more than one search at a time, a unique stream ID is required for each different search. There are two common cases where multiple searches are performed simultaneously:

- A single procedure needs to match two sets of files at the same time. For example, a procedure searches the master file directory of a disk for every top-level directory beginning with PROJECT. Then, for each such directory, the procedure locates all the data files in that directory tree. Two searches are progressing in parallel: the search for top-level project directories and the search within each such directory.
- A procedure locates each file that matches a wildcard spec and then calls another procedure that operates on the file. If the second procedure uses F$SEARCH as part of its file processing, then two searches are in progress simultaneously.

Whenever multiple searches are in progress at the same time, each one must use a different stream ID in its calls to F$SEARCH.

The following example illustrates the first scenario:

```
$10:    dir = f$search("$disk1:[000000]project*.dir;",10)
$       if dir .eqs. "" then goto 19
$       file_spec = "$disk1:[" + f$parse(dir,,,"NAME") + -
                   "...]*.dat;"
$20:    file = f$search(file_spec,11)
$       if file .eqs. "" then goto 29
$       display file
$       goto 20
$29:    goto 10
$19:
```

The outer loop searches for directories whose names begin with PROJECT. The stream ID for the directory search is 10. The inner loop searches for data files in the directory tree found by the outer loop. The stream ID for the file search is 11. The file spec for the inner search is constructed using the name of a directory found by the outer search. For example, if directory PROJECT_DRIVER is found, the file spec $DISK1:[PROJECT_DRIVER...]*.DAT; is constructed. This spec will locate all the data files in the directory tree under the PROJECT_DRIVER directory.

Each stream ID is an arbitrary positive integer. The only requirement is that each simultaneous search use a different ID.

13.3 Searching Directories

13.4 File Protection

OpenVMS provides a comprehensive scheme for protecting files from unauthorized access. This scheme is called *file protection* and is complex enough to merit its own chapter (Chapter 18).

13.5 File Attributes

Each file has a set of descriptive information associated with it. These items of information are called *file attributes*. The file attributes include some well-known items such as the file's creation time and owner UIC. There are also many items that are rarely used by DCL procedures.

The F$FILE_ATTRIBUTES lexical function can be used to obtain the attributes of a file. It requires two arguments: a file spec and an item keyword. The file spec must identify a single existing file. The item keyword is chosen from among a fixed set of keywords that specify the file attributes. Table 13.1 describes some of the common file attributes.

The following example requests a file spec from the user and displays important dates associated with the file.

Table 13.1 F$FILE_ATTRIBUTES items

Keyword	Type	Description of result
"BDT"	String	Backup date/time.
"CDT"	String	Creation date/time.
"EDT"	String	Expiration date/time.
"EOF"	Integer	Number of blocks occupied by data.
"LOCKED"	Boolean	Determines if the file is deaccess locked. This attribute does not indicate that files are locked by an application that is using the OpenVMS lock manager.
"MRS"	Integer	Maximum record size.
"ORG"	String	Organization: "SEQ" for sequential, "REL" for relative, "IDX" for indexed.
"PRO"	String	Protection mask.
"RDT"	String	Revision date/time.
"RVN"	Integer	Number of times file has been modified.
"UIC"	String	Owner UIC string.

```
$10:    libcall ask xda_file s "File spec:"
$       if f$search(xda_file) .nes. "" then goto 19
$       libcall signal xda w filnotfnd -
                        "File ''xda_file does not exist."
$       goto 10
$19:
$       display "Creation time:   ", f$file_attr(xda_file,"CDT")
$       display "Revision time:   ", f$file_attr(xda_file,"RDT")
$       display "Revision count:  ", f$file_attr(xda_file,"RVN")
$       display "Backup time:     ", f$file_attr(xda_file,"BDT")
$       display "Expiration time: ", f$file_attr(xda_file,"EDT")
```

After asking the user for a file spec, the procedure uses the F$SEARCH function to check that the file exists. If not, the user is asked again. The check is important because the F$FILE_ATTRIBUTES function signals an error if given a file that does not exist.

A complete list of the attributes of a file can be displayed with the DCL command DIRECTORY/FULL.

The LOCKED option is listed in Table 13.1 solely because it is not useful for the situations you might initially think it is intended for: files that are locked by other applications. Rather, LOCKED determines if the file is deaccess locked, a state that arises with the failure of an application originally designed for the RSX-11 operating system. This problem rarely arises with native OpenVMS files and applications.

13.6 File Operations

OpenVMS provides a comprehensive set of utilities for manipulating files and directories. These utilities are described in detail in the *OpenVMS DCL Dictionary*, and you are advised to consult that book to learn about the utilities and their various features. The *Dictionary* will sometimes refer you to another OpenVMS document when the utility is complicated and requires many pages of description. Table 13.2 summarizes the operations performed by the file utilities. The descriptions are given in terms of a single file, but most utilities can operate on a set of files using wildcard file specs.

In addition to most accepting wildcard file specs, most file utilities accept a standard group of command qualifiers, which further select and restrict the target files. These qualifiers provide a powerful facility for selecting files according to single or multiple criteria. Table 13.3 describes these file selection qualifiers.

Table 13.2 OpenVMS file utilities

Command	Description
ANALYZE/RMS_FILE	Allows you to interactively peruse the structure and contents of a file. Has a mode that checks the structural integrity of a file. Has another mode that generates a File Definition Language description of the file.
APPEND	Appends a file to the end of an existing file.
BACKUP	Performs various kinds of disk and file backup operations.
CONVERT	Copies one file to another, changing the organization and structure of the file in the process.
COPY	Makes a copy of a file, placing the new file on the same disk or another one. Can also concatenate a set of files into one output file.
CREATE	Creates a sequential file.
CREATE/DIRECTORY	Creates a new directory on a disk.
DELETE	Deletes a file.
DIFFERENCES	Determines the differences between the contents of two files.
DIRECTORY	Locates and displays a list of files, and the associated file attributes.
DUMP	Displays the raw contents of the file, regardless of the file format or record structure.
EDIT/FDL	Invokes a file format editor, allowing the particular record structure of a file to be defined.
EDIT	Invokes a text editor, allowing a file to be created or altered.
MERGE	Combines two or more sorted files, producing an output file with all records sorted.
PURGE	Deletes older (lower-numbered) versions of a file, leaving only the newest version or versions.
RENAME	Changes a file's name or type. Can also move a file from one directory to another on the same disk.
SEARCH	Searches the contents of a file for records matching certain patterns and displays the matching records.
SET DEFAULT	Changes the working device and directory.
SET DIRECTORY	Changes the attributes of a directory.
SET FILE	Changes the attributes of a file.
SET SECURITY	Alters various file security settings.
SHOW DEFAULT	Displays the working device and directory.
SORT	Sorts the records in a file according to various criteria, producing a new file of sorted records.
TYPE	Displays the contents of a file.

Table 13.3
File selection qualifiers

Qualifier	Description
/BACKUP	Selects files based on their backup time. Used in conjunction with the /BEFORE and /SINCE qualifiers.
/BEFORE=*time*	Selects files that are dated before a given time. Used in conjunction with the /BACKUP, /CREATED, /EXPIRED, or /MODIFIED qualifiers.
/BY_OWNER=*uic*	Selects files owned by a particular UIC.
/CREATED	Selects files based on their creation time. Used in conjunction with the /BEFORE and /SINCE qualifiers.
/EXCLUDE=*file-spec*	Does not select files that match the excluded file spec. A list of file specs may be specified, and they may contain wildcards.
/EXPIRED	Selects files based on their expiration time. Used in conjunction with the /BEFORE and /SINCE qualifiers.
/MODIFIED	Selects files based on their revision time. Used in conjunction with the /BEFORE and /SINCE qualifiers.
/SINCE=*time*	Selects files that are dated after a given time. Used in conjunction with the /BACKUP, /CREATED, /EXPIRED, or /MODIFIED qualifiers.

Most OpenVMS commands and utilities also support writing output to a file, typically using a qualifier such as /OUTPUT. Various of the more complex utilities, particularly those with command prompting, often support commands for redirecting the output to a user-specified file, via a utility-specific command.

Chap. 15, p. 189

Chap. 17, p. 215

OpenVMS also has a set of commands for creating, reading, and writing files from a DCL procedure.

13.6 File Operations

CHAPTER 14
Logical Names

A LOGICAL NAME IS A NAMED ENTITY that you can create and assign a value. The name then stands for the value when the logical name is used in certain contexts, such as file specifications. In these contexts, OpenVMS *automatically* replaces the logical name with its value. A logical name may appear to be the same as a symbol, but there are important differences:

- Logical names are created, maintained, and deleted using a different set of OpenVMS commands from those used for symbols.

- Logical names reside in *logical name tables*. A given logical name table can be made available to a single process, a family of processes, or every process on the system. In this way, unlike symbols, logical names can be shared by multiple processes.

- When a logical name appears in an appropriate context, such as a file spec, OpenVMS uses its value automatically. This differs from apostrophe substitution, which must be requested explicitly, although it is similar to personal command substitution.

- Symbols are implemented within the DCL command interpreter and can be substituted only when the command is processed by DCL, and not within the prompts of a utility. Logical names can be used within utility prompts, and within processes that do not have a command interpreter (such as DCL) loaded.

The most common use for a logical name is to stand for part or all of a file spec. For example, the logical name SYS$HELP stands for the system device and directory containing the help libraries and release notes for OpenVMS and its layered products. If you want to view the release notes for DEC/CMS Version 3.8, you can use the following command:

```
$ type sys$help:cms038.release_notes
```

The logical name SYS$HELP is used in place of an explicit device and directory to refer to the file. OpenVMS automatically uses the value of the logical name to complete the file spec and locate the release notes.

One purpose of logical names in file specs is to save the user from having to remember the device and directory. Another purpose is to allow the contents of a directory to be moved to a new directory. Once the logical name is redefined to refer to the new directory, users can work as usual, unaware that a change has been made. This technique will only succeed, however, as long as users always refer to files in the directory via the logical name.

14.1 Defining and Using Logical Names

A logical name is created with the DEFINE command. The basic form of the DEFINE command is as follows:

```
$    define logical-name value
```

The first parameter specifies a sequence of characters that name the logical name. The name can consist of letters, digits, dollar sign ($), and underscore (_). The second parameter specifies the value of the logical name. The value can be composed of any characters and must be enclosed in double quotes if it contains characters other than those that may appear in a file spec. The value is sometimes called the *equivalence string*.

When a logical name is defined for use in file specs, its value can comprise any or all of the components of the file spec. Here are some related examples:

```
$!   Define a logical name for the disk used by the marketing
$!   department.  Such definitions are rarely necessary,
$!   because a logical name is automatically defined when a
$!   disk is mounted.
$
$    define disk_market dka100:
$
$!   Define a logical name for the directory on the marketing
$!   disk that contains monthly reports.  Notice how one
$!   logical name can be defined in terms of another.  Define
```

```
$!     a synonym for the logical name.
$
$      define market_reports disk_market:[reports]
$      define market_documents market_reports
$
$!     Define a logical name for the latest monthly report.
$
$      define market_latest_report market_reports:monthly.txt;
```

In each of these examples, the value of the logical name consists of some or all of the components of a file spec: the device; the device and directory; or the device, directory, file name, type, and version. The components may be specified explicitly or derived in turn from other logical names. Once a logical name is defined, a file can be accessed using a file spec beginning with the logical name. In this case, OpenVMS looks up, or *translates*, the logical name and uses its value to obtain components missing from the file spec. If the value of the logical name contains a second logical name, OpenVMS uses the value of the second name to obtain components for the first, and then uses all the components in the final file spec. This is called *iterative translation.* All of this logical name translation is performed by the OpenVMS file spec parsing service, available to the DCL programmer through the F$PARSE lexical function. Section 14.2 describes the complete file spec parsing algorithm.

Sec. 13.2, p. 152

Here are some sample file specs, shown with the final spec resulting from a parsing operation:

```
disk_market:[archive]history.dat
DKA100:[ARCHIVE]HISTORY.DAT;
```

—or—

```
market_reports:history.dat
DKA100:[REPORTS]HISTORY.DAT;
```

—or—

```
market_documents:history.dat
DKA100:[REPORTS]HISTORY.DAT;
```

—or—

```
market_latest_report
DKA100:[REPORTS]MONTHLY.TXT;
```

The value of the logical name can include components that are not necessarily adjacent in the file spec. For example:

14.1   Defining and Using Logical Names

```
$!     Define a logical name for the monthly report directory
$!     and include the file type TXT to refer to text files
$!     without a specific name.
$
$      define market_report_texts market_reports:.txt
```

This logical name can be used to refer to all the text files in the reports directory, or to a specific one:

```
market_report_texts
DKA100:[REPORTS].TXT;
```

—or—

```
market_report_texts:;-1
DKA100:[REPORTS].TXT;-1
```

—or—

```
market_report_texts:summary
DKA100:[REPORTS]SUMMARY.TXT;
```

Every logical name resides in a logical name table. Section 14.11 describes logical name tables in detail. There are four logical name tables accessible to every process:

Process   Each process has a private logical name table whose logical names are used only by the process. The `DEFINE/PROCESS` command enters logical names in the process table. If no table qualifier is specified on the `DEFINE` command, logical names are entered in the process table by default.

Job   Each job has a logical name table whose logical names are available to the processes in the job. A job consists of the detached process created when you log in to OpenVMS, plus any subprocess created by the main process. The `DEFINE/JOB` command enters logical names in the job logical name table.

Sec. 20.4, p. 264

Group   All processes belonging to a particular UIC group have a group logical name table whose logical names are shared by those processes. This allows processes in the same group to communicate with one another via logical names. The `DEFINE/GROUP` command enters logical names in the group logical name table.

System   There is a single system logical name table shared by all processes on the system. Logical names needed by every process reside in the system logical name table. This includes the standard OpenVMS logical names and those defined by DIGITAL and third-party software products. The

`DEFINE/SYSTEM` command enters logical names in the system logical name table.

Users can define logical names in their process or job tables. The `GRPNAM` or `SYSPRV` privilege is required to define group logical names. The `SYSNAM` or `SYSPRV` privilege is required to define system logical names.

When you use `DEFINE` to define a logical name that already exists, Open-VMS issues a message to remind you that the old value is being superseded. Such a message can confuse the user if it appears during the execution of a command procedure. The `/NOLOG` qualifier suppresses the message.

The `ASSIGN` command is a second command that can be used to define logical names. It expects its parameters in reverse order: first the equivalence string and then the logical name. The order of parameters to the `DEFINE` command is more natural, so people occasionally reverse the parameters to the `ASSIGN` command by mistake. The authors suggest that you always use the `DEFINE` command.

14.2 Complete File Spec Parsing Algorithm

Chapter 13 included a simplified description of how the parse system service parses a file spec. A parsing operation is performed whenever a file spec must be prepared to access a file or group of files. A parse operation can be explicitly requested by the DCL programmer through the `F$PARSE` lexical function. In either case, parsing involves up to three file specs: the primary spec, which is to be fleshed out to a full spec; a default spec, which provides components missing from the primary spec; and a related spec, which provides additional missing components.

Once logical names are introduced, the parsing algorithm becomes more complicated, because logical names need to be translated and their values used in the file spec. Here is a slightly simplified description of the complete file spec parsing algorithm:

1. Begin with the primary file spec:
    - If a node name is present and is a logical name, replace the logical name with its translation. If a node name is still present, then the spec must be parsed on the remote node. This procedure is described below.
    - Otherwise, if a device name is present and is a logical name, replace the logical name with its translation.
    - Otherwise, if the primary spec is composed of a logical name by itself, replace the logical name with its translation.

2. Obtain missing components from the default spec:
   - Translate any logical names in the default spec, but do not worry about node names that may appear.
   - If any components are missing from the primary spec, use the corresponding components from the default spec (if they are included).
3. Obtain additional missing components from the related spec in the same manner as the default spec.
4. Obtain any missing device and directory components as follows:
   - Fill in any missing device component from the value of the logical name SYS$DISK.
   - Fill in any missing directory component from SYS$DISK or, if it does not include a directory, from the working directory.

When the primary file spec includes a node component, then the file spec must be parsed on the remote node. Components missing from the primary spec are filled in from the default and related specs, but *without translating any logical names*. If the primary spec is being used to access a file, it is then transmitted to the remote node for final parsing and processing. If the primary spec is being parsed with the F$PARSE lexical function, the partially parsed spec is simply returned without further processing.

As an example, the default system authorization file is:

SYS$SYSTEM:SYSUAF.DAT

Using F$PARSE and the logical name SYSUAF, you can create a file spec for an authorization file in another location:

```
$    uaf = f$parse("SYSUAF","SYS$SYSTEM:.DAT")
```

If no SYSUAF logical name is defined, F$PARSE returns the usual file spec SYS$SYSTEM:SYSUAF.DAT. But, if the SYSUAF logical name is defined as FIRE_RESCUE_EMS:SYSUAF, then the parsing process takes .DAT from the default spec and the final spec becomes FIRE_RESCUE_EMS:SYSUAF.DAT.

14.3 Displaying Logical Names

The value of a logical name can be displayed with the SHOW LOGICAL command. This command displays the logical name and its equivalence string:

```
$ show logical market_reports
  "MARKET_REPORTS" = "DISK_MARKET:[REPORTS]"
                                         (LNM$PROCESS_TABLE)
```

—or—

```
$ show logical market_documents
  "MARKET_DOCUMENTS" = "MARKET_REPORTS"
                                        (LNM$PROCESS_TABLE)
1 "MARKET_REPORTS" = "DISK_MARKET:[REPORTS]"
                                        (LNM$PROCESS_TABLE)
```

If the value of a logical name is another logical name, iterative translation is performed and the value of the second logical name is displayed in turn. Therefore, you can see the true value of a logical name when synonyms have been defined.

By default, the SHOW LOGICAL command looks for the specified logical name in all four logical name tables in order: process, job, group, system. It displays the translation for each occurrence of the logical name. The logical name table qualifiers /PROCESS, /JOB, /GROUP, and /SYSTEM can be used to restrict the search to a particular logical name table. For example, the logical name SYS$DISK resides in both the process and system logical name tables. The following command restricts the display to the logical name in the process table:

```
$ show logical/process sys$disk
  "SYS$DISK" = "DUA2:" (LNM$PROCESS_TABLE)
```

An asterisk (*) can be used in the logical name as a wildcard to specify all the logical names beginning with a certain string:

```
$ show logical market*

(LNM$PROCESS_TABLE)

  "MARKET_DOCUMENTS" = "MARKET_REPORTS"
  "MARKET_LATEST_REPORT" = "MARKET_REPORTS:MONTHLY.TXT;"
  "MARKET_REPORTS" = "DISK_MARKET:[REPORTS]"
  "MARKET_REPORT_TEXTS" = "MARKET_REPORTS:.TXT"

(LNM$JOB_802EA710)

(LNM$GROUP_000260)

(LNM$SYSTEM_TABLE)
```

When an asterisk is used in the logical name, iterative translation is not performed. Only one level of translation is performed, so that each logical name is displayed with its own value rather than with the value obtained by translating through any synonyms. The display is therefore easier to comprehend, because it illustrates the relations among all the logical names shown.

14.4 Access Modes

A OpenVMS process can run in any of four *access modes* supported by the VAX and Alpha architectures. The four access modes range from least privileged to most privileged, as follows:

User Most OpenVMS utilities and user-written programs run in user mode.

Supervisor Command language interpreters such as DCL run in supervisor mode.

Executive The RMS record management system runs in executive mode.

Kernel The OpenVMS operating system runs in kernel mode.

When a logical name is defined, it is associated with a particular access mode. A given logical name table can contain multiple definitions for the same logical name in different access modes. Table 14.1 describes the commands used by a DCL procedure to define a logical name at each of the access modes. When a request is made to translate a logical name, the access mode plays a role in determining which logical name is actually translated:

- If the translation request does not include a specific access mode, then the logical name table is searched for a logical name in user mode, then supervisor, executive, and kernel modes.

- If the request includes a specific access mode, the search begins with that mode, then the next most privileged, then the next, and so on. Logical names at less privileged modes are ignored.

The four logical name access modes are employed by OpenVMS in the following manner:

User A logical name defined in user mode exists until the next program image completes. All user mode logical names are deleted during image exit. Thus, user mode logicals provide a means of overriding, for the duration of one program, a logical name defined at a more privileged mode.

Supervisor When a logical name is defined with the DEFINE command, it is entered in supervisor mode by default. These logical names exist for the duration of the process.

Table 14.1
Defining logical names in different modes

Access mode	Command	Privileges
User	DEFINE/USER_MODE	(none)
Supervisor	DEFINE/SUPERVISOR_MODE (default)	(none)
Executive	DEFINE/EXECUTIVE_MODE	SYSNAM
Kernel	Cannot be created from DCL	—

Executive Many of the logical names defined by the RMS file system are entered in executive mode. These include the process-permanent logical names, such as SYS$INPUT. They also include the family of logical names that refer to system directories (e.g., SYS$SYSTEM).

Kernel Logical names referring to logical name tables are often defined in kernel mode. Kernel mode logical names are typically not created by OpenVMS users.

14.5 Standard Logical Names

When you log in to OpenVMS, certain process and job logical names are automatically defined. These are described in Table 14.2.

The process-permanent logical names SYS$COMMAND, SYS$INPUT, SYS$OUTPUT, SYS$PIPE, and SYS$ERROR are extremely important to the operation of command procedures. They specify the standard input sources and output destinations for the procedures.

Sec. 20.5, p. 269

14.6 MOUNT Logical Names

Each native OpenVMS disk has an associated character string known as the *volume label*, which uniquely identifies the contents of the disk device. The label is determined by the system manager when the volume is initialized, and can also be changed using the SET VOLUME/LABEL command.

The volume label must be specified to the MOUNT utility whenever a disk volume is made available for user access. As part of the MOUNT operation, OpenVMS uses the disk volume label to transparently construct a unique logical name, DISK$*volumelabel*. This logical name is created by MOUNT regardless of any user-specified logical name that might be specified, and it always translates to the physical device name of the device that contains the volume.

Table 14.2
Standard process and job logical names

Logical name	Table	Description
SYS$COMMAND	Process	The original source of commands for the process.
SYS$DISK	Process	The device containing the process's current working directory. This logical name is redefined whenever a SET DEFAULT command is issued. The working directory can be accessed using the file spec SYS$DISK:[].
SYS$ERROR	Process	The device or file to which OpenVMS displays messages.
SYS$INPUT	Process	The default input source for the process.
SYS$LOGIN	Job	The login device and directory for the process. A reference to the login directory can be made with this logical name regardless of the current working directory.
SYS$LOGIN_DEVICE	Process	The login device for the process.
SYS$OUTPUT	Process	The default output destination for the process.
SYS$PIPE	Process	A command procedure running in a pipe reads pipe input from this logical name, not SYS$INPUT.
SYS$SCRATCH	Job	The default device and directory in which temporary files are created. A procedure should always create temporary files in this directory. By default, this is SYS$LOGIN.

OpenVMS supports a similar mechanism for magnetic tapes, with the logical name TAPE$*volumelabel* that is derived from the tape volume label.

You can use the MOUNT logical names to create a command procedure that is device-independent: a procedure that does not contain any hard-coded physical device names. And further, you can also avoid having to maintain a set of device logical names.

For more information on the MOUNT logical names available on your system, you can use the SHOW DEVICE D command to view the volume labels of the mounted disk volumes and the SHOW LOGICAL DISK$* command to view the associated logical names. You can also ask your system manager for assistance with the local system configuration.

14.7 Other Uses for Logical Names

The following sections describe some additional uses for logical names. These uses clarify the distinction between logical names and symbols.

14.7.1 Root Directories

A *root directory* is a directory whose fundamental purpose is to act as the parent for a related set of subdirectories. The root directory may contain a few data files, but it exists primarily to "root" a collection of subdirectories that contain the files for a software product or application. The root directory allows the files to be accessed or manipulated through a single known point rather than through an unrelated collection of directories.

A logical name is used to refer to the root directory. It is defined as follows:

```
$    define xda_root disk$products:[xda.]
```

The XDA directory on disk DISK$PRODUCTS is the root directory for the XDA application. The fact that it is a root directory is indicated by the trailing period in the directory portion of the spec. The trailing period is required when defining a logical name for a root directory. Assume that three subdirectories exist under the root directory: PROGRAMS, DATA, and USER. A reference to one of the directories can be made using the logical name XDA_ROOT:

```
$ directory xda_root:[user]

Directory DISK$PRODUCTS:[XDA.][USER]
USER-DATA1.DAT     USER-DATA2.DAT     USER-DATA3.DAT
   .
   .
```

Notice how OpenVMS displays the directory spec. There are two directory components, [XDA.] representing the root directory and [USER] representing the subdirectory. This double directory syntax appears whenever rooted directories are used, and is another reason why file specs must only be parsed with the F$PARSE lexical function, which knows how to deal with the double directory.

Sec. 13.2, p. 152

It is possible to hide the equivalence string of the logical name by using the /TRANSLATION_ATTTRIBUTES qualifier on the DEFINE command:

```
$    define xda_root disk$products:[xda.] -
             /translation_attributes=concealed
```

The CONCEALED attribute specifies that the equivalence string is not to be displayed. Instead, OpenVMS displays the root logical name without translation:

```
$ directory xda_root:[user]

Directory XDA_ROOT:[USER]
USER-DATA1.DAT;1    USER-DATA2.DAT;1    USER-DATA3.DAT;1
   .
   .
```

The `CONCEALED` attribute is associated with the equivalence string, not with the logical name as a whole. This is the reason the qualifier appears after the equivalence string in the `DEFINE` command.

In order to refer to the root directory itself, you use the convention adopted for referring to the master file directory of a disk. The special directory name 000000 is reserved to signify that the directory reference is to the root directory (not to a subdirectory named 000000):

```
$ directory xda_root:[000000]

Directory XDA_ROOT:[000000]
DATA.DIR;1         PROGRAMS.DIR;1          USER.DIR;1

Total of 3 files.
```

The root directory contains the three subdirectories mentioned above.

14.7.2 User Addresses

A *user address* is a string that identifies the location and name of an OpenVMS user. For example, `NODE1::SMITH` specifies that user `SMITH` resides on DECnet node `NODE1`. OpenVMS utilities such as `MAIL` and `PHONE` require user addresses as the destination of mail messages and phone calls. Utilities that work with user addresses are designed to accept a logical name in place of an explicit user address. When a utility receives a logical name, it translates the name and uses the resulting equivalence string as the user address.

Because a logical name can be used in place of an address, you can define personal logical names for your friends and associates:

```
$     define Bill node1::node2::Smith
$     define Cynthia node13::Jones
$     define Joe node42::Taylor
```

Once these logical names are defined, you can use them with the `PHONE` and `MAIL` utilities:

```
$ phone cynthia
```

—or—

```
$ mail message.txt bill,joe -
      /subject="Here is the info I promised."
```

Be aware that the presence of these logicals also affects the behavior of other utilities, such as the unexpected creation of a file on another node:

```
$     edit cynthia.txt
```

14.7.3 Search Lists

A logical name with more than one equivalence string is called a *search list*. Here is a logical name used to search two of the XDA subdirectories:

```
$    define xda_files xda_root:[data],xda_root:[user]
```

The two equivalence strings are separated by a comma. Once this logical name is defined, it can be used in a file spec just like any other logical name. When the file spec refers to a single file, OpenVMS searches the directories in order until the first matching file is located. Once it is located, the search stops:

```
$ type xda_files:user-data2.dat
```
: *contents of file XDA_ROOT:[USER]USER-DATA2.DAT;1*

On the other hand, if the file spec contains wildcards, thus naming multiple files, OpenVMS will process all the files that match in any of the directories:

```
$ dir xda_files:*2.dat

Directory XDA_ROOT:[DATA]
XDA_DATA.DAT;1    XDA_SUMMARY.DAT;3

Total of 2 files.

Directory XDA_ROOT:[USER]
USER-DATA2.DAT;1

Total of 1 file.
```

Search lists are useful when the files you want to access are spread across multiple directories whose organization is not obvious. Search lists are also useful when you want to access files in a public directory but supersede some of them with files in a personal directory. In this case, a search list can be defined whose first equivalence string is the personal directory and whose second equivalence string is the public directory. OpenVMS will locate a file in the public directory unless a file with the same name exists in the personal directory.

When a search list logical name appears in a file spec being used to create a file, the file is always created in the *first* directory. It does not matter whether a file with the same name and type appears in some other directory in the search list.

14.7.4 Product Parameters

Because system logical names are available to everyone on an OpenVMS system, they are sometimes used as a repository for product parameters. A *product parameter* is an item of information required by a software product in order to control its operation. A good example is the Universal Coordinated Time (also known by the French-language acronym UTC) and associated time zone support provided in OpenVMS V6.0 and later. This support relies on the system manager to establish various logical names, including ones that contain the local time zone name and the local time offset from UTC, using the `SYS$MANAGER:UTC$CONFIGURE_TDF.COM` procedure.

Various applications and run-time libraries then depend directly or indirectly on the settings of these UTC logical names.

You should give careful consideration to the idea of using logical names for product parameters before you embark on such a scheme. There are a few problems inherent in the technique:

- Someone has to ensure that the logical names are defined whenever the system is booted. The product installation procedure or the system manager must create a procedure containing the logical name definitions. The system manager must remember to invoke the procedure from the site-specific startup procedure.

- If the product has many parameters, the system logical name table will become cluttered with logical names. This takes up system memory and can be annoying when someone is displaying system logical names. When a product has more than a few parameters, it might be better to place them in a data file that the product reads when it starts up. As an alternative to the use of the system logical name table, an application-specific logical name table can be used.

14.8 Obtaining Logical Name Information

Information about a logical name can be obtained with the `F$TRNLNM` lexical function. The acronym `TRNLNM` stands for "translate logical name." The function has the following format:

f$trnlnm(*logical-name*, *table*, *index*, *mode*, *case*, *item*)

The only required argument is *logical-name*. It is a string that specifies the logical name for which information is desired. When only the first argument is specified, OpenVMS searches the process, job, group, and system logical name tables for a definition of the logical name. The equivalence string of the first definition is returned; iterative translation is not performed. If the logical name is not defined in any table, the null string is returned.

Here is an example:

```
$!    The logical name parameter XDA_MANAGER specifies the
$!    user who manages the XDA system.
$
$     xda_manager = f$trnlnm("xda_manager")
$     if xda_manager .eqs. "" then xda_manager = "SYSTEM"
```

The F$TRNLNM function is used to translate the logical name XDA_MANAGER, a product parameter that specifies the user who manages XDA. If the logical name is not defined, the SYSTEM user is assumed.

The second argument, *table*, specifies the logical name table to search for the logical name. By default, the process, job, group, and system tables are searched, in that order. To restrict the search to a particular table, specify a *table* argument of "LNM$PROCESS", "LNM$JOB", "LNM$GROUP, or "LNM$SYSTEM". Section 14.11 describes logical name tables in more detail.

The third argument, *index*, specifies the index of the equivalence string to be returned. The default value is 0, which is the index of the first or only equivalence string. When the logical name is a search list, the additional equivalence strings are numbered 1, 2, and so on. The following code displays all the equivalence strings for the logical name XDA_FILES:

```
$     i = -1
$10:  i = i + 1
$     string = f$trnlmn("xda_files",,i)
$     if string .eqs. "" then goto 19
$     display "#", i, ": ", string
$     goto 10
$19:
```

The symbol I is used as the index argument to the F$TRNLNM function. Each equivalence string is displayed. The loop terminates when F$TRNLNM returns the null string, signifying that there are no more equivalence strings.

The fourth argument, *mode*, is used to select the access modes that are searched for the logical name. The argument is one of the following keyword strings: "USER", "SUPERVISOR", "EXECUTIVE", or "KERNEL". The lexical function first looks for a logical name defined at the specified mode, then at the next most privileged mode, and so on. Logical names defined at less privileged modes are ignored. The default is user mode, which means that all logical names are searched and the value of the least privileged one is returned. Trusted logical names and logical name tables are defined

Table 14.3 F$TRNLNM items

Keyword	Type	Description of result
`"ACCESS_MODE"`	String	One of the following keywords to specify the access mode of the translated logical name: `"USER"`, `"SUPERVISOR"`, `"EXECUTIVE"`, `"KERNEL"`.
`"CONCEALED"`	Boolean	`"TRUE"` or `"FALSE"` to indicate whether the CONCEALED attribute was specified on the equivalence string.
`"LENGTH"`	Integer	The length of the equivalence string.
`"MAX_LENGTH"`	Integer	The largest equivalence string index associated with the logical name. Note that this is 1 less than the number of equivalence strings, because the index is zero-based.
`"TABLE"`	Boolean	`"TRUE"` or `"FALSE"` to indicate whether the logical name is the name of a logical name table (see Section 14.11).
`"TABLE_NAME"`	String	The name of the table where the logical name was located.
`"VALUE"`	String	The equivalence string.

in executive or kernel mode. Access modes are described in detail in Section 14.4.

The fifth argument, *case*, determines whether the logical name search is sensitive to the case of the letters in the logical name. By default, the search is case-blind, which means that the case of the *logical-name* argument can be ignored. OpenVMS first searches for a logical name that matches the case of the first argument. If this fails, it searches for a logical name ignoring the case of the argument. When the search is case-sensitive, OpenVMS searches only for a logical name whose case exactly matches the first argument. The *case* argument is specified as a keyword string, either `"CASE_BLIND"` or `"CASE_SENSITIVE"`.

The sixth argument, *item*, specifies which item of information about the logical name is to be returned by the function. This argument is a keyword string; some choices are described in Table 14.3. The default item is VALUE, which returns the equivalence string.

Prior to OpenVMS Version 4, logical names were translated with the F$LOGICAL function. The F$LOGICAL function is superseded by F$TRNLNM, and should no longer be used.

14.9 Deleting Logical Names

A logical name is removed from a logical name table with the `DEASSIGN` command. The command requires a single parameter, the logical name to be deleted:

```
$    deassign market_report_texts
```

The `DEASSIGN` command accepts the same logical name table qualifiers as the `DEFINE` command: `/PROCESS`, `/JOB`, `/GROUP`, `/SYSTEM`. The process table is the default.

The `DEASSIGN` command corresponds to the `ASSIGN` command, which is not used in this book. In order to create a command that corresponds more closely to the `DEFINE` command, the following personal command can be defined:

```
$    undefine = "deassign"
```

Then a logical name can be deleted as follows:

```
$    undefine market_report_texts
```

14.10 Overview of OpenVMS System Directory Organization

Logical names are the key to referencing the OpenVMS system directories. The OpenVMS system directories are organized under a root directory on the system disk. The system disk device is referred to with the logical name `SYS$SYSDEVICE`. The root directory is actually a search list defined by the logical name `SYS$SYSROOT`. Because all OpenVMS files are located under the root directory, `SYS$SYSDEVICE` is rarely used, `SYS$SYSROOT` being the preferred method of accessing the files.

A system disk can contain multiple OpenVMS systems; each is given a root number. The root directory for system 0 is `SYS0`. The following explanation will concern itself with system 0. The logical name `SYS$SYSROOT` is a search list whose equivalence strings are the logical names `SYS$SPECIFIC` and `SYS$COMMON`. These logical names, in turn, refer to two root directories, one for the system-specific system directories and one for the common system directories shared by all systems. This double root scheme is quite powerful.

The majority of OpenVMS files reside in subdirectories under the common root directory. The logical name `SYS$COMMON` refers to this directory, whose complete spec is `SYS$SYSDEVICE:[SYS0.SYSCOMMON.]`. Under the common root directory are subdirectories, such as `SYSEXE` and `SYSHLP`, which contain the OpenVMS files. When your OpenVMS system is part of a VMScluster, it can share the same common root as the rest of the nodes in the VMScluster (there are exceptions to this rule). In this way, all the nodes in the cluster run the same version of OpenVMS and share clusterwide data files, such as the `SYSUAF` system user authorization file typically located in the `SYSEXE` directory. (The logical name `SYS$TOPSYS` refers to the particular top-level root directory used by the OpenVMS system.)

The logical name `SYS$SPECIFIC` refers to a second root directory whose complete spec is `SYS$SYSDEVICE:[SYS0.]`. Under the specific root directory is another complete set of OpenVMS directories, also including `SYSEXE`, `SYSHLP`, and so forth. This is a separate collection of directories from the ones under the common root. In these directories reside files that are specific to the incarnation of OpenVMS running on the local node. Because the search list `SYS$SYSROOT` specifies `SYS$SPECIFIC` before `SYS$COMMON`, a file in the specific directories will supersede one with the same name and type in the common directories. This allows the local node to have a private copy of a file normally found in the common directories and shared by all nodes. In a VMScluster, each node has its own set of specific system directories. The specific directories contain only a few files, those which are specific to the node and which must supersede the common files.

As an example, assume a VMScluster with two nodes named HUMPTY and DUMPTY. HUMPTY is assigned root 0 on the system disk and DUMPTY is assigned root 1. On both nodes, `SYS$SYSROOT` is a search list whose equivalence strings are the logical names `SYS$SPECIFIC` and `SYS$COMMON`. On HUMPTY, the `SYS$SPECIFIC` logical name translates to `SYS$SYSDEVICE:[SYS0.]`, while on DUMPTY it translates to `SYS$SYSDEVICE:[SYS1.]`. Under these two specific roots are separate sets of the system directories `SYSEXE`, `SYSHLP`, and so on. Because the system directories are separate, each node can contain private copies of system files, which will supersede the common files because the specific directory is mentioned first in the search list. On HUMPTY, `SYS$COMMON` translates to `SYS$SYSDEVICE:[SYS0.SYSCOMMON.]`, while on DUMPTY it translates to `SYS$SYSDEVICE:[SYS1.SYSCOMMON.]`. These two directories act as the root for a third, *shared* set of system directories, which contains the majority of OpenVMS files. Because both roots share the same subdirectories, both nodes are accessing the same copy of system files.

Assume that HUMPTY attempts to access the system user authorization file `SYSUAF.DAT` that resides in the `SYSEXE` directory. If it has its own copy of the file in the specific directory `SYS$SYSDEVICE:[SYS0.SYSEXE]`, that

Table 14.4 System logical names

Logical name	Description
SYS$COMMON	The root directory of the system directories common to all nodes in a VMScluster.
SYS$EXAMPLES	A directory containing various system examples.
SYS$HELP	The directory of system help files.
SYS$LIBRARY	The directory of system macro and text libraries.
SYS$MANAGER	The directory of the system manager files.
SYS$MESSAGE	The directory of the system message files.
SYS$NODE	The DECnet node name of the local system.
SYS$SPECIFIC	The root directory of the system directories specific to the local node.
SYS$SYSDEVICE	The disk containing the system directories.
SYS$SYSROOT	The search list used to access all files in the system directories. Its equivalence strings are SYS$SPECIFIC and SYS$COMMON.
SYS$REM_NODE	Created in SET HOST sessions; contains the name of the originating node.
SYS$REM_USER	Created in SET HOST sessions; contains the name of the originating user.
SYS$SYSTEM	The directory containing system programs and procedures.
SYS$TOPSYS	The name of the system root directory containing the local node's operating system.
SYS$UPDATE	The directory containing system installation and update files.

copy is accessed. If it does not, the shared copy in SYS$SYSDEVICE:[SYS0.SYSCOMMON.SYSEXE] is accessed. The shared copy is available to the entire cluster.

This specific/common directory scheme is used on every OpenVMS V5.0 and later system, regardless of whether it is a cluster. Each of the system directories SYSEXE, SYSHLP, and so on has its own logical name defined so that files in these directories can be accessed with no need to understand the whole scheme. Table 14.4 describes many of the system logical names.

14.10.1 OpenVMS System Directory Aliases

Although common system directories and the files they contain are referenced with logical names and roots such as SYS$SYSDEVICE:[SYS1.SYSCOMMON.], they are actually located under different directories, using file aliases. File aliases are duplicate references to the same file or directory, often using a different name, a location in a different directory, or both. Alias entries can be established with the SET FILE/ENTER command, and removed with the SET FILE/REMOVE command.

The OpenVMS files are located under the top-level common directory SYS$SYSDEVICE:[SYSCOMMON] on OpenVMS V4 systems, under SYS$SYSDEVICE:[V5$COMMON] on V5 systems, and under SYS$SYSDEVICE:[VMS$COMMON] on V6 and later systems. This common directory is entered as a file alias in the SYS$SYSDEVICE:[SYS0] and all other system roots, using the directory name SYSCOMMON.DIR.

Three implications of the use of file aliases within the OpenVMS system disk structure involve significant disk space savings, the requirement for care during file deletions, and misleading results from DIRECTORY/SIZE commands for system directories.

The use of file alias entries avoids the unncessary duplication of files when additional systems are booted from the same system disk in a VMScluster. This includes OpenVMS files, layered product files, and site-specific files. Without these alias entries, each system would require its own complete set of files, greatly increasing storage requirements.

Because files that appear to be local to a system root, such as SYS$SYSROOT:[SYS0.SYSCOMMON...], are actually shared among all OpenVMS systems using the system disk, the modification or deletion of files in a system root should be performed with care. Further, the removal of an obsolete system root should be performed only via a procedure such as CLUSTER_CONFIG or CLUSTER_CONFIG_LAN. because an erroneous DELETE command can delete some or all of the system common files, including those shared with and used by other systems sharing the same system disk.

Also, the DIRECTORY/SIZE SYS$SYSDEVICE:[*...] command will repeatedly locate the same set of shared common files via each SYSCOMMON.DIR alias entry, providing greatly increased and misleading total usage figures. For the same reason, the use of the DELETE command in any system root directory requires extreme caution.

All access to the OpenVMS system directories should be made using the logical names in Table 14.4.

14.11 Overview of Logical Name Tables

Every logical name resides in a logical name table. Each logical name table is assigned a name so that it can be specified in various commands and system requests. For example, a logical name can be looked up in a table by specifying the name of the table and the name of the logical name. There are four standard logical name tables available to every process:

Process The process logical name table is called `LNM$PROCESS_TABLE`.

Job The job logical name table is called `LNM$JOB_`*jjj*, where *jjj* is a unique number for the job.

Group The group logical name table is called `LNM$GROUP_`*ggg*, where *ggg* is the group number.

System The system logical name table, that which is shared by all processes, is called `LNM$SYSTEM_TABLE`.

In order to determine the value of the system logical name `SYS$HELP`, you must ask the system to "look up the logical name `SYS$HELP` in the logical name table `LNM$SYSTEM_TABLE`." This is referred to as translating the logical name. In a command procedure, logical name translation is performed with the `F$TRNLNM` lexical function.

To eliminate the requirement that you know the obscure names of various logical name tables such as `LNM$JOB_8021BC60`, four logical names are defined to refer to the four standard logical name tables. Note the recursive nature of this scheme: logical names refer to logical name tables, which contain logical names. The logical names for the standard logical name tables are as follows:

Process The logical name `LNM$PROCESS` refers to the process logical name table.

Job The logical name `LNM$JOB` refers to the job logical name table.

Group The logical name `LNM$GROUP` refers to the group logical name table.

System The logical name `LNM$SYSTEM` refers to the system logical name table.

This scheme, although it is already complex, has two shortcomings:

- There is no place for the logical names that refer to logical name tables to reside.
- In order to look up a logical name, the user has to know in which logical name table it resides.

Both of these shortcomings are eliminated with the introduction of *logical name table directories*. A logical name table directory, or simply directory, contains a list of logical name tables and logical names that refer to logical name tables. Instead of requesting OpenVMS to "look up this logical name in this table," you can now request it to "look up this logical name in certain tables listed in this logical name table directory." This request is inherently easier to formulate, because there are far fewer directories than there are logical name tables.

In fact, there are two logical name table directories. The first is associated with a process and contains the name of the process logical name table. It also contains logical names that refer to the process, job, and group logical name tables. In addition, it contains the name of the process logical name table directory itself: LNM$PROCESS_DIRECTORY.

The second directory is the system logical name table directory. There is one such directory for the entire system, shared by all users. The system directory contains the names of all the job logical name tables, all the group logical name tables, and the system logical name table. It contains various logical names that refer to collections of logical name tables. And finally, it contains the name of itself: LNM$SYSTEM_DIRECTORY.

Three of the logical names in the system directory are of particular interest:

LNM$FILE_DEV This logical name is defined as a search list of logical name tables that are to be used when parsing a file spec. The default value of this logical name is the list LNM$PROCESS, LNM$JOB, LNM$GROUP, LNM$SYSTEM. It is this default list that causes the file spec parsing service to search for logical names first in the process table, then in the job, group, and system tables.

LNM$DCL_LOGICAL This logical name is used by the SHOW LOGICAL command and F$TRNLNM lexical function to determine which logical name tables to search for the logical name being translated. By default, LNM$DCL_LOGICAL refers in turn to the logical name LNM$FILE_DEV.

LNM$DIRECTORIES This logical name is defined as a search list of the two logical name table directories: first LNM$PROCESS_DIRECTORY and then LNM$SYSTEM_DIRECTORY.

The logical name table scheme presented here makes logical names relatively easy for the average user to deal with. But never let it be said that the scheme is simple. The following is a list of the contents of the two logical name table directories on a small OpenVMS system:

```
(LNM$PROCESS_DIRECTORY)

   "LNM$GROUP" = "LNM$GROUP_000260"
   "LNM$JOB" = "LNM$JOB_802E9DD0"
   "LNM$PROCESS" = "LNM$PROCESS_TABLE"
   "LNM$PROCESS_DIRECTORY" [table] = ""
   "LNM$PROCESS_TABLE" [table] = ""
```

```
(LNM$SYSTEM_DIRECTORY)

    "LMF$LICENSE_TABLE" [table] = ""
    "LNM$DCL_LOGICAL" = "LNM$FILE_DEV"
    "LNM$DIRECTORIES" = "LNM$PROCESS_DIRECTORY"
      = "LNM$SYSTEM_DIRECTORY"
    "LNM$DT_FORMAT_TABLE" [table] = ""
    "LNM$FILE_DEV" [super] = "LNM$PROCESS"
      = "LNM$JOB"
      = "LNM$GROUP"
      = "LNM$SYSTEM"
    "LNM$FILE_DEV" [exec] = "LNM$SYSTEM"
    "LNM$GROUP_000001" [table] = ""
    "LNM$GROUP_000010" [table] = ""
    "LNM$GROUP_000201" [table] = ""
    "LNM$GROUP_000260" [table] = ""
    "LNM$JOB_802E8E00" [table] = ""
    "LNM$JOB_802E94E0" [table] = ""
    "LNM$JOB_802E9DD0" [table] = ""
    "LNM$JOB_802E9E80" [table] = ""
    "LNM$JOB_802E9F30" [table] = ""
    "LNM$JOB_802F0C80" [table] = ""
    "LNM$JOB_802F3880" [table] = ""
    "LNM$JOB_802F3EB0" [table] = ""
    "LNM$JOB_802F4380" [table] = ""
    "LNM$PERMANENT_MAILBOX" = "LNM$SYSTEM"
    "LNM$STARTUP_TABLE" [table] = ""
    "LNM$SYSTEM" = "LNM$SYSTEM_TABLE"
    "LNM$SYSTEM_DIRECTORY" [table] = ""
    "LNM$SYSTEM_TABLE" [table] = ""
    "LNM$TEMPORARY_MAILBOX" = "LNM$JOB"
    "LOG$GROUP" = "LNM$GROUP"
    "LOG$PROCESS" = "LNM$PROCESS"
      = "LNM$JOB"
    "LOG$SYSTEM" = "LNM$SYSTEM"
    "TRNLOG$_GROUP_SYSTEM" = "LOG$GROUP"
      = "LOG$SYSTEM"
    "TRNLOG$_PROCESS_GROUP" = "LOG$PROCESS"
      = "LOG$GROUP"
    "TRNLOG$_PROCESS_GROUP_SYSTEM" = ""LOG$PROCESS"
      = "LOG$GROUP"
      = "LOG$SYSTEM"
    "TRNLOG$_PROCESS_SYSTEM" = "LOG$PROCESS"
      = "LOG$SYSTEM"
```

14.11 Overview of Logical Name Tables

CHAPTER 15

Sequential File Operations

CHAPTERS 13 AND 14 DESCRIBED OPENVMS FILES and presented methods for manipulating files as a whole. This chapter begins the presentation of DCL commands that operate on the contents of files: commands for reading, writing, and updating files. In particular, this chapter addresses sequential files, which are collections of data that can only be accessed in order from beginning to end. Chapter 17 addresses indexed files.

When a program performs file operations such as reading and writing, the operations are carried out by the OpenVMS *Record Management System*, or RMS. This chapter and later chapters will refer to RMS when discussing file operations.

A *sequential file* is a file made up of a sequence of individual *records*. Each record contains some logically related information, while all the records taken together contain the sum total of information in the file. One of the distinguishing features of sequential files is that the records are arranged in a particular sequence and can only be accessed in that order. The file is written one record at a time, from beginning to end, and afterwards can only be read in the same order.

The records in a sequential file can be composed of free-format text, or they can be laid out in a predefined format called a *record structure*. This chapter assumes that sequential files contain free-format text; record structures are described in the next two chapters. In a sequential, free-format text file, or simply *text file*, each record can contain a different amount of text; the length of all records need not be the same. Such records are called *variable-length* records. A text file can also have *fixed-length* records, but those files are not as common.

A program source file is one example of a text file. In particular, a DCL procedure is contained in a text file. Text files can be created and modified using a text editor such as LSEDIT, EVE, TPU, or Emacs.

15.1 Reading an Existing File

Before the records in an existing file can be read, the file must be *opened*. The process of opening a file prepares it for future input operations. In DCL, files are opened with the OPEN command, which ensures that the file exists and determines whether the process is allowed to read the file. The OPEN command requires two parameters, a logical name and the specification of the file to be opened:

```
$    open/read xda_data_file sys$manager:user-list.dat;
```

The /READ qualifier specifies that the file is to be opened for read access. Records can be read from the file, but the file cannot be modified. The first parameter is a logical name (not a symbol), which is assigned by the OPEN command to refer to the opened file. The logical name is used in subsequent commands that need to access the open file (e.g., the READ command to obtain records from the file). The second parameter is a file spec that identifies the particular file to be opened.

Sec. 20.5, p. 269

The file is opened as a process-permanent file, which means that it remains open until it is explicitly closed by a subsequent CLOSE command or until the user logs out. The logical name is not equated to the full file spec of the open file. Instead it is equated to a binary-coded string containing an internal reference to the file. If, after the file is opened, you use the logical name in other DCL commands, the command will operate on the open file. In particular, the READ command will read records from the file.

If the file does not exist or cannot be opened for some other reason, an error status is returned by the OPEN command and the procedure's error handler is invoked. This fatalistic behavior may not be acceptable in a sophisticated procedure, particularly if the file spec was entered by the user in response to a query. The /ERROR qualifier can be used on the OPEN command to specify a label at which execution should proceed if an error occurs. The following code continually prompts the user for a file spec until the file can be opened:

```
$10:    libcall ask xda_file s "Enter a file spec:"
$       open/read xda_data_file 'xda_file /error=15
$       goto 19
$15:    libcall signal xda w badfile -
                "File ''xda_file cannot be opened." '$status
$       goto 10
$19:
```

If any error occurs while opening the file, DCL continues execution at label FILE_ERROR rather than with the command following the OPEN. A warning is signaled and the user is prompted for another file spec. The warning message includes a second line containing the RMS status message.

Once a file has been opened successfully, records can be retrieved from it with the READ command. Each READ command obtains the next sequential record from the file and stores its contents in a symbol. The command requires two parameters: the logical name defined by the open operation, and the symbol in which the retrieved record is stored:

```
$       read xda_data_file line
```

The next record is read from the file specified by logical name XDA_DATA_FILE, and then the record is stored in the symbol LINE. In a fashion identical to the OPEN command, any errors are returned by the READ command and cause the procedure's error handler to be invoked. The /ERROR qualifier can be used to override this behavior; it specifies a label at which execution should continue if an error occurs:

```
$       read xda_data_file line /error=20
```

If the entire file has been read and no more records are available, the *end-of-file* condition occurs. DCL treats this condition as an error, so an error status is returned from the READ command or, if the /ERROR qualifier is present, execution continues at the error label. Because end-of-file is a common condition that is often not treated as an error, a separate qualifier is provided to name a handler for it. The /END_OF_FILE qualifier specifies a label to which DCL branches when end-of-file is detected:

```
$       read xda_data_file line /error=20/end_of_file=30
```

If end-of-file occurs on this read operation, execution continues at label FILE_EOF. If any other error occurs, execution continues at label FILE_READ_ERROR.

Once all the necessary records have been read from a file, it must be closed. The close operation relinquishes access to the file and deassigns the logical name defined by the open operation:

15.1 Reading an Existing File

```
$       close xda_data_file
```

The following loop reads and displays the file specified by symbol FILE_SPEC:

```
$       open/read xda_data_file 'file_spec /error=5
$       goto 10
$5:     libcall signal xda w openerr -
                "Unable to open file ''file_spec'" '$status
$       goto 20
$10:    read xda_data_file line /end_of_file=19
$       display line
$       goto 10
$19:    close xda_data_file
$20:
```

It is crucial that an application close every file it opens. If a file is not closed explicitly by the application, it will not be closed automatically when the main procedure exits, because files opened by DCL are process-permanent files. The file remains open until the process terminates; in particular, it is still open if the application is run again. You might think that the second OPEN command would "reopen" the file by first closing and then opening it, but in fact the second OPEN command does absolutely nothing: it does not close the file, it does not open it a second time, nor does it return any kind of error status. Because a file is opened as a process-permanent file, DCL assumes that any subsequent OPEN commands using the same logical name need to access the file that is already opened. Therefore, the file remains in the state it was when the application terminated the first time, perhaps partly read or at end-of-file.

To ensure that all files are closed, a procedure that opens a file should close it in two places. First, the procedure should close the file as soon as it has no further need for the file. This means that a file is closed as soon as possible so that unused open files don't take up system resources. Second, the procedure should include cleanup code to close the file. This guarantees that the file is closed regardless of whether the procedure terminates normally or due to an error or interrupt. The CLOSE command in the cleanup code should include the /NOLOG qualifier, which suppresses any error messages if the file was already closed by the procedure in its normal course of execution. Here is the preceding example with cleanup code added:

```
$       open/read xda_data_file 'file_spec' /error=5
$       goto 10
$5:     libcall signal xda w openerr -
                "Unable to open file ''file_spec'" '$status
$       goto 20
```

Sec. 20.5, p. 269

```
$10:    read xda_data_file line /end_of_file=19
$       display line
$       goto 10
$19: close xda_data_file
$20:
        .
        .
        .
$exit:
$       set noon
$       close/nolog xda_data_file   ! Close file if left open.
$       exit status .or. $x10000000
```

15.2 Creating and Writing a New File

A DCL application can create a new sequential file and write records to it. The create operation is distinct from the write operation. There are many ways to create a new file, but the simplest way is to let the OPEN command do it:

```
$       open/write xda_new_file -
            sys$system:xda_user-data.dat; /error=20
```

When the /WRITE qualifier is specified, the OPEN command either creates the specified file or returns an error. The rules are simple:

- If the specified file does not exist, it is created.
- If the specified file does exist:
    - If an explicit version is not included in the file spec (as in the preceding example), then a new version of the file is created with a version number higher than all existing versions.
    - If an explicit version is included and that version of the file does not exist, it is created.
    - If an explicit version is included and that version already exists, an error status is returned. The OPEN/WRITE command cannot be used to overwrite an existing file or to add records to it.

Once the file is created, the OPEN/WRITE command behaves exactly like the OPEN/READ command. The logical name is defined to refer to the file, so that subsequent WRITE and CLOSE commands can use it.

The WRITE command has been covered in previous chapters as it pertains to displaying information at the terminal. The same command is used to write records to a sequential file:

```
$       write xda_new_file line
```

The first parameter is the logical name defined by the OPEN command. The second parameter is an expression or list of expressions whose values are to be written together as one record. In the preceding example, the symbol LINE contains the record to be written. A write operation always creates exactly one record in the file.

The following example creates a new data file containing a list of the files in the system manager's directory. The list includes the modification dates of the files.

```
$      open/write xda_new_file sys$manager:file-list.dat
$10:   file = f$search("sys$manager:*.*;")
$      if file .eqs. "" then goto 19
$      write xda_new_file file, " ", -
                   f$file_attributes(file,"RDT")
$      goto 10
$19:   close xda_new_file
```

Notice that the argument to the F$SEARCH function includes an explicit semicolon so that only the latest version of each file is located. This prevents the list from containing multiple versions of the same file.

The WRITE commands illustrated above are limited to writing records of 1,024 bytes or less. Furthermore, the value of each individual expression is limited to 255 bytes. These limitations can be relaxed by including the /SYMBOL qualifier on the command, which allows expressions and records of up to 2,048 bytes. However, use of the /SYMBOL qualifier places another restriction on the WRITE command: the expressions specified in the command must be symbols; no string literals, lexical functions, or operators are allowed. When you want to write more than 1,024 bytes, you must build the output string in a symbol and then specify the symbol on the WRITE command.

The WRITE command exhibits one quirk when it creates a new file. Programmers familiar with OpenVMS would expect it to create a standard sequential file with the *carriage return carriage-control* attribute, a file normally referred to as a text file. Such a file can be displayed, printed, edited with all available editors, and otherwise processed by any OpenVMS utility or application. In fact, however, the command creates a sequential file containing records in the *variable with fixed control* (VFC) format. Each record has a 16-bit header whose contents are not available to the DCL programmer.

Some editors and utilities cannot deal with VFC files. If you encounter a problem with VFC files, use the CREATE command to create the file, rather than allowing the WRITE command to do so. The CREATE command creates a standard text file and then reads lines from SYS$INPUT to populate the file. During execution of a procedure, SYS$INPUT is directed to the procedure file, so data lines in the procedure will end up as records in the file. If there are no data lines, the file will be empty:

```
$       create sys$manager:file-list.dat
$!      There are no data lines, so the file will be empty.
```

Once the empty file is created, you can add records by opening the file and appending new records.

15.3 Appending to an Existing File

Additional records can be added to an existing sequential file by opening the file *for append*. Once a file is opened for append, write operations cause records to be added to the end of the file:

```
$       open/append xda_data_file sys$manager:file-list.dat;
```

In all other respects, a file opened for append behaves identically to a file opened for write.

The /APPEND qualifier is particularly useful when writing to an empty file made with the CREATE command. The file is a standard text file, not a VFC file, and thus DCL will write standard text records into it. Here is another example of creating a file list using the CREATE command:

```
$       create sys$manager:file-list.dat
$       open/append xda_new_file sys$manager:file-list.dat
$10:    file = f$search("sys$manager:*.*;")
$       if file .eqs. "" then goto 19
$       write xda_new_file file, " ", -
                        f$file_attributes(file,"RDT")
$       goto 10
$19:  close xda_new_file
```

15.4 Temporary Files

A DCL application often needs a *temporary file* to contain data for a short period of time. A temporary file is created by the procedure, filled with records, processed, and then deleted. The file does not exist after the application terminates. There are two important differences between temporary and permanent files.

The first difference concerns the location and name chosen for the temporary file. A temporary file should not be placed in the working directory or the directories dedicated to the OpenVMS system and other software products. Temporary files will clutter those directories and confuse anyone looking in them. Don't forget that many users may be running your application or other similar applications. Temporary files should be placed in a directory dedicated to containing short-lived data. OpenVMS provides a standard logical name, `SYS$SCRATCH`, which can be defined to refer to such a directory. When you log in, `SYS$SCRATCH` refers to your `SYS$LOGIN` login directory, but you can certainly redefine it to a personal or systemwide directory created expressly for the purpose of containing temporary files. The authors recommend that you redefine `SYS$SCRATCH` to reference a scratch directory, to ease the task of cleaning up any remaining temporary files.

The file name of a temporary file must be carefully chosen so that it does not duplicate the name of another temporary file. If two DCL applications create the file `TEMP.DAT` in the same directory, the results will surely be unpredictable. A unique name must be generated with a zero or vanishingly small probability of duplication. The process of generating a unique name is performed often enough that it deserves a subroutine in the subroutine library. The subroutine is called `UNIQUE_NAME` and requires two parameters: a global symbol to be set to the generated name, and a pattern specifying how the name is formatted. The pattern can contain arbitrary text, but must include a question mark (?) to specify the position in which the unique portion of the name is inserted. The unique portion of the name is a ten-digit number. The subroutine is used in the following example:

```
$    libcall unique_name xda_temp sys$scratch:xda_?.dat
```

The global symbol `XDA_TEMP` will be set to the unique name, which consists of the prefix `SYS$SCRATCH:XDA_` plus the unique portion plus the suffix `.DAT`. The unique portion consists of ten decimal digits, which are generated from the current time. The preceding subroutine call might return the following file spec:

SYS$SCRATCH:XDA_1643296105.DAT

The second difference between temporary and permanent files is that temporary files must be deleted before the application terminates. It is best to delete them as soon as they are no longer needed. In order to ensure that a temporary file is deleted, the `DELETE` command should be placed in the cleanup code of the procedure that created it. The following code creates a temporary file containing the names of the data files in the system manager's directory and mails it to the system manager:

```
$    libcall unique_name xda_data_list sys$scratch:xda_?.lis
$    directory/output='xda_data_list sys$manager:*.dat;
```

```
$       mail 'xda_data_list system -
        /subject="List of data files in SYS$MANAGER"
```
  : *continue processing*

```
$exit:
$       set noon
$       if f$type(xda_data_list) .nes. "" then -
          if f$search(xda_data_list) .nes. "" then -
            delete 'xda_data_list;*
```
  : *more cleanup*

A temporary file spec is generated and used in the /OUTPUT qualifier of the DIRECTORY command. The list of data files is therefore placed in the temporary file. The MAIL command sends this file to the system manager with an appropriate subject. The procedure's cleanup code includes three lines that delete the temporary file. These lines perform the following functions:

1. The first line ensures that the global symbol XDA_DATA_LIST exists. It is possible that an interrupt or error occurred before the symbol was created by UNIQUE_NAME subroutine and therefore there is no file to delete.

2. The second line ensures that the temporary file does indeed exist. It is possible that an interrupt occurred between the call to UNIQUE_NAME and the completion of the DIRECTORY command.

3. The third line deletes the temporary file. Note that it deletes all versions of the file, just in case more than one was created.

The following example illustrates the technique for handling temporary files created with the OPEN command:

```
$       libcall unique_name xda_data_file sys$scratch:xda_?.tmp
$       open/write xda_data_file 'xda_data_file
```
  : *process file*
```
$       close xda_data_file
```

```
$exit:
$       set noon
$       close/nolog xda_data_file
$       if f$type(xda_data_file) .nes. "" then -
          if f$search(xda_data_file) .nes. "" then -
            delete 'xda_data_file;*
```
  : *more cleanup*

15.4 Temporary Files

A unique file spec is generated and used in the OPEN command to create a temporary file and prepare it for writing. There is no reason to believe that the OPEN command will fail, so no /ERROR qualifier is specified; an error will cause the usual error handler to be invoked. Once open, the file is processed and eventually closed. The cleanup code must perform two operations on the temporary file. It must close the file if still open, and it must delete the file.

The SYS$SCRATCH directory exists as a standard place in which to put scratch files. OpenVMS does *not* automatically delete files in this directory. By default, SYS$SCRATCH is your SYS$LOGIN directory, which is one of most obvious reasons why the contents of SYS$SCRATCH are not deleted.

15.5 Displaying a File

There are two ways in which a procedure can display a sequential file at the terminal. If the records are to be displayed exactly as they appear in the file, and if the file is to be displayed in its entirety, then the TYPE command can be used. The TYPE command writes the file's records to SYS$OUTPUT, which normally refers to the terminal screen. The records are displayed without pausing, unless the /PAGE qualifier is included, in which case the records are displayed one screenful at a time. The following example asks the user for a file spec and displays the file screen by screen:

```
$       libcall ask xda_file s "File to display:"
$       type/page 'xda_file
```

> Sec. 9.1, p. 105

It is courteous to allow the user to cancel the file display with CTRL/Y. Only two lines must be added to this example:

```
$       libcall ask xda_file s "File to display:"
$       on control_y then goto 19
$       type/page 'xda_file
$19:    on control_y then goto control_y
```

Another way to display sequential files is to read them one record at a time and display each record individually. This method allows much finer control over which records are displayed, how many are displayed, and the format of the display. The disadvantage is that the method is significantly slower than using TYPE. The following code displays the first five nonblank lines in a file:

```
$10:    libcall ask xda_file s "File to summarize:"
$       open/read xda_file 'xda_file /error=15
$       goto 19
```

Sequential File Operations

```
$15:    libcall signal xda w filnotfnd -
                        "File ''xda_file does not exist."
$       goto 10
$19:
$   n = 0
$20:    read xda_file line /end_of_file=29
$       if f$edit(line,"TRIM") .eqs. "" then goto 20
$       n = n + 1
$       display line
$       if n .lt. 5 then goto 20
$29: close xda_file
```

The F$EDIT function is used to trim the trailing spaces from the line. If this results in the null string, then the line is blank and another line is immediately read. The loop terminates after the fifth nonblank line is displayed.

15.6 Searching Files

Certain DCL applications, particularly those in the domain of code management, system building, or system testing, require that text files be searched for occurrences of specific character sequences. For example, a procedure may need to search a set of files generated by a testing procedure for occurrences of the sequence "ERROR". OpenVMS provides the SEARCH utility to assist with searching files. You could read and scan the lines of a text file directly in DCL, but such a procedure would be unacceptably slow for all but the smallest files.

The SEARCH utility requires two parameters: the specification of the files to be searched, and an indication of what to search for (known as the search *pattern*). The utility can search a single file or any number of files that match a wildcard spec. The output from the utility consists of a listing of those lines in the files that match the search pattern. The output is normally directed at the terminal but can be redirected, as usual, with the /OUTPUT qualifier.

The search pattern is specified as one or more character strings in conjunction with the /EXACT and /MATCH qualifiers. The /EXACT qualifier determines whether the pattern strings must match the text exactly (/EXACT) or may match without regard to uppercase and lowercase letters (/NOEXACT). The default is /NOEXACT. Table 15.1 describes how the /MATCH qualifier determines the method of searching when used in conjunction with the pattern strings.

The SEARCH command accepts various other qualifiers, which control the amount and format of its output. One important feature of the command is the status code it returns. If any matches are found, the status code includes a

Table 15.1
How /MATCH affects searching

Qualifier	Default?	Method of matching
/MATCH=OR	✓	A text line matches if it contains *any* of the pattern strings.
/MATCH=AND		A text line matches if it contains *all* of the pattern strings.
/MATCH=NOR		A text line matches if it contains *none* of the pattern strings.
/MATCH=NAND		A text line matches if it contains *some* but not *all* of the pattern strings.

success severity. If no matches are found, the status code includes an informational severity. Neither status is an error, but the two cases can be distinguished by the severity of the status.

The following example repeatedly asks the user for a file spec and tells the user whether the file contains the sequence "ERROR" or "WARNING":

```
$10:    libcall ask xda_file s "File to be searched:"
$       if f$search(xda_file) .nes. ""
$       then
$         search/output=nla0: 'xda_file -
                            "error","warning"/match=or
$         match = $severity .eq. 1
$         if match then display "The file contains errors."
$         if .not. match then display -
                            "The file contains no errors."
$       else
$         libcall signal xda w filnotfnd -
                            "File ''xda_file' does not exist."
$       endif
$       goto 10
```

The /OUTPUT qualifier is used to discard all the output from the SEARCH command by directing it to the null device. Therefore, the only interesting result of the command is the status code it returns. If a success status is returned, then the file contains the pertinent sequences. If an informational status is returned, the file does not contain the sequences.

200   Sequential File Operations

CHAPTER 16

Data Manipulation

THIS CHAPTER PRESENTS VARIOUS TECHNIQUES and tricks for manipulating data in DCL. The techniques include methods for performing simple arithmetic operations, character string manipulation, and calculations related to dates and times.

16.1 Arithmetic Techniques

DCL provides only rudimentary arithmetic operations on integer values. Applications often require more sophisticated operations, which must be built up out of the operations that DCL provides. This section illustrates a few of the advanced operations and how they can be achieved in DCL.

The "maximum" function examines two or more integers and returns the largest one. The "minimum" function is similar but returns the smallest integer. These functions are not provided by DCL but can be implemented as follows:

```
$!     Determine the largest of the values A, B, and C.
$
$      max = a
$      if b .gt. max then max = b
$      if c .gt. max then max = c
```

```
                    —or—

        $!      The block count is equal to the total file blocks,
        $!      but can be no larger than 600. In other words,
        $!      block_count = minimum(total-file-blocks, 600).
        $
        $       block_count = total_file_blocks
        $       if block_count .gt. 600 then block_count = 600
```

Sometimes it is necessary to round a number to a multiple of a particular integer. For example, when calculating the number of bytes a file will occupy, it makes sense to round up to a multiple of 512, since disk space is always allocated in units of 512-byte blocks. The following code rounds up the value in BYTES to a multiple of 512:

```
        $       bytes = (bytes + 511) / 512 * 512
```

Because division truncates the quotient toward zero, the result of the division is always an integer. The multiplication is therefore guaranteed to produce an integer multiple of 512. Adding 511 first means that the division operation will round up rather than down. In general, if the number b is to be rounded up to a multiple of m, the command is

```
        $       b = (b + m-1) / m * m
```

A variation on this expression can be used to calculate the remainder upon dividing one number by another. The following command determines the remainder when dividing A by B:

```
        $       remainder = a - a/b*b
```

Note that the remainder has the same sign as the dividend.

DCL does not provide floating-point numbers, and it is rather tedious to simulate them with integers. However, there is one floating-point calculation that is often useful: determining the ratio of two numbers. This can be accomplished by multiplying the numerator by 100 and then performing the division:

```
        $       ratio = blocks_used*100 / total_blocks
```

This command calculates the ratio of disk blocks used to total disk blocks. The ratio is an integer in the range 0–100, so it can also be displayed as a percentage. Note that the percentage is rounded down to the nearest integer.

16.2 Lists

For the purposes of this section, a *list* is a sequence of data items separated by commas or some other delimiting character. A character string can contain a list of items like the following:

"CYNTHIA,PAT,DIRK,TIM,MARK,BILL,MEREDITH"

—or—

"TXT,DAT,LIS,EXE,OBJ,CLD"

The first example is a list of people's first names, and the second is a list of file types. The first list might represent the names of friends to be invited to a party. The second list might represent the types of files found in a particular directory.

The following code builds a list of all the file types found in the directory whose file spec is in the symbol DIRECTORY:

```
$       type_list = ""
$10:    file = f$search(directory+"*.*;")
$       if file .eqs. "" then goto 19
$       type = f$parse(file,,,"TYPE") - "."
$       type_list = type_list + "," + type
$       goto 10
$19:
$       type_list = f$extract(1, 9999, type_list)
```

The list is constructed in the symbol named TYPE_LIST, which is initialized to the null string before the loop. File types are added to the list by concatenating each type to the character string in the TYPE_LIST symbol, along with a comma to separate it from the previous type. When the loop terminates, TYPE_LIST contains a list of all the file types found in the directory, each separated by a comma. There will also be a comma at the beginning of the list, which is removed using the F$EXTRACT function. The function receives a starting index of 1, thus excluding the first character, and a length of 9,999 so that all remaining characters are included.

The list constructed by the previous example will contain duplicates when there is more than one file with the same type. Eliminating duplicates requires a little more code in the loop:

```
$       type_list = ""
$10:    file = f$search(directory+"*.*;")
$       if file .eqs. "" then goto 19
$       type = f$parse(file,,,"TYPE") - "."
```

```
$       if f$locate(","+type+",", type_list+",") .eq. -
            f$length(type_list)+1 then -
$         type_list = type_list + "," + type
$       goto 10
$19:
$       type_list = f$extract(1, 9999, type_list)
```

In order to determine whether a type is already in the list, the F$LOCATE function is used to scan the list for a duplicate type. The F$LOCATE function takes two arguments: a pattern string and a target string. The target string is scanned for an occurrence of the pattern string. If the pattern is found, its index in the target string is returned. If the pattern is not found, the length of the target is returned. Upon first consideration you might think it would suffice to use the file type as the pattern and the list as the target, thus scanning for the type in the list. However, this would fail in the case of two types where one was a substring of the other.

Take the file types DAT and STAR-DATA, for example. If the type list contained STAR-DATA and a file with type DAT was encountered, it would appear that the DAT type was already in the list because F$LOCATE would find the "DAT" in "STAR-DATA". In order to prevent this problem, you must search for the file type surrounded by commas. Requiring the matches to include a comma on each end of the file type ensures that only complete file types are matched.

Once a list is constructed, you may want to split it apart into its individual components. The F$ELEMENT function is perfect for this task, as illustrated by the following code, which displays the file types in the list, one per line:

```
$       i = -1
$20:    i = i + 1
$       type = f$element(i, ",", type_list)
$       if type .eqs. "," then goto 29
$       display type
$       goto 20
$29:
```

Imagine the type list as a sequence of types, each with a numerical index. The leftmost one is number 0, the next 1, and so on. The F$ELEMENT function takes three arguments: the first is the index of the desired list element; the second, the delimiter character, and the third, the list itself. The function extracts the element specified by the index from the list and returns it. If the index specifies an element that does not exist, the function returns the delimiter (it does not return a null string, because a null string is a perfectly valid list element).

The code uses I as the element index, initializing it to -1 before the loop. Each iteration of the loop increments the index and extracts the next type from the list. If F$ELEMENT returns a comma, then the list is exhausted and the loop terminates. If the function does not return a comma, then it returns a file type, which is displayed. The following table shows the values returned by each call to F$ELEMENT when the type list is "TXT,LSP,EXE,STAR-DATA,CLD,DAT":

Value of I	Return value
0	"TXT"
1	"LSP"
2	"EXE"
3	"STAR-DATA"
4	"CLD"
5	"DAT"
6	","

Do not be tempted to use F$ELEMENT to analyze or split apart such things as file specs. Assume a file spec is stored in the symbol FILE_SPEC. It is incorrect to extract the file type and version from the file spec with the following command:

```
$!    Extract everything after the dot before the file type.
$
$     type_version = f$element(1, ".", file_spec)
```

The directory portion of the file spec might contain a dot, and the command would fail to perform as expected. Even something so apparently foolproof as extracting the file name/type/version can backfire:

```
$!    Extract everything after the directory's close bracket.
$
$     name_type_version = f$element(1, "]", file_spec)
```

Remember, angle brackets (< >) are also valid directory delimiters. If they were present, the command would fail. Further, though your parsing might work in the cases you are aware of, future changes to the supported file name character set or to file name delimiters within OpenVMS can have unforseen implications to your code. File specs must be split up using the F$PARSE lexical function.

Sec. 13.2, p. 152

16.2 Lists

16.3 Keywords

A *keyword* is a character string chosen from among a fixed set of valid strings. Keywords are used to represent commands or options when the repertoire of such choices is finite. A keyword is more meaningful than a number (imagine if DCL commands were chosen by number rather than by verb!). Keywords are used in lexical functions to control the behavior of the function (e.g., the F$EDIT function requires keywords to control the kind of string editing performed). Keywords can also be used by DCL applications when asking the user to choose among several possible actions. For example, an application that creates many files in a directory might incorporate a feature to clean up the directory from time to time. The cleanup function can be controlled by a query such as

```
$     libcall ask xda_clean_option s -
            "Directory cleanup option (DELETE, PURGE, NONE):"
```

App. E, p. 347

The user must enter DELETE, PURGE, or NONE to choose the desired action. It is usually helpful if the application allows the keyword to be abbreviated. And a message should be displayed if the user enters an invalid option. All this "keyword manipulation" is embodied in the library subroutine LOOKUP_KEYWORD. This subroutine requires three arguments: a global symbol, which is set to the result of the lookup; the user's original input; and a list of valid keywords in alphabetical order. If the user's original input is a full or abbreviated keyword in the list, the global symbol is set to the full keyword. If the user's input is not a valid keyword or is an ambiguous abbreviation of a keyword, the global symbol is set to the null string.

Here is the cleanup example expanded to include keyword checking:

```
$10:   libcall ask xda_clean_option s -
            "Directory cleanup option (DELETE, PURGE, NONE):"
$      libcall lookup_keyword xda_clean_option -
            "''xda_clean_option'" DELETE,NONE,PURGE
$      if xda_clean_option .eqs. "" then goto 10
$
$      goto 20_'xda_clean_option
$
$20_DELETE:
            : delete files
$      goto 29
$
$20_NONE:
$      goto 29
```

206   Data Manipulation

```
$20_PURGE:
    .
    . purge files
    .
$29:
```

Once a valid option is obtained from the user, the keyword is used in a GOTO command to select the appropriate cleanup code. In the case of the NONE option, the cleanup code does nothing.

A GOTO command that employs apostrophe substitution to select one of a number of labels is called a *case statement*. The value of a symbol is substituted in the GOTO command to provide part or all of the label name. DCL then alters the procedure's flow of control to continue at the selected label. The procedure must be careful to ensure that the label that results after the substitution is present in the procedure. If not, an error is signaled. When keywords are used to form the labels, as in the previous example, the use of LOOKUP_KEYWORD guarantees that the keyword is valid and therefore that the GOTO will work as expected.

16.4 Dates and Times

Dates and times are important data items in many applications. OpenVMS uses the terms *time* or *date* interchangeably to refer to dates, times, or combinations of the two. Various customizable, application, and language-specific date and time formats are available to OpenVMS users; the OpenVMS default formats are used in this book.

DCL provides facilities to manipulate times, which are represented as character strings in the following format:

dd-mon-yyyy hh:mm:ss.cc

In this format, *dd* is the day of the month, *mon* is a three-letter abbreviation for the month, *yyyy* is the year, *hh* is the hour in 24-hour form, *mm* is the minute, *ss* is the second, and *cc* is the hundredth of a second. This time is called an *absolute time* because it denotes a specific time, past, present, or future. There are also three special absolute times that are relative to the current time. Note that these are absolute times and therefore represent specific points in time, not time spans:

TODAY   The current day at 00:00:00 (midnight).

TOMORROW   The next day at midnight (24 hours after TODAY).

YESTERDAY   The previous day at midnight (24 hours before TODAY).

The F$TIME lexical function returns the current absolute time. It requires no arguments and returns the current time as a character string:

```
$    display "The current time is: ", f$time()
```

This command could produce the following display:

```
The current time is 17-SEP-1998 12:53:36:29
```

Certain other functions can return times when given the appropriate arguments. For example, F$FILE_ATTRIBUTES returns the creation time of a file when the "CDT" keyword is used:

```
$    create_time = f$file_attributes(file_spec,"CDT")
```

Occasionally you may want to compare two absolute times to determine which one is later. To continue the example with F$FILE_ATTRIBUTES, you may want to determine which of two files was most recently modified. The modification time of a file can be obtained with F$FILE_ATTRIBUTES, but it will be in absolute time format. Absolute format is not suitable for comparison because the fields are not in sort order: the year field is not first and the month field is alphabetic. The F$CVTIME function can be used to convert an absolute time to a *comparison time*, which has the following format:

yyyy-mm-dd hh:mm:ss.cc

A comparison time differs from an absolute time in two ways. The fields are in sort order, from most significant to least significant. And the month is represented as a number rather than as an abbreviation. One comparison time A is greater than another comparison time B if and only if A is later in time than B. A simple string comparison operator will suffice.

The F$CVTIME function can accept a rather complex combination of arguments. In order to convert an absolute time to a comparison time, the first argument must be the absolute time. The second argument is a keyword string specifying the type of conversion to be performed; the "COMPARISON" keyword requests that the absolute time be converted to comparison format and returned. The modification times of two files can be compared as follows:

```
$    time1 = f$cvtime(f$file_attr(file1,"RDT"),"COMPARISON")
$    time2 = f$cvtime(f$file_attr(file2,"RDT"),"COMPARISON")
$    if time1 .gts. time2 then action when first later than second
```

Always convert times to comparison format before trying to compare them. Comparision times are useful for purposes other than comparisons, such as incorporation into file specifications.

OpenVMS provides another time format called the *delta time*. A delta time specifies the difference between two absolute times. Another way to look at it is that a delta time specifies a time span, a certain amount of time. The format of a delta time is as follows:

dddd-hh:*mm*:*ss*.*cc*

In this format, *dddd* denotes some number of days, *hh* some number of hours, and so on. Taken together, the fields specify an amount of time from one hundredth of a second up to 9,999 days and 24 hours.

Delta times are rarely used by themselves; rather, they are usually used in combination with absolute times. An absolute time and a delta time specified together is called a ***combination time***. A combination time has one of the following formats:

"*absolute+delta*"
"*absolute-delta*"

In these formats, *absolute* represents an absolute time and *delta* represents a delta time. The combination time must often be enclosed in quotation marks, so it is best always to do so. The first format specifies a time that is "delta" later than the absolute time, that is, a specific time some interval after the absolute time. The second format specifies a time that is "delta" earlier than the absolute time.

The following example sets the expiration date of a file to be 30 days after midnight tomorrow:

```
$ set file/expiration="tomorrow+30-00:00:00.00" myfile.dat
```

The combination time consists of the absolute time TOMORROW plus the delta time 30-00:00:00.00. DCL has a complex set of rules to allow you to omit certain fields from times when they are unnecessary. In this example, the minutes, seconds, and hundredths fields can be omitted from the delta time:

```
$ set file/expiration="tomorrow+30-00" myfile.dat
```

The authors recommend that you specify all time fields until you become familiar with the rules for forming and abbreviating times. The rules are given in the *OpenVMS User's Manual*.

The F$CVTIME function can also be used to convert a combination time to an absolute time. The first argument is the combination time and the second argument is the keyword "ABSOLUTE". The following example asks the user for a new file expiration date based on the file's creation date:

```
$    created = f$file_attributes(file_spec,"CDT")
$    display "The file was created ", created
$    libcall ask xda_delta s -
             "How long until it expires (delta time):"
```

16.4 Dates and Times

```
$       expires = f$cvtime(created+"+"+xda_delta, "ABSOLUTE")
$       display "The file will expire on ", expires
$       set file/expiration="''expires'" file_spec
```

The file's creation time is obtained and displayed. Then the user is asked for a delta time, which is used as the file's lifetime. The absolute expiration date is determined using the F$CVTIME function. Note how the combination time is constructed by concatenating the absolute time, a plus sign, and the delta time. The expiration date is then displayed and the file set.

The F$CVTIME function has many other features, which are described in the *OpenVMS DCL Dictionary*.

16.5 Record Structures

Chapter 15 presented sequential files whose records contain textual information. Chapter 17 will introduce indexed files whose records are structured. Both sequential and indexed files can contain structured records, although such records are more common in indexed files. A structured record, or simply *structure*, is a record whose contents are formatted into *fields*, each field containing a single item of information. All the fields, except perhaps for the last one, are of fixed size. The last field can have variable size if the records in the file have variable length. The sizes of all the fields except the last are fixed, and the last field occupies the rest of the variable-length record.

The records in an index file are almost always structured. The records in a sequential file can contain textual information, as was the assumption in Chapter 15, or they can be structured. Sequential files with structured records are not specifically addressed in this book because the techniques are the same as for indexed files.

Using structures in DCL is somewhat difficult because there is no direct support for them. However, with the careful use of features already described, you can create new structures and access the fields from existing ones. For purposes of illustration we will use the record structure illustrated in Table 16.1.

In order to access and store the fields in a structure, we need to know the position, size, and data type of each field. This information is represented using one or two symbols for each field. The value of the first symbol is the field's position; the value of the second symbol is the field's size. The name of the first symbol also contains a one-letter code that identifies the data type of the field. The conventions for structure symbols are explained below. Here is the code that sets up the symbols for the sample structure:

Table 16.1
Fields in a record structure

Position	Size	Type	Description
0	12 bytes	String	User name.
12	17 bytes	Date	Date this record was created, in the form *dd-mm-yyyy hh:mm*.
29	17 bytes	Date	Date this record was last modified.
46	64 bytes	String	Device/directory owned by this user.
110	32 bits	Integer	Number of files in the directory.
114	32 bits	Integer	Block count of files in the directory.
118	8 bits	Boolean	1 if the user is a student, 0 if not.

```
$       ufr_t_username  =  0
$       ufr_s_username  =  12
$       ufr_t_created   =  12
$       ufr_s_created   =  17
$       ufr_t_modified  =  29
$       ufr_s_modified  =  17
$       ufr_t_devdir    =  46
$       ufr_s_devdir    =  64
$       ufr_l_count     =  110*8
$       ufr_l_blocks    =  114*8
$       ufr_b_student   =  118*8
```

The record contains information about a user's files, so it is called a user file record, or UFR. This structure has four different types of fields: integer, text, date, and Boolean. The definition symbols required for each type are as follows:

Text A field containing a text string is described by two symbols. The first symbol name contains a T to identify a text field, and its value is the byte position of the beginning of the field. The value of the second symbol is the size of the field, and the symbol name contains an S to identify it as a size symbol.

Date A field containing a date and time is described by two symbols. The first symbol name contains a T to identify a text field, and its value is the byte position of the beginning of the field. The second symbol again specifies the size of the field.

Integer An integer is a 32-bit integer quantity. A field containing an integer is described by one symbol. The symbol name contains an L to identify a longword integer field, and its value is the *bit* position of the beginning

16.5 Record Structures

of the field. The reason for using the bit position will become apparent later. No size symbol is needed, because a longword integer field is always a four-byte (32-bit) field.

Boolean A field containing a Boolean value is described by one symbol. The symbol name contains a B to identify a Boolean field, and its value is the *bit* position of the field. No size symbol is needed, because a Boolean field is always a one-byte (eight-bit) field. The field contains a 0 for false, or a 1 for true.

The letters used to identify the field type are dictated by the OpenVMS modular programming standard, which is described in the *Guide to Creating OpenVMS Modular Procedures*.

16.5.1 Creating a Structure

A record is created by storing the values of its constituent fields into a character string, one at a time, from first to last. The substring and bit-field assignment statements are used to store the data into the character string. The following code will construct one of our sample records:

> Sec. 3.7, p. 45

```
$       date = f$extract(0,ufr_s_created,f$time())
$       record = ""
$       record[ufr_t_username,ufr_s_username]  := "DJONES"
$       record[ufr_t_created,ufr_s_created]    := "''date'"
$       record[ufr_t_modified,ufr_s_modified]  := "''date'"
$       record[ufr_t_devdir,ufr_s_devdir]      := "$DISK3:[DJONES]"
$       record[ufr_l_count,32]                  = file_count
$       record[ufr_l_blocks,32]                 = file_blocks
$       record[ufr_b_student,8]                 = false
            .
            .    write record
            .
```

Before the record is created, the current time is retrieved, truncated after the minutes field, and stored in the symbol DATE. The record will be the value of the symbol RECORD, so the symbol is initialized by setting it to the null string. Then each field is stored in the symbol, beginning with the one at position zero and continuing until all fields have been stored. Text and date fields are stored using a substring assignment statement. The substring's byte position and length are specified by the two symbols that define the field. Note that each assignment automatically extends the record to the required length so that the field will fit in it. The value assigned to a text or date field is extended with spaces to occupy the entire field. In this manner, every character of the record is filled with good data.

Integer and Boolean fields are stored using a bit-field assignment statement. The field's *bit* position is specified by the symbol that defines the field. The field's size is always 32 bits for a longword integer and eight bits for a Boolean. Remember that a substring position is specified by the starting byte position. Once all the fields have been stored, a complete record exists in the symbol RECORD. The record can now be written to a file or manipulated in some other fashion.

The character string representing a structure is composed of both textual fields and binary fields. If you display the string on a terminal, the textual fields will be apparent, but the binary fields may cause the terminal to behave strangely. This is because the binary fields may appear to the terminal as control sequences or other nontextual data.

16.5.2 Extracting Fields from a Structure

In order to use the information in an existing record, the data in the record's fields must be extracted and assigned to symbols. Once the data is assigned to symbols, it can be manipulated by all the normal DCL facilities. Lexical functions are used to extract the fields of a record:

```
     : read record as described in Chapter 17
$    user_name   = f$edit(f$extract(ufr_t_username,-
                                    ufr_s_username, record),-
                          "TRIM")
$    create_date = f$extract(ufr_t_created, ufr_s_created,-
                             record)
$    modify_date = f$extract(ufr_t_modified, ufr_s_modified,-
                             record)
$    dev_dir     = f$edit(f$extract(ufr_t_devdir,-
                                    ufr_s_devdir, record),-
                          "TRIM")
$    file_count  = f$cvsi(ufr_l_count,32,record)
$    file_blocks = f$cvsi(ufr_l_blocks,32,record)
$    student     = f$cvsi(ufr_b_student,8,record)
```

Text and date fields are extracted with the F$EXTRACT function. The field's position and size are specified by the two symbols that define the field. If the data might not fill the field, as is the case with user name and device/directory, the F$EDIT function is used to trim the trailing spaces present in the field.

Integer and Boolean fields are extracted with the F$CVSI function. The acronym CVSI stands for "convert signed bit-field to integer." This function requires three arguments: a bit position, a size, and a value. The value is treated as a sequence of bits, and the bit-field specified by the position and size is extracted, assumed to represent a signed integer, and converted to an integer. This is exactly what we need when extracting an integer or Boolean field, because the field was stored as a series of bits with a bit-field assignment statement.

There is a companion to the F$CVSI function, called F$CVUI, which extracts unsigned bit fields. The F$CVUI function can be used in place of F$CVSI when the field is known to be positive. It is not used in this book because all bit fields are assumed to contain signed (potentially negative) integers.

CHAPTER 17
Indexed File Operations

THIS CHAPTER CONTINUES THE DISCUSSION of file operations begun in Chapter 15. It deals with indexed files, which have a much richer structure than sequential files.

An indexed file consists of a set of *records*, each of which is composed of individual *fields*. A field is a portion of a record containing one item of information, such as a user name or a Social Security number. An indexed file record can contain any number of fields. There is no requirement that all the records in a file have the same field layout; there can be various types of records, each with its own layout. If all the records in a file have the same length, then the indexed file can have *fixed-length records*. Otherwise the file must contain *variable-length records*.

What distinguishes indexed files from sequential files are the *key fields* in a record. A key field, or simply *key*, is a field whose values are to be indexed for fast lookup. An index for each key field is maintained in a section of the file separate from the data records. The index for a particular key contains an entry for each record in the file, the entry matching the record's key with the record's location in the file. The index is sorted such that a given key can be found quickly and the corresponding record or records retrieved. The indexes thus allow records to be retrieved randomly by key.

Every indexed file has at least one key, called the *primary key*. There may be up to 254 additional keys, called *alternate keys*. Information describing the keys is kept at the beginning of the indexed file in the *file prologue*. The primary key has some important attributes associated with it:

Name A string describing the key. It can be up to 32 characters in length.

Number An integer that specifies the number of the index. The primary index is number 0; alternate indexes are numbered starting with 1.

Type A keyword that specifies the data type of the key. The OpenVMS record management system supports binary, decimal, and character string keys, but DCL can only handle files with character string keys.

Position An integer specifying the starting position of the key in the record. The first position is zero.

Length An integer that specifies the length of the key. A string key can be up to 255 characters in length.

Duplicates A Boolean value that controls whether duplicate keys are allowed. When the value is true, there can be more than one record with the same key value.

There are additional attributes not discussed here. A complete description of all indexed file attributes can be found in the *Guide to OpenVMS File Applications*.

Alternate keys have all the attributes of the primary key, plus some additional ones:

Changes A Boolean value that controls whether the value of the key can be changed when a record is updated.

Null key A Boolean value that controls whether a *null value* is allowed in the key field. If a null value is present in an alternate key field, that field is not entered into the index for the key.

Null value A character specifying the null value for the key field. The field is considered null if it is full of this character. Typical null values are the NUL and space characters.

17.1 Sample File

The remainder of this chapter focuses on index file features that are supported by DCL. There are other features available in conventional programming languages that are not described here. The examples in this chapter are based on an indexed file named XDA_USER-FILE.DAT. The records in this file are formatted as illustrated in Table 17.1. The file has two keys. The primary key is an OpenVMS user name, which is a string 12 characters in length. The alternate key is the user's department, which is a string 16 characters in length.

Table 17.1 Fields in the sample indexed file

Name	Position	Size	Type	Description
XUF_T_USER	0	12	String	OpenVMS user name, the primary key.
XUF_T_DEPT	12	16	String	Department name, an alternate key.
XUF_T_PROJECT	28	16	String	Project name.
XUF_L_PEOPLE	44	4	Integer	Number of direct reports, if user is a manager.

Duplicate keys are not allowed for the user name key, but they are allowed for the department key.

In order to read and write records in the indexed file, a command procedure must define the structure of the records. The technique for defining the fields in a structure can be used to define the fields in a record. One or two assignment commands are required to define the symbols for accessing each field. These assignment commands are included in the initialization code of the application's main procedure:

> Sec. 16.5, p. 210

```
$!    Define the fields in a user file record. The symbols for
$!    each field are prefixed with XUF, for "XDA User File".
$
$     xuf_t_user    = 0
$     xuf_s_user    = 12
$     xuf_t_dept    = 12
$     xuf_s_dept    = 16
$     xuf_t_project = 28
$     xuf_s_project = 16
$     xuf_l_people  = 44*8
```

17.2 Reading an Existing File

In order to read an existing indexed file, you must first open it. This is accomplished with the OPEN command, as with sequential files:

```
$    open/read xda_user_file xda_system:xda_user-file.dat;
```

The OPEN command checks that the file exists, determines whether the process is allowed to read it, and prepares it for reading. The /READ qualifier requests read access to the file, so writing will not be allowed.

Once an indexed file is open, there are two ways to read records from it: randomly by key or sequentially. In order to read a record by one of its keys, you must specify the key index number and the key value. If a record exists with that key, it is read from the file:

```
$       libcall ask xda_user s "Which user:" "" u
$       user = f$fao("!#AS",xuf_s_user,xda_user)
$       read xda_user_file/index=0/key="''user'" record /error=5
$       goto 9
$5:     libcall signal xda e nosuchuser -
                        "User ''xda_user does not exist."
$9:
            .
            : display information
            .
```

In this example, the user is prompted for a user name. The user name is supplied as the primary key value when reading a record. If the record is found, the procedure displays information contained in it. If the record is not found, the error branch is taken and an error is signaled. The procedure's error handler will be invoked in the latter case.

The /INDEX qualifier specifies the number of the index in which the key lookup is performed. The /KEY qualifier specifies the value of the key enclosed in quotation marks. In order to find a record whose key exactly matches the specified key value, the key value must be prepared according to the following rules:

- The key lookup is sensitive to the case of the key. In the sample file, user names are stored in uppercase letters, so the call to ASK includes the U option to convert the input to uppercase.

- The value specified with the /KEY qualifier must be of the same length as the key. In the preceding code, the F$FAO function is used to pad the user name to a full 12 characters. This is accomplished with the sharp sign (#) character in the field-width position of the !AS directive. Instead of using an explicit width, the sharp sign indicates that the width is specified by the next argument to the lexical function. In this case, the field width is specified as the size of the user field: XUF_S_USER.

There are ways to perform key lookup other than by exact match. These are described in Section 17.2.1.

Once a record is retrieved by key, additional records can be read sequentially. When the READ command is used without the /INDEX and /KEY qualifiers, DCL will read the record whose key is next in alphabetical order in the same index. This is useful if you want to read some or all of the records in alphabetical order. It is also useful when an index has duplicate keys: you can read all the records having the same key. The following code prompts the user for a department and displays all the users in that department:

```
$       libcall ask xda_dept s "Which department:" "" u
$       dept = f$fao("!#AS",xuf_s_dept,xda_dept)
$       read xda_user_file/index=1/key="''dept'" record /error=5
$       goto 9
$5:     libcall signal xda e nodept -
                        "There are no users in ''xda_dept."
$9:
$       display "Users in department ", xda_dept, ":"
$10:    display f$extract(xuf_t_user,xuf_s_user,record)
$       read xda_user_file record /end_of_file=19
$       if f$extract(xuf_t_dept,xuf_s_dept,record) .eqs. dept-
            then goto 10
$19:
```

The user is prompted for a department name, which is converted to uppercase letters and padded with spaces to 16 characters. A random read is performed to obtain the first record with the requested department. If no such record is found, an error is signaled. If there is at least one such record, a loop is executed to read all of them. The loop first displays the user name from the previous record. It then reads the next record from the file. Because the alternate index has been established as the current one, RMS tries to read the next record in alphabetical order by department. There are three possible outcomes:

- There are no more records in the file. The /END_OF_FILE qualifier causes a branch to the end of the loop.

- There is another record and the department field matches the requested one. The IF command branches to the beginning of the loop.

- There is another record, but the department field does not match. The IF command does not branch and thus falls through to the end of the loop.

You must concern yourself with these three cases whenever you read duplicate records from an index.

If a procedure performs a sequential read without first establishing an index and key, RMS reads records according to the primary index, beginning with the first record in alphabetical order.

17.2.1 Key Matching

The method used by RMS to select a record by key depends upon the length of the supplied key and the value of the /MATCH qualifier. The supplied key may be equal in length to the record keys, or it may be shorter. An error is signaled if it is longer. The /MATCH qualifier takes the values EQ (equal), GE (greater than or equal), or GT (greater than). The default is /MATCH=EQ. There is no facility for matching records whose keys are less than the supplied key, because indexed files cannot be read backwards.

If the supplied key is equal in length to the record keys, RMS selects a record based on the full key. If /MATCH=EQ is specified, RMS selects the first (or only) record with an exactly matching key. If /MATCH=GE is specified, RMS selects the first record with an exactly matching key, or the next key in order if there is no exact match. Finally, if /MATCH=GT is specified, RMS selects the next key in order, *skipping any and all exact matches*.

If the supplied key is shorter than the record keys, RMS selects records based on the first *n* characters of the key, where *n* is the length of the supplied key. This is called a *generic match*. The /MATCH qualifier is used in the same way as full matches, except that "equal" and "greater than" comparisons are performed using only the first *n* characters of the record keys.

If no records match the specified key, an error or end-of-file condition is signaled.

Assume that the sample file contains records with following department keys: DEVELOPMENT, SALES, SERVICE, SERVICE. Note that there are two records for the service department. Here are examples of READ commands that access records by the department index:

```
$!      Read the record for the SALES department:
$
$       read xda_user_file /index=1/key="SALES        "/match=eq-
            record
```

—or—

```
$!      Read the record for the SALES department:
$
$       read xda_user_file /index=1/key="S            "/match=ge-
            record
```

—or—

```
$!      Read the first record for the SERVICE department:
$
$       read xda_user_file /index=1/key="SALES        "match=gt-
            record
```

—or—

```
$!      Use a generic match and read the record for the
$!      DEVELOPMENT department:
$
$       read xda_user_file /index=1/key="D"/match=eq record
```

—or—

```
$!     Read the record for the SALES department:
$
$      read xda_user_file /index=1/key="E"/match=ge record
```

—or—

```
$!     Read the first record for the SERVICE department:
$
$      read xda_user_file /index=1/key="SA"/match=gt record
```

17.3 Creating a File

Unlike sequential files, indexed files cannot be created with the OPEN command. DCL does not provide a way to specify all the information needed to create the file and construct its indexes. The DCL programmer must therefore use the File Definition Language Facility to characterize and create an indexed file. This facility is described in the *OpenVMS Record Management Utilities Reference Manual*. The File Definition Language (FDL) is a language in which all the attributes of an indexed file can be specified. The specification resides in a text file, which is assigned the file type FDL by convention. The CREATE command can create an indexed file according to the specifications in such an FDL file.

A complete description of FDL is beyond the scope of this book. However, the following points summarize the steps that must be taken to create an indexed file in DCL:

1. Use the FDL editor to create the text file, which describes the desired indexed file. The EDIT/FDL command invokes the FDL editor. It will ask a series of questions about the indexed file and ultimately generate an FDL file to describe it.

2. Include the FDL file with your DCL application files.

3. When the application needs to create the indexed file, it uses the CREATE/FDL command. This command creates an empty indexed file according to the specifications in the FDL file.

4. The application can then open the empty indexed file and write records in it.

The CREATE/FDL command is used as follows:

```
$      create/fdl=xda_system:xda_user-file.fdl -
       xda_system:xda_user-file.dat
```

The /FDL qualifier specifies the FDL file containing the specification of the indexed file. The parameter specifies the indexed file to be created. The new file has no records in it. The next section describes how to write records in an indexed file.

Here is the FDL description of the sample file:

```
TITLE "XDA Sample File"

IDENT " 9-MAY-1997 10:55:09   OpenVMS FDL Editor"

SYSTEM
    SOURCE                      OpenVMS

FILE
    ORGANIZATION                indexed

RECORD
    CARRIAGE_CONTROL            carriage_return
    FORMAT                      fixed
    SIZE                        48

AREA 0
    ALLOCATION                  29
    BEST_TRY_CONTIGUOUS         yes
    BUCKET_SIZE                 2
    EXTENSION                   6

AREA 1
    ALLOCATION                  4
    BEST_TRY_CONTIGUOUS         yes
    BUCKET_SIZE                 2
    EXTENSION                   2

AREA 2
    ALLOCATION                  13
    BEST_TRY_CONTIGUOUS         yes
    BUCKET_SIZE                 1
    EXTENSION                   3

KEY 0
    CHANGES                     no
    DATA_AREA                   0
    DATA_FILL                   100
    DATA_KEY_COMPRESSION        yes
```

```
            DATA_RECORD_COMPRESSION      yes
            DUPLICATES                    no
            INDEX_AREA                    1
            INDEX_COMPRESSION             yes
            INDEX_FILL                    100
            LEVEL1_INDEX_AREA             1
            NAME                          "Username"
            PROLOG                        3
            SEGO_LENGTH                   12
            SEGO_POSITION                 0
            TYPE                          string
      KEY 1
            CHANGES                       no
            DATA_AREA                     2
            DATA_FILL                     100
            DATA_KEY_COMPRESSION          yes
            DUPLICATES                    yes
            INDEX_AREA                    2
            INDEX_COMPRESSION             yes
            INDEX_FILL                    100
            LEVEL1_INDEX_AREA             2
            NAME                          "Department"
            SEGO_LENGTH                   16
            SEGO_POSITION                 12
            TYPE                          string
```

17.4 Writing a File

Before an application can write records in an indexed file, it must open the file for write operations:

```
$    open/read/write xda_user_file -
             xda_system:xda_user-file.dat;
```

The /WRITE qualifier specifies that write operations will be performed. The /READ qualifier is also necessary so that DCL will assume that the file already exists. If just the /WRITE qualifier is specified, DCL will create a *new sequential* file, superseding the indexed file. Always open an existing indexed file with an OPEN/READ/WRITE command.

In order to write a new record in an indexed file, you must first construct a character string containing the record's contents. Once the record is constructed, it is written with the WRITE command:

Sec. 16.5, p. 210

```
       obtain user name and department
$      record = ""
$      record[xuf_t_user,xuf_s_user]       := "'"user'"
$      record[xuf_t_dept,xuf_s_dept]       := "'"dept'"
$      record[xuf_t_project,xuf_s_project] := ""
$      record[xuf_l_people,32]              = 0
$      write/symbol xda_user_file record
```

The record is constructed in the symbol RECORD. The symbol is first cleared to make sure that any previous data is removed. Substring and bit-field assignment commands are used to initialize the four fields in the record. The substring assignment command (:=) requires the use of apostrophe substitution to assign the user name and department to their respective fields. Once the record is constructed, the WRITE command adds it to the indexed file. The /SYMBOL qualifier allows the symbol RECORD to contain records of up to 2,048 bytes, rather than restricting it to 255 bytes. Although a particular indexed file may contain short records, it is best to specify the /SYMBOL qualifier to avoid any future problems with record length.

Sec. 3.6, p. 43

If a procedure attempts to write a record with a duplicate key, and the index for that key does not allow duplicates, an error is signaled.

17.5 Updating a File

The WRITE command can be used to *update* an existing record in an indexed file. A record is updated by first reading it, then altering the data in the record, and finally rewriting the record. The following example increases by 1 the number of people reporting to a particular manager:

```
$      libcall ask xda_user s "Manager with new person:" "" u
$      user = f$fao("!#AS",xuf_s_user,xda_user)
$      read xda_user_file/index=0/key="'"user'" record /error=5
$      goto 9
$5:    libcall signal xda e nosuchuser -
                         "User ''xda_user does not exist."
$9:
$      people = f$cvui(xuf_l_people,32,record)
$      record[xuf_l_people,32] = people + 1
$      write/symbol/update xda_user_file record
```

Once the record is read, the people count is extracted with the F$CVUI function. The people field is then increased by 1. Finally, the record is updated with the WRITE/UPDATE command. The /UPDATE qualifier specifies that the record just read should be rewritten with new information. An update option always rewrites the record last read.

An alternate key field may be updated with a new value only if the corresponding index was created with the "changes" attribute. A primary key can never be changed.

17.6 Deleting Records

Records can be individually deleted from an indexed file without the need to copy the entire file. The READ/DELETE command first reads a record from the file and then deletes the record. Once a record is deleted, there is no way to restore it except by rewriting it. The following example deletes a user record from the sample file:

```
$       libcall ask xda_user s "User to delete:" "" u
$       user = f$fao("!#AS",xuf_s_user,xda_user)
$       read/delete xda_user_file/index=0/key="''user'" -
                record /error=5
$       goto 9
$5:     libcall signal xda e nosuchuser -
                    "User ''xda_user does not exist."
$9:
```

You must be careful when writing a procedure to delete records from an indexed file. It is quite easy to delete the wrong record or, when deleting multiple records, to delete too many records. Avoid using generic matching to delete records; specify exact key matches whenever possible. The following example deletes all users in a given department:

```
$       libcall ask xda_dept s "Delete which department:" "" u
$       dept = f$fao("!#AS",xuf_s_dept,xda_dept)
$       count = 0
$10:    read/delete xda_user_file/index=1/key="''dept'" -
                record /error=19
$       count = count + 1
$       goto 10
$19:
$       display "Users deleted: ", count
```

This code uses a loop to delete each record with the given department. Note that exact key matching is used, even though multiple records are being deleted. As soon as an error occurs, it is presumed to be a "key not found" error and the loop is terminated.

17.7 File Sharing

RMS provides a facility for *file sharing*, which allows multiple processes to access and modify an indexed file simultaneously. If a file contains data that can potentially be accessed by more than one user at a time, that file must be shared among all users. It is the OPEN command that determines whether a file can be shared.

By default, a file is opened so as to disallow file sharing. To allow sharing, you must specify the /SHARE qualifier on the OPEN command. This qualifier takes a value, either READ or WRITE. If you specify /SHARE=READ, other users are allowed to read the file but not to modify it. If you specify /SHARE=WRITE, others users are allowed to read and modify the file:

```
$   open/read/write/share=write xda_user_file -
                        xda_system:xda_user-file.dat;
```

This OPEN command allows other processes to read and modify the file. When a file is shared, every procedure that opens the file must cooperate by specifying the /SHARE qualifier. If some procedure does not cooperate, one of two things can happen:

- If the uncooperative procedure opens the file first, no other procedure will be able to open it. When a file is opened without sharing, no other process can open it without signaling an error.

- If the uncooperative procedure attempts to open the file after some other procedure has opened it, the uncooperative procedure will fail. When a file is opened with sharing, every process must open it with sharing.

Once a file is opened for sharing, many processes can access and modify it simultaneously. This opens up a host of possibilities for damaging the contents of the file. Suppose two processes attempt to update a record at the same time? One process will update the record first, but its update will be immediately lost as the second process performs another update. RMS provides a facility called *record locking*, which helps maintain the integrity of shared files.

The concept behind record locking is simple: when a record is read from the file, it is locked. A locked record cannot be read or written by any other process. When the record is updated by the original reader, it is unlocked, allowing other processes to access it again. This simple concept gets more complicated, however, when all the various combinations of record accessing are considered. The /LOCK qualifier specifies whether a record is to be locked after it is read. A record is locked if /LOCK is specified on the READ command (the default). It is not locked if /NOLOCK is specified. When you are reading a record that will not be updated, use /NOLOCK to prevent other processes from being locked out of the record.

Here is the record update example with record locking:

```
$    libcall ask xda_user s "Manager with new person:" "" u
$    user = f$fao("!#AS",xuf_s_user,xda_user)
$    read/lock xda_user_file/index=0/key="''user'" -
             record /error=5
$    goto 9
$5:  libcall signal xda e nosuchuser -
                      "User ''xda_user does not exist."
$9:
$    people = f$cvui(xuf_l_people,32,record)
$    record[xuf_l_people,32] = people + 1
$    write/symbol/update xda_user_file record
```

The record is locked by the READ command and remains locked until it is updated by the WRITE command. No other processes can read or update the record while it is locked.

A record is locked when it is read with the READ/LOCK command (remember, /LOCK is the default). The record remains locked until the procedure takes one of the following actions:

- The record is updated with the WRITE/UPDATE command.
- The record is deleted with the READ/DELETE command.
- Another record is read, with or without locking.
- A new record is written to the file with the WRITE command.
- The file is closed.

When a process attempts to read a record that is locked by another process, one of two things happens. If the record is read with a READ/LOCK command, an error is signaled. If the record is read with a READ/NOLOCK command, the record is read in spite of the lock. This latter behavior allows a procedure to read a record regardless of other process activity, as long as the procedure does not intend to update the record. If the procedure will update the record, it *must* lock it first or the record may be corrupted.

An error is signaled if a process attempts to lock a record that is already locked. This presents a problem to the procedure that wants to wait until the record is unlocked. The /ERROR qualifier can be used on the READ command to detect the lock error and jump to an error handler. However, any error will jump to the error handler, not just lock errors. The simplest solution to this problem is to write procedures that do not wait for locked records but rather just allow the error to be signaled. If this is unacceptable for your application, you must write an error handler that distinguishes lock errors from other errors.

The error status for locked records is called RMS$_RLK and has the hexadecimal value %X000182AA. Define this error status in the main procedure as follows:

```
$    rms$_rlk = %x000182aa
```

The error handler for the READ command can check for this status and retry the read operation:

```
$10:    read/lock xda_user_file/index=0/key="''user'" -
                record /error=15
$       goto 19
$15:    status = $status
$       if status .eq. rms$_rlk then goto 10
$       libcall signal xda e nosuchuser -
                        "User ''xda_user does not exist."
$19:
        ; update the record
```

The read loop will repeat until the record is successfully read and locked. Then the record can be updated.

The sample application in Appendix D illustrates the use of shared indexed files and record locking.

CHAPTER 18

File Protection

DATA SECURITY IS AN IMPORTANT ASPECT of many applications, particularly those involving the confidential data of your organization. OpenVMS provides a data protection facility, which allows you to control which users can access a collection of data and which operations those users can perform on the data. The data protection facility is composed of two independent protection mechanisms: *user identification code* (UIC) protection and *access control list* (ACL) protection.

The UIC-based protection mechanism was the original data protection mechanism in OpenVMS. It is grounded in the idea that each protected object is owned by a particular UIC. The relation between the owner UIC and the UIC of the user who is attempting to access the object determines if and how the user can access the object. UIC-based protection can be applied to the following kinds of objects:

- Devices
- Data volumes
- Files and directories
- Logical name tables
- Queues
- Global sections

The ACL-based protection mechanism was introduced in OpenVMS Version 4 to provide a more flexible data security facility. The acronym ACL stands for access control list: an arbitrary list of associations between user identifiers and access capabilities. When the user who is attempting to access the object appears in the object's ACL, then the ACL determines if and how the user can access the object. An ACL can be associated with all the kinds of objects listed above except for data volumes.

This chapter describes those features of the two protection mechanisms that are most often needed by OpenVMS users, and DCL programmers in particular. The discussion is restricted to the protection of files and directories because these objects are the ones most commonly manipulated by DCL applications. The protection of the other kinds of objects is quite similar and should not pose a problem for a DCL programmer familiar with the information in this chapter. The *OpenVMS Guide to System Security* describes the OpenVMS protection mechanism in complete detail.

18.1 UIC-Based Protection

Every OpenVMS user has a user identification code assigned by the system manager and specified in the user's record in the user authorization file. Every file and directory has an associated UIC, called its *owner UIC*. It is the relation between the file's owner UIC and the UIC of the user who is attempting to access the file that determines whether the user can actually access the file and which operations can be performed on it.

> Sec. 2.6, p. 16

Consider the relation between the file's owner UIC and the accessing user's UIC. OpenVMS defines four *access categories* based on the possible relation:

System   The accessor is in a system UIC group or has special privileges (described below).

Owner   The accessor is the owner.

Group   The accessor is in the same group as the owner (but is not the owner).

World   The accessor is in a different group than the owner.

The system category is the most privileged, or highest, access category, and the world category is the lowest. OpenVMS places the accessor in the highest possible category when determining access capability. For example, if an accessor is the owner of the file but is also in a system UIC group, OpenVMS places the accessor in the system category.

Once the accessor is placed in the appropriate category, OpenVMS determines the operations that the accessor can perform by consulting the *protection mask* associated with the file. The protection mask contains four access flags for each of the four access categories, a total of 16 flags. The four access flags and the operations they permit are as follows:

Read   The accessor can read the file.

Write   The accessor can write or update the file.

Execute   The accessor can execute the file (pertinent to executable images and DCL procedures).

Delete   The accessor can delete the file.

The accessor can perform an operation on the file if the operation is permitted by the category to which the accessor was assigned. Furthermore, the accessor can perform the operation if it is permitted by any lower category. For example, if the accessor was assigned to the group category and wants to delete the file, the accessor can do so if either the group or the world category allows delete access. You must keep in mind, however, that it is not just the protection mask of the data file that matters. In order to get at the file, OpenVMS must begin at the device, travel down through the directory hierarchy, and finally arrive at the file itself. The protection masks on the device, directories, and file all play a part in determining how the file can be accessed. Table 18.1 lists the operations that can be performed on a directory and describes how the various protection masks determine whether an accessor can perform the operation. Table 18.2 does the same for operations on data files.

Starting with OpenVMS V6.0, any file creation operation that supersedes an existing file version also requires write access to the version of the file being superseded. Superseding the existing file with a new version is tantamount to replacing the contents of the existing file. Also, if any file or directory version limits are enabled, and the lowest version must be deleted when the new version is created, then delete access to the deleted version is required.

There is a fifth type of access, called control access, which has no explicit flags in the protection mask. A user with control access to a file can change the file's protection or other characteristics just as the owner of the file can. It is inherent in the UIC-based protection scheme that users in the system and owner categories have control access, while users in the group and world categories do not. When you need to grant control access in any other fashion, you must use an access control list.

If the accessor has certain privileges, UIC-based protection checking is altered in fundamental ways. The following privileges affect the protection-checking methodology:

Table 18.1
Access needed for directory operations

Operation	Grandparent directories	Parent directory	Directory
Create directory	R or E	W	—
Create file	R or E	R or E	R and W
Look up single file	R or E	R or E	R or E
Use wildcards or list directory	R or E	R or E	R
Rename file	R or E	R or E	R and W
Change directory attributes	R or E	R or E	C
Delete directory	R or E	W	D

Table 18.2
Access needed for file operations

Operation	Grandparent directories	Directory	File
Read file	R or E	R or E	R
Write or modify file	R or E	R or E	R and W
Execute file	R or E	R or E	R or E
Change file attributes	R or E	R or E	C
Delete file	R or E	W	D

BYPASS All protection checking is completely bypassed. The accessor can perform any operation whatsoever on the file.

GRPPRV If the accessor is in the same group as the owner, the accessor is placed in the *system* category (not the group category).

READALL The accessor can read the file regardless of its protection.

SYSPRV The accessor is treated as if accessor's UIC is in the system category, regardless of the actual UIC. A system UIC is determined by the setting of the MAXSYSGROUP parameter.

18.1.1 Protection Mask Format

The protection mask for a file is specified and displayed in the following format:

(system:*rwed*, owner:*rwed*, group:*rwed*, world:*rwed*)

The access categories are listed from highest to lowest. In each category, the letter R indicates read access, W write access, E execute access, and D delete access. A letter is present if its corresponding access is allowed in that category, absent if not. Remember that control access is always allowed in the system and owner categories and disallowed in the group and world categories.

When you specify a protection mask, you can abbreviate the access category name down to one letter (e.g., G for group). Here is a protection mask that allows all access for the system and owner category, read/write access for the group category, and no access for the world category:

```
(s:rwed,o:rwed,g:rw,w)
```

When no access is allowed, the colon is omitted along with the access letters.

18.1.2 Setting the Protection Mask

Some commands allow the protection mask to be specified when a file is created. These commands include APPEND, BACKUP, CREATE, and COPY. The following example creates a new file with a specified protection mask:

```
$    create xda_songs.dat -
         /protection=(s:rwed,o:rwed,g:rwe,w:r)
```

The /PROTECTION qualifier includes the protection mask that is assigned to the file.

If a command does not allow a protection mask to be specified, then it must be established separately with the SET FILE or SET SECURITY command. The OPEN command does not accept a protection mask:

```
$    open/write xda_file xda_songs.dat
$    set file xda_songs.dat -
         /protection=(s:rwed,o:rwed,g:rwe,w:r)
```

The SET FILE command can be used to change a file's protection mask at any time (when the file is not locked). Table 18.2 describes the file access that is required to change its owner or protection mask.

18.1.3 Displaying the Protection Mask

The DIRECTORY command can be used to display the protection mask for a file. It is also useful to display the file's owner at the same time:

```
$ directory/owner/protection xda_songs.dat
```

This command will display the file spec, owner, and protection mask.

To view all security attributes associated with the file, use the DIRECTORY/SECURITY command:

```
$ directory/security xda_songs.dat
```

18.1.4 Obtaining the Protection Mask

⚓ Sec 13.5, p. 160

A DCL procedure can obtain the protection mask for a file with the lexical function F$FILE_ATTRIBUTES. The function returns the mask as a character string in the following format:

"SYSTEM=*rwed*, OWNER=*rwed*, GROUP=*rwed*, WORLD=*rwed*"

Note the presence of a space after each comma. Also note the use of an equal sign (=) rather than a colon after the category names. When a procedure needs to determine whether a particular type of access is allowed for an access category, it must parse the protection mask. The following code determines whether delete access is allowed for the world category:

```
$    mask = f$file_attributes(file_spec,"PRO")
$    world = f$element(3, ",", mask) - "WORLD"
$    world_can_delete = f$locate("D",world) .ne. -
                 f$length(world)
```

⚓ Sec. 16.2, p. 203

The first line obtains the protection mask for the file whose file spec is stored in the symbol FILE_SPEC. The second line determines the information for the world category by extracting the final comma-separated element from the protection mask (remember that the F$ELEMENT function numbers elements beginning with zero, so the final one is number 3). The category name "WORLD" is removed from the element, leaving only the equal sign and the access flags. The third line attempts to locate a "D" in the flags. If present, the world category has delete access. If absent, the world category does not have delete access.

The authors suggest that you avoid parsing protection masks if at all possible. The problem with doing so is that the protection mask does not tell the whole story about the protection of the file, and so the procedure may obtain a false picture of the access allowed (or denied) a particular user. The protection mask does not tell the whole story because the file may also have an access control list.

18.2 Access Control Lists

The ACL-based protection mechanism is used to grant or deny access to a file in a more fine-grained fashion than that allowed by UIC-based protection. An access control list consists of one or more entries that specify the access allowed a particular user or set of users. Each entry is called an *access control entry* (ACE). What makes the ACL more flexible than the UIC-based protection mask is the way in which sets of users can be identified.

Individual users or sets of users are identified by *rights identifiers*. Rights identifiers, or simply identifiers, are defined and maintained by the system manager using the AUTHORIZE utility. There are four kinds of identifiers:

- Each user is assigned an identifier whose name is usually identical to the user name. The value of the identifier is the user's UIC.

- Each user group is assigned an identifier. The value of the identifier is the UIC [*group-number*,*].

- There are some special system identifiers that name the various environments in which programs can run. These include BATCH, DIALUP, INTERACTIVE, LOCAL, NETWORK, and REMOTE.

    Systems also typically have an identifier identifier that identifies the particular node, SYS$NODE_nodename.

- The system manager can define additional identifiers that name various collections of users or that are associated with particular applications.

When a user logs in, OpenVMS creates a process to run the user's programs. Various identifiers are associated with this process, just as the user's UIC is. The process identifiers always include the identifier assigned to the user name by the system manager. The process identifiers also include some of the environment identifiers. For example, a normal interactive process has the INTERACTIVE and LOCAL identifiers. In addition, the system manager can assign other identifiers, which name applications that the user can run or groups of files that the user can access. This last category of identifier is open-ended: the system manager can invent all kinds of identifiers to associate with users.

When a user attempts to access a file that has an ACL, the user's process identifiers are matched against the ACEs making up the ACL. The matching is performed from left to right, starting with the first ACE and ending with the last. The leftmost ACE whose identifiers *are all held by the process* is the ACE used by OpenVMS to determine the access allowed the user. No other ACEs are considered once a matching one is found. It is possible that no ACEs match any of the process identifiers. There are three potential outcomes of the matching attempt:

- If there is a matching ACE and it allows the access requested by the user, then the access is granted.

- If there is a matching ACE and it does not allow the access, then the access is denied except in certain special cases. See Section 18.4 for a description of the special cases.

- If there are no matching ACEs, then the UIC-based protection mask is used to determine whether access is granted.

It is important that the UIC-based protection be set to an appropriate value even when an ACL is used. If access is to be controlled using an ACL, the UIC-based protections will typically deny all access to users in the group and world categories, while allowing access only to the system and owner categories.

The following sections describe two types of ACE.

18.2.1 Identifier ACEs

An identifier ACE controls the type of access allowed to users with particular identifiers. The identifier ACE has the following format:

(IDENTIFIER=*identifiers*,ACCESS=*access-types*)

The *identifiers* portion of the ACE specifies one or more rights identifiers that this ACE matches. The identifiers can be specified in UIC format or as simple identifier names. The *access-types* portion of the ACE specifies the type of access allowed to users with the identifiers listed. The access types are READ, WRITE, EXECUTE, CONTROL, DELETE, and NONE. If multiple identifiers or access types are specified, they must be connected with plus signs (+).

Here are some examples of ACEs that might appear on a file. The following ACEs allow read, write, execute, and control access for all members of group DEVELOPMENT. A group can be specified in UIC format or simply as the name of the group.

(identifier=[development,*],access=read+write+execute+control)

—or—

(identifier=development,access=read+write+execute+control)

Assume that the system manager has defined an identifier called PAYROLL, which is associated with the payroll application and assigned to those users who have access to the application. The following ACE allows those users to read, write, and control a file:

(identifier=payroll,access=read+write+execute)

The payroll administrator decides that the payroll application can only be used by people logged in at the office. It cannot be used by people who have dialed in over a modem or logged in remotely from another node in the network. The following ACEs can be added to the files to prevent unauthorized access:

```
(identifier=network,access=none),
(identifier=dialup,access=none),
(identifier=remote,access=none),
(identifier=payroll,access=read+write+execute)
```

The first three ACEs disallow access to network processes (i.e., to people trying to access the file from a remote node), users on dialup terminals, and users hosted from another network node. If an accessor does not match any of the first three ACEs, then the accessor is logged in at a local terminal. The final ACE matches users with the PAYROLL identifier, just as in the previous example. The order of these four ACEs is critical. If the payroll ACE were first, then any user with the PAYROLL identifier could access the payroll application regardless of how the user had logged in. Remember, OpenVMS selects the first ACE whose identifiers match those of the accessor.

Alternatively, the following ACE could be used to permit access to the payroll files only from local authorized users:

```
(identifier=payroll+local,access=read+write+execute)
```

The following example allows any batch jobs to read a file, except that users DEXTER and SINISTER cannot access the file at all:

```
(identifier=dexter,access=none)
(identifier=sinister,access=none)
(identifier=batch,access=read)
```

Again, the order of the ACEs is critical. Specific user identifiers must be matched before more general identifiers so that access is denied to the specific users even if they have the general identifiers.

A special kind of identifier ACE, called a default identifier ACE, can be placed in the ACL associated with a directory. This ACE is automatically included on the ACLs of any files *subsequently* created in that directory. The format of a default identifier ACE is as follows:

```
(IDENTIFIER=identifiers,OPTIONS=DEFAULT,ACCESS=access-types)
```

It is identical to a normal identifier ACE except for the inclusion of the string OPTIONS=DEFAULT between the identifiers and the access types. Once this ACE is added to a directory's ACL, any new files created in the directory are automatically assigned the ACE (minus the DEFAULT option). If there are multiple ACEs with the DEFAULT option, the file is assigned all the default ACEs in order.

Other ACE options are described in the following section and in the *OpenVMS Guide to System Security*.

18.2.2 Default Protection ACEs

A default protection ACE can reside only on the ACL of a directory. It specifies the UIC-based protection mask to be assigned to new files in the directory when no explicit mask is given. The default protection ACE applies to files that are created in the directory or in any of its subdirectories with no default protection ACE of their own. A default protection ACE has the following format:

(DEFAULT_PROTECTION, *protection-mask*)

The *protection-mask* portion of the ACE is specified in the standard system, owner, group, world format.

The following ACE, appearing on the ACL of a directory, will assign the specified protection mask to files created in that directory. The mask allows full access to the system and owner categories, read/write access to members of the group, and no access to others:

(default_protection,s:rwed,o:rwed,g:rw,w)

18.2.3 Modifying an ACL

There are two ways to modify the ACL of a file. The first method is to use the ACL editor. The ACL editor allows you to add, modify, and delete ACL entries interactively, in a manner similar to text editing. You can invoke the ACL editor with the following command:

$ edit/acl *file-spec*

The ACL editor is not described in detail in this book. See the *OpenVMS System Management Utilities Reference Manual* for a description of the ACL editor.

The second method of modifying an ACL is to use the SET SECURITY command. The command requires one parameter, a file spec that identifies one or more files whose ACLs are to be modified. The command also accepts a host of qualifiers, which specify operations to be performed on the ACLs, along with existing or new ACEs involved in the operations. The SET SECURITY command is used in a DCL procedure to add new ACEs to an ACL or to delete existing ones. Table 18.3 describes many of the qualifiers accepted by the SET SECURITY command.

Some of the qualifiers to SET SECURITY specify ACEs that are to be removed from the ACL. In this case, only the identifier portion of the ACE need be included; the options and access types do not participate in selecting ACEs to be removed.

The SET SECURITY command replaced various other commands, including SET ACL, in OpenVMS V6.0.

Table 18.3 SET SECURITY command qualifiers

Qualifier	Description
/ACL=*list-of-aces*	Specifies a list of ACEs to participate in the operation. If neither the /DELETE nor the /REPLACE qualifiers are included, the ACEs are added to the ACL at the position specified by the /AFTER qualifier.
/AFTER=*ace*	Specifies the position in the ACL at which the ACEs specified by the /ACL qualifier are inserted. They are inserted after the ACE whose identifiers are named by this qualifier. If no /AFTER qualifier is included, the ACEs are inserted at the beginning of the ACL.
/DEFAULT	If the file being modified is a directory, its ACEs are removed and replaced with the ACEs of its parent directory. If the file being modified is not a directory, its ACEs are removed and replaced with the *default* ACEs of its parent directory (those specified with OPTIONS=DEFAULT).
/DELETE	The ACEs specified by the /ACL qualifier are deleted.
/NEW	All existing ACEs are removed from the ACL before the operation specified by the other qualifiers is performed.
/REPLACE=*list-of-aces*	The ACEs specified by the /ACL qualifier are removed, and then the ACEs listed in this qualifier are inserted at the position occupied by the rightmost ACE removed.

In the following example, three ACEs are added to the ACL of a file. They are added to the beginning of the ACL because the /AFTER qualifier is not included:

```
$ set security/acl=((identifier=dexter,access=none), -
_$                  (identifier=sinister,access=none), -
_$                  (identifier=batch,access=read)) -
_$      payroll.dat
```

If these are the first ACEs ever added to the file, everything works fine. However, assume that the payroll file already had the following ACL:

```
(identifier=taylor,access=read)
(identifier=payroll_dept,access=read+write+execute+control)
```

The DEXTER and SINISTER ACEs can be added at the beginning of the ACL. However, the BATCH ACE must be added at the end so that people in the payroll department receive full access even when running batch jobs. The following two SET SECURITY commands are required to add the new ACEs correctly:

```
$ set security/acl=((identifier=dexter,access=none), -
_$                 (identifier=sinister,access=none)) -
_$      payroll.dat
$ set security/acl=(identifier=batch,access=read) -
_$           /after=(identifier=payroll_dept) payroll.dat
```

Here is the data file's ACL so far:

```
(IDENTIFIER=[AMCDEV,DEXTER],ACCESS=NONE),
(IDENTIFIER=[AMCDEV,SINISTER],ACCESS=NONE),
(IDENTIFIER=[AMCDEV,TAYLOR],ACCESS=READ),
(IDENTIFIER=PAYROLL_DEPT,ACCESS+READ+WRITE+EXECUTE+CONTROL),
(IDENTIFIER=BATCH,ACCESS=READ)
```

If the SET SECURITY command specifies an ACE that already exists in the ACL, the old ACE is replaced with the new one. However, its position in the ACL is not maintained; you must specify the position with the /AFTER qualifier. The following example replaces the batch ACE to allow both read and execute access:

```
$ set security/acl=(identifier=batch,access=read+execute) -
_$           /after=(identifier=payroll_dept) payroll.dat
```

And now the payroll file's ACL looks like this:

```
(IDENTIFIER=[AMCDEV,DEXTER],ACCESS=NONE),
(IDENTIFIER=[AMCDEV,SINISTER],ACCESS=NONE),
(IDENTIFIER=[AMCDEV,TAYLOR],ACCESS=READ),
(IDENTIFIER=PAYROLL_DEPT,ACCESS+READ+WRITE+EXECUTE+CONTROL),
(IDENTIFIER=BATCH,ACCESS=READ+EXECUTE)
```

The payroll department decides to split its personnel into two categories, those who can read the payroll file and those who can write it. The PAYROLL_DEPT identifier is replaced with two new identifiers that are named PAYROLL_READ and PAYROLL_WRITE. The following command removes the old identifier and adds the new ones in the same position:

```
$ set security/acl=(identifier=payroll_dept) -
_$           /replace=((identifier=payroll_read, -
_$                      access=read+execute), -
_$                     (identifier=payroll_write,-
_$                      access=read+write+execute+control))-
_$      payroll.dat
```

The final ACL on the payroll data file is:

```
(IDENTIFIER=[AMCDEV,DEXTER],ACCESS=NONE),
(IDENTIFIER=[AMCDEV,SINISTER],ACCESS=NONE),
(IDENTIFIER=[AMCDEV,TAYLOR],ACCESS=READ),
```

```
(IDENTIFIER=PAYROLL_READ,ACCESS=READ+EXECUTE),
(IDENTIFIER=PAYROLL_WRITE,ACCESS=READ+WRITE+EXECUTE+CONTROL),
(IDENTIFIER=BATCH,ACCESS=READ+EXECUTE)
```

18.3 Default File Protection

Sections 18.3.1 and 18.3.2 describe how OpenVMS determines the default protection mask and ACL for a new directory or file. A default protection mask is only required when you do not specify one explicitly in the command that creates the directory or file. A default ACL is always required, because there is no way to specify one in the commands that create directories and files.

18.3.1 Directories

The default protection mask for a new directory is determined as follows:

- It is always identical to the protection mask of its parent directory.

The default ACL for a new directory is determined as follows:

- It is identical to the ACL of its parent directory, except that ACEs with the `NOPROPAGATE` option are not included in the default ACL.

The `NOPROPAGATE` option can be included in a directory ACE to prevent it from being propagated to new subdirectories.

18.3.2 Files

The default protection mask for a new file is determined by following these steps:

1. If the file is a new version of an existing file, its protection mask is the same as the previous version.
2. Otherwise, if the parent directory has a default protection ACE, the protection mask is taken from the ACE.
3. Otherwise, the process default protection mask is used.

The process default protection mask is specified by the OpenVMS system generation (`SYSGEN` parameter `RMS_FILEPROT`), which is established by your system manager. You can determine its value by using the following command:

```
$ show protection
   SYSTEM=RWED, OWNER=RWED, GROUP=RE, WORLD=NO ACCESS
```

The protection mask shown in this example is the standard default. You can change the process default with the SET PROTECTION/DEFAULT command:

```
$ set protection=(s:rwed,o:rwed,g,w) /default
```

This new protection mask denies access to users in the same group. Once the default protection mask is set, it is used in step 3 above.

The authors recommend that you do not change the process default protection in a command procedure. First, it is better to be explicit and to specify the protection mask on the command that creates the file. Second, if the procedure changes the default protection, then it is responsible for restoring it to its original value before the procedure exits. This is more trouble than it is worth. Remember, even if you do change the default protection mask, the file may still receive its mask from the parent directory's default protection ACE. If the procedure requires a particular protection mask, it must specify it explicitly.

The default ACL for a new file is determined by following these steps:

1. If the file is a new version of an existing file, its ACL is the same as the ACL of the previous version. However, ACEs with the NOPROPAGATE option are not included in the new ACL.

2. Otherwise, if the parent directory has any identifier ACEs with the DEFAULT option, these ACEs make up the ACL of the new file.

3. Otherwise, the new file has no ACL.

The NOPROPAGATE option can be included in an ACE to prevent it from being propagated to new versions of the file.

A special rule is applied when you create a file whose owner is not your own UIC (e.g., using the /OWNER_UIC qualifier on the CREATE command). In this case, the file receives an additional ACE, which grants the owner's access capabilities to your UIC. In addition, it grants control access to your UIC. Therefore, regardless of the owner of a file, its creator retains control over the file.

18.4 The Access Algorithm

The exact algorithm used by OpenVMS to perform UIC-based and ACL-based protection checking is relatively complex. In particular, there are some not-so-obvious interactions between the two protection mechanisms. Assume that a particular user (the accessor) is requesting a particular type of access (e.g., write access) to a file. OpenVMS takes the following steps to determine whether access is granted:

1. If the file has no ACL, go to step 2. Otherwise perform the ACL-based protection check:
   (a) If the ACL includes an identifier ACE that grants access, then access is granted.
   (b) If the accessor is not identified in the ACL, go to step 2.
   (c) The ACL includes an identifier ACE that denies access. However:
      i. If the accessor is the owner of the file and the owner category in the protection mask grants access, then access is granted. If it does not grant access, then go to step 3.
      ii. If the accessor is in the same group as the file's owner, then go to step 3.
      iii. Go to step 3b.

2. Perform the UIC-based protection check:
   (a) If the accessor is the owner of the file and the owner category of the protection mask grants access, then access is granted.
   (b) If the world category of the protection mask grants access, then access is granted.
   (c) If the accessor is in the same group as the file's owner and the group category of the protection mask grants access, then access is granted. If it does not grant access, then go to step 3.
   (d) Go to step 3b.

3. Check various privileges that affect access:
   (a) If the accessor has GRPPRV privilege and the system category of the protection mask grants access, then access is granted.
   (b) If the accessor has system access, via a system UIC or via SYSPRV privilege, and the system category of the protection mask grants access, then access is granted.
   (c) If the accessor has BYPASS privilege, then access is granted.
   (d) If the accessor has READALL privilege and wants only read and/or control access, then access is granted.
   (e) Access is denied.

When working to debug unexpected security behaviors or access control questions, privileged users can use OpenVMS security auditing features to great advantage. Using the SET AUDIT command, audits and alarms can be enabled for many security-related user activities, and can help point to the security attributes involved.

Audits and alarms are available in OpenVMS Version 5. Additional audits and alarms are present in Version 6 and later systems. For further information, see the *OpenVMS Guide to System Security* manual.

18.5 Mandatory Access Controls

Environments requiring higher levels of system security than are available with OpenVMS can use the mandatory access controls available with SEVMS, a separately installed product.

SEVMS is a security-enhanced version of OpenVMS and implements all of the discretionary UIC- and ACL-based access control mechanisms of OpenVMS. SEVMS adds nondiscretionary object security and integrity controls, controls that are configured by the site security manager. These mandatory controls cannot be reconfigured by nonprivileged system users. The controls prevent unauthorized access to system information, and more importantly the unauthorized release of system information.

SEVMS security and security management are covered in the SEVMS documentation.

CHAPTER 19
Devices

IN CLASSICAL TERMS, A *DEVICE* is a hardware component attached to a computer for purposes of data storage or input/output. Such devices include disk drives, magnetic tape drives, printers, terminals, and so on. In the OpenVMS environment, the term *device* includes all these hardware components, along with *virtual devices* created by the OpenVMS software. Examples of virtual devices are the mailboxes used for interprocess communication, DECterm windows on VAXstation and AlphaStation monitors, and a shadowset disk device.

The purpose of some devices, particularly disk and tape drives, is to store permanent information. The magnetic medium on which information is stored is called a *volume*. Tape drives and certain disk drives have removable volumes, so a drive may contain different volumes at different times. Many newer disk drives have fixed volumes that cannot be removed from the drive, though an entire StorageWorks drive can be swapped.

DCL applications often describe or manipulate devices, usually hardware components. For example, an application might display information about the disks on a system or mount a tape volume on a tape drive. This chapter describes methods for obtaining device information and manipulating devices in DCL.

19.1 Device Names

Each device on an OpenVMS system and each device within an OpenVMS Cluster configuration has a unique *device name*. The name is used to refer to the device in file specs and DCL commands that require a device name, such as `MOUNT`. In the early days of OpenVMS, the format of device names was quite simple. The name consisted of two letters, which identified the type of device; a single letter, which identified the device controller; and an integer, which identified the particular unit attached to the controller. For example, the device name TTB3 identified a hard-wired terminal (TT) attached to the B controller and having unit number 3. Users began to *assume* that all device names consisted of four characters and that the type of device could be deduced from the first two letters.

With the advent of OpenVMS Cluster systems, terminal servers, workstations, and other innovations, such assumptions about the device name format are no longer valid. Here are some of the developments that render the assumptions obsolete:

- Not all devices have physical incarnations. A mailbox, for example, is a logical device used for communication between processes. A window on a Digital Personal Workstation display screen is a logical device, which is similar to a terminal, but many such devices may be assigned to the same display screen.

- Devices that are available to all nodes in an OpenVMS Cluster system have a segmented name. The first segment is the name of the node to which the device is connected, or the system or port allocation class of the device. The second segment is a conventional device name. The segments are separated by a dollar sign. A disk connected to node `WILTON` might have the name `WILTON$DKA200`. A disk served by two OpenVMS systems in allocation class 1 might have the name `$1$DKA500`.

- A terminal server supports many physical terminals that are not connected directly to an OpenVMS system. The terminal server is a single device that appears to the user as multiple devices.

It is not valid to assume that a device name is four characters long, that the first two characters accurately identify the type of device, that the device is physically connected to the local VAX or Alpha system, or that the device is accessable via only a single controller or host path.

19.2 Device Information

The characteristics of a device cannot be determined from its name, but they can be determined using the `F$GETDVI` lexical function. This function requires two arguments. The first is a string containing the device name. The

Table 19.1 F$GETDVI items	Keyword	Type	Description of result
	`"ALL"`	Boolean	True if the device is allocated to a user, false if it is available.
	`"DEVCLASS"`	Integer	The class of the device. See the *OpenVMS DCL Dictionary* for a list of classes.
	`"DEVBUFSIZ"`	Integer	The device buffer size, and the width of the line on a terminal.
	`"DEVNAM"`	String	The name of the device.
	`"DEVTYPE"`	Integer	The type of the device. See the *OpenVMS DCL Dictionary* for a list of types.
	`"EXISTS"`	Boolean	True if the device exists, false if not.
	`"FREEBLOCKS"`	Integer	The number of available blocks on a disk device.
	`"FULLDEVNAM"`	String	The fully qualified device name, which includes the node name in a OpenVMS Cluster environment.
	`"MAXBLOCK"`	Integer	The number of blocks on a disk device.
	`"MNT"`	Boolean	True if a volume is mounted on a disk or tape device, false if not.
	`"TT_PAGE"`	Integer	The length of the page setting on a terminal.
	`"VOLNAM"`	String	The name of the volume mounted on a disk or tape drive.

second is a keyword string specifying the item of information desired. The information is returned as an integer, string, or Boolean, depending upon the item requested.

The device name is usually specified as the name by itself, but you can also specify a file spec or a logical name that includes the device. The lexical function ignores everything but the device name. Table 19.1 describes a few of the item keywords; many more are available.

If `F$GETDVI` is called with an invalid device name, it signals an error. If you are not absolutely sure that a device name is valid (e.g., it was entered by a user), call `F$GETDVI` with the `"EXISTS"` keyword. This is the one exception to the rule that the function signals an error for invalid devices. Instead, it returns a true value if the device exists, a false value if it does not. If the device does not exist, you cannot use `F$GETDVI` to obtain any other information about it.

Once you know that a device exists, you can use any of the item keywords to obtain information about that device. One important item is the device class (`"DEVCLASS"`). The device class denotes the general category of device, such as disk, tape, terminal, or line printer. Each class is represented by an integer;

a complete list of device classes is available in the *OpenVMS DCL Dictionary*. The device class is useful when the user has entered a device to be used for a specific purpose, such as the target of a backup operation. In this case, the procedure can verify that the device is a disk or tape.

Another important item is the device name ("DEVNAM"). It may seem silly to have an item that returns the device name, but remember that the first argument to F$GETDVI need not be a device name by itself. It may be a logical name or a full file spec. In these cases, the device name item is used to extract the actual device name, by itself, without any other elements of the file spec.

Here is an example of the use of F$GETDVI:

```
$10:    libcall ask xda_dev s "Backup device:"
$       dev_ok = f$getdvi(xda_dev,"EXISTS")
$       if dev_ok
$       then
$         backup_dev_name  = f$getdvi(xda_dev,"DEVNAM")
$         backup_dev_class = f$getdvi(xda_dev,"DEVCLASS")
$         dev_ok = backup_dev_class .eq. 1 .or. -
                  backup_dev_class .eq. 2
$         if .not. dev_ok then libcall signal xda i baddevcl -
                              "Device must be a disk or tape."
$       else
$         libcall signal xda i nosuchdev -
                              "Device ''xda_dev does not exist."
$       endif
$       if .not. dev_ok then goto 10
$19:
```

This example uses a loop to repeatedly ask the user for a backup device until a valid disk or tape name is entered. Once the loop terminates, the symbol BACKUP_DEV_NAME contains the device name and BACKUP_DEV_CLASS contains its class number. (The device class constant values are included in the system Macro32 definition libraries, in the SYS$LIBRARY:LIB.MLB module $DCDEF.)

The F$GETDVI lexical function can return an astounding amount of information about a device. You should consult the *OpenVMS DCL Dictionary* for complete details.

19.3 Obtaining a List of the Devices on a System

You may find yourself implementing a particularly sophisticated DCL application, which needs to obtain a list of every device on the system or perhaps all the disks or terminals. For example, an application that monitors the free space on mounted disks needs a list of all disks. Unfortunately, there is no straightforward way to obtain such a list in DCL. You must obtain the list using a somewhat devious technique.

First of all, generate a list of all devices, using the SHOW DEVICE command. The output from the command can be directed to a file with the /OUTPUT qualifier. The /MOUNTED qualifier can be used to restrict the list to only those devices with volumes mounted on them. The file will contain a list in roughly the following format:

Device Name	Device Status	Error Count	Volume Label	Free Blocks	Trans Count	Mnt Cnt
WILTON$DKA0:	Mounted	0	WILTONSYS	2654550	494	1
WILTON$DKA100:	Online	1				
WILTON$DKA200:	Online wrtlck	0				
WILTON$DKA400:	Online wrtlck	0				
WILTON$DVA0:	Online	0				

Device Name	Device Status	Error Count	Volume Label	Free Blocks	Trans Count	Mnt Cnt
WILTON$MKA500:	Online	1				

Device Name	Device Status	Error Count
FTA0:	Offline	0
FTA1:	Online	0
FTA5:	Online	0
.		
.		
WSA0:	Offline	0
WSA1:	Online	0
WSA2:	Online	0

Note that there are blank lines, heading lines, and lines describing devices. A list of devices is obtained by opening the file and reading the lines, one at a time, looking for those lines that contain a device description. The device name is extracted from the line and added to the list. The following code builds a list of all tape drives:

```
$       libcall unique_name xda_show sys$scratch:xda_?.lis
$       show device/output='xda_show
$       open/read xda_show 'xda_show
$       tape_list = ""
$10:    read xda_show line /end_of_file=19
$       if f$locate(":", line) .eq. f$length(line) then -
            goto 10
$       dev = f$edit(f$element(0, ":", line), "COLLAPSE")
```

19.3 Obtaining a List of the Devices on a System 249

```
$          if f$getdvi(dev,"EXISTS") then -
$              if f$getdvi(dev,"DEVCLASS") .eq. 2 then -
$                  tape_list = tape_list + dev + ","
$          goto 10
$19:   close xda_show
$      delete 'xda_show;*
```

Notice how careful the code is to ensure that what it finds is indeed a tape device. If the line does not contain a colon, then it is blank or a heading and is ignored. Once the device name is extracted, F$GETDVI is used to ensure both that the name represents an existing device *and* that the device is a tape drive. The existence check may seem superfluous, but it serves two purposes. First, it guarantees that a real device name has been extracted from the device listing. Second, it guards against a device that existed when the SHOW DEVICE was performed but has subsequently disappeared (e.g., a temporary mailbox or remote terminal). When the loop terminates, the symbol TAPE_LIST contains a list of the tape drives available to the system.

(Note that this example, along with others in the book, does not take into account the possibility that a string such as TAPE_LIST might ultimately exceed the maximum length allowed for a string.)

Do not extract any additional information from the device listing file; instead use F$GETDVI. The format of the listing file may change in a future release of OpenVMS. We are taking enough of a chance with the assumption that the device name begins in column zero and ends with a colon. Never extract information from listing files unless *absolutely necessary*. OpenVMS makes no guarantee that the format of listings will remain the same.

The SHOW DEVICE command accepts a generic device name parameter, in which case it includes only those devices in the listing. For example, SHOW DEVICE T produces a listing of devices whose name begins with the letter T. It is tempting to use this command to produce a list of the terminals on the system. Don't forget, however, that many terminal names will begin with T; DECserver LAT terminals begin with LT, and virtual terminals begin with VT. Further, you may find that a command intended to list the tape devices on the system, SHOW DEVICE M, will also find a variety of MB mailbox devices. Always use F$GETDVI to determine the class of a device.

19.4 Terminal Characteristics

Associated with each terminal device is information called the *terminal characteristics*. Some of the characteristics specify features of the terminal, for example, whether it accepts ANSI escape sequences or is connected to a modem. Other characteristics control the behavior of the terminal, for example, whether line editing is allowed or whether lines wrap when the cursor reaches the right margin. Terminal characteristics can be modified with the SET TERMINAL command, and there is an F$GETDVI item keyword that can be used to obtain each characteristic. Most terminal characteristics do not affect a DCL procedure, because DCL has only rudimentary facilities for dealing with terminal displays and keyboards.

One characteristic that a DCL application might use is the "ANSI CRT" characteristic ("TT_ANSICRT"). This is a Boolean characteristic that is true if the terminal accepts ANSI standard control sequences, false if not. An application that sends control sequences to the terminal for screen formatting should first check the terminal to determine whether the sequences will be obeyed:

See Sec. 6.2, p. 76

```
$!   Make sure we have an ANSI terminal to display on.
$
$    output_dev = f$getdvi("sys$output","DEVNAM")
$    if f$getdvi(output_dev,"DEVCLASS") .eq. 66
$    then
$      if .not. f$getdvi(output_dev,"TT_ANSICRT") then -
          libcall signal xda f notansi -
              "This application runs only on ANSI terminals."
$    else
$      libcall signal xda f notterm -
              "This application requires a terminal."
$    endif
```

The code determines the device to which output will be displayed. It then checks to make sure the device is a terminal, in particular an ANSI terminal. If either check fails, a fatal error is signaled and the application terminates.

19.5 Device Allocation

A procedure can request exclusive use of a device by *allocating* the device. Once a device is allocated to a process, no other process can use the device until the original process deallocates it. The devices most commonly allocated are disk and tape drives. A procedure might allocate a disk drive in order to initialize a new disk volume and prepare it for use by some application. A procedure might allocate a tape drive for use in a disk backup operation.

A device is allocated with the ALLOCATE command. The ALLOCATE command has three forms, described in the following paragraphs.

In its simplest form, the ALLOCATE command accepts a list of devices, one of which it allocates. It checks the devices in the order specified and allocates the first one available. The command also accepts an optional second parameter, which must be a logical name. This logical name is defined to refer to the allocated device, so you can tell which one was actually allocated. The following example requests exclusive use of tape drive MKA0 or MKA100:

```
$    allocate mka0,mka100 xda_tape_drive
```

OpenVMS first tries to allocate MKA0 and then MKA100. The first available drive is allocated to the process. If neither are available, an error is signaled. The process logical name XDA_TAPE_DRIVE is defined as MKA0: or MKA100:, as appropriate.

The ALLOCATE command can also accept a group of devices; it will try to allocate one of the devices in that group. A group can consist of all the devices with a particular two-letter type (e.g., MK), or all the devices on a particular controller (e.g., DUA). The following example attempts to allocate a SCSI disk drive:

```
$    allocate dk scsi_disk_drive
```

OpenVMS tries to allocate any device whose name contains the device type DK, that is, a SCSI disk drive. If one is allocated, the logical name SCSI_DISK_DRIVE is defined to refer to it.

The first two letters of a device name do not always refer to a specific type of device. For example, DU is used for the name of the entire RA and RD families of disks, including the RA90, RA92, and RD54, whereas the DK prefix is used for SCSI disks. If you want to allocate a specific type of device, use the third form of the ALLOCATE command. Include the /GENERIC qualifier and a list of device types rather than device names:

```
$    allocate/generic ra92 xda_disk_drive
```

OpenVMS tries to allocate any RA92 device, ignoring all other disk types, including the RA90.

The /LOG qualifier can be used to control information displayed by the ALLOCATE command. If /LOG is specified (the default), then the command displays the name of the allocated device. In addition, if the logical name is already defined, the command displays a message explaining that the logical name's value is being superseded. The /NOLOG qualifier suppresses both of these messages.

The following example asks the user for the type of a device to be allocated and performs the allocation:

```
$10:    libcall ask xda_dev s "Type of device to allocate:"
$       set noon
$       allocate/generic/nolog 'xda_dev xda_device
$       status = $status
```

```
$       set on
$       if status then goto 19
$       libcall signal xda i cantalloc -
                "No ''xda_dev can be allocated." 'status
$       goto 10
$19:
$       display "Device ''f$trnlnm("xda_device") was allocated."
```

The code contains a loop, which asks the user for a device type and attempts to allocate such a device. Once the allocation is successful, the procedure displays the name of the device by translating the logical name XDA_DEVICE. Note the use of the /NOLOG qualifier on the ALLOCATE command to prevent its status messages from being displayed.

A device is deallocated using the DEALLOCATE command. The logical name defined by the ALLOCATE command is specified as the name of the device to deallocate:

```
$       deallocate xda_device
```

The /ALL qualifier can be used to deallocate all devices allocated by the current process:

```
$       deallocate/all
```

All devices allocated to a process are deallocated when the process is deleted. In particular, all devices allocated during an interactive session are deallocated when the user logs out.

19.6 Volume Initialization

A new disk or magnetic tape volume must be *initialized* before data can be recorded on it. The INITIALIZE command prepares a formatted volume for use by OpenVMS. The command requires two parameters, the first of which is the name of the device on which the new volume is mounted. The second parameter is the *volume label* for the new volume. The volume label is limited to 12 characters for a disk volume, six for a magnetic tape volume. The label is recorded on the volume and identifies it for future use.

The INITIALIZE command formats the volume for use by OpenVMS. By default, a disk is formatted according to "Files-11 Structure Level 2." This is the standard format for disks that will contain OpenVMS directories and files. Again by default, a tape is formatted according to "level 3 of the ANSI standard for magnetic tape labels and file structure for informational interchange" (ANSI X3.27-1978). This is the current standard format for magnetic tapes.

Within these standards there are many options, which affect the logical format of the volume. These options can be specified using a large number of qualifiers to the `INITIALIZE` command. These qualifiers are described in the *OpenVMS DCL Dictionary*.

The following example allocates a nine-track magnetic tape drive and initializes a new magnetic tape volume:

```
$    allocate mt xda_tape_drive
$    libcall ask xda_label s "Label for new tape volume:" -
              "" u
$    display "Please load a new tape volume on drive ", -
             f$trnlnm("xda_tape_drive")
$    libcall ask xda_ s "Press RETURN when ready:" continue
$    initialize/density=6250 xda_tape_drive 'xda_label
```

This code allocates an `MT` tape drive, typically a nine-track magnetic tape. It then asks the user for a label for the new volume and requests that the volume be mounted on the drive. Finally, the new volume is initialized. The `/DENSITY` qualifier specifies the density (in bits per inch) at which the nine-track magnetic tape volume is written.

A volume cannot be initialized if it has already been mounted with the `MOUNT` command, described in the next section.

19.7 Volume Mounting

The term *mounting* refers to the process by which the system recognizes a data volume on a storage device, such as a disk or magnetic tape drive. Not until a volume is mounted can its files be created and manipulated by OpenVMS programs. Before a volume can be mounted it must be physically **loaded** on the device by a human being, or by a media library robot. Be careful to distinguish the physical loading process from the system's mounting process.

The `MOUNT` command is used to mount a volume. It has the following general format:

```
$    mount device label logical-name
```

The *device* parameter specifies the device on which the volume is to be mounted. The parameter can name a specific device, or it can specify a device group, as in the `ALLOCATE` command. The *label* parameter specifies the label of the volume being mounted. This parameter is only required in some circumstances, described below. The *logical-name* parameter specifies a logical name, which is defined to refer to the device on which the volume is ulti-

Table 19.2 MOUNT command qualifiers

Qualifier	Default?	Description
/ASSIST	✓	Operator intervention is requested if a failure occurs during the mount operation.
/NOASSIST		The command will immediately terminate on failures, and the user must intervene if a failure occurs.
/FOREIGN		The magnetic tape volume is not in standard ANSI format, or the disk volume does not use a standard OpenVMS file structure. No volume label or header checking is performed. Tapes used by the BACKUP utility are mounted foreign.
/GROUP		The volume is made available to other users in the same UIC group. This qualifier requires GRPNAM privilege.
/LABEL	✓	The volume is in standard ANSI format. Volume label and header checking are performed.
/OVERRIDE		This qualifier accepts keyword values, which specify steps in the mount sequence that are to be bypassed. The keyword IDENTIFICATION specifies that volume label checking is not performed. In this case, no label needs to be specified on the MOUNT command.
/SHARE		The disk volume is made shareable. The device is not allocated by the current process.
/SYSTEM		The volume is made public; all system users can access it. This qualifier requires SYSNAM privilege.

mately mounted. All future references to the device should be made through this logical name.

The MOUNT command accepts a number of qualifiers, some of which are described in Table 19.2. You should familiarize yourself with the qualifiers before reading further.

The MOUNT command performs the following steps:

1. If a specific device is named, the command ensures that the device is unallocated or already allocated to the current process. If a device group is specified, the command locates an available device in that group. (The command does not search for a device containing the volume with the requested label; it merely locates one that is unallocated.)

2. If the /GROUP, /SHARE, or /SYSTEM qualifiers are specified, the command deallocates the device if necessary. Otherwise, it is allocated to the current process.

3. The command ensures that a volume is physically loaded on the device.

4. Unless the /FOREIGN or /OVERRIDE=IDENTIFICATION qualifiers are specified, the command checks the volume label against the label specified on the MOUNT command.

5. The command prepares the volume for input/output operations.

6. The command defines one or two logical names to refer to the mounted device. The logical names are defined in the process logical name table by default, the group table if /GROUP is specified, or the system table if /SYSTEM is specified. If a logical name is specified in the MOUNT command, it is defined. Regardless of the specification of a logical name by the user, the MOUNT command defines logical name DISK$*label* or TAPE$*label*, as appropriate. The *label* portion of the name is identical to the volume label.

The MOUNT command has many more options than are described here. Also note that qualifier defaults vary by the mode—batch or interactive—of the procedure performing the MOUNT command. The *OpenVMS System Management Utilities Reference Manual* describes the command in complete detail.

CHAPTER 20
Processes

THE OPENVMS ENVIRONMENT in which DCL commands are executed and programs are run is called the *process*. A process provides the structure and information necessary to run the program images that make up DCL, OpenVMS utilities, and application software. A component of OpenVMS called the *scheduler* is responsible for periodically choosing a process to run on each VAX or Alpha processor. The scheduler must ensure that all processes get their fair share of the VAX or Alpha execution cycles. The following components are associated with every OpenVMS process:

- A set of data structures containing control information for the process. These structures are maintained by OpenVMS in an area of system memory called *S0 space*. Some of the control information is described in the next section.

- A private area of virtual memory called *P0 space*. A program image invoked with the RUN command or directly with its own command (e.g., PHONE) is executed in P0 space.

- A private area of virtual memory called *P1 space*. When a process is being controlled by the DCL command interpreter, the DCL program image is located and running in P1 space. Symbols and process logical names are maintained in P1 space. Information about executing command procedures, as well as temporary stack storage for images, is also maintained in P1 space.

OpenVMS supports various kinds of processes, five of which you are likely to encounter in your adventures with OpenVMS:

Interactive An *interactive process* is created when you log in to OpenVMS at a terminal. The DCL command interpreter resides in P1 space and reads commands from the terminal. OpenVMS treats an interactive process as an autonomous entity, which remains in existence until you log out.

Batch A *batch process* is created when you submit a batch job to a job queue with the `SUBMIT` command. The batch queues and jobs are controlled by the OpenVMS job controller.

⚑ Chap. 21, p. 277

Network A *network process* is created when a process on another DECnet node attempts to communicate with the local node. This communication may result from copying a file to or from the local node, sending mail to a user, or calling the user with the `PHONE` utility. A network process is also created when a remote user logs in to the local node with the `SET HOST` command.

⚑ Chap. 23, p. 299

Subprocess A *subprocess* is a separate OpenVMS process, which is created and owned by another process. Subprocesses are described in this chapter.

Other An "other process" is a separate OpenVMS process that uses the DCL command interpreter, but does not have an associated terminal or interactive user. Detached processes running the DCL interpreter, as well as the system startup process, are examples of other processes.

Interactive, batch, network, and other processes are collectively called *detached processes* because they are not attached to or owned by any other process. A subprocess is not a detached process because it is owned by some other process.

20.1 Information about the Current Process

OpenVMS maintains a plethora of information about each process. The information is used to identify the process and control its execution. Much of the important information can be obtained from within a DCL procedure using one of two techniques.

The primary technique for obtaining information about the current process is the `F$GETJPI` lexical function. The acronym `GETJPI` stands for "get job and process information." The lexical function requires two arguments. The first is a process identifier, which for the current process is the null string. The second is a keyword string specifying the desired item of informa-

Table 20.1 F$GETJPI items

Keyword	Type	Description of result
"ACCOUNT"	String	The billing account, padded with spaces to eight characters. The billing account is stored in the user's record in the user authorization file (UAF).
"AUTHPRIV"	String	A list of the authorized privileges of the process. These are stored in the user's UAF record.
"CPUTIM"	Integer	The CPU time used by the process, in hundredths of a second.
"CURPRIV"	String	A list of the current privileges of the process.
"GRP"	Integer	The group number of the UIC. This is stored in the user's UAF record.
"LOGINTIM"	String	The date and time the process was created.
"MEM"	Integer	The member number of the UIC. This is stored in the user's UAF record.
"MODE"	String	The process mode: "INTERACTIVE", "BATCH", "NETWORK", or "OTHER".
"PRCNAM"	String	The process name.
"TERMINAL"	String	The terminal at which an interactive user logged in.
"USERNAME"	String	The user name, padded with spaces to 12 characters. This is the name used to log in to OpenVMS and is the key to the user's UAF record.

tion. Table 20.1 describes some of the commonly used process information items. The F$GETJPI function returns the current value of the requested item, as either an integer or a character string. The following code displays the user name, billing account, and login time for the current process:

```
$    display "User Name: ", f$getjpi("","USERNAME")
$    display "Account:   ", f$getjpi("","ACCOUNT")
$    display "Login Time: ", f$getjpi("","LOGINTIM")
```

One of the items that F$GETJPI can return is the *process mode*. The mode is a keyword string: "INTERACTIVE" for an interactive process and its subprocess; "BATCH" for a batch process and its subprocesses; "NETWORK" for a network process and its subprocesses; "OTHER" for all other kinds of processes. The mode can be used in a procedure to determine, for example, whether an interactive user is available to answer questions:

```
$    interactive = f$getjpi("","MODE") .eqs. "INTERACTIVE"
       .
       .
```

```
$     if interactive
$     then
         ⋮ ask some questions
$     endif
```

The F$GETJPI function obtains the mode of the process and the assignment command sets the symbol INTERACTIVE to true if the mode is interactive, false otherwise. The symbol is tested later in the procedure to determine whether to ask questions of the interactive user.

An alternative method that deals with all four process modes is often useful to structure the commands present in a login command procedure:

```
$     goto 10_'f$getjpi("","MODE")
$10_INTERACTIVE:
         ⋮ perform steps only valid for interactive processes; fall through
$10_BATCH:
         ⋮ equate symbols and invoke various supporting procedures; fall through
$10_NETWORK:
         ⋮ set up various logical names; fall through
$10_OTHER:
         ⋮ perform just the most basic steps needed in all modes
$     exit
```

Three items of information available with F$GETJPI can also be obtained with other lexical functions. The process mode can be obtained with F$MODE, the name with F$PROCESS, and the UIC with F$USER. These functions were available before F$GETJPI was introduced into DCL. The authors suggest that you use F$GETJPI rather than the three other lexical functions, both for consistency and because the names F$PROCESS and F$USER are potentially misleading.

Additional process information, mostly related to the DCL environment, can be obtained with the F$ENVIRONMENT lexical function. This function takes one argument, a keyword string specifying the desired item. It returns the current value of the item as an integer or character string. Table 20.2 describes some important items of environment information, most of which have already been described in previous chapters. The following example uses F$ENVIRONMENT:

```
$     this_proc = f$environment("PROCEDURE")
$     proc_dir = f$parse(this_proc,,,"DEVICE") + -
                 f$parse(this_proc,,,"DIRECTORY")
```

Table 20.2 F$ENVIRONMENT items

Keyword	Type	Description of result
"CAPTIVE"	Boolean	True if the process was created by logging in to a captive user account.
"DEFAULT"	String	The working device and directory, as established with the SET DEFAULT command.
"MESSAGE"	String	The current message settings, as established with the SET MESSAGE command.
"PROCEDURE"	String	The full file spec of the executing command procedure.
"VERIFY_IMAGE"	Boolean	True if the SET VERIFY=IMAGE command is in effect.
"VERIFY_PROCEDURE"	Boolean	True if the SET VERIFY=PROCEDURE command is in effect.

```
$    define xda_system 'proc_dir
     .
     .
$    @xda_system:xda_another-proc
```

The F$ENVIRONMENT function obtains the file spec of the executing procedure. The logical name XDA_SYSTEM is defined to refer to the device and directory containing the procedure. This logical name can then be used to refer to any file in the procedure directory, such as another procedure that must be invoked by the current one.

20.2 Information about Other Processes

The F$GETJPI lexical function can be used to obtain information about processes other than the current one. Its first argument is a *process identifier*, or PID. A PID is an integer that uniquely identifies a process from among all the processes on the system. In fact, in an OpenVMS Cluster configuration, the PID uniquely identifies a process from among all processes on all nodes of the cluster. OpenVMS assigns a PID during the creation of each process. The format and the allocation sequence of the PID is opaque and undocumented; you should not make any assumptions around it.

If you know the PID of a process, you can obtain information about the process. However, it is rarely the case that a procedure can determine the PID of some arbitrary process. It could attempt to ask the user for one, but the user probably doesn't know either. Instead of trying to determine the

PID of a specific process, the procedure uses the F$PID lexical function to obtain information about *every* process, perhaps selecting some subset of the processes to display or alter.

The F$PID function requires a single argument, called the ***context symbol***. The context symbol must be initialized to the null string before the first call. On the first call, F$PID returns the PID of the first process in the system's process table. The PID is returned as a *string* containing the external representation of the integer identifying the process (e.g., "%X02000024"). The fact that it is returned as a string is a holdover from the time when DCL represented integers as character strings. The F$PID function also updates the context symbol, so on the next call it returns the PID of the second process in the table. This continues until there are no more processes, at which point the function returns the null string.

The F$PID function returns the identifiers of some or all of the processes on the system, depending upon the privileges of the requesting process. If the process has WORLD privilege, every PID is returned. If it has GROUP but not WORLD privilege, only the PIDs of processes in the same group are returned. If it has neither, then only the PIDs of processes with the same UIC are returned.

The F$GETJPI function expects a PID as its first argument (as a special case, it accepts the null string or a PID of zero to identify the current process). The function can accept either an integer or a string as the PID, which allows the string returned by F$PID to be used as the first argument to F$GETJPI. In this way, F$GETJPI can obtain information about a process whose identifier was returned by F$PID.

Suppose you are writing a procedure to shut down the system. As part of the shutdown sequence, the procedure lists the processes that still exist on the system. However, it does not want to include system processes or system users, those processes with UICs in groups MAXSYSGROUP and below. The following code accomplishes this task:

```
$       display "Non-system processes:"
$       process_count = 0
$       context = ""
$10:    pid = f$pid(context)
$       if pid .eqs. "" then goto 19
$       if f$getjpi(pid,"GRP") .le. -
            f$getsyi("MAXSYSGROUP") then goto 10
$       display f$fao("!16AS (!AS)", f$getjpi(pid,"PRCNAM"), -
                                    f$getjpi(pid,"MODE"))
$       process_count = process_count + 1
$       goto 10
$19:
```

```
$       if process_count .eq. 0 then -
            display "There are no such processes."
$       if process_count .ne. 0 then -
            display "Process count: ", process_count
```

When this example is run, it produces output something like the following:

```
Non-system processes:
CAPTIVE1_1          (INTERACTIVE)
MARION              (INTERACTIVE)
MARION_1            (INTERACTIVE)
BATCH_1922          (BATCH)
LES_1               (INTERACTIVE)
AMC_MAINT           (INTERACTIVE)
CAPTIVE1            (INTERACTIVE)
HOFFMAN             (INTERACTIVE)
LES                 (INTERACTIVE)
BASE                (INTERACTIVE)
BASE_1              (INTERACTIVE)
Process count:   11
```

The F$PID and F$GETJPI functions provide a powerful mechanism for determining the status of any processes on an OpenVMS system or OpenVMS Cluster. There is no way to obtain the DCL environment information for a process other than the current one (the F$ENVIRONMENT function does not accept a PID).

20.3 Setting Process Information

OpenVMS provides various commands to establish or alter the current process environment. These commands are listed in Table 20.3, along with the chapters in which they are described. All but two have been described in previous chapters.

The SET PROCESS/PRIVILEGES command can be used to set the current process privileges to a specified list of privileges. This command is rarely used in procedures because it does not provide a straightforward way to save the user's privilege settings, alter them, and then restore them to the original settings. The F$SETPRV lexical function is designed to serve exactly this purpose. It should be used in place of the SET command to establish the privileges for a procedure.

Sec. 7.1.4, p. 86

The process name can be altered with the SET PROCESS/NAME command. The name is composed of any characters, including lowercase letters, but is restricted to 15 characters in length. OpenVMS chooses a process name for

Table 20.3 Commands to set process environment

Environment item	Command	Chapter
Default directory	SET DEFAULT	7
Message settings	SET MESSAGE	7
Privileges	SET PROCESS/PRIVILEGES=*list*	20
Process name	SET PROCESS/NAME="*name*"	20
User identification code (UIC)	SET UIC (obsolete)	7
Process rights	SET RIGHTS	18
Verification	SET VERIFY	12

each process as it is created. In the case of interactive processes, the process name is the same as the user name for the user's first process and the same as the terminal name for subsequent processes. In the case of batch processes, the process name consists of the word BATCH with a numeric suffix.

20.4 Subprocesses

A subprocess is a separate OpenVMS process, created by an existing process and owned by that process. The owner is called the *parent* and the subprocess is called the *child*. A process that is not a subprocess is a detached process: the interactive process created when you log in is a detached process.

A DCL procedure creates a subprocess using the SPAWN command. The SPAWN command is complex, and you probably will become comfortable with it only after some experimentation. The following paragraphs describe the command in detail. Table 20.4 lists many of the qualifiers accepted by SPAWN. A process must have the TMPMBX or PRMMBX privilege in order to use the SPAWN command.

When a subprocess is created with the SPAWN command, it inherits some of the environment of the parent process. In particular:

- The child always inherits the parent's current process privileges, as both its current and authorized privileges.

- The child always inherits the working disk and directory.

- The child always inherits the message settings established with the DCL command SET MESSAGE.

- The child can inherit the parent's global, prompt-level, and procedure-level symbols, as controlled by the /SYMBOLS qualifier. The child never inherits the $RESTART, $SEVERITY, or $STATUS symbols.

Sec. 21.4, p. 283

Table 20.4 SPAWN command qualifiers

Qualifier	Default?	Description
/INPUT=*file-spec*		Specifies a procedure file containing commands to be executed by the subprocess. If neither this qualifier nor a command string is included on the SPAWN command, input is taken from the terminal.
/LOGICAL_NAMES	✓	The child inherits the parent's logical names.
/NOLOGICAL_NAMES		The child does not inherit the parent's logical names.
/OUTPUT=*file-spec*		Specifies a file that receives the output from the subprocess. If not included, output is directed to the same destination as the parent's SYS$OUTPUT.
/PROCESS=*name*		Specifies a name for the subprocess. If not specified, the name consists of the parent's name with an integer suffix.
/SYMBOLS	✓	The child inherits the parent's global, prompt-level, and procedure-level symbols.
/NOSYMBOLS		The child does not inherit the parent's symbols.
/TRUSTED		The SPAWN operation is trusted and is permissible from within a captive command procedure.
/WAIT	✓	The parent suspends execution until the child terminates.
/NOWAIT		The parent and child execute simultaneously.

- The child can inherit the process logical names and name tables, as controlled by the /LOGICAL_NAMES qualifier.

It is also important to note the environment items that are *not* inherited by the subprocess:

Sec. 20.5, p. 269

- The child does not inherit the standard process-permanent files SYS$COMMAND, SYS$INPUT, SYS$OUTPUT, and SYS$ERROR. These files are established separately for the subprocess.

- The child does not inherit the parent's current DCL command table. It always uses the standard table unless changed by the subprocess itself.

- The child does not execute a LOGIN.COM procedure.

- The child does not inherit the parent's authorized privileges.

20.4 Subprocesses

The `SPAWN` command creates a subprocess with the described environment. The child runs independently of the parent, executing commands determined by the parameters and qualifiers to the `SPAWN` command:

- The `SPAWN` command accepts an optional command string consisting of a single DCL command to be executed by the child. If the command string is present, the command is executed immediately after the child process is created and initialized. This command can be a procedure invocation using @.

- The `SPAWN` command accepts an optional /INPUT qualifier, which specifies a procedure file. The procedure file becomes the child's process-permanent SYS$INPUT file, thus causing the child to execute the procedure.

- If both the command string and the /INPUT qualifier are present, the command string is executed first, then the input procedure.

- If neither are present, the child reads commands from the terminal. In the case of a subprocess spawned from a batch job, however, the process terminates immediately, having no source of commands to execute.

Subprocess input and output is described in more detail in Section 20.5.

The subprocess executes its commands independently of the parent. The action taken by the parent during the execution of the child depends on the /WAIT qualifier. If /WAIT is specified on the `SPAWN` command (it is the default), then the parent ceases execution until the child is done. If /NOWAIT is specified, the parent and child execute simultaneously. When the `SPAWN` command is entered at the DCL prompt, both forms of the qualifier are useful. You may want to use the /WAIT qualifier to suspend the main process while you do some other work in a subprocess. Or you may want to use the /NOWAIT qualifier to execute a time-consuming command in a subprocess while continuing to edit a file in the main process. On the other hand, when the `SPAWN` command is used in a procedure, the /NOWAIT qualifier is almost always used so that the two processes can execute simultaneously.

The use of the /NOWAIT qualifier requires some synchronization between the parent and child processes; one method of synchronization is described in Sections 20.6 and 20.7.

20.4.1 Examples

Sec. 9.1, p. 105

The `SPAWN` command is one of the DCL commands that can be executed at the temporary command level created by a CTRL/Y interrupt. When you press CTRL/Y during the execution of a program, a temporary command level is created by DCL. The SPAWN command can be entered at this level in order to create a subprocess. The subprocess can execute arbitrary DCL commands without affecting the parent process. When you log out of the subprocess and enter the CONTINUE command at the temporary command level, the command level is canceled and the original program resumes execution. This technique allows you to interrupt a lengthy program, perform some other activities (e.g., read a new mail message), and then resume the program.

Here is an example of a temporary command level:

```
$ search xda_system:*.com error
        .
        . output from search
        .
```
Interrupt
```
$ spawn
%DCL-S-SPAWNED, process HOFFMAN_1 spawned
%DCL-S-ATTACHED, terminal now attached to process HOFFMAN_1
$ mail
        .
        . read your mail
        .
MAIL> exit
$ logout
   Process HOFFMAN_1 logged out at  3-APR-1998 19:30:21.04
%DCL-S-RETURNED, control returned to process HOFFMAN
$ continue
        .
        . more output from search
        .
```

During the search operation, the user presses CTRL/Y to create a temporary command level. The SPAWN command creates a subprocess in which the MAIL utility can be used. The subprocess is ultimately terminated with the LOGOUT command, and the search operation is resumed with the CONTINUE command.

The /NOWAIT qualifier can be used on a SPAWN command entered at the DCL prompt in order to initiate the simultaneous execution of a time-consuming command:

```
$ spawn/nowait/output=error.sea search xda_system:*.com error
```

In this case, the same search operation is performed in a subprocess executing at the same time as the parent process. The /OUTPUT qualifier is used to direct the subprocess output to a file so that the output does not clutter the terminal screen and also so that it is collected in one place for future reference.

The SPAWN command can be used in a procedure to create a parallel flow of execution when an application needs to do two things at once. Section 20.7

presents a complete example of this technique. Here are a few examples of just the SPAWN command:

```
$!    Create a subprocess to execute the background sampling
$!    procedure.  Don't let it inherit any symbols.
$
$     spawn/nowait/nosymbols @xda_system:xda_sampler
```

—or—

```
$!    The same thing can be accomplished using the /INPUT
$!    qualifier, but it really isn't as clear to the reader.
$
$     spawn/nowait/nosymbols /input=xda_system:xda_sampler
```

—or—

```
$!    In particular, if the procedure requires any parameters,
$!    they can only be passed using the first form of the
$!    command:
$
$     spawn/nowait/nosymbols @xda_system:xda_sampler -
                    sys$sysdevice 1:00:00
```

20.4.2 Inheriting Symbols and Logical Names

When a child subprocess is created with the SPAWN command, the subprocess normally inherits the symbols and logical names of its parent. The /NOSYMBOLS qualifier prevents symbols from being inherited, while the /NOLOGICAL_NAMES qualifier prevents logical names from being inherited.

Symbol inheritance should be avoided if at all possible. A procedure should not pass information to a child subprocess by creating symbols with the information and then allowing the subprocess to inherit the symbols. This implicit method of passing information to the subprocess is not at all obvious to a reader of the procedure and may be difficult to maintain in the future. Instead, the parent procedure can pass information to the child procedure in the form of procedure parameters. Another reason to avoid symbol inheritance is that it takes significant time during subprocess creation to pass the symbols from the parent to the child.

Neither global nor local symbols are visible across processes, and the values are passed from the parent to the child subprocess only as a result of the SPAWN command. Symbols cannot be used to communicate from the child subprocess to the parent.

Logical name inheritance is also dangerous and inefficient, although it is sometimes the case that the subprocess must rely on logical names defined by the parent. If at all possible, use the /NOLOGICAL_NAMES qualifier to prevent logical name inheritance and pass the necessary information as procedure parameters. Section 20.7 contains an example of passing parameters to a subprocess.

Process logical names are inherited by the subprocess by default, but the contents of the subprocess's private logical name tables are not propogated back to the parent process. If you plan to use logical names to share information among processes, avoid the use of inheritence and use logical names located in a shared logical name table, such as the LNM$JOB job logical name table.

20.4.3 Subprocess Termination

A subprocess created with the SPAWN command terminates when it has no more commands to execute. There are three possibilities:

- When the SPAWN command includes a command to execute but does not include the /INPUT qualifier, the subprocess terminates after executing the single command. Note, however, that the command can be the at-sign command to invoke a procedure in the subprocess; in this case, the entire procedure executes.

- When the SPAWN command includes the /INPUT qualifier, the subprocess terminates when the specified command procedure exits.

- When neither a command nor the /INPUT qualifier is included, the subprocess must be terminated with the LOGOUT command. In the case of a batch process, however, the spawned subprocess terminates immediately, because it has no source of commands.

The action taken by the parent process during the lifetime of the subprocess depends upon the /WAIT qualifier. If /WAIT was specified, the parent process suspends execution until the subprocess terminates. If /NOWAIT was specified, both processes execute simultaneously with no automatic synchronization.

20.5 Process-Permanent Files

A *process-permanent file* is a file that is opened by a process and that remains open until either it is explicitly closed or the process terminates. There are two common uses for process-permanent files (PPFs). First, the four standard logical names SYS$COMMAND, SYS$INPUT, SYS$OUTPUT, and SYS$ERROR, which define the inputs and outputs for a process, are PPFs. The SYS$PIPE PPF is available within the context of the PIPE command; see Section 20.8 for

Table 20.5
Standard PPFs:
Interactive procedure

PPF	Detached process	Subprocess
SYS$COMMAND	The terminal.	(1) The terminal; or (2) the command procedure specified with the /INPUT qualifier on the SPAWN command.
SYS$INPUT	The command procedure executing in the detached process.	The command procedure executing in the subprocess.
SYS$OUTPUT	(1) The terminal; or (2) the file specified with the /OUTPUT qualifier on the at-sign command that invoked the procedure.	(1) The same as the parent's destination; or (2) the file specified with the /OUTPUT qualifier on the SPAWN command.
SYS$ERROR	The terminal.	Same as SYS$OUTPUT.

more information. Additionally, any file opened with the OPEN command is a PPF.

The four standard files listed above are automatically opened by OpenVMS during the creation of a process. They remain open until the process terminates. The sources for SYS$COMMAND and SYS$INPUT and the destination of SYS$OUTPUT and SYS$ERROR are determined by OpenVMS using some standard rules along with optional information given by the creator of the process. The sources and destinations for these logical names are not always obvious, particularly in the case of a subprocess spawned from within a DCL procedure. Table 20.5 lists the PPFs for a procedure running in an interactive process. Table 20.6 lists the PPFs for a procedure running in a batch process. Remember that these tables pertain only to a process running a DCL procedure.

When a process-permanent file is specified as a source or destination for a program, the program performs input/output operations on the file that is already open. In particular, when a PPF is specified as an output file, data is appended to the existing file. No new file is created.

20.6 Jobs

OpenVMS uses the term *job* to refer to a detached process and all of its subprocesses. The detached process can be an interactive, batch, or network process; the word *job* has nothing to do with the traditional term *batch job*. When a procedure uses the SPAWN command to create a subprocess, both the parent and the child are members of the same job.

Table 20.6
Standard PPFs:
Batch procedure

PPF	Detached process	Subprocess
SYS$COMMAND	The command procedure executing in the detached process.	(1) The null device (NLA0:); or (2) the command procedure specified with the /INPUT qualifier on the SPAWN command.
SYS$INPUT	Same as SYS$COMMAND.	The command procedure executing in the subprocess.
SYS$OUTPUT	(1) The log file; (2) the null device (NLA0:) if no log file was requested; or (3) the file specified with the /OUTPUT qualifier on the at-sign command that invoked the procedure (subprocedures only).	(1) The same as the parent's destination; or (2) the file specified by the /OUTPUT qualifier on the SPAWN command.
SYS$ERROR	(1) The log file; or (2) the null device (NLA0:) if no log file was requested.	Same as SYS$OUTPUT.

Associated with each job is a *job logical name table*. Logical names defined in this table can be accessed by any process in the same job as the defining process. Thus, if a parent process defines a job logical name, any children created with SPAWN can access the logical name, and vice versa. The following command defines the job logical name XDA_JOB_INFO:

```
$    define/job xda_job_info step_1
```

The job logical name table is deleted when the job's detached process is deleted.

Job logical names can be used to communicate between parent and child subprocesses. The following section presents an example of the SPAWN command used in conjunction with the job logical name table.

20.7   An Example with SPAWN

Suppose you have a procedure that creates and deletes many files on a particular disk. It might be interesting to monitor the minimum number of free blocks on the disk as the procedure runs. A subprocess can be used to "watch" the disk as the parent process executes. At the end of the file manipulation, the subprocess can report the free block count to the parent. Note that the free block count might be affected by other users on the system.

Here is the command procedure that is run in the subprocess:

```
$!     This is the XDA_WATCH-DISK procedure.
$!     P1, the first parameter, is the disk to be watched.
$
$      min_free = 999999999
$10:   if f$trnlnm("xda_watch_disk_blocks") .eqs. "" then -
           goto 19
$      wait 00:00:00.50
$      curr_free = f$getdvi(p1,"FREEBLOCKS")
$      if curr_free .lt. min_free then min_free = curr_free
$      goto 10
$19:
$      define/job xda_watch_disk_blocks 'min_free
$      exit
```

Here is part of a DCL application that uses the disk watcher:

```
$      define/job/nolog xda_watch_disk_blocks in-progress
$      spawn/nosymbols/nological_names/nowait -
           @xda_system:xda_watch-disk 'disk
       .
       . perform file manipulation
       .
$      undefine/job xda_watch_disk_blocks
$10:   if f$trnlnm("xda_wath_disk_blocks") .eqs. ""
$       then
$         wait 00:00:01.00
$         goto 10
$       endif
$      display "Minimum free blocks: ", -
           f$trnlnm("xda_watch_disk_blocks")
$      undefine/job xda_watch_disk_blocks
```

The job logical name XDA_WATCH_DISK_BLOCKS provides the communication and synchronization between the parent process and the subprocess watching the disk. The following sequence of events occurs when this application runs:

1. The parent process defines the logical name XDA_WATCH_DISK_BLOCKS in the job logical name table, assigning it an arbitrary value such as the word IN-PROGRESS.

2. The parent spawns a subprocess. There is no reason for the child to inherit the symbols or logical names of the parent, so the /NOSYMBOLS and /NOLOGICAL_NAMES qualifiers are used. The /NOWAIT qualifier allows the parent and child to run simultaneously.

3. The parent begins to perform its file manipulation activities.
4. The XDA_WATCH-DISK procedure running in the child repeatedly performs the following steps:
   (a) It checks to see whether the parent has deleted the job logical name. If so, this is the signal to stop watching the disk, report the result to the parent, and exit.
   (b) It waits one-half second.
   (c) It determines the number of free blocks on the disk and resets MIN_FREE if a new low has been attained.
5. Eventually the parent deletes the job logical name. The subprocess ceases executing the disk-watching loop and redefines the job logical name so that its value is the minimum number of free blocks. The procedure then exits and the child is deleted.
6. After the parent deletes the job logical name, it must wait until the child redefines it. This is done with a loop that checks for the logical name once per second.
7. The parent determines the minimum free blocks by translating the logical name.
8. The parent deletes the logical name so that it does not clutter the job logical name table.

20.8   PIPE

Another option for creating and executing commands in subprocesses is the PIPE command. The PIPE command has a number of similarities to the SPAWN/WAIT SPAWN/NOWAIT commands, and several key differences. As with SPAWN, you can execute commands synchronously and asynchronously. And you can use the PIPE qualifiers /LOGICAL_NAMES and /SYMBOLS qualifiers to control the availability and propogation of process logical names and process symbols available within the PIPE processing. Unlike the SPAWN commands, the PIPE command permits the direct specification of multiple commands, permits the redirecting the SYS$OUTPUT of one command into the SYS$INPUT of the next, and allows you to specify conditional execution of the commands specified.

You can control the operation and behavior of the command segments within the PIPE command using *separators*. Each separator indicates the particular processing applied to the *command segments* within the `PIPE` command. Information on the available separators is included in Table 20.7.

The general format of the `PIPE` command is:

    $ `pipe` *command separator command*   ...

Within the `PIPE` command, you can execute commands individually, or you can use parentheses to group commands within a *subshell*. An example of using a subshell is:

    $ `pipe` (*command* ; *command* ; *command*)

The two conditional separators are "&&" and "||". You can use the "&&" separator to control the execution of the commands following the separator: these commands are executed only if the preceding commands succeed. The "||" separator is similar, but the commands are executed only when preceding commands fail. As an example, the following `PIPE` command performs a compilation, and conditionally performs a link upon successful compilation:

```
$    pipe cc/decc sourcefile/object=objectfile && -
         link objectfile
```

The three separators that control the flow of processing are ";", "&", and "( )". The semicolon acts as a checkpoint, and waits for all prior processing to complete before proceeding. The ampersand causes the earlier commands to execute in a *background shell*, asynchronously with the remaining commands. The parentheses are used to group commands together into a subshell, executing the commands as a group. The `PIPE` separators are summarized in Table 20.7.

The `PIPE` command was introduced in OpenVMS V7.1.

20.8.1 Creating a Tee

There are times when you need to duplicate the output of one stage of a pipe, writing one copy of the output into a file and passing another copy of the output to the next stage of the pipe. A common solution is a construct known as a *tee*, analogous to the plumbing connection with one input and two outputs. A tee is useful for logging output or even for debugging the operation of a `PIPE` command.

OpenVMS does not provide a tee within the `PIPE` command, but it does provide the `SYS$PIPE` logical name that you can use to easily implement one with the following command procedure:

Table 20.7 PIPE separators

Characters	Description
|	Sequential command execution. Data written to SYS$OUTPUT by the command preceding the bar can be read from SYS$INPUT by the command following the bar.
&	Background execution. Commands preceding the ampersand are executed in the background, asynchronously.
;	Command completion sequence point. Commands preceding the colon must be completed before proceeding. To differentiate this separator from a file version number, a space must precede the colon.
&&	Commands following this separator are only executed upon successful completion of the commands preceding it.
||	Commands following this separator are only executed upon the failure of the commands preceding it.
<	SYS$INPUT is redirected, reading input from the specified file.
>	SYS$OUTPUT is redirected, writing output to the specified file.
2>	SYS$ERROR is redirected, writing errors to the specified file.
(...)	Parenthesized commands are executed as a unit within a subshell.

```
$!     TEE.COM usage: pipe cmd1 | @tee file | cmd2
$
$      open/write file 'p1
$
$10:   read/end_of_file=19 sys$pipe text
$      write sys$output text
$      write file text
$      goto 10
$19:   close file
$      exit
```

20.8 PIPE

CHAPTER 21

Batch Jobs

This chapter describes the batch facility of OpenVMS, which allows a process to run "unattended," without being connected to an interactive terminal. DCL applications can take advantage of the batch facility to perform time-consuming tasks without tying up the user's terminal. It is important for the DCL programmer to understand the batch environment in order to coordinate the interactive and batch portions of an application and ensure their consistency.

21.1 The Batch Environment

A *batch job* is a process that runs in the OpenVMS batch environment rather than in the interactive environment. The batch-processing facility is supported by a special program called the *queue manager*, which runs in its own OpenVMS process. The queue manager is responsible for maintaining a set of *batch queues* to which users submit batch and print jobs for processing. The remainder of this chapter discusses techniques for using the queue manager and queues to run batch jobs.

A given OpenVMS system can have one or more batch queues, each with its own unique name. Associated with a queue is a set of attributes, which determine how the queue manager selects and runs jobs from the queue. It is up to your system manager to set up the batch queues and define their attributes; this book does not discuss the creation of queues. Almost every OpenVMS system has a standard batch queue named `SYS$BATCH`.

When you submit a batch job for execution, what you are submitting is a DCL procedure that the queue manager is to execute in a batch process. A batch process is similar to the interactive process described in this book, but there are important differences. Once you understand the differences, you can write DCL applications that run both interactively and in batch. The following points describe the differences between a batch process and an interactive one:

- There is no terminal associated with a batch process. Its input comes from a command procedure and its output goes to a *log file*.

- The logical names `SYS$COMMAND` and `SYS$INPUT` refer to the DCL procedure being run in the batch process.

- The logical names `SYS$OUTPUT` and `SYS$ERROR` are directed to a log file. A log file is a text file whose purpose is to contain all the output generated by the batch job. The log file can be retained after the job completes.

- The `F$GETJPI` lexical function can be used to determine whether a procedure is being run interactively or in batch. When called with the item keyword `"MODE"`, the function returns the string `"INTERACTIVE"` or `"BATCH"`, depending upon the current environment.

  Sec. 20.1, p. 258

- Certain commands often found in `LOGIN.COM` procedures, such as `SET TERMINAL/INQUIRE`, will return errors if used in the batch environment.

A fundamental consequence of the batch environment is that a procedure cannot ask questions of the interactive user. Instead, any information the procedure requires to operate must be passed to it in the form of parameters.

One important similarity between the batch and interactive environments is the login procedure. If the procedure `LOGIN.COM` exists in your login directory, OpenVMS automatically invokes it when you log in. The same is true when a batch job is submitted: OpenVMS automatically invokes your `LOGIN.COM` immediately after it creates the batch process. If parts of the login procedure should be skipped in batch, use the `F$GETJPI` function to check for batch mode and exclude those parts.

21.2 Submitting a Batch Job

A batch job is submitted to a batch queue using the `SUBMIT` command. The `SUBMIT` command accepts many qualifiers, which control how and when the job is executed. The basic form of the command is as follows:

```
$    submit procedure-spec
```

The *procedure-spec* is a file spec that names the DCL procedure to be run in batch. The procedure must exist at the time the SUBMIT command is entered. Table 21.1 describes many of the important qualifiers for the SUBMIT command.

Here are a few things to note about the SUBMIT command:

- Unless you specify the /AFTER qualifier, the job is run as soon as possible, depending on the jobs queued before it.
- By default, a log file is generated, printed to the SYS$PRINT queue, and deleted. It is usually easier to review the log file with an editor. This is specified by the following combination of qualifiers:

    $ submit /log_file=*file-spec*/keep/noprinter *procedure*

Table 21.1 SUBMIT command qualifiers

Qualifier	Default?	Description
/AFTER=*time*		The job is held in the queue and not run until the specified time.
/DELETE		The command procedure is deleted after the job finishes.
/NODELETE	✓	The command procedure is not deleted.
/HOLD		The job is held in the queue until it is explicitly released by the SET QUEUE/ENTRY command.
/NOHOLD	✓	The job is not held.
/IDENTIFY	✓	The job name, queue, and entry number are displayed after the job is submitted.
/NOIDENTIFY		The job information is not displayed.
/KEEP	(depends)	The log file is retained after the job completes. This is the default if /NOPRINTER is specified.
/NOKEEP	(depends)	The log file is deleted after the job completes. This is the default if /PRINTER is specified.
/LOG_FILE=*spec*	✓	Specifies the file to contain the job log. The default device/directory is the submitter's login directory. The default file name is the name of the job. The default file type is LOG.
/NOLOG_FILE		No job log file is produced.
/NAME="*name*"		Specifies the name of the job. The name can contain any characters but is limited to 39 characters in length. The default name is the name of the command procedure.
/NOTIFY		A message is broadcast to your terminal when the job completes.

Table 21.1 (continued) SUBMIT command qualifiers

Qualifier	Default?	Description
/NOTIFY		A message is broadcast to your terminal when the job completes.
/NONOTIFY	✓	No completion message is broadcast.
/PARAMETERS		Provides up to eight parameters to the command procedure. The parameters are separated by commas and enclosed in parentheses. If a parameter contains any characters other than letters or digits, it must be enclosed in double quotes (" ... ").
/PRINTER=queue	✓	The log file is queued for printing. The default print queue is SYS$PRINT. *Note that this qualifier is present by default.*
/NOPRINTER		The log file is not printed.
/QUEUE=queue		Identifies the batch queue on which the job is queued. The default queue is SYS$BATCH.
/RESTART		Specifies that the batch job is restartable (see Section 21.4).
/USER=user		Names the user on whose behalf the job is run. The default is the submitting user. The CMKRNL privilege is required to submit a job for another user.

Sec. 15.2, p. 193

If the log file spec does not include a directory, the log file is placed in your login directory. The log file is in VFC (variable with fixed control) format, not in the standard variable-length text format.

- If the /LOG_FILE qualifier does not include a log file name, the name of the command procedure is used. However, if the /NAME qualifier is present, then the job name is used. In the latter case, the job name must be a valid file name.

- To use the /USER qualifier to submit a job on behalf of another user, you must have CMKRNL (change mode to kernel) privilege and read access to the user authorization file.

- The entry number is an opaque numeric value. When large numbers of jobs are queued or executing in parallel, the queue manager can extend the range of entry numbers available automatically. You should not make any assumptions around the allocation, scale, or ordering of entry numbers.

The SUBMIT command is used by a DCL application to run a portion of an application in batch. For example, an application that generates accounting reports might do so in batch because the `ACCOUNTING` utility takes a long time to format reports from large accounting files. The application could use the following `SUBMIT` command:

```
$   submit /name=xda_accounting_reports -
        /log_file=xda_logs:xda_accounting_reports.log -
        /keep/noprinter -
        xda_system:xda_accounting/parameters=(all,summary)
```

21.3 Sending Mail about Job Status

The success or failure of a batch job can always be determined by saving a log file and checking it after the job completes. However, because a batch log is nothing more than a snapshot of the output produced by the job, it can be difficult for a naive user to understand. In addition, it may contain a lot of extraneous information that is not of direct concern to the user. Another way to summarize the status of a batch job is for the job to produce a succinct log of important events and mail the log to the user who submitted the job. This status log can be customized for the task being performed, using terminology and summarizing events that the user understands.

A status log is relatively easy to produce. The command procedure creates a temporary file at the beginning of the job. As it proceeds, it writes summary information to the file. When the procedure is finished it closes the file, mails it to the submitter, and deletes it. The following command procedure is designed to run in batch. It accepts a wildcard file spec, which identifies a set of files whose internal structure is to be checked with the `ANALYZE` utility. The output produced by each analysis is collected in a status log and mailed to the user.

```
$!      @XDA_ANALYZE file-spec
$
$       analyze = "analyze"
$       delete = "delete"
$       mail = "mail"
$       xda__status  = %x10428000
$       xda__success = xda__status + %x0001
$       xda__ctrly   = xda__status + %x000c
$       status = xda__success
$       log_file = ""
$       on control_y then goto control_y
$       on warning then goto error
$
$       libcall = "@xda_system:subroutine-library"
```

```
$       libcall unique_name xda_ sys$scratch:xda_?.log;
$       log_file = xda_
$       open/write xda_log 'log_file
$       write xda_log ""
$       write xda_log "Analysis performed with ANALYZE/RMS/CHECK."
$
$10:    file = f$search(p1)
$       if file .eqs. "" then goto 19
$       set noon
$       analyze/rms_file/check/output=xda_log 'file
$       set on
$       goto 10
$19:
$
$       close xda_log
$       set noon
$       mail 'log_file 'f$getjpi("","USERNAME") -
            /subject="Batch analysis of ''p1'"
$       set on
$       delete 'log_file'*
$
$control_y:
$       status = xda__ctrly
$       goto exit
$error:
$       status = $status
$       goto exit
$exit:
$       set noon
$       close/nolog xda_log
$       if log_file .nes. "" then -
            if f$search(log_file) .nes. "" then delete 'log_file'*
$       exit status .or. %x10000000
```

The status log is opened with the logical name XDA_LOG. Any number of WRITE commands can be used to add lines to the status log. In addition, the logical name can be specified in the /OUTPUT qualifier of a command so that the output produced by a utility is directed to the status log. This is the case with the ANALYZE command in the procedure. The output from each use of the ANALYZE utility is appended to the status log.

This job is submitted using a command such as the following:

```
$ submit/nolog_file -
_$ xda_system:xda_analyze/parameter=user_disk:[smith]*.dat
```

The SUBMIT command specifies that no log file is to be produced; the status log mailed by the job is sufficient. The /PARAMETER qualifier specifies the files that are to be analyzed.

21.4 Restartable Batch Jobs

In some applications, it is imperative that a batch job run to completion even if it is terminated prematurely. There are at least two reasons why a batch job can terminate prematurely without running its cleanup code. First, the OpenVMS system might crash. Second, the operator or some other user might cancel the batch job. A batch job can be made *restartable* so that it will always run to completion.

The queue manager guarantees to resubmit a restartable job if the job does not complete its execution. The job will be resubmitted if the system crashes while it is executing. The job will also be resubmitted if the operator cancels it, as long as it is canceled with the following command:

```
$ stop/queue/entry=number/requeue queue-name
```

The /REQUEUE qualifier requests that the job be restarted.

A batch job is made restartable by including the /RESTART qualifier on the SUBMIT command. This single qualifier is all that is required to ensure that the job is resubmitted if it does not complete the first time. However, if the batch job does terminate prematurely and restarts, it will run again from the beginning, repeating the code that was already executed during the original submission. This may be harmless, but in many cases it is not. The programmer must design the batch procedure to be restartable, skipping those portions of the code that have already been executed and that must not be reexecuted.

DCL includes some simple features to aid the programmer in designing restartable procedures. Two special symbols are involved:

$RESTART   This symbol is always defined. It has a Boolean value, false if this is the original execution of a batch job, true if this is a restarted job. The symbol does not specify whether the job is startable, but rather whether it has in fact been restarted.

BATCH$RESTART   This symbol is only defined during the execution of a restarted job. Its value is determined by the procedure during its *original execution*, as explained below.

A procedure can test the $RESTART symbol to determine whether it has been restarted. If it has, it can use the value of BATCH$RESTART to control which parts are executed and which are skipped. The value of BATCH$RESTART is established with the SET RESTART_VALUE command. Upon restart, the symbol has the last value that was set during the original execution of the procedure. Using the SET RESTART_VALUE command, the procedure can be divided into steps as follows:

```
         . procedure initialization
$step1:
$       set restart_value=step1
         . perform first step of procedure
$
$step2:
$       set restart_value=step2
         . perform second step
$
$step3:
$       set restart_value=step3
         . perform third step
$       goto exit
$
$exit:
$       set restart_value=exit
         . cleanup code
```

Each step begins with a SET RESTART_VALUE command, which saves the step name. The step name is included as a label at the beginning of the code that performs the step. When the procedure is about to exit, a SET RESTART_VALUE command saves the label EXIT as an indication that the procedure is effectively complete. All you need to make this procedure restartable is some code to test the value of $RESTART and to skip to the appropriate step:

```
         . procedure initialization
$       if $restart then if f$type(batch$restart) .nes. "" then-
            goto 'batch$restart
$
$step1:
$       set restart_value=step1
         . perform first step of procedure
```

```
$
$step2:
$       set restart_value=step2
        .
        . perform second step
        .
$
$step3:
$       set restart_value=step3
        .
        . perform third step
        .
$       goto exit
$
$exit:
$       set restart_value=exit
        .
        . cleanup code
        .
```

After procedure initialization, the value of $RESTART is tested. If it is true, the procedure has been restarted. In this case, the F$TYPE lexical function is used to determine whether BATCH$RESTART has a value from a SET RESTART_VALUE command. If so, the procedure skips to that label, effectively bypassing the steps completed during the original execution of the batch job. If BATCH$RESTART does not exist, then the original job did not even get to the first step, and execution takes up at the beginning. In the event that the procedure almost finished during its original execution, BATCH$RESTART contains the label EXIT and execution skips immediately to the cleanup code and the procedure exits.

The only difficult aspect of designing restartable jobs is in breaking the procedure into steps. Here are a few guidelines:

- Do not assume that BATCH$RESTART exists, because the first step might not be reached before the system crashes. Test BATCH$RESTART with the F$TYPE function to make sure it is defined.

- Each step must be restartable. When the system crashes in the middle of a step, the job is restarted at the beginning of that step. It must be harmless to reexecute the step from the beginning.

- If a step of the procedure cannot be rerun, then you must arrange for the procedure never to restart at the beginning of that step. Assume that step 3 cannot be rerun. Instead of performing a SET RESTART_VALUE=STEP3 at the beginning of step 3, you can perform a SET RESTART_VALUE=STEP4 so that step 3 is skipped in the event of a restart.

- After the last step, make sure to set BATCH$RESTART to indicate that the procedure is effectively complete. Performing a SET RESTART_VALUE= EXIT command will ensure that the procedure immediately exits if it is restarted after the last step.

21.5   Periodic Batch Jobs

Some applications require that a batch job run periodically, perhaps once an hour or once a day. The OpenVMS queue manager does not provide a facility for direct implementation of periodic batch jobs, so the batch job must take the responsibility for resubmitting itself. The simplest technique is for the batch job to resubmit itself just before it exits:

```
$!     Procedure to monitor system resources every 4 hours.
$
$!     Remember the time at which the job started.
$
$      start_time = f$time()
         . additional initialization
$
         . procedure activities
$exit:
$      set noon
$      submit/nolog_file/after="''start_time+0-04:00" -
               'f$environment("PROCEDURE")
         . more cleanup
$      exit status .or. %x10000000
```

At the very beginning of the procedure, the current time is saved in the symbol START_TIME. The cleanup code includes a SUBMIT command to resubmit the job for execution 4 hours after the starting time. The SUBMIT command is included in the cleanup code so that it is guaranteed to be executed regardless of the reason for procedure exit. A combination time is specified on the /AFTER qualifier: it includes the job starting time as its absolute time component and the delta time "4 hours from now" as its delta time component. The resulting absolute time is 4 hours from the original job starting time.

This job rescheduling technique is almost foolproof, but it has one flaw. If the batch job terminates before it has had a chance to resubmit itself, perhaps because of a system crash, the periodicity of the job is broken. In order to reduce the chances of this happening, you could reorganize the procedure to resubmit itself at the beginning rather than at the end. This may indeed significantly reduce the "window" in which termination prevents resubmission, but it does not eliminate it. The system might crash at the very beginning of the job. In addition, resubmitting the job at the beginning of the procedure opens up the possibility that the first job is not finished before the second one begins (what if the first job occasionally runs for more than 4 hours?).

You can guarantee that the batch job will resubmit itself by making it restartable. The technique used to make the procedure restartable is a variation on the scheme presented in the previous section. Here is the preceding procedure modified to guarantee that it is resubmitted:

```
$!     Procedure to monitor system resources every 4 hours.
$
$!     Remember the time at which the job started.
$
$      start_time = f$time()
$
$!     If this is a restart and we already resubmitted the
$!     procedure, exit immediately.  Otherwise skip to the
$!     cleanup code and resubmit.
$
$      if $restart
$      then
$        if f$type(batch$restart) .nes. "" then -
             if batch$restart .eqs. "RESUBMITTED" then exit
$        goto exit ! To resubmit the job.
$      endif
```
          : *additional initialization*
```
$
```
          : *procedure activities*
```
$
$exit:
$      set noon
$      submit/nolog_file/after="''start_time+0-04:00"/restart -
               'f$environment("PROCEDURE")
$      set restart_value=resubmitted
```
          : *more cleanup*
```
$      exit status .or. %x10000000
```

21.5 Periodic Batch Jobs

During the normal execution of this procedure, nothing special happens until after the job is resubmitted by the cleanup code. Once the job is resubmitted, the restart value is set to "RESUBMITTED" to indicate that the resubmittal has occurred. If the job then exits normally, the restart value is never employed. Note that the SUBMIT command includes the /RESTART qualifier so that the next batch job is also restartable.

If the system crashes while the procedure is executing, the batch job is restarted. Here is what happens:

1. The starting time is saved.

2. The procedure detects that it was restarted.
   (a) If the symbol BATCH$RESTART exists and has the value "RESUBMITTED", then the original job got far enough to resubmit itself. There is nothing left to do, so the restarted job exits immediately.
   (b) If the symbol BATCH$RESTART does not exist or has some other value, then the original job did not get far enough. The procedure skips to the exit code to resubmit itself.

3. Under no circumstances does the job execute its initialization code or procedure activities

With the addition of only a few lines of code, the procedure can guarantee that the batch job is executed every 4 hours regardless of how each job terminates.

21.6 Preventing Duplicate Jobs

The previous section demonstrated a method to ensure that a periodic batch job is resubmitted exactly once every period. This does not rule out the possibility of duplicate jobs, however, because a user might accidentally submit the job while it is already active or queued for its next run. Or an operator might submit it after a system crash, not realizing that the job is restarted after crashes. If you want to ensure that only one copy of a batch job can ever run at one time, additional code is needed in the procedure.

The additional code is quite straightforward. It makes use of the group or system logical name table. The fundamental idea is that a particular group or system logical name will always be defined while the job is running. This logical name acts as a "lock" on the batch procedure. If another job detects that the logical name exists when it starts up, it immediately cancels itself.

The group logical name table can be used if the batch procedure is used only by the members of a particular UIC group. If anyone can submit the procedure, then the system logical name table must be used so that all submitters can access the logical name. The only reason to use a group logical name is that it requires only GRPNAM privilege, while use of a system logical name requires SYSNAM privilege. A cluster-wide logical name table can be used on OpenVMS V7.2 systems, assuming you have sufficient privilege to write to the table.

Here is the periodic batch job from the previous section with the addition of a logical name lock:

```
$!     Procedure to monitor system resources every 4 hours.
$
$!     If this procedure is already running, exit immediately.
$!     Otherwise define the system logical name to lock the
$!     procedure.
$
$      if f$trnlmn("xda_batch_lock") .nes. "" then exit
$      define/system xda_batch_lock running ! Any value
$
$!     Remember the time at which the job started.
$
$      start_time = f$time()
$
$!     If this is a restart and we already resubmitted the
$!     procedure, exit immediately.  Otherwise skip to the
$!     cleanup code and resubmit.
$
$      if $restart
$      then
$         if f$type(batch$restart) .nes. "" then -
              if batch$restart .eqs. "RESUBMITTED" then goto exit2
$         goto exit ! To resubmit the job.
$      endif
           .
           . additional initialization
           .
$
           .
           . procedure activities
           .
$
$exit:
$      set noon
$      submit/nolog_file/after="''start_time+0-04:00"/restart -
              'f$environment("PROCEDURE")
$      set restart_value=resubmitted
           .
           . more cleanup
           .
```

21.6 Preventing Duplicate Jobs

```
$exit2:
$    undefine/system xda_batch_lock ! Remove lock.
$    exit status .or. %x10000000
```

The first thing the procedure does is check to see if the XDA_BATCH_LOCK logical name is defined. If so, it assumes that another batch job is running the same procedure and exits immediately. If the logical name is not defined, the procedure defines it. These two commands act as a lock to prevent more than one copy of the batch job from running at the same time. Any copies other than the first simply fade away without resubmitting themselves.

The cleanup code must delete the logical name so that it does not prevent future batch jobs from running. If the system crashes during the job, the system logical name will not be defined after the system reboots. Therefore, the restarted batch job will run normally. The only problem arises when the operator cancels the job without restarting it. When the job runs again, the logical name is still defined and the job exits immediately. In this case someone must delete the logical name by hand.

If the GRPNAM and SYSNAM privileges are not available to the users of a batch job that must be locked, and there is no shared logical name table writable by the users, a file can be used instead of a logical name. The presence of the "lock file" signifies that the batch job is running; its absence signifies that the job is not running. To reduce the chances of a false lock-out that can result from a lock file that was erroneously left undeleted, the PID of the batch job can be written into the lock file. Accessors can then test for the presence of the lock file, and can also read and verify that the PID is valid on the system.

CHAPTER 22
Arrays

IN MOST PROGRAMMING LANGUAGES, AN *ARRAY* is a collection of data elements of the same type. In the C language, for example, you can create an array of integers, an array of floating-point numbers, or an array of characters. Two items of information are needed to refer to an individual element of an array. The first is the name of the array, and the second is an identifier for the particular element in question. This identifier is called an *index* or *subscript*. Most languages, C included, require that an index be an integer. A few languages, MUMPS being a notable example, allow an index to be any value whatsoever. The array is elevated from a simple ordered sequence of elements to an associative array that maps one value (the index or key) to another value (the data item).

DCL does not provide built-in array facilities. However, using apostrophe substitution, you can simulate an array with a collection of symbols. A portion of the symbol name serves as the array name and a portion serves as the index. There is no requirement that all the array elements be of the same type, because each symbol can contain any type of data.

22.1 Arrays with Integer Indexes

Most programming languages provide arrays whose index values are integers. This can be simulated in DCL with a collection of symbols, one for each array element, whose names consist of a fixed alphabetic part (the array name) and an integer part (the index). For example, an array of file specifications might use the symbols FILE_SPEC1, FILE_SPEC2, FILE_SPEC3, and so on. The array name is FILE_SPEC and the indexes are the integer suffixes 1, 2, and 3. If the symbol I is set to the desired index, the correct array symbol is obtained using the following form of apostrophe substitution:

```
... file_spec'i ...
```

When the symbol I is set to the value 2, the symbol named after substitution is

```
... file_spec2 ...
```

Note carefully that the apostrophe substitution results in the *name* of the array symbol containing the desired value. The substitution does not produce the value itself. Here is a complete example, which builds a file spec array from all the data files in the system manager's directory:

```
$       i = 0
$10:    file = f$search("sys$manager:*.dat;")
$       if file .eqs. "" then goto 19
$       i = i + 1
$       file_spec'i = file        ! Create an array element.
$       goto 10
$19:
$       file_count = i            ! Remember the array size.
```

The symbol I is used as an index into the FILE_SPEC array. It is initialized to zero and incremented each time an array element is created. Therefore, the array elements will be named FILE_SPEC1, FILE_SPEC2, and so on, as desired. The command that creates an array element is an example of an assignment statement containing apostrophe substitution; array manipulation is one of the few operations that necessitates substitution in the left-hand side of an assignment statement.

The following loop scans the file specs in the array and eliminates any spec containing a dollar sign in its file name by replacing the spec with a placeholder string:

```
$       i = 0
$10:    i = i + 1
$       if i .gt. file_count then goto 19
$       name = f$parse(file_spec'i,,,"NAME")
$       if f$locate("$",name) .ne. f$length(name) then -
            file_spec'i = "(system file)"
$       goto 10
$19:
```

As in the first example, the symbol I is used to index the array. The loop terminates when I becomes greater than the number of file specs in the array, as specified by FILE_COUNT. The name portion of the file spec is extracted using the F$PARSE lexical function and then examined for a dollar sign. If a dollar sign is found, the array element is set to the string "(system file)".

It cannot be overemphasized that apostrophe substitution produces the name of the symbol containing an array element, not the value of the array element. After substitution in the preceding examples, a command includes the name of the symbol containing a file spec. It does not include the file spec itself, nor does it include a string literal containing the file spec. In these examples, it is convenient that substitution results in the name of the symbol, because it is precisely the name that is required on the left-hand side of an assignment statement or as an argument to a lexical function. When you want to assign a value to an array element or use an existing value in an expression, it is the name of the array element symbol that must appear after substitution.

But what if you need an array element in a command that does not accept an expression? If the command does not accept an expression, then it will not take the name of the array element symbol and automatically extract its value. It must directly receive the value of the element. You could decide that two substitutions are required, one to produce the array symbol name and then another one to substitute the symbol's value in the command. With this in mind, you might think that the following command would work:

```
$       delete 'file_spec''i
$!              ^---------^         left substitution
$!                         ^^       right substitution
```

Unfortunately, the left substitution is performed first, so DCL attempts to substitute the value of the symbol FILE_SPEC. This symbol has nothing to do with the array elements, which are named FILE_SPEC1, FILE_SPEC2, and so forth. The symbol FILE_SPEC probably does not exist, or it is does, it contains a value that is unrelated to the problem at hand. There is no way to force DCL to perform the right substitution (of I) first, using apostrophe substitution. The solution is to use ampersand substitution, or to perform the substitution in two steps. The authors recommend using apostrophe substitution, and two commands:

Sec. 5.3, p. 72

```
$       file = file_spec'i
$       delete 'file
```

The appropriate array element is copied to the temporary symbol FILE, and that symbol is substituted in the DELETE command.

22.1 Arrays with Integer Indexes

The contrast between substitution in expressions and substitution outside of expressions can be demonstrated clearly using procedure parameters. One array that is always present in a procedure is the parameter array. Because the procedure parameters are named P1–P8, they naturally form an array of eight character strings. The following procedure will display the values of its parameters:

```
$!      Display all the parameters passed to this procedure.
$
$       i = 0
$10:    i = i + 1
$       if i .gt. 8 then goto 19
$       if p'i .nes. "" then display "P", i, ": ", p'i
$       goto 10
$19:
```

The second IF command displays the value of a parameter if it is not null. On the third cycle through the loop, for example, when I has the value 3, the IF command becomes:

```
$       if p3 .nes. "" then write sys$output "P", i, ": ", p3
```

Because the IF and WRITE commands accept expressions, the *value* of P3 is used where its name is specified.

Compare the previous procedure to the following one, which assumes its parameters are file specs and displays the contents of the files:

```
$!      Display the contents of files specified as parameters.
$
$       i = 0
$10:    i = i + 1
$       if i .gt. 8 then goto 19
$       file = p'i
$       if file .nes. "" then type/page 'file
$       goto 10
$19:
```

The TYPE command expects a file spec as its parameter, not an expression. Therefore, two commands are required: one to assign the parameter value to a temporary symbol, and a second one to test the symbol and type the file. An attempt to combine the two commands in a fashion similar to the first example:

```
$       if p'i .nes. "" then type/page p'i
```

would result in the following line after substitution:

```
$       IF P3 .NES. "" THEN TYPE/PAGE P3
```

The TYPE command will attempt to display a file named P3, rather than the file specified by the third procedure parameter. It does not evaluate P3 because it does not accept an expression.

22.2 Arrays with String Indexes

In the previous section, substitution was used to insert the names of array symbols into commands. The symbol names consisted of a fixed alphabetic portion and a variable integer portion, the index. There is no reason why the index has to be an integer. It can be an arbitrary string, as long as it is composed of the alphanumeric characters valid in a symbol name. An array whose indexes are strings are called a *symbolic array*, because it associates the index string, which is presumably meaningful, or symbolic, with some other data item. The index string is often called the "key" and the associated data item the "value."

A symbolic array can be used to maintain information about the CPU time consumed by users currently logged in to OpenVMS. The information can be stored in symbols of the form CPU_*xxx*, where *xxx* is the name of a particular user. Because user names are composed of alphanumeric characters, they will always form a valid symbol name. The following loop collects the elapsed CPU time for each user on the system (assuming the user has WORLD privilege):

Sec. 20.1, p. 258

```
$       context = 0
$10:    pid = f$pid(context)
$       if pid .eqs. "" then goto 19
$       if f$getjpi(pid,"GRP") .le. MAXSYSGROUP then goto 10
$       username = f$edit(f$getjpi(pid,"USERNAME"), "TRIM")
$       if f$type(cpu_'username) .eqs. "" then -
            cpu_'username = 0
$       cpu_'username = cpu_'username + f$getjpi(pid,"CPUTIM")
$       goto 10
$19:
```

The procedure uses the F$PID lexical function to obtain the process IDs for all processes on the system, one at a time. System processes in groups 0 and 1 are ignored. In turn, the process ID is used to obtain the user name, say "JONES". If the symbol CPU_JONES does not exist, it is created and initialized to zero. The value of the symbol CPU_JONES is then incremented by the elapsed CPU time for the process. After the loop is complete, the total CPU time for each user will be accumulated, regardless of the number of times each user is logged in.

There are two problems connected with symbolic arrays, which reduce their usefulness. The first is that the key can be composed only of letters, digits, dollar signs, and underscores. DCL syntax errors occur if any other characters creep in. A file name, for example, could potentially result in problems if used as a key, as depending on the disk file structure, file names can contain hyphens and potentially other characters, and these other characters are not permissible in symbol names.

The second problem has to do with the collection of symbols that are created for a symbolic array. In the preceding example, each distinct user name results in a symbol whose name includes that user name. Because the user names are arbitrary, there is no way to predict which symbols are created. Therefore, when you want to cycle through the array later on, say to print a report, you don't know which symbols to inspect. How do you know which user names were encountered? There are two possible solutions. The first is to search all the processes again and use the resulting user names to index the array. Unfortunately, in the meantime, some users may have logged out and new ones logged in. There is a mismatch between your array and reality.

The other solution is to build a separate list of user names as the array is created. This list can be used later to cycle through the array. Here is the preceding example, modified to keep a list:

```
$     user_list = ""
$     context = 0
$10:  pid = f$pid(context)
$       if pid .eqs. "" then goto 19
$       if f$getjpi(pid,"GRP") .le. MAXSYSGROUP then goto 10
$       username = f$edit(f$getjpi(pid,"USERNAME"), "TRIM")
$       if f$type(cpu_'username) .eqs. ""
$       then
$         cpu_'username = f$getjpi(pid,"CPUTIM")
$         user_list = user_list + username + ","
$       else
$         cpu_'username = cpu_'username + -
                          f$getjpi(pid,"CPUTIM")
$       endif
$       goto 10
$19:
```

The logic is similar, but with the addition of one action. Each time a new user is encountered, the user name is appended to USER_LIST, along with a comma. When the loop terminates, USER_LIST will contain a list of all the distinct user names encountered as the processes were searched. For example, if JONES, SMITH, and SNORK were logged in, USER_LIST will contain the string "JONES,SMITH,SNORK,". Note the trailing comma.

The following code will print a simple report showing the total CPU times for the users:

```
$       display f$fao("!12AS  !10AS", "User", " Total CPU")
$       i = -1
$10:    i = i + 1
$       username = f$element(i, ",", user_list)
$       if username .eqs. "" then goto 19
$       display f$fao("!12AS  !10UL", username, cpu_'username)
$       goto 10
$19:
```

After a heading is printed, the symbol I is used to index the list of users. The F$ELEMENT function extracts each user name, which is assigned to USERNAME. When USERNAME finally contains the null string, every user name has been examined and the loop terminates. The value of USERNAME is used in two ways. First, it is displayed so that the user name is included in the report. Second, it is used as the index in the CPU array to extract the user's total CPU time and display it. The USER_LIST symbol contains the definitive list of users who have an entry in the CPU array.

There is one potential problem with the USER_LIST approach, however. Each individual DCL symbol is limited in its total capacity, and systems with a large number of processes and a large number of users can easily exceed the capacity of a symbol such as USER_LIST. A more appropriate solution, specific to the maintenance of an array of user or process information, would involve the use of the F$GETJPI itemcode PROCESS_INDEX. This itemcode returns a unique value for each process on the system, limited by the SYSGEN parameter MAXPROCESSCNT, the maximum number of processes permissible. This numeric value is well suited for use as a numeric array index. This approach is better suited for OpenVMS systems with large MAXPROCESSCNT values and large numbers of processes, and thus avoids exceeding the capacity of the DCL symbol table.

Symbolic arrays are a powerful tool, but must be used with care.

22.3 The DCL Symbol Table

All symbols you create using DCL are kept in an area of memory called the *symbol table*. Even though OpenVMS is a virtual memory system, the amount of memory set aside for the symbol table is fixed. This amount is determined by the system generation (SYSGEN) parameter CLISYMTBL and is measured in units of 512-byte pages. Whenever OpenVMS creates a process, it uses the parameter to determine the number of pages to set aside for the symbol table. Once the process is created, the symbol table cannot be enlarged.

When you develop a complex DCL application that requires many symbols, you may find that the symbol table space is exhausted during execution of the application. In this case, you have two choices: reduce the number of symbols, or ask the system manager to increase the value of the system SYSGEN parameter CLISYMTBL. Any new processes created after the system manager increases the parameter will have a larger symbol table.

CHAPTER 23

DECnet Communications

THIS CHAPTER COVERS APPLICATION COMMUNICATIONS over a network, using DECnet. This chapter builds on the file operations discussed in Chapters 15 and 17.

OpenVMS systems are commonly configured into networks of computer systems that consist of machines running OpenVMS and various other operating systems. These systems and these networks use a variety of networking protocols, such as DECnet, the Open Systems Interconnect (OSI), and Internet Protocol (IP). And a OpenVMS Cluster is a form of a network, running a networking protocol known as system communications services (SCS).

DECnet Phase IV and DECnet-Plus are two of the networking packages commonly used on many OpenVMS systems, and on DIGITAL Unix and ULTRIX systems, as well as on various other systems. DECnet-Plus can operate over various transports, including DECnet Phase IV, OSI, and IP. For the purposes of this book, both DECnet packages are sufficiently similar and will be referred to collectively as DECnet. DECnet network terms are used throughout this book.

Computer systems configured in a network are refered to as host *nodes*. The networking software on these nodes provide a variety of services to users, such as network terminals, remote file access, and disk and tape access. These services are all based on software layered onto the basic interprocess communications services provided by the networking package. These services all require software running on each node. In DECnet terms, these network services are

Table 23.1 Network service commands

Command	Description
COPY	Remote file access via DECnet when a node name is included in one or both of the command parameters. specified, via DECnet.
COPY/FTP	Remote file access via the IP FTP protocol.
MAIL	Send mail via IP, DECnet, or locally.
SET HOST	DECnet network command terminal.
SET HOST/TELNET	Network command terminal via the IP TELNET protocol.
SHOW NETWORK	Display the current network status.

known as tasks, these tasks are running on various nodes in the network, and these services are based on task-to-task communications. Examples of network commands are included in Table 23.1.

This chapter will concentrate on the capabilities of DECnet and DECnet task-to-task communications.

23.1 Clients and Servers

Within any distributed application such as a network task-to-task application, there are client tasks and there are server tasks. When you are using a network application, you are directly using a client task. The client task then communicates with the server task, requesting the assistance of the server.

Within a distributed application, you normally start up and use the client task directly. The client task then connects itself to the networking software and requests communications with the specified server task on the specified remote node. On the remote node, the networking software passes the incoming connection request to the specified server task. The server can then accept or reject the connection and can communicate with the client as needed.

A server can be designed in a variety of different ways. A server can be designed to run continuously, and handle a number of connections in parallel. A server can also be designed to handle a single connection, and to be started up by the network software in response to an individual incoming connection request from a client.

The server normally writes any output into a log file, NETSERVER.LOG, located in the default directory on the node the server is running on. (From the perspective of the client and the user, the NETSERVER.LOG file is created on the remote node.)

23.2 Task-to-Task Communications

The task-to-task communications between a client and a server occur over a connection called a *network channel*. The client opens up a channel to the network software, specifying the target server. The server accepts the incoming connection using a channel made available by the network software. On OpenVMS, the channel available to the server is specified by the SYS$NET logical name.

Using the network channel, the client and the server exchange information, reading and writing messages as needed. These messages are often ordinary text strings and can be variable in length. The messages can contain user names, file names, or almost any other information that might be of interest to the client and the server task.

With simple network applications, the client and the server tasks must be designed with a predetermined protocol for the exchange of messages. These tasks have a particular series and number of messages that are exchanged between the client and the server. When one task is writing a message, the other task must be reading the message. This means that tasks can switch between writing and reading, or that the tasks can have a "turn-around" message, indicating that the task that is currently writing is about to start reading messages. The simplest case is when one tasks writes all the messages and the other task reads all the messages.

23.3 DECnet Networking

By now, you are probably familiar with a variety of network service applications, such as SET HOST. What you may not realize is that DCL is fully capable of performing basic DECnet network *task-to-task communications*.

Here is an example of a command procedure that displays the system error counts using the SHOW ERROR command:

```
$!     SHOWERR.COM
$
$      if f$getjpi("","MODE") .nes. "NETWORK"
$      then
$         show error
$      else
$         define/user sys$output sys$net
$         show error
$      endif
$      exit
```

The `SHOWERR.COM` command procedure is sensitive to the process mode, handling network mode slightly differently than interactive or the other modes. You can invoke this procedure directly, or you can invoke it indirectly, as a server task.

To invoke this particular command procedure as a server, you can use the `TYPE` command. In place of the typical file name, the following `TYPE` command includes a specification of a node, a user name and password, and something new, the name of a remote DECnet task. This `TYPE` command invokes the `SHOWERR.COM` procedure:

```
$ type wilton"hoffman openvms$faq"::"task=showerr"
```

The `TYPE` command displays the contents of the specified file. When you specify the `SHOWERR.COM` procedure as the task, the `TYPE` command displays the output generated by the `SHOWERR.COM` procedure: the system error counts for node `WILTON`. (The maximum length of the DECnet task specification field, and thus the file name, is documented as 12 characters.) This example server task uses a logical name to redirect the output of the `SHOW ERROR` command to `SYS$NET` and through to the client task, but you can also often accomplish this redirection using `/OUTPUT=SYS$NET` or other similar techniques.

The remote task, `SHOWERR.COM`, must be located in the default login directory on the remote node. If you are not sure which directory is the default directory on the remote node, you can use a command similar to the following to find out:

```
$ directory wilton"hoffman openvms$faq"::
```

Displaying information from a remote node can be useful in simpler cases, but many applications require more interaction between the client and the server. These applications need to read and write messages: they need *bidirectional communications*.

To implement communications over DECnet, DCL procedures use the same commands used for file access: `OPEN`, `CLOSE`, `READ`, and `WRITE`.

The following is an example of a simple client used for bidirectional communications:

```
$       open/read/write server -
                wilton"hoffman openvms$faq"::"task=server"
$       write server "Hello"
$       read server string
$       close server
$       exit
```

And in the default directory on the remote node, the associated server:

```
$       open/read/write client sys$net
$       read client string
$       write client "Good-bye"
$       close client
```

Notice that the client initiates the DECnet connection, writes the first message, then reads a message from the server and closes the channel. The server reverses this process: it receives the connection, reads the first message from the client, then writes a message and closes the channel.

23.4 Advanced Considerations

You might find it useful to have a single procedure act both as a client and a server. And you might want to incorporate version checks, so that a client does not try to communicate with a different and incompatible version of the server.

The following procedure XQTYPE.COM is both the client and the server, based on the process mode. The procedure looks at the XQA0: device on the remote system to determine if it is a DELQA or DEQNA Ethernet controller, if there is no XQA0: network controller configured on the system, or if the XQA0: device is of a type that the procedure does not recognize.

```
$!  XQTYPE.COM
$
$!  Uses DCL DECnet task-to-task to check the device type of
$!  the XQA0: controller on the remote system, if any. Can
$!  return <unknown>, <none>, <DELQA>, or <DEQNA>. Requires
$!  V5.0 or better, as this procedure uses block-structured
$!  IF syntax.
$!
$!  Calling:
$!     @XQTYPE node
$!
$!  Procedure must be named XQTYPE.COM and must reside in the
$!  default login directory on both the local and the remote
$!  nodes. Note that the remote login may occur either in the
$!  directory specified by a proxy, if one exists, or in the
$!  DECnet directory. If you're not sure, the default
$!  directory is determined by entering the command:
$!     "DIRECTORY node::".
$!  Requires access to the DECnet TASK object on the remote
$!  end either by the default DECnet user name/password or
$!  via a proxy.
```

```
$       set noon
$       vers = "0000|XQTYPE"
$       goto 'f$getjpi("","MODE")
$
$INTERACTIVE:
$10:    p1 = f$edit(p1,"COLLAPSE,UPCASE") - "::"
$       if f$length(p1) .eq. 0
$       then
$         msg = "Error reading input"
$         read/prompt="Node? "/error=exit sys$command p1
$         goto 10
$       endif
$
$       msg = "Error creating network connection"
$       open/read/write/error=exit net 'p1::"task=xqtype"
$       read net remvers
$       if remvers .nes. vers Then goto exit
$       write net vers
$       read net xqtype
$       close net
$       write sys$output -
                "XQA0: Device type on node ''p1:: is ''xqtype'"
$       msg = ""
$       goto exit
$
$NETWORK:
$!      display some information into the NETSERVER.LOG
$       show process/all
$       msg = "Error receiving network connection"
$       open/read/write/error=exit net sys$net
$       write net vers
$       read net remvers
$       if remvers .nes. vers then goto exit
$       if f$getdvi("XQA0:","EXISTS")
$       then
$         devtype = f$getdvi("XQA0:","DEVTYPE")
$         xqtype = "<unknown>"
$         if devtype .eq. 33 then xqtype = "DELQA"
$         if devtype .eq. 22 then xqtype = "DEQNA"
$       else
$         xqtype = "<none>"
$       endif
$       write net xqtype
$       close net
$
```

```
$BATCH:
$OTHER:
$     msg = "Unsupported mode"
$
$exit:
$     if f$length(msg) .ne. 0 then write sys$output msg
$     close/nolog net
$     stop
$     exit
```

23.5 DECnet Access Controls

When you access a remote system using DECnet, you must use a valid user name and password on the system you are accessing. A valid user name and password indicate that you are authorized to access the system.

To provide for the user to specify the access control information, a DECnet node specification includes the name of the node, an optional quoted string called the DECnet access control string, and a pair of colons (::). The quoted access control string can be omitted, can contain nothing, can contain only a user name, or can contain a user name and a password. With OpenVMS V6.2 and later, and the integrated IP support features, IP access control specifications operate in an analogous fashion.

Using the access control string, DECnet supports three main access control mechanisms for incoming connection requests. The first mechanism allows you to specify a user name and a password for the remote system. This technique works well for interactive use, but has several limitations when used within command procedures. The explicit specification can expose the user name and password to any user that can read the command procedure. The technique also requires all command procedures that reference the user name and password to be altered whenever the password is changed, and this tends to discourage users from changing the password as frequently as it should be.

An example of an explicit specification of the user name HOFFMAN and the password OPENVMS$FAQ:

```
$     directory wilton"hoffman openvms$faq"::
```

The second access control mechanism, default DECnet access, involves using the default DECnet user name and password configured on the remote system, or the default DECnet task user name. Relatively few OpenVMS systems have a default DECnet user name or a DECnet task user name configured, because having these default accounts means that any remote user can directly access the system. To request access using the default DECnet user name:

```
$    directory wilton::
```

When configured, the default DECnet user name and password are set up in the DECnet database for the node by the system manager.

The third and often most appropriate DECnet access control mechanism is the DECnet *proxy*. The DECnet proxy examines the user and the node that is requesting access and then maps the requestor into one or more local user names. The need to explicitly specify the user name and password is eliminated. The proxy eliminates unrestricted access to the system.

Two varieties of proxies exist: the default proxy and the non-default proxy. There can be at most one default proxy configured for each remote user. There can be zero or more non-default proxies configured, each mapping the remote user into a specific local user name. The default proxy is selected when no access control string is specified. A non-default proxy can be selected by specifying the user name that is associated with the desired proxy in the access control string. In either case, the specification of the password is not required.

You may notice that a default proxy is selected using the same syntax as in a request for default DECnet access:

```
$    directory wilton::
```

When non-default proxies are configured, a specific non-default proxy, such as a proxy to the SYSTEM user name, can be requested with the command:

```
$    directory wilton"system"::
```

If the requesting user name and node are listed in the proxy database, and access to the SYSTEM user name is permitted, the access will occur under the SYSTEM user name.

Because of the similarity of the syntax for the default DECnet request and the default proxy request, the authors recommend that all requests for the default DECnet user name assume that proxies are configured and use the following alternate syntax:

```
$    directory wilton""::
```

The NETSERVER.LOG is created in the default directory: the directory associated with the explicit user name and password, the directory for the DECnet default user name, or the directory associated with the default or non-default proxy.

DECnet proxies are configured using the AUTHORIZE utility, using the ADD/PROXY, MODIFY/PROXY, and REMOVE/PROXY commands. For additional information, see the DECnet documentation and the documentation of the `AUTHORIZE` utility. Please see your system manager for assistance in creating and configuring proxies. The DECnet default user name exists in `SYSUAF` using `AUTHORIZE`, and configured in DECnet using `NCP` or `NCL`.

23.6 DECnet Object Specifications

Client applications specify the target for the connection to DECnet using a DECnet object number. DECnet provides a number of predefined objects for various purposes, and applications and system managers can configure additional objects as needed. Typical objects include the objects used by `MAIL` and `SET HOST`, and an object central to many task-to-task applications communications, the `TASK` object. Each DECnet object is assigned an object number, with the `TASK` object assigned object number zero. Information on configuring and using objects other than object zero is included in 24.

DCL typically uses the task object, but DECnet can be configured to use others. As you have already seen, the task object can be referenced using `TASK=` and a task name:

```
$ type wilton::"task=server"
```

In this context, the task name is the name of the DCL command procedure to invoke.

Because objects can be referenced using numbers, you can also refer to the `SERVER` command procedure using the command:

```
$ type wilton::"0=server"
```

Each DECnet object can be assigned a user name and password and can be assigned the name of a procedure or an image to invoke. The task object is a special case, because it allows the remote user to specify the name of a procedure to invoke. Because of this, the task object is often configured *without* a default user name and password, because allowing general access can leave the system vulnerable to nefarious activity.

For additional information, please see the DECnet documentation.

23.7 Troubleshooting Task-to-Task Problems

A variety of problems can arise when you are working with interprocess communications. Here are some of the more common problems and how they can be resolved:

- Commands in the remote `SYLOGIN.COM` or `LOGIN.COM` can cause problems with the remote task. Check `NETSERVER.LOG` for details on the failure. Use the process mode to conditionalize the execution of the commands, or remove the commands.

- When the `READ` and `WRITE` commands are mismatched, it is possible for the client or the server to hang indefinitely on a command. Check the `NETSERVER.LOG` log file, and use procedure verification to determine the cause of the hang.

- Messages indicating that the network partner has exited usually indicate problems on the remote node, such as invalid commands in the remote server, the remote `SYLOGIN.COM`, or the remote `LOGIN.COM`. Check the `NETSERVER.LOG` on the remote node for further information.

- There are various reasons why a `NETSERVER.LOG` log file might be missing. Check for problems with file protections and disk quotas, and use the `DIRECTORY` command to locate the remote default directory. Also check for a log with the highest permissible file version, `NETSERVER.LOG;32767`, and check for any site-specific commands that might be automatically deleting the log file. If you are unable to determine the problem, ask your system manager to use system auditing or system security alarms to determine if the `NETSERVER.LOG` is being written, and where.

- Access or login failures can be caused by an invalid user name or password, by the specification of an incorrect destination node, or by OpenVMS breakin evasion processing.

23.8 Advanced Networking Applications

DCL has difficulty performing various tasks that are required for more advanced networking tasks. The following list contains some of the application designs that are not normally implemented in DCL (designs that require the use of executable images):

- Applications that can post read and write messages in parallel, for example, having a `READ` operation outstanding while a `WRITE` operation is performed.

- Servers that support multiple connection requests, having multiple clients connected to a single server.

- Clients and servers that use IP protocols and interfaces.

- Applications that use communication designs other than the client/server designs discussed in this chapter. This includes applications that use peer-to-peer designs, designs where server tasks communicate directly with other server tasks.

These tasks are beyond the capabilities of DCL and also beyond the scope of this book. These advanced applications are typically based on executable images, often implemented using OpenVMS asynchronous system traps (ASTs), or threads. DCL, for instance, does not have the ability to issue a write on a channel with a read request outstanding; DCL would pause on the READ command, blocking the write.

For information on designing and creating advanced networking applications, see the DECnet documentation, the *DIGITAL TCP/IP Services for OpenVMS* documentation, and the various example programs available in SYS$EXAMPLES.

CHAPTER 24

Security

SYSTEM SECURITY AND INTEGRITY are of critical importance as we enter the new millennium. This chapter presents information that helps the DCL programmer create procedures that maintain system security. It also explain how to use DCL to control access to files and other resources of an OpenVMS system, while preventing the user from gaining unrestricted access to the system.

OpenVMS security features can be used to permit access to information and to system resources, and can also be use to prevent access. Additional security features also provide the ability to audit system activity.

Most commonly, you will be called upon to develop a procedure that will allow access to files or to system resources, access that a user would not ordinarily possess. System security and integrity will be important considerations during this development process. Security refers to which users and which applications can access the system and the data. Integrity is equally important, as it indicates the level of trust users can place in the system and the data.

This chapter assumes DECnet Phase IV command syntax. Equivalent capabilities are available under DECnet-Plus, though a different command syntax is required.

24.1 Captive and Restricted Logins

OpenVMS users are typically not restricted: they can enter DCL commands interactively. There may be times when you will not want certain users to have unrestricted command access, however. As an example, you may want to allow a user to perform a fully privileged operation, such as a file system backup, but without allowing general access to the file system.

To perform a task such as a system backup, you have probably already considered including various commands in the LOGIN.COM of a dedicated user name. This works nicely, but the user can potentially use CTRL/Y to interrupt the procedure, even if you place a SET NOCONTROL=Y command or similar at the start of the procedure. Further, if the user finds or can induce an error in the procedure, it may be possible to exit to the DCL interpreter. And once at DCL, the user can use the privileges for almost any purpose, appropriate or otherwise.

The OpenVMS AUTHORIZE utility and the OpenVMS security policy provides two mechanisms, called *captive* and *restricted logins*, that can be useful here. Using flags in the system authorization file, specific user names can be marked as either captive or restricted. Both mechanisms ensure that SYLOGIN.COM and LOGIN.COM execute fully. Should any error condition or code path arise that would allow the user to directly access DCL, a captive user process will be automatically logged out with a NOCMDPROC error.

Captive users are prevented from performing a variety of operations. Table 24.1 provides a list of the more commonly encountered prohibitions. The user is also forced to execute the SYLOGIN.COM and LOGIN.COM procedures, if present.

Table 24.1 Prohibitions for CAPTIVE users

Action	Restrictions
CTRL/Y	The interrupt sequence is disabled by default.
INQUIRE	All access to this rather idiosyncratic command is disabled.
SPAWN	Subprocess creation with SPAWN is permitted only when the /TRUSTED qualifier is specified. Spawning from utilities such as MAIL and LSEDIT is prohibited.
/CLI	Login qualifier; uses an alternate command line interpreter.
/COMMAND	Login qualifier; requests an alternate login command procedure.
/DISK	Login qualifier; that specifies an alternate default login device.
/LGICMD	Login qualifier; selects a nondefault login procedure.
/TABLES	Login qualifier; utilizes an alternate command table.

Restricted users have many similarities to captive users, but restricted users can reach DCL. Restricted configurations are chosen in situations where you wish the user to always execute the SYLOGIN.COM and LOGIN.COM procedures, but when DCL access is permissible. You can place logging routines, checks for the source of remote logins (such as via the F$GETDVI itemcode TT_ACCPORNAM), or other operations in these procedures.

You can also use restricted logins, in conjunction with a feature of OpenVMS authentication, to provide the login command procedure with enhanced privileges while denying the user access to these privileges. To configure this, enable the enhanced privileges in the default privilege mask for the user using AUTHORIZE, but do not enable the privileges in the authorized privileged mask. The login procedure can use the privileges as needed. When the use of the privileges has completed, the procedure then issues a SET PROCESS/PRIVILEGE command or F$SETPRV lexical function to disable the privileges at any time prior to exiting to DCL. Because the privileges are not in the authorized mask and are disabled prior to exiting to DCL, the extra privileges cannot be used or reenabled by the user.

An example of setting up enhanced privileges for use by a restricted login follows:

```
$ set default sys$system
$ run authorize
UAF> modify targetuser -
_UAF> /privilege=(tmpmbx,netmbx) -
_UAF> /defprivilege=(sysnam,cmexec,tmpmbx,netmbx) -
_UAF> /flags=(nodisuser,nocaptive,restrict)
```

The behavior of captive logins described here was first implemented in V5.2. Further, the behavior of restricted logins effectively matches the behavior of captive logins on OpenVMS versions prior to V5.2.

Here is an example captive command procedure:

```
$      on control_y then continue
$      on warning then logout/brief
       .
       procedure activities
       .
$      logout
```

This procedure does not establish an interrupt handler as described in Chapter 9. Instead, it specifies the CONTINUE command as the handler. The CONTINUE command effectively ignores interrupts and continues execution of the procedure and any image that may be running at the time. Thus, CTRL/Y interrupts are disabled. (It is possible to use CTRL/Y interrupt the procedure just prior to the ON CONTROL_Y command.)

The procedure also does not handle errors in the normal fashion. Instead, the error handler executes a `LOGOUT` command, which immediately logs the user out of the system. More sophisticated error handling is certainly possible in a captive procedure, but you run the risk of opening a hole through which the user can escape to DCL.

Captive user procedures cannot issue certain DCL commands, such as the `INQUIRE` and `SPAWN` command. The prohibition against spawning prevents a tool such as a text editor that might support a `SPAWN` command from allowing a user to escape to DCL. Procedures and commands can explicitly override this behavior using the `SPAWN/TRUSTED` command.

24.2   Controlled Access via DECnet

Sec. 23.5, p. 305

DECnet task-to-task command procedures can be used to provide a nonprivileged user with access to a privileged account, in a controlled and secure fashion. Because you are configuring OpenVMS to allow this access, elevated privileges are required. In particular, various `AUTHORIZE` and DECnet NCP commands in this section require privileges. Please check with your system manager for assistance with these privileged commands, and for guidance on the local site security policies and associated requirements.

Using what you have learned in Chapter 23, set up a DECnet proxy to an appropriately privileged user name. For example, the following associates user `GREEK` on node `WILTON` with the local user `HOFFMAN`.

```
$ set default sys$system
$ run authorize
UAF> add/proxy wilton::greek hoffman
```

You can also specify a wildcard for the remote node, for the remote user name, or for both fields. The following command example sets up a proxy that allows any remote user anywhere on the network to access the local user `HOFFMAN`:

```
UAF> add/proxy *::* hoffman
```

Wildcard proxies should be used with caution, as they can permit the specified access to a wide variety of remote users.

Now that you have the proxy configured, place the server command procedure in the default directory for the user name. Use care to avoid including any command procedures in the default directory other than the intended procedures, as a remote user will be able to use the proxy to invoke any procedures in the directory.

As an alternative to proxies, you can set up a DECnet object. You have already seen various DECnet objects, including the task object in Chapter 23. Various server tasks, such as MAIL, are assigned DECnet objects. Using similar techniques, you can assign your own network object for a particular task, including a specific user name and password, and the name of the command procedure.

The following example creates a dedicated user name FOOSERVER and an associated directory. It sets up a DECnet object FOO in both the DECnet permanent and volatile databases. As part of this DECnet object creation, the user name, password, and file name are specified.

```
$ set default sys$system
$ run authorize
UAF> add fooserver/password=tunafish$gel -
_UAF> /uic=[376,370] -
_UAF> /device=sys$sysdevice:/directory=[fooserver] -
_UAF> /privilege=(tmpmbx,netmbx) -
_UAF> /defprivilege=(tmpmbx,netmbx) -
_UAF> /flags=(nodisuser,nocaptive,restrict)/lgicmd=nla0: -
_UAF> /nobatch/nointeractive -
_UAF> /owner="The Foo Server"
$ create/directory sys$sysdevice:[fooserver]
$ run sys$system:ncp
NCP> define object foo user fooserver password tunafish$gel
NCP> set object foo user fooserver password tunafish$gel
```

When no file is specified with the DECnet object, the file name is assumed to match the object name, with a default of SYS$SYSTEM:.COM. In this example, the command procedure would be SYS$SYSTEM:FOO.COM. Also, the above example shows a nonprivileged user name, but the creation and use of a privileged user name is equally possible.

To invoke the FOO.COM command procedure using the FOO object, use the DECnet specification WILTON::"FOO=". As a result of all this configuration effort, you now have a way for a nonprivileged user to invoke a procedure under a privileged user name. Now, using techniques from Chapter 23, you can exchange data with the procedure, communicating commands, options, or parameters as required.

Both the proxy-based login and the object-based access work equally well, though the object-based approach allows more direct control over the particular procedures available to the remote users. Conversely, the proxy-based approach allows direct control over which specific users are permitted to use the access.

24.3 Automatic Logins

OpenVMS supports a mechanism, known as an *automatic login*, that permits any user accessing the OpenVMS system from a specified terminal to automatically log in. An automatic login, most commonly used with a captive command procedure, is used to allow a user to avoid having to specify a user name and password.

To establish an automatic login at terminal TXA0: under user name FOOUSER, you can use the SYSMAN automatic login facility (ALF) commands:

```
$ SYSMAN
SYSMAN> ALF ADD TXA0 FOOUSER
```

User FOOUSER would be configured as a captive user name, with a login command procedure that performs the necessary operations.

24.4 System Resources

Tracking the usage of system resources, and particularly of disk storage, is often of interest. OpenVMS supports a mechanism, called a *disk quota,* that can be used to track disk storage usage. Quotas are enabled by the system manager on a disk volume basis, with an entry for each user who will store files on the volume. Quotas can be used to limit storage, and also to track storage by simply setting each user's quota limit to a value larger than the total capacity of the disk volume.

On systems with disk quotas established, you may want to set up a shared storage area. This area can be used as a scratch storage area, or it could be used for common project files. Users creating files in the common area would not be charged for the storage; it would be assocated with a type of identifier known as a *resource identifier*.

The following example shows how to create a resource identifier SCRATCH, permit the users HOFFMAN and GREEK to charge resources to it, set up the disk storage associated with the identifier, and set up a scratch directory and its associated ACL. The ACL includes a number of access control entries (ACEs):

- The specification of the default protection assigned to all files created in the directory.
- The access permitted to users that possess the SCRATCH identifier.
- The default ACE that will be added to any new files created in the directory.

- The access that will he granted to the creator of any file created in the directory.

```
$ set default sys$system
$ run authorize
UAF> add/identifier scratch/attributes=resource
UAF> grant/identifier scratch hoffman/attributes=resource
UAF> grant/identifier scratch greek/attributes=resource
UAF> ^Z
$ sysman
SYSMAN> diskquota add scratch/permquota=10000/overdraft=1000
SYSMAN> ^Z
$ create/directory scratchdisk:[scratcharea]/owner=scratch
$ set security scratchdisk:[scratcharea] -
_$ /acl=((default_protection,s:rwed,o:rwed,g:rwed,w),-
_$ (identifier=scratch,access=read+write+delete),-
_$ (identifier=scratch,options=default,-
_$   access=read+write+delete),-
_$ (creator,access=read+write+delete))
```

When using a resource identifier, the creator ACE specifies the access granted to the creating process, as the file will be owned by the resource identifier. To disable the creation of this ACE, use the ACCESS=NONE keyword on the creator ACE.

If an application you are working with creates temporary files, the creating process must have sufficient disk quota on the target device, or disk quotas must not be enabled on the target device. Temporary files, as differentiated from standard files that are created in a scratch directory, are not created in a directory; they exist in the file structure outside of any directory. Because these files are not in a directory, they do not and cannot honor any established resource identifiers.

Disk quotas are not supported on the OpenVMS system disk and should not be enabled on it.

24.5 Guidelines for Maintaining Security

The following are general guidelines for maintaining system security within your command procedure:

- Do not insert OpenVMS passwords directly into command procedures, because the contents of procedures can be viewed by users. Furthermore, you are unlikely to change the passwords periodically, as you should, if they are "hardwired" in procedures.

- Procedures should avoid asking passwords of the user and recording these in a data file, as users are likely to use their OpenVMS password here. This data file could thus expose valid OpenVMS passwords. If you must store passwords in a file, use an image that calls the OpenVMS password hashing routine to hash the passsword before storing or comparing it, and only compare the hashed version of the password against the saved hashed passsword.

- Avoid using the `INQUIRE` command, as it has a variety of potentially unexpected and undesired behaviors. Instead, use the `READ` command. The `INQUIRE` command is prohibited in captive command procedures.

  Sec. 11.1, p. 126

- Do not allow a captive command procedure to write to its own local directory. Overwriting some or all of the files associated with the command procedure can have undesirable effects on system security. This includes preventing the user from issuing a command such as `EXTRACT/NOHEADER SYS$LOGIN:LOGIN.COM` from within `MAIL`, and other similar techiques of replacing existing files or procedures.

- Never accept and directly execute any user input. Always filter it to exclude any characters that are not in the required character set, before including the input in any executed command. This particularly involves avoiding characters such as the apostrophe (`'`) and the ampersand (`&`) in the input text.

- Ask the system manager to enable security auditing on key application files, using alarm and audit ACEs, to detect and log any modifications to the application files.

- Do not permit system access unnecessarily: avoid wildcard DECnet proxies and issuing or enabling privileges unnecessarily.

CHAPTER 25
The World Wide Web

THE WORLD WIDE WEB has become part of our life. This chapter offers guidelines for using DCL within the framework of the *World Wide Web* (WWW). It builds on information from Chapter 6 on displaying output and from Chapter 23 on DECnet communications.

A complete description of the World Wide Web is beyond the scope of this chapter. Various good books exist on this subject, and a wealth of information exists online, including the information available via the World Wide Web Consortium's site at www.w3c.org.

To make full use of the information in this chapter, you will need access to a package known as a web server and to a package known as a web browser. Commercial and noncommercial web server and web browser packages are available for OpenVMS from various sources. Various features common to most web servers are assumed; you will want to check your specific web server documentation for the features available, and for any specific requirements or restrictions.

The World Wide Web is commonly called simply the "web," which is what we will call it. The web is a collection of computers that, in cooperation with each other, retrieve and display pages of text for users. They can also gather simple input from the users. The text pages contain information and links to other related pages that can reside in the same document or in documents on other computers anywhere in the world. These links, called *hyperlinks,* are among the most powerful features of the World Wide Web.

Sec. 23.1, p. 300

The web is a client/server environment. The client portion of the web is the most familiar of the various components; it is the software that you use to read web pages. On the web, these clients are called *web browsers,* or often simply browsers. Browsers can access local web pages directly, but more commonly access web pages by connecting to a web server on the local node or on another node in the network. The browsers and the servers typically communicate using an IP-based protocol known as the *hypertext transport protocol* (HTTP).

Within the web, clients locate servers and servers reference other servers using network addresses known as uniform or *universal resource locators* (URL). The major components of the URL include the protocol to use for the access, such as HTTP or FTP, the host IP address, and the specific web page of interest. Various parts of the URL can be omitted, and the web server and web browser can be configured to provide defaults. An example of a simple URL follows:

```
http://www.openvms.digital.com/
```

The protocol used in this example URL is HTTP, and the IP address is `www.openvms.digital.com`. Since the port and the web page are not specified, default values for both are applied by the web server. Additional examples of URLs are presented in Section 25.8.

Web pages are most commonly written in a language called *Hypertext Markup Language* (HTML). HTML is a text formatting language, consisting of text with embedded tags. These tags provide various functions, including text formatting and hyperlinks. The available HTML tags, as well as the format of the language, are defined in the evolving HTML standards; various web browsers and web servers can include nonstandard extensions to HTML.

On OpenVMS and on various other operating systems, each HTML web page is organized into a separate text file. These HTML files are located in a set of directories that are configured to be accessable to the web browser.

For information on the type and the configuration of the local web server, and for the location of the directories that contain the HTML files, please contact your local system manager.

25.1 HTML

An example of the HTML contents of the file `SIMPLE.HTML` follows. This HTML generates among the simplest web pages possible:

```
<html>
<p>Simple web page.
</html>
```

The `<html>` and `</html>` tags indicate the begining and end of the web page document. The `<p>` indicates the beginning of a paragraph. The rest of the text, `Simple web page.`, is output directly.

To view this file directly from within a web browser on OpenVMS, you can use the following URL:

```
file:///sys$login/simple.html
```

The `file` protocol used in this URL requests that the web browser directly access and view a local file. This approach entirely avoids the use of a web server, and avoids the need to locate the file `SIMPLE.HTML` in a directory visible to the web server. The three consecutive slash (/) characters used in this URL indicate that the host name has been omitted. Not all web browsers support this syntax.

25.2 HTML Tags

The HTML standard provides for a wide variety of HTML tags. Some of the most common tags are listed in Table 25.1. Additional tags are described in Appendix D.

Various nonstandard HTML extension tags are available. These tags are specific to a particular web browser. The authors recommend that you avoid nonstandard extensions whenever feasible, because the use of any of these extensions can prevent your pages from being viewed at all, or from being viewed correctly, using web browsers that do not support the extensions.

Web servers can contain extensions as well. These extensions can be general in nature, or the web server can be tailored for specific tasks. Server extensions should be treated with the same caution as other extensions, as they can restrict your pages to the services of a particular web server.

For information on the current HTML standards, visit the World Wide Web Consortium's site at www.w3c.org. This book follows the HTML V3.2 standard and avoids the use of any vendor-specific HTML extensions.

25.3 Common Gateway Interface (CGI)

The contents of a basic HTML web page are static and the text displayed when the web page is accessed changes only when you change the file containing the web page.

Table 25.1 HTML tags

Tag	Description
<A> ... </A>	Marks the begining and end of an anchor. Anchors are used to implement internal hyperlinks within the current web page, as well as hyperlinks to other web pages elsewhere.
<BODY> ... </BODY>	Delimits the body of the document. The body contains the body text, as well as various tags.
 	Forces a line break in the text.
<FORM> ... </FORM>	Delimits a group of HTML tags that prompts for and processes user input.
<IMG>	Marks the inclusion of an image, usually a GIF (typically pronounced "JIF") file. Also optionally provides alternate text that can be displayed for the web browser, when the image is not visible.
<INPUT>	Processes user input within a form.
<H1> ... </H1>	These tags denote the beginning and the end of a header. The header text can be a section or paragraph header. Six levels of header tags are permitted, with <H1> being the largest and most significant, and <H6> being the smallest and least significant.
<HEAD> and </HEAD>	Marks the beginning and end of the document headers. The header contains the document header information.
<HTML> and </HTML>	Marks the beginning and the end of the HTML document.
<HR>	Includes a horizontal rule in the display.
<P>	Marks the beginning of a paragraph.
<PRE> ... </PRE>	Marks the beginning and end of a section of preformatted text.
<SELECT> ... </SELECT>	Allows user selections within a form.
<TITLE> ... </ENDTITLE>	Denotes the beginning and the end of the document title.

You might want to make the information more dynamic, generating the information based on the output from an application image or a command procedure. One obvious way to display more dynamic information would be to regenerate the contents of the web page by periodically invoking a program or a DCL command procedure that rewrites the file containing the text and HTML tags used for the web page. This will certainly work, but there is a better method. You can avoid writing a file by creating the web page automatically each time it is viewed. This method uses the *Common Gateway Interface* (CGI), and a CGI script. A CGI script can be a DCL command procedure or an application image.

CGI directly uses the output from the command procedure or the application image as the source for the contents of the web page. It also uses HTML. Rather than creating and storing the HTML in a file, the CGI script skips the file and simply displays the HTML, and the web server then reads and processes the HTML for display on the web browser. The CGI script typically runs as a subprocess of the web server.

CGI scripts are involved by the web server in response to a URL reference such as the following:

```
http://wilton.zko.dec.com/cgi-bin/script.com
```

Most web servers support CGI.

Like HTML files, CGI procedures must be executed from a particular directory or subdirectory. On OpenVMS and on most other systems, this directory is typically called `cgi-bin`, the CGI binary directory.

The next example is almost identical to the one before. The only addition is a tag to the inform the web server how to process the document, followed by a blank line. With web pages stored in files, the file type tells the web server and the web browser how to display the file. With a CGI script, the `content-type` tag provides the same necessary information. The blank line denotes the end of the CGI header, and the beginning of the HTML document.

```
content-type: text/html

<html>
<p>Simple web page.
</html>
```

The simple DCL CGI script to generate this HTML is:

```
$    display = "write sys$output"
$    display "content-type: text/html"
$    display ""
$    display "<html>"
$    display "<p>Simple web page."
$    display "</html>"
$    exit
```

25.3 Common Gateway Interface (CGI)

Table 25.2
CGI symbols

Symbol	Description
GATEWAY_INTERFACE	The CGI interface protocol.
HTTPS	Indicates if the secure version of the HTTP protocol is in use.
HTTP_ACCEPT	Indicates the content types that are supported.
HTTP_HOST	The host address and port.
HTTP_USER_AGENT	Information on the web browser.
PATH	The current default device and directory.
REMOTE_ADDR	The remote IP address.
REMOTE_HOST	The remote IP host name.
REQUEST_METHOD	The request type indicates how the data is passed from the web browser to the web server.
SCRIPT_NAME	The Unix-format directory specification for the CGI script.
SERVER_NAME	The IP host name for the web server host.
SERVER_PORT	The IP port number for the web server.
SERVER_PROTOCOL	The transport protocol name and version.
SERVER_SOFTWARE	The name of the web server package.
SERVER_URL	The URL used to reach the web server.

25.4 CGI Symbols

On OpenVMS, web servers pass information into CGI scripts using symbols. Information on the user that has requested the script, on the type of the remote web browser, on the local web server, and other information of interest to the CGI script is available via DCL symbols created by the web server when the CGI script is invoked; these symbols are intended for use by the CGI script. Table 25.2 contains some of the global symbols created by one particular vendor's web server. Check your web server documentation for information on the specific symbols available to you.

25.5 CGI File Types

Web servers and web browsers cooperate to display various file formats, based on the file type specified or defaulted in the URL. HTML is the most common of the file formats, and file types, that can be displayed. Other formats that can be processed by various web browsers include graphical images, various

Table 25.3
CGI file types

Type	Description
AVI	Video images.
BMP	Bitmap images.
GIF	Graphic images. Often used to display pictures and icons.
JPEG or JPG	Graphic images.
MPEG or MPG	Movies and video images.
HTML or HTM	Hypertext markup language documents. These files are the basis for most web pages. HTM is common on systems with restrictive file name requirements.
PDF	Adobe portable document format documents. A format used for documentation.
PS	Adobe Postscript format documents. A format used for printed material.
TXT	Text document.

document formats, movies, audio, and many others. Table 25.3 summarizes the most common file types. Not all web browsers can process all formats.

The web browser is responsible for interpreting the particular applications or viewers that should be used to display the file. Unrecognized file types typically result in the display of a dialog that controls the downloading the file from the web server to the local system. Various file formats can be combined within a single HTML document, allowing graphic images and text to be combined.

Individual web browsers can be configured to recognize various additional file types when an application is available to display the file.

File types can have different meanings on different platforms. One of the common file type conflicts involves DCL: the .COM file type. On OpenVMS, this file type indicates a DCL common procedure. On other operating systems, this type can be associated with other file content, such as an executable image. Most web browsers support a preferences menu, to allow you to tie a specific file type to a specific viewing tool.

File downloads typically occur via the *File Transfer Protocol* (FTP). an IP-based file transfer utility. FTP is the IP equivalent of the OpenVMS COPY command. FTP supports two basic file transfer modes: image and text. Image mode is used to transfer data. Text files, source code, and such are transferred using text mode. Transferring a file using the incorrect transfer mode can lead to file corruptions.

When FTP is specified directly within a URL, the transfer mode is selected based on the file type, as determined by defaults set in preferences menu of

25.5 CGI File Types

the web browser. This mechanism fulfills a role for FTP similar to the role the `content-type` tag performs for the `HTTP` protocol: it describes how to interpret the file data.

Specific web browsers will recognize different sets of file types. Different browsers can also different sets of preferences for file types, both across different browsers, and across the platforms that the browsers support. Because of this, and because of the differing extensions supported by various browsers, basic testing with several different common browsers is recommended.

25.6 Advanced CGI Processing

The following CGI script, `CGI_DEMO.COM`, displays all global symbols present in the current process, including the symbols that are created by the web server. It also demonstrates a techique for converting the output of a DCL command (`SHOW SYMBOL`, in this example) directly into the web page output for display on the remote web browser.

```
$!   CGI_DEMO.COM: CGI-DCL Demonstration
$!   Displays various information about the web server.
$!   Example URL:
$!      http://wilton.zko.dec.com:port/cgi-bin/cgi_demo.com
$
$    display = "write sys$output"
$
$    display "content-type: text/html"
$    display ""
$    srvsoft = f$element(0,"/","''server_software'")
$    srvvers = f$element(1,"/","''server_software'")
$    display "<H1>Fun with DCL</H1>"
$    display -
        "<p>This is a DCL procedure running under CGI.<br>"
$    display "<HR>"
$    display "<pre>"
$    show symbol/all/global
$    display "</pre>"
$    display "<IMG SRC=""/images/ball.gif""> " + -
            "This web server is running " + srvsoft + -
            " version " + srvvers + "<br>"
$    display "<IMG SRC=""/images/ball.gif""> " + -
            "This web server is running on " + SERVER_NAME + -
            "<br>"
$    display "<HR>"
```

```
$       display "<p>This procedure was brought to you by "
$       display -
          "<A HREF=""http://wilton.zko.dec.com/author.html"">" + -
          "Hoff</A>. Your "
$       display "<A HREF=""mailto:dcl@wilton.zko.dec.com"">" + -
                "feedback</A> is welcome<br>"
$       exit
```

25.7 CGI Subprocesses

CGI scripts run as subprocesses of the web server, under a user name set up specifically for the web server. When designing a CGI script, you must consider the security access available to the web server and to the CGI subprocess. This includes setting up the appropriate file protections and ACLs to allow the CGI script to access any files it might require. You must also consider the settings of the process quotas associated with the web server user name, as these quotas may not reflect the quotas necessary for your particular application. In other words, you must be aware that the CGI script does not execute under your user name.

Most web servers include a logging mechanism, which can be invaluable for troubleshooting problems within CGI scripts. The logs can also be used to track hits, that is, individual web page accesses. See your web server documentation for information on the log file, and see your system manager for the specific location of the log on your system.

25.8 URLs

The following URLs show various more complex URLs, and various URL formats:

```
http://wilton.zko.dec.com:80/www.html#fragment
http://wilton.zko.dec.com/www.htmlparameter=value
http://wilton.zko.dec.com/www.htmlspace=contains%20space
```

The first URL shows the specification of the IP port number 80, and a reference to the label of a text fragment `fragment` contained within the `www.html` document. The second URL demonstrates passing parameters. The third shows a space character, hexadecimal 20, embedded in a parameter. Additional information on parameters and parameter encoding will be covered shortly.

IP port 80 is the default port used for most standard web servers. Secure web servers typically use port 443. Ports 1024 and higher are typically non-privileged, and web servers using these ports may or may not be operating with the sanction or knowledge of the local system manager.

Additional URLs are:

```
file://localhost/direct.html
file:///direct.html
ftp://wilton.zko.dec.com/saveset.bck
mailto:dcl@wilton.zko.dec.com
```

The first is a direct access to a local file, `direct.html`. The second is similar, but the reference to `localhost` is defaulted. Note the extra slash. The third is an FTP file transfer: a file copy operation for `saveset.bck`. The final URL invokes the local mail utility to send mail to the specified address.

The `file` protocol is useful for direct access to files and avoids the use of a web server. This can be useful for allowing access to files on a local disk or CD-ROM using a web browser.

File transfers via the FTP protocol allow the user to perform a download of the specified file to the system running the browser.

The `mailto` protocol invokes the local mail utility and prompts the user for the text of a mail message to send to the specified Internet address. This URL is most often used to obtain feedback for a specific web page or web site.

25.9 Input

When you write a DCL procedure to directly query the user for data, you would use the READ or occasionally the INQUIRE command, displaying a prompt and directly reading the user input into a DCL symbol. By now, this interactive series of reads, prompts, and output should be very familiar to you.

Processing user input via the web is not interactive; it more closely parallels processing by terminals with local editing capabilities, such as the older forms-oriented terminals. All questions and prompts are displayed on a web page; the user reads the prompts and answers the questions and then submits the form for processing. The results are then transferred from the CGI script down to the web browser and are displayed on another form. This new form can obviously display the results of the form queries to the user and can include the display of additional prompts and questions. Or the form can simply thank the user for providing the input.

With web servers and web browsers, prompting and reading user input involves processing parameters, either specified directly via embedded hyperlinks, or via HTML forms. HTML forms are designed to accept user input and pass the results to the CGI script via the URL, or via input channel. Forms input passed to the CGI script via the URL is called *GET data,* while input passed with the input channel is called *POST data.*

When input data is passed by GET data, the data is encoded and appended to the URL. This is called *URL encoding.* Only a specific set of characters are permitted within the text of the URL. Any characters that might affect the processing of the URL are translated into other, permitted, characters. The question mark (?) delimits the beginning of the argument list, and the ampersand (&) separates parameters. The space character is translated into a plus (+) character. Characters such as the ampersand (&), plus (+), and percent sign (%) are translated into a percent sign followed by the two-character hexadecimal representation of the ISO Latin-1 character value.

The following example is an HTML page that contains a form. The form prompts the user for input using a text box, a set of radio buttons, a selector, and a submission button. When the user selects the submit button, the user input is transfered to the `CGI_DEMO_FORM.COM` command procedure. Because the form method is `GET`, the input is transfered as parameters on the URL that invokes `CGI_DEMO_FORM.COM` procedure. The parameters are passed to the procedure by the web server using the `QUERY_STRING` symbol.

Text Input Box: [   ]

Radio Buttons: ○ Button1 ● Button2 ○ Button3

Selector: [Option1 ▼]

[Submit Query]

The following command procedure is called by the previous form. Notice that it is similar to the earlier `CGI_DEMO.COM` command procedure. This procedure differs primarily in addition of the `URLDECODE` subroutine, a routine to decode the data from the URL-encoded parameters passed into the procedure by the `QUERY_STRING`.

```
$!   CGI_DEMO2.COM: CGI-DCL Demonstration
$!   Displays various information about the web server.
$!   Example URL:
$!      http://wilton.zko.dec.com:port/cgi-bin/cgi_demo_form.com
$
```

```
$       display = "write sys$output"
$
$       display "content-type: text/html"
$       display ""
$       srvsoft = f$element(0,"/","''server_software'")
$       srvvers = f$element(1,"/","''server_software'")
$       display "<H1>Fun with DCL</H1>"
$       display "<p>This is a DCL procedure running under CGI.<br>"
$       display "<HR>"
$       display "<pre>"
$       call URLDECODE "''query_string'"
$       display "</pre>"
$       display "<IMG SRC=""/images/ball.gif""> " + -
                "This web server is running " + srvsoft + -
                " version " + srvvers + "<br>"
$       display "<IMG SRC=""/images/ball.gif""> " + -
                "This web server is running on " + -
                server_name + "<br>"
$       display "<HR>"
$       display "<p>This procedure was brought to you by "
$       display -
           "<A HREF=""http://wilton.zko.dec.com/author.html"">" + -
           "Hoff</A>. Your "
$       display "<A HREF=""mailto:dcl@wilton.zko.dec.com"">" + -
                "feedback</A> is welcome<br>"
$       exit
$
$URLDECODE: subroutine
$       count = 0
$       qs = ""
$10:
$       ! process the query string, one character at a time
$       chr = f$extract(count,1,p1)
$       if chr .eqs. ""
$       then
$         if qs .nes. ""
$         then
$           ! no more characters; we are done
$           ! display and then create the symbol
$           display "''qs'"
$           'qs
$           qs = ""
$         endif
$         goto 19
$       endif
```

```
$       if chr .eqs. "+"
$       then
$         ! process a space character
$         qs = qs + " "
$         goto 15
$       endif
$       if chr .eqs. "%"
$       then
$         ! convert hexadecimal back into ASCII
$         x = " "
$         asc = "%x" + f$extract(count+1,2,p1)
$         x[0,8] = 'asc
$         qs = qs + x
$         count = count + 2
$         goto 15
$       endif
$       if chr .eqs. "="
$       then
$         ! create a global symbol
$         qs = qs + ":=="
$         chrnxt = f$extract(count+1,1,p1)
$         if chrnxt .eqs. "&" .or. chrnxt .eqs. "" then -
            qs = qs + """"""
$         goto 15
$       endif
$       if chr .eqs. "&"
$       then
$         ! the ampersand delimits parameters
$         ! display and then create the symbol
$         display "'qs'"
$         'qs
$         qs = ""
$         goto 15
$       endif
$       qs = qs + chr
$15:
$       count = count + 1
$       goto 10
$19:
$   exit
$   endsubroutine
```

The URLDECODE subroutine translates a URL-encoded parameter list into separate parameters. The procedure extracts and then creates a series of symbols, based on the parameters passed into the routine.

25.9 Input

`CGI_DEMO_FORM.COM` creates DCL global symbols based on the parameters specified in the input form. Great care should be taken to avoid using parameters with names that will match any symbols used within the procedure.

25.10 HTML Page Design Considerations

HTML is designed to allow control over page *contents*, and not specifically over the page *layout*. The format of the text display can be changed by the browser, as can the font and the colors associated with the text. Further, users can disable the viewing of icons and of other graphic images.

When displaying icons, always provide alternate text. This allows users to view the web page without having the icons loaded. Users may be using a web browser that does not support icons, such as Lynx, or the user may have disabled loading the icon for performance or for various other reasons.

Avoid distracting the reader from the information. The use of flashing text, animated or dancing GIFs, multiple fonts and font attributes, and the use of many colors will all tend to distract the user from the information and will detract from the overall appearance of the web page. "Angry fruit salad" is one of the epithets used to describe the more garish web pages.

Avoid changing any attributes set by the user of the web browser. This includes changing the text or background colors and changing the font. As in the use of nonstandard HTML extensions, you cannot be assured that your choice of colors will be viewable on the web browser, or that the colors will appear as you expect. More than a few web page designers have unintentionally set the page background color to the user's text color, rendering the page entirely invisible.

Users often set up the font and the text colors to match what they prefer, and what their systems and software are capable of supporting. This can include specific font sizes for the size of the display, and the use of specific colors. The settings of users who have unusually large or small displays, who have specific colors available, or who might have specific color or general vision problems should be respected. If you want a page layout language, HTML is not your implementation choice.

APPENDIX A

Hexadecimal Notation

MODERN DIGITAL COMPUTERS operate in the binary number system, so they represent data internally as quantities in base 2. Each binary digit is called a *bit*. DCL supports integer quantities, which occupy 32 bits. In both the VAX and the Alpha architectures, a collection of 32 bits is called a *longword*, so DCL supports longword integers.

Programming languages such as DCL allow integers to be represented externally as decimal numbers, performing the necessary conversion to binary when the programs are prepared for execution. Decimal integers are appropriate for most situations, but occasionally the actual bit patterns within the integer are important. An example of this is the OpenVMS status code, a longword integer that is divided into several bit fields. When the bit patterns are important, the decimal number system is not a particularly useful external representation.

Picture the longword integer 96,877 in binary:

```
00000000000000010111101001101101
```

A programming language might allow integers to be specified in binary, but doing so would require the programmer to type a sequence of 32 ones and zeros. The chance of making an error in the number is high. In order to reduce the length of the digit sequence, the base 16, or hexadecimal, number system is employed. Since the hexadecimal base, 16, is a power of the binary base, 2,

333

the conversion from binary to hexadecimal is nothing more than a grouping operation. Begin by separating the binary digits into groups of 4:

| 0000 | 0000 | 0000 | 0001 | 0111 | 1010 | 0110 | 1101 |

Each group contains 4 binary digits and has 1 of 16 possible values from 0 through 15. This is exactly the number of possible values of a single digit in a base-16 number. So a 32-digit binary number can be represented as an 8-digit hexadecimal number.

A single printable character must be chosen to represent each of the 16 hexadecimal digit values. The digit characters 0 through 9 are chosen for the digit values 0 through 9, and the letters A through F are chosen for the digit values 10 through 15. Now the groups of binary digits can be replaced by their equivalent hexadecimal digits:

| 0 | 0 | 0 | 1 | 7 | A | 6 | D |

The hexadecimal number 00017A6D is equivalent to the decimal number 96,877. DCL allows a number to be represented in hexadecimal by preceding its hexadecimal digits with a percent sign (%) and an X:

```
$    value = %x00017a6d
```

As with decimal numbers, leading zero digits are not required:

```
$    value = %x17a6d
```

Both of these assignment commands set the symbol VALUE to the hexadecimal value %X00017A6D. DCL converts the hexadecimal value to binary before setting the symbol.

APPENDIX B

Character Sets

Various character sets are used on OpenVMS systems, including Unicode, ISO Latin-1, ASCII, the DEC Multinational Character Set (MCS), and the DEC Technical Character Set.

The specific character sets used for your applications will depend on which characters you need to display, and which characters can be displayed on your terminals and terminal emulators. Most applications will use the Latin-1 and the MCS character sets.

The Latin-1 and MCS character sets are closely related, and both are effectively extensions to the ASCII character set. In Latin-1, MCS, and ASCII, each character consists of 1 byte of data, 8 bits. Traditional ASCII applications use 7 of these bits in each byte. All 128 characters available in 7-bit ASCII have been assigned. Latin-1 and MCS have additional characters, characters assigned 8-bit values. One 7-bit ASCII character you will see through this book is the escape character, with an ASCII value of 27.

New characters are assigned or reassigned within the Latin-1 character set on occasion. Among the newer characters is the Euro currency character. These newer characters may or many not be displayed by your terminals.

The Latin-1 and MCS character sets provide the majority of the characters necessary for Romance languages. Most current terminals and the DECwindows DECterm terminal emulator use the ISO Latin-1 character set. Other terminals and terminal emulators use the DEC MCS or ASCII character sets. These are the character sets that you will be using with most DCL applications and with most terminals.

Unicode uses multiple bytes to represent each character and supports a much larger variety of characters, including characters used for languages other than the Romance languages. DCL does not directly support reading and displaying Unicode characters. Initial Unicode support was added in OpenVMS V7.2.

The following procedure displays a table of characters on your terminal:

```
$! This procedure displays various character sets on the local
$! terminal.  This procedure can display only those printable
$! characters that are supported by the local terminal.
$!
$! Parameters that specify the requested character set and
$! the display radix are permitted:
$!
$!   @CHAR_SETS <charset> <radix>
$!
$! The <charset> parameter:
$!   ASCII    ASCII character set (default)
$!   LATIN1   ISO Latin-1
$!   MCS      Multinational Character Set
$!   TCS      Technical Character Set
$!   VT       VT100 series terminal charset
$!
$! The <radix> parameter:
$!   Decimal
$!   Hexidecimal (default)
$!   Octal
$!
$! Parameter specifications can be truncated.
$
$ display = "write sys$output"
$ so[0,8]  = %x0E
$ si[0,8]  = %x0F
$ esc[0,8] = %x1B
$
$! Because we alter the displayed character set, we must
$! set up a few things: we need to reset the display,
$! and we then make an effort to return the user's default
$! character set back to the expected settings on exit.
$
$ on control_y then goto exit
$ on warning then goto exit
$
$! Process the character set option parameter: P1
$! The default character set to display is ASCII.
```

```
$!
$!      The following section could be enhanced to use LIBCALL
$!      ASK XDA_CLEAN_OPTION to clean up the parameters.
$
$       charset = f$extract(0, 1, f$edit(p1, "COLLAPSE,UPCASE"))
$       if charset .eqs. "" then charset = "A"
$       charsetcode = ""
$       if charset .eqs. "A" then charsetcode = "B"  ! ASCII
$       if charset .eqs. "L" then charsetcode = "<"  ! ISO Latin-1 (8-bit)
$       if charset .eqs. "M" then charsetcode = "<"  ! MCS (8-bit)
$       if charset .eqs. "T" then charsetcode = ">"  ! TCS
$       if charset .eqs. "V" then charsetcode = "0"  ! VT100 terminals
$       if charsetcode .eqs. ""
$       then
$          display "P1 must be ""ASCII"", ""LATIN1"", ""MCS," +-
                    """TCS"", ""VT"", or blank"
$          goto exit
$       endif
$
$!      Process the radix option parameter: P2
$!      The default radix for the display is HEXIDECIMAL
$
$       radix = f$extract(0, 1, f$edit(p2, "COLLAPSE,UPCASE"))
$       if radix .eqs. "" then radix = "H"
$       format = ""
$       if radix .eqs. "O" then format = "!AS[!UB;!UBH!OB   !AS!AS!AS"
$       if radix .eqs. "D" then format = "!AS[!UB;!UBH!UB   !AS!AS!AS"
$       if radix .eqs. "H" then format = "!AS[!UB;!UBH!XB   !AS!AS!AS"
$       if format .eqs. ""
$       then
$          display "P2 must be 'Octal', 'Decimal, 'Hex', or blank"
$          goto exit
$       endif
$
$       screen_column = 3
$       column = %x00
$
$!      Comment-out the following column assignment line to enable the
$!      display of control characters.  When enabled, the control characters
$!      are processed through the f$fao lexical before it is displayed on
$!      the terminal.
$
$       column = column + %x20
$
$!      Select the character set to use, based on the character set
```

Character Sets   337

```
$!      the user has requested.
$
$       display esc + ")" + charsetcode
$
$!      charset options L and M both select ISO Latin-1.
$!      Use it as the default label for the display.
$
$       table_label = "ISO Latin-1 and DEC MCS chart:"
$       if charset .eqs. "A" then table_label = "Ascii chart:"
$       if charset .eqs. "T" then table_label = "DEC TCS chart:"
$       if charset .eqs. "V" then table_label = "DEC VT100 chart:"
$       display esc + "[H" + ESC + "[J" + table_label
$
$
$30:    row = 0
$40:      char[0,8] = column + row
$         display f$fao(format, esc, row+3, -
                        screen_column, column + row, so, char, si)
$         row = row + 1
$         if row .lt. %x10 then goto 40
$       column = column + %x10
$       screen_column = screen_column + 10
$       if column .lt. %x80 then goto 30
$
$exit:
$       display esc + "[18;0H"
$       exit
```

American National Standards Institute (ANSI) control sequences are used in the procedure. For information on these control sequences, see the DECterm documentation or the documentation with your specific terminal or terminal emulator. A subset of the available control sequences are listed in the Screen Management (SMG) text database SYS$SYSTEM:SMGTERMS.TXT. (SMGTERMS.TXT is a text-format file used as a source file when an SMG binary database is updated. The format and contents of the file are readable and are suitable for quick reference. The file does not contain tutorial or explanatory text.)

Both 7- and 8-bit control sequences are available. Seven-bit sequences use the escape character plus a character such as the open square bracket ([), while equivalent 8-bit sequences use the CSI character alone. Seven-bit control sequences are used here.

APPENDIX C

Dates and the Year 2000

AT THE TIME OF THIS WRITING, date-related programming issues likely to arise in the years 2000 and 2038 are of interest to many system managers and software developers. This appendix discusses some of the problems and common issues, as well as the procedures that can be used to test for and to locate date-related issues within DCL procedures. Many of the testing and review issues discussed in this appendix are general, and are not specific to DCL procedures.

Date-related programming issues and problems are not new in the computer industry. Because of the ways in which programmers can store, retrieve, and utilize dates within programs, it is quite possible for latent date-related bugs to arise in many applications and to occur at various application- or system-specific dates. Programs that have been coded to assume the current century is any particular century contain the classic 2-digit year limitation. When the century changes from 1900 to 2000, for instance, programs that store and retrieve the values of years as 2-character values can incorrectly assume that the year 00 is 1900, and not 2000. Also, applications that have been incorrectly coded to assume that all century years are not leap years can incorrectly handle 2000, which is a leap year.

Applications that manipulate dates 15, 30, or even 40 years in the future will obviously tend to reach date-related limits earlier than applications that manipulate only the current date. Applications that work with future dates include various financial applications for mortgage loans, for bonds, and for retirement calculations, as well as applications that track licenses or passports, documents that might be renewed only every 5 or 10 years.

Some applications and some application users can use specific dates, such as 9-Sep-1999 (9/9/99) or 31-Dec-1999 (12/31/99), to represent a specific condition within the application, rather than a specific date. An application programmer, or even an application user, might choose to use one of these dates to represent an unknown date, a non-expiring date, or a date believed (correctly or incorrectly) to be beyond the range of dates supported by the application.

More subtle problems can and have occured within specific applications, within specific programming languages, and even in operating systems. In languages such as C, one of the program-specific representations of time can use a signed longword field to contain the number of seconds since 1 Jan 1970. (On OpenVMS, `time_t` is `unsigned int`, but applications can erroneously use an `int`.) This format overflows early in the year 2038. The Global Positioning System (GPS) satellites and satellite receivers use a fixed-width field for the transmission of the number of weeks since the GPS base date. This field will overflow the week of 21 Aug 1999, and this can potentially result in problems for GPS users, both for positioning and for a time base. Many date-related problems have appeared over the years, and more will arise in the future.

All computer systems and all languages have a base date, the oldest date that can be directly stored and represented within the system. The OpenVMS operating system, as well as the VAX and Alpha architectures, use a base date of 17 Nov 1858, the base date of the Smithsonian Astrophysical Calendar. The C language and various Unix operating systems use 1 Jan 1970 as the base date.

Dates can be stored and manipulated in software, and can also be present in system hardware. Examples of hardware storage of dates are the system hardware clocks: the VAX time of year register (TOY), and the Alpha battery-backed watch register `BB_WATCH`.

Operating systems, applications, hardware clocks, and languages all have a specific range of dates that can be stored, based on the size of the storage area used for the dates. This range is sometimes referred to as the *epoch*. The OpenVMS VAX and OpenVMS Alpha operating systems use a quadword to contain the number of centiseconds since the base date. This format supports dates for tens of millennia. As mentioned previously, C and Unix store the number of seconds since 1 Jan 1970 in a longword. When viewed as a signed longword, the Unix epoch overflows in 2038.

Of course, system and application code can have date-related limits much lower than the upper limits imposed by the operating system or the hardware clock. An example within OpenVMS is the standard text date format. This text format uses a 4-digit year, a limit that will be exceeded on 1 Jan 10000. C on OpenVMS, as well as applications and components of OpenVMS that are written in or dependent on C code, and C on various other operating system platforms, can all contain the 2038 limit. Also, applications that directly perform mathematical operations on binary dates can encounter failures well before the end of the epoch supported by the particular format.

C.1 OpenVMS and the Year 2000

OpenVMS Engineering has completed an evaluation of Year 2000 issues within the OpenVMS operating system and has warranted the operating system free of date-related problems prior to 2038. Various versions of OpenVMS require an update kit that corrects the (minor) Year 2000 incompatibilities that were found in the release. For details, please see the information with the update kit, and see the OpenVMS Year 2000 warrantee information.

The most obvious limit within DCL itself is the 4-character limit common to OpenVMS date-related system services and lexical functions: 31 Dec 9999. DCL applications, however, can be coded with various other limitations prior to this date, including the 2-digit year limitations previously mentioned.

Here are three ways that you might extract a 2-digit year from a date and immediately run into trouble:

```
$    year = f$extract(2,2,f$cvtime(,,"YEAR"))
$    year = f$cvtime(,,"YEAR") - "19"
$    year = f$extract(9, 2, f$time())
```

OpenVMS Year 2000 information is available via the World Wide Web at www.openvms.digital.com.

C.2 Code Review and Testing

The most reliable means to locate date-related problems in existing applications is to review the design and the code, and then to test the code with the system time set to various dates.

Areas of DCL procedures that should be reviewed obviously include any areas of the code that process, use, or store dates. Dates can be used for display, for file names, for sorting information, for recording the times when events occur, and for a wide variety of other uses.

Various directly time-related lexical functions exist, including F$CVTIME and F$TIME. Less obviously, F$GETJPI, F$FILE_ATTRIBUTES, and a variety of other lexical functions can retrieve and process dates. A few applications also capture and process the output from various utilities, and this output can contain dates.

There are, of course, many other possible date-related activities and date-related coding constructs possible. These date-related activities may not use `date` or `time`, or any other obvious and easily-located keyword.

The following dates are often associated with problems involving 2-character years and with the correct calculations for leap years. Remember, 2000 is a leap year. Testing with at least these dates is recommended:

- 31 Dec 1999 through 1 Jan 2000
- 29 Feb 2000 through 1 Mar 2000
- 28 Feb 2001 through 1 Mar 2001
- 29 Feb 2004 through 1 Mar 2004

Properly preparing the OpenVMS operating system for date-related testing, and for properly restoring the system environment after the testing has been completed, is beyond the scope of this book. Information on BACKUP-related and testing-related procedures are available in the *OpenVMS System Manager's Manual: Essentials* manual, as well as via the World Wide Web at www.openvms.digital.com.

Performing OpenVMS- or application-related date testing in the years 2038 and later is not presently recommended by the authors.

C.3 Code Changes

Various changes may be required to resolve date-related problems in applications. Most obviously, this could involve moving from 2 to 4 characters in display fields and in calculations, and moving to 4-character years in files and other storage areas. Use of the full 4-digit year value is the best solution, but this may not always be workable.

Another approach involves working with a transition year value, such as 57, as the cutoff between the years interpreted as after 1900, and the years interpreted as after 2000. Two-digit values equal or larger than 57 are assumed to be after 1900, while smaller values are assumed to be after 2000. The 2-digit year 98 would be assumed to be 1998, while the 2-digit year 23 would be assumed to be 2023. The transition value should be chosen based on the smallest 2-digit year expected or that is currently in use. Within OpenVMS, the transition year is typically 57.

The transition year mechanism can be used in conjunction with the storage of the date file records in the 2-character format, and it can be converted and rewritten into the record in the 4-digit format. The 4-digit year is stored in a new and formerly unused field within the file record, while existing applications continue to read the date from the 2-digit field. This approach can allow a suite of related applications to be incrementally converted to the use of 4-digit years. This obviously works only if there are a few specific areas that write these dates.

The authors recommend both code review and code testing for Year 2000 problems, and for other date-related problems that might be latent in your systems and your applications. Testing with the dates specified in this appendix, as well as with any other dates that might be relevant to your applications, is strongly recommended. The authors recommend testing for and resolving any problems found in the application code, as well as your supporting and code development routines: for example, your source code management systems, your application build procedures and tools, and any other supporting procedures.

APPENDIX D

Hypertext Markup Language

THE COMMON HTML TAGS are described in the following table. For further information on HTML and the related standards, please visit the World Wide Web Consortium's site at www.w3.org.

Tag	Description
`<A> ... </A>`	Marks the begining and end of an anchor. Anchors are used to implement internal hyperlinks within the current web page, as well as hyperlinks to other web pages elsewhere.
`<ADDRESS> ... </ADDRESS>`	The enclosed text is an address.
`<BLOCKQUOTE> ... </BLOCKQUOTE>`	Delimits a block quotation.
`<BODY> ... </BODY>`	Delimits the body of the document. The body contains the body text, as well as various tags.
` `	Forces a line break in the text.
`<CENTER> ... </CENTER>`	Marks text to be centered on the page.
`<CODE> ... </CODE>`	Contains text to be formatted as example source code.
`<FORM> ... </FORM>`	Delimits a group of HTML tags that prompts for and processes user input.
`<IMG>`	Marks the inclusion of an image, usually a GIF file. Also optionally provides alternate text that can be displayed for the web browser, when the image is not visible.

`<INPUT TYPE=CHECKBOX>`	Processes checkbox input within a form.
`<INPUT TYPE=FILE>`	Processes file selection input within a form.
`<INPUT TYPE=PASSWORD>`	Processes hidden text input within a form.
`<INPUT TYPE=TEXT>`	Processes text input within a form.
`<H1>`...`</H1>`	These tags denote the beginning and the end of a header. The header text can be a section or paragraph header. Six levels of header tags are permitted, with `<H1>` being the largest and most significant, and `<H6>` being the smallest and least significant.
`<HEAD>`...`</HEAD>`	Marks the beginning and end of the document headers. The header contains the document header information.
`<HTML>`...`</HTML>`	Marks the beginning and the end of the HTML document.
`<HR>`	Displays a horizontal rule in the display.
`<LI>`	Marks an entry in a list.
`<OPTION>`	Defines an option within a `<SELECT>`.
`<P>`	Marks the beginning of a paragraph.
`<PRE>`...`</PRE>`	Marks the beginning and end of a section of preformatted text.
`<SELECT>`...`</SELECT>`	Allows user selections within a form.
`<SMALL>`...`</SMALL>`	Marks a section of smaller text.
`<STRONG>`...`</STRONG>`	Delimits text to be displayed with strong emphasis.
`<TABLE>`...`</TABLE>`	Marks the boundaries of a table.
`<TD>`...`</TD>`	Marks the contents of a data cell within a table.
`<TH>`...`</TH>`	Marks the contents of a header cell within a table.
`<THEAD>`...`</THEAD>`	Sets up a table header.
`<TR>`...`</TR>`	Sets up a row of cells within a table.
`<UL>`...`</UL>`	Delimits an unordered list. Entries use `<LI>`.
`<TITLE>`...`</ENDTITLE>`	Denotes the beginning and the end of the document title.

APPENDIX E

Subroutine Library

THIS APPENDIX CONTAINS A COMPLETE LISTING of the subroutine library described and used throughout this book. The subroutine library resides in a single, self-sufficient procedure containing a collection of DCL subroutines that can be used by DCL applications to perform common but nontrivial operations. The library is yours to modify and expand as required by your applications.

Each subroutine includes a block comment describing its function, parameters, and any return value. When the library is used for production applications, the comments should be moved to the end of the procedure so that they do not slow down its execution.

The general format of a call to a subroutine is as follows:

```
$    @directory:subroutine-library name parameter ...
```

The *directory* portion specifies the disk and directory containing the subroutine library. The first parameter, *name*, is the name of the desired subroutine. Additional *parameters* are required to specify the exact operation to be performed.

The examples in this book assume that the personal command LIBCALL is defined in the application's initialization code. The command is defined as follows:

```
$    libcall = "@directory:subroutine-library"
```

This personal command improves the readability of a subroutine call and takes up less space on the command line:

```
$       libcall name parameter ...
```

The subroutine library is self-sufficient and does not depend on any symbols or logical names defined by its caller.

```
$!      DCL Subroutine Library
$
$       sublib__status = %x10000000
$       sublib__success = sublib__status + %x0001
$       on control_y then exit sublib__status + %x0004
$       on warning then exit $status .or. %x10000000
$
$       display = "write sys$output"
$       goto 'p1
```

```
$! Title:        Ask a Question
$!
$! Synopsis:     This subroutine asks the user a question and returns
$!               the answer.  The prompt for the question is composed
$!               of a query string and optionally a default answer.
$!
$! Parameters:   P2: A global symbol to receive the answer.
$!               P3: The data type of the answer.  B for boolean
$!                   (yes/no); I for integer; S for string.
$!               P4: The query string for the question.  It must end
$!                   with a punctuation character and no space.
$!               P5: The default answer (optional; if not specified
$!                   then an answer must be entered).
$!               P6: A comma-separated list of options:
$!                       H: Display help before asking question.
$!                       S: Skip a line before asking question.
$!                       U: Upcase the input string.
$!                       Z: Allow CTRL/Z as an answer.
$!               P7: The help specifier (optional).  It must be in
$!                   the form "procedure [parameter...]".  The
$!                   procedure is invoked with the at-sign command.
$!
$! Result:       For Boolean data type, a 0 (no) or 1 (yes).  For
$!               Integer data type, the integer.  For String data
$!               type, the string.  If CTRL/Z is allowed and entered,
$!               the string "^Z" is returned.
$
$ASK:
$
$       signal = "@" + f$environment("PROCEDURE") + " signal ask"
$       if p3 .eqs. "B" .and. p5 .nes. "" .and. -
            f$type(p5) .eqs. "INTEGER" then -
          p5 = f$element(p5,"/","NO/YES")
$       if p5 .nes. "" then p4 = f$extract(0,f$len(p4)-1,p4) + -
                    " [" + p5 + "]" + f$extract(f$len(p4)-1,1,p4)
$       if f$locate("S",p6) .ne. f$length(p6) then display ""
$       if f$locate("H",p6) .ne. f$length(p6) then @'p7
$
$a10:   read sys$command /prompt="''p4 " input /end_of_file=a_eof
$       if input .eqs. "" then input = p5
$       input = f$edit(input,"TRIM")
$       if input .eqs. ""
$       then
$           signal w inputreq -
                "Please enter a value; there is no default."
```

```
$              else if input .eqs. "?"
$              then
$                if p7 .nes. "" then @'p7
$                if p7 .eqs. "" then display -
                    "There is no help for this question."
$              else
$                goto a_'p3
$a_B:          input = f$edit(input,"UPCASE")
$              if f$locate(input,"YES") .eq. 0 .or. -
                    f$locate(input,"NO") .eq. 0
$              then
$                input = input .and. 1
$                goto a19
$              else
$                signal w yesnoreq "Please answer YES or NO."
$              endif
$              goto a15
$
$a_I:          if f$type(input) .eqs. "INTEGER"
$              then
$                input = f$integer(input)
$                goto a19
$              else
$                signal w intreq "The input must be an integer."
$              endif
$              goto a15
$
$a_S:          if f$locate("U",p6) .ne. f$length(p6) then -
                    input = f$edit(input,"UPCASE")
$              goto a19
$a15:
$              endif
$              endif
$              goto a10
$a_eof:
$              input = "^Z"
$              if f$locate("Z",p6) .ne. f$length(p6) then goto a19
$              signal i invctrlz "End-of-file is not a valid response."
$              goto a10
$a19:
$          'p2 == input
$          exit sublib__success
```

350   Subroutine Library

```
$! Title:        Look Up a Keyword in a List
$!
$! Synopsis:     This subroutine looks up a keyword or its
$!               abbreviation in a list of valid keywords.
$!               If the keyword exists in the list and is
$!               unique, the full keyword is returned.
$!
$! Parameters:   P2: A global symbol to receive the result.
$!               P3: The keyword or a unique abbreviation thereof.
$!               P4: A comma-separated list of valid keywords.
$!
$! Result:       If the (abbreviated) keyword is valid and unique,
$!               the full keyword is returned.  If the keyword is
$!               invalid or null, the null string is returned.
$
$LOOKUP_KEYWORD:
$
$       'p2 == ""
$       if p3 .eqs. "" then exit sublib__success
$       p3 = "," + f$edit(p3,"UPCASE")
$       p4 = "," + f$edit(p4,"UPCASE") + ","
$       p4_tail = f$extract(f$locate(p3,p4)+1, 999, p4)
$       if f$locate(p3,p4_tail) .eq. f$length(p4_tail) then -
            'p2 == f$element(0,",",p4_tail)
$       exit sublib__success
```

Subroutine Library

```
$! Title:          Signal an Informational or Error Message
$!
$! Synopsis:       This subroutine "signals" a message, producing one
$!                 or more message lines in the standard OpenVMS format.
$!                 It also exits with a status whose severity matches
$!                 that of the message.
$!
$! Parameters:     P2: The message facility code.
$!                 P3: The message severity (S, I, W, E, or F).
$!                 P4: The message identification.
$!                 P5: The message text.
$!                 Pn: Optional message lines or status codes whose
$!                     corresponding message lines are to be included.
$!
$! Status:         The severity of the exit status is equal to the
$!                 message severity, except in the case of warnings.
$!                 If the message severity is W, an informational
$!                 severity is included in the status so that the
$!                 caller's error handler is not invoked.
$
$SIGNAL:
$
$       prefix = f$fao("%!AS-!AS-!AS, ", p2, p3, p4)
$       i = 4
$s10:   i = i + 1
$       if i .gt. 8 then goto s19
$       if p'i .eqs. "" then goto s19
$       text = p'i
$       if f$type(text) .eqs. "INTEGER" then -
            text = f$message(text)
$       if f$ext(0,1,text) .nes. "%" then text = prefix + text
$       if i .gt. 5 then text[0,1] := "-"
$       display text
$       goto s10
$s19:
$       if p3 .eqs. "W" then p3 = "I"
$       exit sublib__status + f$locate(p3,"WSEIF")
```

```
$! Title:         Generate a Unique Name
$!
$! Synopsis:      This subroutine generates a unique name suitable for
$!                use in creating a temporary file.
$!
$! Parameters:    P2: The global symbol to receive the result.
$!                P3: The pattern specifying the format of the unique
$!                    name. It must contain a question mark (?), which
$!                    is replaced with a unique number.
$!
$! Result:        A unique name consisting of the pattern with the
$!                question mark replaced with a 10-digit number.
$!                The number is composed of 8 digits of time and a
$!                2-digit counter.
$
$UNIQUE_NAME:
$
$       if f$type(sublib_counter) .eqs. "" then sublib_counter == 0
$       sublib_counter == (sublib_counter+1) - -
                        (sublib_counter+1)/100*100
$       'p2 == f$fao("!AS!8AS!2ZL!AS", f$element(0,"?",p3), -
                f$extract(12,11,f$time())-":"-":"-".", -
                sublib_counter, f$element(1,"?",p3))
$       exit sublib__success
```

Subroutine Library

```
$! Title:         Check the Validity of a Symbol
$!
$! Synopsis:      This subroutine checks the validity of a string
$!                representing the name of a symbol.  It checks the
$!                length and the individual characters.
$!
$! Parameters:    P2: The global symbol to receive the result.
$!                P3: The symbol to be checked.
$!                P4: Optional maximum length of symbol (default 31).
$!                P5: Optional valid characters in addition to the
$!                    standad letters, digits, dollar, and underscore.
$!
$! Result:        The null string if the symbol is okay.  Otherwise a
$!                message fragment describing the error.
$
$VERIFY_SYMBOL:
$
$       p3 = f$edit(p3,"TRIM,UPCASE")
$       if p4 .eqs. "" then p4 = 31
$       'p2 == f$fao("is limited to !UL characters", f$integer(p4))
$       if f$length(p3) .gt. p4 then exit sublib__success
$       v = "$0123456789ABCDEFGHIJKLMNOPQRSTUVWXYZ_" + p5
$       'p2 == ""
$       i = -1
$vs10:  i = i + 1
$          if i .ge. f$length(p3) then exit sublib__success
$          if f$locate(f$extract(i,1,p3),v) .lt. f$length(v) then -
              goto vs10
$       'p2 == f$fao("contains the invalid character ""!AS""", -
                   f$extract(i,1,p3))
$       exit sublib__success
```

APPENDIX F

Sample Application

THE MANAGER FOR ORGANIZED DISTRIBUTION LISTS (MODL) is a DCL application that helps you manage distribution lists for the MAIL utility. A *distribution list* is a text file containing a list of users who are to receive mail about a particular topic. For example, you might have a distribution list for a software project; the list contains the user names of all the developers working on the project. You might have another list containing the names of all the managers in your organization. Distribution lists tend to proliferate, and the same people can appear in multiple lists. It quickly becomes difficult to manage the updating of distribution lists, and it can even take some time to locate the particular list you need.

The MODL system introduces the idea of a single distribution file containing a record for each user in the organization. The organization might be a project group, a department, or the entire company. The larger the organization encompassed by a MODL distribution file, the fewer distribution files there are. In addition to user records, the MODL file contains records for keywords, which are mnemonic identifiers for particular groups or projects. A keyword can be associated with one or more users who are members of the group or project for which the keyword stands. For example, the keyword MANAGER might signify people who are managers in the department. Once this keyword is associated with the users who are managers, mail can be sent to the managers by asking MODL to "send mail to all users with keyword MANAGER." Another example is the keyword CONSULTANT. This keyword can be associated with the users who are outside consultants rather than employees. Then when you are sending mail about a new company policy, you can ask MODL to "send mail to all users who are not a CONSULTANT."

MODL distribution files are created and maintained through a set of commands supported by the MODL system.

F.1 Using MODL

The MODL system provides a command-oriented interface, which makes MODL behave like other command-oriented utilities such as MAIL. In order to invoke MODL, enter the MODL command:

```
$ modl

    Manager for Organized Distribution Lists

MODL>
```

MODL responds with a prompt. At the prompt you may enter one of the following:

- A MODL command. A command begins with a command verb and may require some parameters. If a parameter is omitted, MODL will prompt for it. See Section F.2 for a description of MODL commands.

- A OpenVMS command. If the line you enter begins with a dollar sign ($), MODL assumes the rest of the line contains an OpenVMS command. The command is executed.

- A blank line. A blank line is ignored.

- A CTRL/Z. When CTRL/Z is pressed, MODL exits. The CTRL/Z is equivalent to the EXIT command.

Lines entered at the MODL> prompt may contain comments. A comment begins with an exclamation point (!); the exclamation point and the rest of the line are ignored:

```
MODL> modl add manager shubin ! Phred Shubin got promoted.
```

You can also use MODL to execute a single command and then immediately exit. If, at the DCL prompt, you include a command following the MODL verb, MODL executes the command and then immediately exits without beginning an interactive session.

```
$ modl send policy.txt "not consultant" "Vacation policy."
```

F.2 MODL Commands

The following sections describe the commands available with MODL. The commands are described in alphabetical order.

F.2.1 The ADD Command

The `ADD` command assigns keywords to users.

    ADD *keyword*, ... *user*, ...

The *keyword* parameter is a single keyword or a list of keywords to be added to users. The keywords must have been previously defined with the `REGISTER` command.

    The *user* parameter is a single user or a list of users to receive the keywords. The users must have been previously defined with the `REGISTER` command. The word `SELF` can be used in the list to specify the current user.

F.2.2 The CLOSE Command

The `CLOSE` command closes the current MODL distribution file.

    CLOSE

The current MODL distribution file is closed. After this command is used, no MODL file is selected.

F.2.3 The CREATE Command

The `CREATE` command creates a new MODL distribution file.

    CREATE *file-spec* "*title*"

The *file-spec* parameter provides the specification of the new MODL file. If no device and directory are included, the file is created in the working directory. MODL provides a default file type of `MODL_FILE`.

    The *title* parameter specifies a descriptive title for the new distribution file. The new distribution file contains no registered users or keywords.

F.2.4 The DEREGISTER Command

The `DEREGISTER` command removes the definitions of users or keywords from the MODL distribution file.

    DEREGISTER USER *user* [NOVERIFY]

The *user* parameter is the name of a user to be removed from the distribution file. The word SELF can be used to signify the current user.

MODL normally verifies the deregistration of a user. The optional parameter NOVERIFY specifies that MODL should not verify the operation. If the parameter is not specified, MODL does not prompt for it.

```
DEREGISTER KEYWORD keyword
```

The *keyword* parameter is a keyword to be removed from the distribution file. MODL requires that the keyword not be assigned to any users.

F.2.5 The DISPLAY Command

The DISPLAY command displays a list of all the users who match given selection criteria.

```
DISPLAY "selection"
```

The *selection* parameter is a Boolean expression that specifies which users are to be displayed. All users matching the selection are displayed at the terminal.

The *selection* parameter is a Boolean expression composed of keywords and operators. The keywords must be registered in the distribution file. The Boolean operators are AND, OR, and NOT. The NOT operator is applied first, followed by AND, followed by OR. Parentheses may be used to alter the order in which operators are applied. Unless the *selection* parameter is a single keyword, it must be enclosed in double quotes.

Here are some examples:

```
MODL> ! Select users who are developers.
MODL> display developer
```

—or—

```
MODL> ! Select users who are developers or managers.
MODL> display "developer or manager"
```

—or—

```
MODL> ! Select users who are not managers.
MODL> display "not manager"
```

—or—

```
MODL> ! Select users who are developers; exclude consultants.
MODL> display "developer and not consultant"
```

—or—

```
MODL> ! Invite all developers plus the marketing managers.
MODL> display "developer or marketing and manager"
```

—or—

```
MODL> ! The same expression clarified with parentheses.
MODL> display "developer or (marketing and manager)"
```

—or—

```
MODL> ! Invite all development and marketing managers.
MODL> display "(developer or marketing) and manager"
```

F.2.6 The EXIT Command

The EXIT command causes MODL to exit back to DCL.

```
EXIT
```

F.2.7 The LIST Command

The LIST command creates a OpenVMS MAIL distribution list containing users who match given selection criteria.

```
LIST "selection" output-file "heading"
```

The *selection* parameter is a Boolean expression that selects the users in the MODL distribution file who are to be included in the MAIL distribution list. See the DISPLAY command for a description of the *selection* parameter.

The *output-file* parameter is the file spec for the MAIL distribution list. The default device/directory is the working directory, and the default file type is DIS.

The *heading* parameter is a text string to be used as a heading in the MAIL distribution list.

F.2.8 The MODIFY Command

The MODIFY command updates information about users or keywords.

```
MODIFY USER user "new full name" "new title" new-mail-address
```

The *user* parameter specifies the name of the user to be updated. The word SELF can be used to signify the current user.

The *new full name*, *new title*, and *new-mail-address* parameters specify the new information about the user. See the REGISTER command for a description of these items.

```
MODIFY KEYWORD keyword "new title"
```

The *keyword* parameter specifies the keyword to be updated.

The *new title* parameter specifies a new title for the keyword. See the REGISTER command for a description of these items.

F.2.9 The OPEN Command

The OPEN command selects a MODL distribution file and prepares it for use.

OPEN *file-spec*

The *file-spec* parameter provides the specification of an existing MODL distribution file to be opened.

F.2.10 The REGISTER Command

The REGISTER command registers a new user or keyword in the MODL distribution file.

REGISTER USER *name* "*full name*" "*title*" *mail-address*

The *name* parameter specifies the name to be associated with the new user. The name will usually be identical to the person's OpenVMS user name.

The *full name*, *title*, and *mail-address* parameters specify information about the user. The *full name* is a string containing the person's full name. The *title* is a string containing the person's business title or other identifying information. The *mail-address* is the person's DECnet mail address.

REGISTER KEYWORD *keyword* "*title*"

The *keyword* parameter specifies a string that identifies the keyword being registered. The keyword can be composed of letters, numbers, dollar sign ($), underscore (_), and hyphen (-).

The *title* parameter specifies a string that describes the meaning of the keyword.

F.2.11 The REMOVE Command

The REMOVE command removes keywords from users.

REMOVE *keyword*, ... *user*, ...

The *keyword* parameter is a single keyword or a list of keywords to be removed from users.

The *user* parameter is a single user or a list of users from whom the keywords are to be removed. The users must have been previously defined with the REGISTER command. The word SELF can be used in the list to specify the current user. If this parameter is specified as an asterisk (*), the keywords are removed from all registered users.

F.2.12 The SEND Command

The SEND command sends mail to a group of users who match given selection criteria.

SEND *file-spec* "*selection*" "*subject*"

The *file-spec* parameter is the spec of the file containing the message to be sent. The default device/directory is the working directory. The default file type is TXT.

The *selection* parameter is a Boolean expression that specifies the users in the MODL distribution file who will receive the message. See the DISPLAY command for a description of the *selection* parameter.

The *subject* parameter is a text string specifying the subject of the message.

The method used to send the message is determined by the SET AGENT and SET SEND commands.

F.2.13 The SET Command

The SET command establishes various operating characteristics for MODL.

SET AGENT "*string*"

This command establishes the mailing agent for future SEND commands. The *string* parameter is the code for the mailing agent followed by a percent sign (%). For example, the Zipnet agent might be specified as "zp%". The mailing agent is stored in the MODL distribution file, so all users of the file will use the same agent.

SET NOAGENT

This command specifies that future SEND commands will not use a mailing agent. When there is no mailing agent, the SEND command sends the message by invoking the MAIL utility once for each recipient.

When a new MODL distribution file is created, no mailing agent is stored in it.

SET SEND *copy-self? batch?*

This command establishes the operating characteristics for future SEND commands. The *copy-self?* parameter specifies whether an additional copy of each message should be sent to the user initiating the message. The *batch?* parameter specifies whether message sending should be performed in batch or interactively. This command establishes the operating characteristics for the remainder of the current session; it does not save the characteristics in the MODL distribution file.

If no SET SEND command has been issued during a terminal session, the default for *copy-self?* is false and the default for *batch?* is true.

F.2.14 The SHOW Command

The SHOW command displays information about various aspects of the MODL system.

SHOW FILE

This command displays information about the current MODL distribution file, including its file spec, title, and agent.

SHOW KEYWORD *keyword*

This command displays information about a registered keyword. The *keyword* parameter specifies the keyword in question. The information displayed includes the keyword and its title. The parameter may also be specified as an asterisk (*), in which case information about all registered keywords is displayed.

SHOW SEND

This command displays information about the operating characteristics established with the SET command. The information includes the mailing agent, copy-self status, and batch status.

SHOW USER *name*

This command displays information about a registered user. The *name* parameter specifies the user in question. The information displayed includes the user name, full name, title, mailing address, and keyword list. The parameter can also be specified as an asterisk (*), in which case information about all registered users is displayed.

F.3 File Layout

A MODL distribution file is an indexed file containing three types of records. The file has a single key, which occupies the first field in every record.

A MODL file has a header record, which describes the file and contains information that pertains to the entire file, such as the mailing agent. Table F.1 describes the fields in the header record.

Table F.1
MODL file: Header record

Position	Size	Type	Description
0	16	String	The key of the header record is !HEADER!.
16	12	String	The user name of the user who created the file.
28	17	String	The date and time when the file was created.
45	32	String	The title of the file.
77	32	String	The mailing agent, or blank if no agent is used.

Table F.2
MODL file: Keyword record

Position	Size	Type	Description
0	16	String	The key of the keyword record consists of a sharp sign (#) followed by the keyword.
16	12	String	The user name of the user who registered the keyword.
28	17	String	The date and time when the keyword was registered.
45	32	String	The title of the keyword.

Table F.3
MODL file: User record

Position	Size	Type	Description
0	16	String	The key of the user record consists of the user name.
16	12	String	The user name of the user who registered this user.
28	17	String	The date and time when the user was registered.
45	32	String	The user's business title.
77	32	String	The user's full name.
109	64	String	The user's mailing address.
173	up to 200	String	A comma-separated list of the keywords associated with the user.

There is a record for each keyword registered in the file. The record contains the keyword's title. Table F.2 describes the fields in a keyword record.

There is a record for each user registered in the file. The record contains information that describes the user, the user's mailing address, and a list of the keywords associated with the user. Table F.3 describes the fields in a user record.

F.4 Listings
F.4.1 File MODL.COM

```
$       define = "define/nolog"
$       delete = "delete"
$       mail   = "mail/noself"
$       submit = "submit"
$
$       saved_message = f$environment("MESSAGE")
$       set message/facility/severity/identification/text
$
$       modl__status  = %x11088000
$       modl__success = modl__status + %x001
$       modl__ctrly   = modl__status + %x00c
$       status = modl__success
$       on control_y then goto control_y
$       on warning then goto error
$
$       check_open_file    = -
          "if f$trnlnm(""modl_file"") .eqs. """" then " + -
          "signal e nofileopen ""No MODL file has been opened."""
$       display            = "write sys$output"
$       false              = 0
$       libcall            = "@modl_system:subroutine-library"
$       modlcall           = "@modl_system:modl_subroutines.com"
$       read_lock          = "read/lock modl_file"
$       read_lock_header   = "read/lock modl_file /key=""!HEADER!"""
$       read_nolock        = "read/nolock modl_file"
$       read_nolock_header = -
                             "read/nolock modl_file /key=""!HEADER!"""
$       this_user          = f$edit(f$getjpi("","USERNAME"),"TRIM")
$       true               = 1
$       undefine           = "deassign"
$       update_unlock      = "write/update/symbol modl_file"
$       write_unlock       = "write/symbol modl_file"
$       ask                = libcall + " ask"
$       signal             = libcall + " signal modl"
$
$!      Establish defaults for the copy-self? and batch? settings.
$
$       if f$type(modl_batch) .eqs. "" then modl_batch == true
$       if f$type(modl_copy_self) .eqs. "" then -
          modl_copy_self == false
$
```

```
$           mf_t_key        =   0       ! Key: !HEADER! for the header;
$           mf_s_key        =   16      ! #keyword for a keyword record;
$                                       ! username for a user record.
$           mf_t_doer       =   16      ! User who created/updated record.
$           mf_s_doer       =   12
$           mf_t_time       =   28      ! Date/time of creation/update.
$           mf_s_time       =   17
$           mf_t_title      =   45      ! Title (all records).
$           mf_s_title      =   32
$           mf_t_agent      =   77      ! Mailing agent (header).
$           mf_s_agent      =   32
$           mf_t_name       =   77      ! Full name (user).
$           mf_s_name       =   32
$           mf_t_address    =   109     ! Mailing address (user).
$           mf_s_address    =   64
$           mf_t_keylist    =   173     ! List of keywords (user).
$           mf_s_keylist    =   200
$
$
$!          If a MODL distribution file has been OPENed by the user,
$!          then open the RMS file so we can read and write it.
$
$           if f$trnlnm("modl_opened_file") .nes. "" then -
               open/read/write/share=write modl_file -
                                       modl_opened_file /error=5
$           goto 9
$5:         @modl_system:modl_close
$           signal f errselfile -
            "Error opening MODL file ''f$trnlnm("modl_opened_file")'" -
            '$status
$9:
$           command_list = "ADD,CLOSE,CREATE,DEFINE,DEREGISTER," + -
                           "DISPLAY,EXIT,HELP,LIST,MODIFY,OPEN," + -
                           "REGISTER,REMOVE,SEND,SET,SHOW,UNDEFINE"
$
$           if p1 .nes. ""
$           then ! The command line includes a MODL command.
$              libcall lookup_keyword modl_ "''p1'" 'command_list
$              if modl_ .eqs. "" then signal f unkcmd -
                                "The command ''p1 is unknown or ambiguous."
$              @modl_system:modl_'modl_ "''p2'" "''p3'" "''p4'" -
                                       "''p5'" "''p6'" "''p7'" "''p8'"
$
$           else ! No command, so start a session.
$              display ""
```

```
$           display "    Manager for Organized Distribution Lists
$           display ""
$10:        read sys$command/prompt="MODL> " command /end_of_file=19
$           command = f$edit(command,"TRIM,UNCOMMENT")
$           if command .eqs. "" then goto 10
$           if f$extract(0,1,command) .eqs. "$"
$           then ! It's a DCL command.
$              set noon
$              define/user_mode sys$input sys$command
$              'f$extract(1,999,command)
$              if f$getdvi("SYS$INPUT","DEVCLASS") .ne. 1 then -
$                 deassign/user_mode sys$input ! Undo DEFINE/USER.
$              set on
$              display ""
$
$           else ! It's a MODL command.
$              verb = f$element(0," ",command)
$              libcall lookup_keyword modl_ "''verb'" 'command_list
$              if modl_ .eqs. "EXIT" then goto 19
$              if modl_ .eqs. ""
$              then
$                 signal i unkcmdverb -
                         "The command ''verb is unknown or ambiguous."
$              else
$                 set noon
$                 @modl_system:modl_'modl_ 'f$string(command - verb)
$                 set on
$                 if f$trnlnm("modl_file") .nes. "" then -
                       read_nolock_header junk ! Unlock all records.
$              endif
$           endif
$           goto 10
$19:
$       endif
$       goto EXIT
$
$
$control_y:
$       status = modl__ctrly
$       goto EXIT
$
$error:
$       status = $status
$       goto EXIT
$
```

```
$exit:
$       set noon
$       close/nolog modl_file
$       set message 'saved_message
$       exit status .or. %x10000000
$
$! Title:      Manager for Organized Distribution Lists (MODL)
$!
$! Synopsis:   MODL is a system which helps manage distribution
$!             lists for the MAIL utility.  A MODL distribution
$!             file is an indexed file which cross-references
$!             users and keywords.  A mail message can be sent
$!             to some or all of the registered users by specifying
$!             a keyword or boolean combination of keywords.  MODL
$!             selects the users who fit the keyword selection and
$!             sends the message to them.
$!
$! Usage:      MODL is run by invoking this procedure.  It is best
$!             to define a personal command:
$!
$!                modl == "@modl_system:modl"
$!
$!             When MODL is invoked with no parameters, it
$!             initiates a command loop which reads a command
$!             and executes it.  When MODL is invoked with
$!             parameters, it executes the single command
$!             specified by the parameters and then exits.
$!
$! Author:     Paul C. Anagnostopoulos
$! Created:    July 1988
```

F.4.2   File MODL_ADD.COM

```
$       on control_y then exit modl__ctrly
$       on warning then exit $status .or. %x10000000
$       check_open_file
$
$       new_keys = p1
$       users = p2
$       if new_keys .eqs. "" then ask modl_ s "_Keyword List:"
$       if new_keys .eqs. "" then new_keys = modl_
$       if users .eqs. "" then ask modl_ s "_User List:"
$       if users .eqs. "" then users = modl_
$       new_keys = f$edit(new_keys,"COLLAPSE,UPCASE")
$       users = f$edit(users,"COLLAPSE,UPCASE")
$
$       i = -1
$10:    i = i + 1
$       keyword = f$element(i,",",new_keys)
$       if keyword .eqs. "," then goto 19
$       key = f$fao("!#<#!AS!>", mf_s_key, keyword)
$       read_nolock /key="''key'" rec /error=15
$       goto 10
$15:    signal e undefkey "Keyword ''keyword is not defined."
$19:
$
$       i = -1
$20:    i = i + 1
$       username= f$element(i,",",users)
$       if username .eqs. "," then goto 29
$       if username .eqs. "SELF" then username = this_user
$       key = f$fao("!#AS", mf_s_key, username)
$       read_lock /key="''key'" rec /error=25
$       key_list = f$edit(f$extract(mf_t_keylist,mf_s_keylist,-
                         rec), "TRIM")
$       gosub add_keywords
$       rec[mf_t_keylist,mf_s_keylist] := "''key_list'"
$       update_unlock rec
$       goto 20
$25:    signal w unreguser "User ''username is not registered."
$29:
$       exit modl__success
$
$add_keywords:
$       k = -1
$80:    k = k + 1
```

```
$           keyword = f$element(k,",",new_keys)
$           if keyword .eqs. "," then goto 89
$           if f$locate(","+keyword+",", ","+key_list+",") .eq. -
              f$length(key_list)+2
$           then
$             if key_list .nes. "" then key_list = key_list + ","
$             key_list = key_list + keyword
$           else
$             signal i userhaskey -
              "User ''username'' already has keyword ''keyword''."
$           endif
$           goto 80
$89:    return modl__success
$
$! Module:     Process the ADD Command
$!
$! Synopsis:   This module processes the ADD command, which is
$!             used to associate keywords with users.  Both the
$!             keywords and users must be previously registered
$!             with the REGISTER command.
$!
$! Format:     ADD keyword,... user,...
$!
$! Parameters: keyword:  A registered keyword to be associated with
$!                       the specified user(s).
$!             user      A registered user with whom the keyword is
$!                       associated.  The word SELF can be used to
$!                       specify the current user.
```

F.4 Listings

F.4.3 File MODL_CLOSE.COM

```
$       on control_y then exit modl__ctrly
$       on warning then exit $status .or. %x10000000
$       check_open_file
$
$       close/nolog modl_file
$       undefine modl_opened_file
$       exit modl__success
$
$! Module:      Process the CLOSE Command
$!
$! Synopsis:    This module processes the CLOSE command, which
$!              closes the current MODL file.  After the command
$!              completes, there is no current MODL file.
$!
$! Format:      CLOSE
$!
$! Parameters:  none
```

F.4.4 File MODL_CREATE.COM

```
$       on control_y then exit modl__ctrly
$       on warning then exit $status .or. %x10000000
$
$       file_spec = p1
$       title = p2
$       if file_spec .eqs. "" then ask modl_ s -
                                        "_MODL Distribution File:"
$       if file_spec .eqs. "" then file_spec = modl_
$       if title .eqs. "" then ask modl_ s "_Title:"
$       if title .eqs. "" then title = modl_
$
$       file_spec = f$parse(file_spec,".modl_file",,,"SYNTAX_ONLY")
$       if f$search(file_spec) .nes. "" then signal e fileexists -
                    "The MODL file ''file_spec already exists."
$       create/fdl=modl_system:modl_file.fdl 'file_spec
$
$       open/read/write modl_file 'file_spec
$       hdr = ""
$       hdr[mf_t_key,mf_s_key]     := "!HEADER!"
$       hdr[mf_t_time,mf_s_time]   := "''f$time()'"
$       hdr[mf_t_doer,mf_s_doer]   := "''this_user'"
$       hdr[mf_t_title,mf_s_title] := "''title'"
$       hdr[mf_t_agent,mf_s_agent] := " "
$       write_unlock hdr
$       close modl_file
$
$       @modl_system:modl_open 'file_spec
$       exit modl__success
$
$! Module:      Process the CREATE Command
$!
$! Synopsis:    This module processes the CREATE command, which is
$!              used to create a new MODL distribution file.  The
$!              new file has no registered users or keywords.
$!              There is no mailing agent stored in the file.
$!              The file is automatically opened after creation.
$!
$! Format:      CREATE file-spec "title"
$!
$! Parameters:  file-spec:  The file spec for the new MODL file.
$!                          The default file type is MODL_FILE.
$!              title:      A title for the new MODL file.
```

F.4.5 File MODL_DEREGISTER.COM

```
$       on control_y then exit modl__ctrly
$       on warning then exit $status .or. %x10000000
$       check_open_file
$
$       what = p1
$       if what .eqs. "" then ask modl_ s -
                                "_Deregister KEYWORD or USER:"
$       if what .eqs. "" then what = modl_
$       libcall lookup_keyword modl_ "''what'" KEYWORD,USER
$       if modl_ .eqs. "" then signal e unkwhat -
                        "The item ''what is unknown or ambiguous."
$       goto 'modl_
$
$KEYWORD:
$       keyword = p2
$       if keyword .eqs. "" then ask modl_ s "_Keyword:"
$       if keyword .eqs. "" then keyword = modl_
$       keyword = f$edit(keyword,"TRIM,UPCASE")
$
$       key = f$fao("!#<#!AS!>", mf_s_key, keyword)
$       read_nolock /key="''key'" rec /error=k15
$       goto k19
$k15:   signal e keynotreg "Keyword ''keyword is not registered."
$k19:
$       read_nolock /key="$"/match=ge rec /end_of_file=k29
$k30:     key_list = f$edit(f$extract(mf_t_keylist,mf_s_keylist,-
                                rec), "TRIM")
          if f$locate(","+keyword+",", ","+key_list+",") .ne. -
            f$length(key_list)+2 then -
            signal e keyinuse -
                "At least one user has keyword ''keyword." -
                "Use the REMOVE command first."
$       read_nolock rec /end_of_file=k39
$       goto k30
$k39:
$       read_nolock/delete /key="''key'" rec
$       exit modl__success
$
$
$USER:
$       username = p2
$       verify = p3 .nes. "NOVERIFY"
$       if username .eqs. "" then ask modl_ s "_User:"
```

```
$          if username .eqs. "" then username = modl_
$          username = f$edit(username,"TRIM,UPCASE")
$
$          if username .eqs. "SELF" then username = this_user
$          key = f$fao("!#AS", mf_s_key, username)
$          read_lock /key="''key'" rec /error=u15
$          goto u19
$u15:      signal e usernotreg "User ''username is not registered."
$u19:
$
$          if verify
$          then
$            ask modl_ b -
                  "Are you sure you want to deregister ''username?" no
$            if .not. modl_ then exit modl__success
$          endif
$
$          read_nolock/delete /key="''key'" rec
$          exit modl__success
$
$! Module:      Process the DEREGISTER Command
$!
$! Synopsis:    This module processes the DEREGISTER command, which
$!              is used to remove registered users and keywords from
$!              the MODL file.
$!
$!              When a user is deregistered, the user record is
$!              removed from the MODL file.  No information about
$!              the user remains.
$!
$!              When a keyword is deregistered, the command first
$!              checks to ensure that the keyword is not associated
$!              with any users.  Then the keyword record is removed.
$!
$! Format:      DEREGISTER USER user-name [NOVERIFY]
$!
$! Parameters:  user-name:  The user name of the user.
$!              NOVERIFY:   If this parameter is not specified, the
$!                          command prompts to ensure that you
$!                          want to deregister the user.  If it is
$!                          specified, no prompt occurs.
$!
$! Format:      DEREGISTER KEYWORD keyword
$!
$! Parameters:  keyword:    The name of the keyword.
```

F.4.6 File MODL_DISPLAY.COM

```
$       on control_y then exit modl__ctrly
$       on warning then exit $status .or. %x10000000
$       check_open_file
$
$       selection = p1
$       if selection .eqs. "" then ask modl_ s "_Selection:"
$       if selection .eqs. "" then selection = modl_
$
$       modlcall parse_selection modl_selection "'selection'"
$       read_nolock_header hdr
$       agent = f$edit(f$extract(mf_t_agent,mf_s_agent,hdr),"TRIM")
$
$       fao = "!12AS  !32AS  !32AS"
$       display ""
$       display f$fao(fao, "User", "Full Name", "Mailing Address")
$       display f$fao(fao, "----", "---- ----", "------- -------")
$       count = 0
$       read_nolock /key="$"/match=ge rec /end_of_file=19
$10:    kl = "," + -
              f$edit(f$extract(mf_t_keylist,mf_s_keylist,rec),-
                 "TRIM") + ","
$       if 'modl_selection then gosub display_user
$       read_nolock rec /end_of_file=19
$       goto 10
$19:
$       display f$fao("!/Users displayed: !UL!/", count)
$       exit modl__success
$
$
$display_user:
$       user = f$edit(f$extract(mf_t_key,mf_s_key,rec),"TRIM")
$       name = f$edit(f$extract(mf_t_name,mf_s_name,rec),"TRIM")
$       address = f$edit(f$extract(mf_t_address,mf_s_address,rec),-
                 "TRIM")
$       display f$fao(fao, user, name, agent + address)
$       count = count + 1
$       return
$
$! Module:     Process the DISPLAY Command
$!
$! Synopsis:   This module processes the DISPLAY command, which is
$!             used to display a list of the users who satisfy a
$!             given selection expression. The users are displayed,
```

```
$!                  but no mail message is sent.  The display includes
$!                  the user name, full name, and mailing address.
$!
$! Format:          DISPLAY "selection"
$!
$! Parameters:      selection:  The selection expression specifying the
$!                              users to be displayed.
$!
$! Notes:           See the User's Guide for a description of the
$!                  selection expression.
```

F.4 Listings

F.4.7 File MODL_HELP.COM

```
$       on control_y then exit modl__ctrly
$       on warning then exit $status .or. %x10000000
$
$       define/user_mode sys$input sys$command
$       help/library=modl_system:modl_helplib.hlb -
            /page/noinstruction/prompt -
          'p1 'p2 'p3 'p4 'p5 'p6 'p7 'p8
$       exit modl__success
$
$! Module:     Process the HELP Command.
$!
$! Synopsis:   This module processes the HELP command, which
$!             provides online help for MODL.  The help text
$!             is stored and displayed using the OpenVMS HELP.
$!
$! Format:     HELP [topic ...]
$!
$! Parameters: topic:  A topic or topic hierarchy which selects
$!                     specific help information to be displayed.
$!                     If this parameter is missing, the help
$!                     facility displays the top-level help screen.
$!
$!Notes:       The help text is not included in this appendix.
```

F.4.8 File MODL_LIST.COM

```
$       status = modl__success
$       on control_y then goto CONTROL_Y
$       on warning then goto ERROR
$       check_open_file
$
$       selection = p1
$       output_file = p2
$       heading = p3
$       if selection .eqs. "" then ask modl_ s "_Selection:"
$       if selection .eqs. "" then selection = modl_
$       if output_file .eqs. "" then ask modl_ s "_Output File:"
$       if output_file .eqs. "" then output_file = modl_
$       if heading .eqs. "" then ask modl_ s "_Heading:"
$       if heading .eqs. "" then heading = modl_
$
$       modlcall parse_selection modl_selection "''selection'"
$       read_nolock_header hdr
$       agent = f$edit(f$extract(mf_t_agent,mf_s_agent,hdr),"TRIM")
$       output_file = f$parse(output_file,".DIS",,,"SYNTAX_ONLY")
$
$       create 'output_file
$       open/append modl_list 'output_file
$       write modl_list "! ", heading
$       write modl_list ""
$       write modl_list "! This is a MODL distribution list."
$       write modl_list "! File:         ", -
                         f$trnlnm("modl_opened_file")
$       write modl_list "! Selection: ", selection
$       write modl_list ""
$
$       read_nolock /key="$"/match=ge rec /end_of_file=19
$10:    kl = "," + -
              f$edit(f$extract(mf_t_keylist,mf_s_keylist,rec),-
                 "TRIM") + ","
$       if 'modl_selection then gosub list_user
$       read_nolock rec /end_of_file=19
$       goto 10
$19:
$       goto EXIT
$
$CONTROL_Y:
$       status = modl__ctrly
$       goto EXIT
```

```
$ERROR:
$       status = $status
$       goto EXIT
$EXIT:
$       set noon
$       close/nolog modl_list
$       exit status .or. %x10000000
$
$
$list_user:
$       name = f$edit(f$extract(mf_t_name,mf_s_name,rec),"TRIM")
$       address = agent + -
                f$edit(f$extract(mf_t_address,mf_s_address,rec),-
                "TRIM")
$       s = f$length(address)
$       if s .lt. 32 then s = 32
$       write modl_list f$fao("!#AS !! !AS", s, address, name)
$       return
$
$! Module:       Process the LIST Command.
$!
$! Synopsis:     This module processes the LIST command, which is
$!              used to create a MAIL distribution list.  The users
$!              included in the list are those who satisfy a given
$!              selection expression.  The distribution list is
$!              created, but no mail message is sent.
$!
$! Format:       LIST "selection" output-file "heading"
$!
$! Parameters:   selection:      The selection expression specifying
$!                               the user to be included in the list.
$!              output-file:    The spec of the distribution list.
$!                              The default file type is DIS.
$!              heading:        A heading to be included at the
$!                              beginning of the distribution file.
$!
$! Notes:        See the User's Guide for a description of the
$!              selection expression.
```

F.4.9 File MODL_MODIFY.COM

```
$       on control_y then exit modl__ctrly
$       on warning then exit $status .or. %x10000000
$       check_open_file
$
$       what = p1
$       if what .eqs. "" then ask modl_ s "_Modify KEYWORD or USER:"
$       if what .eqs. "" then what = modl_
$       libcall lookup_keyword modl_ "''what'" KEYWORD,USER
$       if modl_ .eqs. "" then signal e unkwhat -
                        "The item ''what is unknown or ambiguous."
$       goto 'modl_
$
$KEYWORD:
$       keyword = p2
$       new_title = p3
$       if keyword .eqs. "" then ask modl_ s "_Keyword:"
$       if keyword .eqs. "" then keyword = modl_
$       keyword = f$edit(keyword,"TRIM,UPCASE")
$       key = f$fao("!#<#!AS!>", mf_s_key, keyword)
$       read_lock /key="''key'" rec /error=15
$       goto 19
$15:    signal e keynotreg -
                "The keyword ''keyword is not registered."
$19:
$       old_title = f$edit(f$extract(mf_t_title,mf_s_title,rec),-
                        "TRIM")
$       if new_title .eqs. "" then ask modl_ s "_New Title:" -
                                        "''old_title'"
$       if new_title .eqs. "" then new_title = modl_
$       rec[mf_t_title,mf_s_title] := "''new_title'"
$       update_unlock rec
$       exit modl__success
$
$USER:
$       username = p2
$       new_full_name = p3
$       new_title = p4
$       new_address = p5
$       if username .eqs. "" then ask modl_ s "_User Name:"
$       if username .eqs. "" then username = modl_
$       username = f$edit(username,"TRIM,UPCASE")
$       if username .eqs. "SELF" then username = this_user
$       key = f$fao("!#AS", mf_s_key, username)
```

```
$          read_lock /key="''key'" rec /error=55
$          goto 59
$55:       signal e usernotreg "User ''username is not registered."
$59:
$          old_full_name = f$edit(f$extract(mf_t_name,mf_s_name,rec),-
                            "TRIM")
$          old_title = f$edit(f$extract(mf_t_title,mf_s_title,rec),-
                            "TRIM")
$          old_address = f$edit(f$extr(mf_t_address,mf_s_address,rec),-
                            "TRIM")
$          if new_full_name .eqs. "" then ask modl_ s -
                            "_New Full Name:" "''old_full_name'"
$          if new_full_name .eqs. "" then new_full_name = modl_
$          if new_title .eqs. "" then ask modl_ s "_New Title:" -
                                          "''old_title'"
$          if new_title .eqs. "" then new_title = modl_
$          if new_address .eqs. "" then ask modl_ s "_New Address:" -
                                          "''old_address'"
$          if new_address .eqs. "" then new_address = modl_
$          rec[mf_t_name,mf_s_name]       := "''new_full_name'"
$          rec[mf_t_title,mf_s_title]     := "''new_title'"
$          rec[mf_t_address,mf_s_address] := "''new_address'"
$          update_unlock rec
$          exit modl__success
$
$! Module:      Process the MODIFY Command
$!
$! Synopsis:    This module process the MODIFY command, which is
$!              used to modify the information about registered
$!              users and keywords.
$!
$! Format:      MODIFY USER user-name "new full name" "new title" -
$!                            new-address
$!
$! Parameters:  user-name:      The name of the registered user
$!                              to be updated.
$!              new full name:  The full name of the user.
$!              new title       The business title of the user.
$!              new address     The OpenVMS mailing address of the user.
$!
$! Format:      MODIFY KEYWORD keyword "new title"
$!
$! Parameters:  keyword:        The name of the registered keyword
$!                              to be updated.
$!              new title:      A descriptive title for the keyword.
```

```
$!
$! Notes:     As usual, if a parameter is omitted, MODL prompts
$!            for it.  The default answer is the previous value
$!            of the field.
```

F.4.10 File MODL_OPEN.COM

```
$       on control_y then exit modl__ctrly
$       on warning then exit $status .or. %x10000000
$
$       file_spec = p1
$       if file_spec .eqs. "" then ask modl_ s -
                                "_MODL Distribution File:"
$       if file_spec .eqs. "" then file_spec = modl_
$
$       file_spec = f$parse(file_spec,".modl_file",,,"SYNTAX_ONLY")
$       if f$search(file_spec) .eqs. "" then signal e filnotfnd -
                        "MODL file ''file_spec does not exist."
$
$       if f$trnlnm("modl_opened_file") .nes. "" then -
          @modl_system:modl_close
$
$       open/read/write/share=write modl_file 'file_spec /error=5
$       goto 9
$5:     signal e filenotopen "Cannot open MODL file ''file_spec'" -
                        '$status
$9:
$
$       read_nolock_header hdr /error=15
$       goto 19
$15:    close modl_file
$       signal e notmodlfile "File ''file_spec is not a MODL file."
$19:
$       define modl_opened_file 'file_spec
$       exit modl__success
$
$! Module:      Process the OPEN Command
$!
$! Synopsis:    This module processes the OPEN command, which is
$!              used to select a MODL distribution file and prepare
$!              it for use. The MODL file must have been previously
$!              created using the CREATE command.
$!
$! Format:      OPEN file-spec
$!
$! Parameters:  file-spec:      The file spec of the MODL
$!                              distribution file.
$!
$! Notes:       Most other MODL commands require that a MODL
$!              distribution file is already open.
```

F.4.11   File MODL_REGISTER.COM

```
$       on control_y then exit modl__ctrly
$       on warning then exit $status .or. %x10000000
$       check_open_file
$
$       what = p1
$       if what .eqs. "" then ask modl_ s -
                                "_Register USER or KEYWORD:"
$       if what .eqs. "" then what = modl_
$       libcall lookup_keyword modl_ "''what'" KEYWORD,USER
$       if modl_ .eqs. "" then signal e unkwhat -
                        "The item ''what is unknown or ambiguous."
$       goto 'modl_
$
$KEYWORD:
$       keyword = p2
$       title = p3
$       if keyword .eqs. "" then ask modl_ s "_Keyword:"
$       if keyword .eqs. "" then keyword = modl_
$       if title .eqs. "" then ask modl_ s "_Title:"
$       if title .eqs. "" then title = modl_
$
$       keyword = f$edit(keyword,"TRIM,UPCASE")
$       libcall verify_symbol modl_ "''keyword'" -
                                'f$integer(mf_s_key-1) "-"
$       if modl_ .nes. "" then signal e invkey -
                                "Keyword ''keyword ''modl_."
$
$       key = f$fao("!#<#!AS!>", mf_s_key, keyword)
$       read_nolock /key="''key'" rec /error=19
$       signal e keyalrdydef "Keyword ''keyword is already defined."
$19:
$       rec = ""
$       rec[mf_t_key,mf_s_key]     := "''key'"
$       rec[mf_t_time,mf_s_time]   := "''f$time()'"
$       rec[mf_t_doer,mf_s_doer]   := "''this_user'"
$       rec[mf_t_title,mf_s_title] := "''title'"
$       write_unlock rec
$       exit modl__success
$
$
$USER:
$       user = p2
$       full_name = p3
```

F.4   Listings

```
$       title = p4
$       address = p5
$       if user .eqs. "" then ask modl_ s "_User Name:"
$       if user .eqs. "" then user = modl_
$       if full_name .eqs. "" then ask modl_ s "_Full Name:"
$       if full_name .eqs. "" then full_name = modl_
$       if title .eqs. "" then ask modl_ s "_Title:"
$       if title .eqs. "" then title = modl_
$       if address .eqs. "" then ask modl_ s "_Mailing Address:"
$       if address .eqs. "" then address = modl_
$
$       user = f$edit(user,"TRIM,UPCASE")
$       if user .eqs. "SELF" then user = this_user
$       if f$length(user) .gt. mf_s_key then -
            signal e userlen "User name ''user is too long."
$       if f$length(address) .gt. mf_s_address then -
            signal e addrlen "Mailing address ''address is too long."
$
$       key = f$fao("!#AS", mf_s_key, user)
$       read_nolock /key="''key'" rec /error=59
$       signal e useralrdyreg "User ''user is already registered."
$59:
$       rec = ""
$       rec[mf_t_key,mf_s_key]              := "''key'"
$       rec[mf_t_time,mf_s_time]            := "''f$time()'"
$       rec[mf_t_doer,mf_s_doer]            := "''this_user'"
$       rec[mf_t_title,mf_s_title]          := "''title'"
$       rec[mf_t_name,mf_s_name]            := "''full_name'"
$       rec[mf_t_address,mf_s_address]      := "''address'"
$       write_unlock rec
$       exit modl__success
$
$! Module:     Process the REGISTER Command
$!
$! Synopsis:   This module process the REGISTER command, which is
$!             used to register information about users and
$!             keywords. Duplicate users/keywords are not allowed.
$!
$! Format:     REGISTER USER user-name "full name" "title" address
$!
$! Parameters: user-name:       The name of the user.
$!             new full name:   The full name of the user.
$!             new title        The business title of the user.
$!             new address      The OpenVMS mail address of the user.
$!
```

```
$! Format:       REGISTER KEYWORD keyword "title"
$!
$! Parameters:   keyword:        The name of the keyword.
$!               new title:      The descriptive title for keyword.
```

F.4.12 File MODL_REMOVE.COM

```
$       on control_y then exit modl__ctrly
$       on warning then exit $status .or. %x10000000
$       check_open_file
$
$       remove_keys = p1
$       users = p2
$       if remove_keys .eqs. "" then ask modl_ s "_Keyword List:"
$       if remove_keys .eqs. "" then remove_keys = modl_
$       if users .eqs. "" then ask modl_ s "_User List:"
$       if users .eqs. "" then users = modl_
$       remove_keys = f$edit(remove_keys,"COLLAPSE,UPCASE")
$       users = f$edit(users,"COLLAPSE,UPCASE")
$
$       if users .eqs. "*"
$       then
$          read_lock /key="$"/match=ge rec /end_of_file=19
$10:       kl = f$edit(f$extract(mf_t_keylist,mf_s_keylist,rec),-
                  "TRIM")
$          modlcall remove_keywords modl_ "''kl'" "''remove_keys'"
$          rec[mf_t_keylist,mf_s_keylist] := "''modl_'"
$          update_unlock rec
$          read_lock rec /end_of_file=19
$          goto 10
$19:
$       else
$          i = -1
$20:       i = i + 1
$          username= f$element(i,",",users)
$          if username .eqs. "," then goto 29
$          if username .eqs. "SELF" then username = this_user
$          key = f$fao("!#AS", mf_s_key, username)
$          read_lock /key="''key'" rec /error=25
$          kl = f$edit(f$extract(mf_t_keylist,mf_s_keylist,rec),-
                  "TRIM")
$          modlcall remove_keywords modl_ "''kl'" "''remove_keys'"
$          rec[mf_t_keylist,mf_s_keylist] := "''modl_'"
$          update_unlock rec
$          goto 20
$25:       signal w unreguser "User ''username is not registered."
$          goto 20
$29:
$       endif
$       exit modl__success
```

```
$
$!  Module:      Process the REMOVE Command
$!
$!  Synopsis:    This module processes the REMOVE command, which is
$!               used to disassociate keywords from users.
$!
$!  Format:      REMOVE keyword,... user,... | *
$!
$!  Parameters:  keyword:  A keyword to be disassociated from the
$!                         specified user(s).  A list is allowed.
$!               user:     A registered user from whom the keyword(s)
$!                         are removed.  A list is allowed.  If an
$!                         asterisk (*) is specified, the keywords
$!                         are removed from all registered users.
```

F.4 Listings

F.4.13 File MODL_SEND.COM

```
$       status = modl__success
$       on control_y then goto control_y
$       on warning then goto error
$       check_open_file
$       dc$_mailbox = 160
$
$       file_spec = p1
$       selection = p2
$       subject = p3
$       copy_self = p4
$       batch = p5
$       if file_spec .eqs. "" then ask modl_ s "_File to Send:"
$       if file_spec .eqs. "" then file_spec = modl_
$       if selection .eqs. "" then ask modl_ s "_Selection:"
$       if selection .eqs. "" then selection = modl_
$       if subject .eqs. "" then ask modl_ s "_Subject:"
$       if subject .eqs. "" then subject = modl_
$       if copy_self .eqs. "" then copy_self = modl_copy_self
$       if batch .eqs. "" then batch = modl_batch
$       if f$mode() .eqs. "BATCH" then batch = false
$
$!      Parse the message file spec and make sure the file exists.
$!      Allow the spec to be NL: by checking for a mailbox device.
$
$       file_spec = f$parse(file_spec,"sys$disk:[].txt;")
$       if f$getdvi(file_spec,"DEVCLASS") .ne. dc$_mailbox then -
$         if f$search(file_spec) .eqs. "" then -
            signal e filnotfnd "File ''file_spec does not exist."
$
$       if batch
$       then
$!        Submit a batch job to send the message.  First parse the
$!        selection expression to check for errors.  Then create a
$!        little procedure which opens the current MODL file, sends
$!        the message, and exits.  Submit the procedure so that it
$!        is deleted when done.
$
$         modlcall parse_selection modl_ "''selection'"
$         libcall unique_name modl_ sys$scratch:modl_?.tmp
$         temp_file = modl_
$         open/write modl_temp_file 'temp_file
$         write modl_temp_file "$ modl open ", -
                               f$trnlnm("modl_opened_file")
```

```
$            write modl_temp_file "$ modl send ", file_spec, " """, -
                         selection, """ """, subject, """ ", copy_self
$            write modl_temp_file "$ exit"
$            close modl_temp_file
$            submit/identify/nolog/notify 'temp_file/delete
$
$        else
$!           Send the message immediately.  Determine whether there is
$!           a mailing agent and call the appropriate subroutine.  Then
$!           send a self-copy if requested.
$
$            signal i sendfile "File to be sent: ''file_spec'"
$            read_nolock_header hdr
$            agent = f$edit(f$extract(mf_t_agent,mf_s_agent,hdr),-
                         "TRIM")
$            if agent .eqs. "" then gosub send_no_agent
$            if agent .nes. "" then gosub send_agent
$            if copy_self then mail 'file_spec 'this_user -
                         /subject="''subject (MODL self copy)"
$        endif
$        goto exit
$
$control_y:
$        status = modl__ctrly
$        goto exit
$error:
$        status = $status
$        goto exit
$exit:
$        set noon
$        close/nolog modl_temp_file
$        close/nolog modl_log_file
$        exit status .or. %x10000000
$
$
$!       This subroutine sends a message without using an agent.
$!       It does so by invoking MAIL once for each user, thus
$!       preventing one problem from messing up the other recipients.
$!       As it goes, it maintains a log file of the results, which
$!       is mailed back to the sender at the end.
$
$SEND_NO_AGENT:
$        modlcall parse_selection modl_selection "''selection'"
$        libcall unique_name modl_ sys$scratch:modl_?.log;
$        log_file = modl_
```

F.4 Listings   389

```
$         open/write modl_log_file 'log_file
$         fao = "!12AS  !20AS   !40AS"
$         write modl_log_file -
              f$fao(fao, "User", "Mailing Address", "Status")
$         write modl_log_file -
              f$fao(fao, "----", "------- -------", "------")
$         set message sys$message:cliutlmsg
$
$         read_nolock /key="$"/match=ge rec /end_of_file=59
$50:      kl = "," + -
                f$edit(f$extract(mf_t_keylist,mf_s_keylist,rec),-
                    "TRIM") + ","
$         if 'modl_selection
$         then
$           user = f$edit(f$extract(mf_t_key,mf_s_key,rec),"TRIM")
$           address = f$edit(f$extr(mf_t_address,mf_s_address,rec),-
                        "TRIM")
$           set noon
$           mail 'file_spec 'address /subject="''subject'"
$           message = f$message($status)
$           set on
$           write modl_log_file f$fao(fao, user, address, -
                    f$edit(f$element(1,",",message),"TRIM"))
$         endif
$55:      read_nolock rec /end_of_file=59
$         goto 50
$59:
$         close modl_log_file
$         send_log = true
$         if f$getjpi("","MODE") .eqs. "INTERACTIVE"
$         then
$           ask modl_ b "Do you want a copy of the mailing log?" no
$           send_log = modl_
$         endif
$         if send_log then mail 'log_file 'this_user -
                        /subject="''subject (MODL mailing log)"
$         delete 'log_file'*
$         return
$
$
$!        This subroutine sends a message using an agent.  It creates
$!        a MAIL distribution list with the selected users and then
$!        sends the message to them with one invocation of MAIL.
$
$SEND_AGENT:
```

```
$       libcall unique_name modl_ sys$scratch:modl_?.dis;
$       temp_dis = modl_
$       @modl_system:modl_list "''selection'" 'temp_dis -
                "Temporary list for sending by agent."
$       mail 'file_spec "@''temp_dis'" /subject="''subject'"
$       delete 'temp_dis'*
$       return
$
$! Module:      Process the SEND Command
$!
$! Synopsis:    This module processes the SEND command, which is
$!              used to send a message to users who satisfy a given
$!              selection expression.  There are four modes for
$!              sending the message:
$!
$!              Interactive, no agent:  The message is sent while
$!                the user waits.  A separate invocation of MAIL is
$!                used for each recipient.  Errors appear on the
$!                terminal and a log file can be saved.
$!              Interactive, agent:  The message is sent while the
$!                user waits.  A distribution list is created and a
$!                single invocation of MAIL is used.  Errors appear
$!                on the terminal.
$!              Batch, no agent:  A batch job is submitted to send
$!                the mail.  In batch, a separate invocation of MAIL
$!                is used for each recipient.  An error log is
$!                mailed back to the sender.
$!              Batch, agent:  A batch job is submitted to send the
$!                mail.  In batch, a distribution list is created and
$!                a single invocation of MAIL is used.  Errors are
$!                reported by the agent.
$!
$! Format:      SEND message-file "selection" "subject"
$!
$! Parameters:  message-file:   The file spec of the text file with
$!                              the message to be sent.
$!              selection:      The selection expression specifying
$!                              the users to receive the message.
$!              subject:        The subject heading for the message.
$!
$! Notes:       See the User's Guide for a description of the
$!              selection expression.
```

F.4.14 File MODL_SET.COM

```
$       on control_y then exit modl__ctrly
$       on warning then exit $status .or. %x10000000
$       check_open_file
$
$       what = p1
$       if what .eqs. "" then ask modl_ s -
                                "_What (AGENT, NOAGENT, SEND):"
$       if what .eqs. "" then what = modl_
$       libcall lookup_keyword modl_ "'"what'" AGENT,NOAGENT,SEND
$       if modl_ .eqs. "" then signal e unkwhat -
                        "The item ''what is unknown or ambiguous."
$       goto 'modl_
$
$AGENT:
$       agent = p2
$       read_lock_header hdr
$       old_agent = f$edit(f$extract(mf_t_agent,mf_s_agent,hdr),-
                        "TRIM")
$       if agent .eqs. "" then ask modl_ s "_Agent:" "'"old_agent'"
$       if agent .eqs. "" then agent = modl_
$       hdr[mf_t_agent,mf_s_agent] := "'"agent'"
$       update_unlock hdr
$       exit modl__success
$
$
$NOAGENT:
$       read_lock_header hdr
$       hdr[mf_t_agent,mf_s_agent] := ""
$       update_unlock hdr
$       exit modl__success
$
$
$SEND:
$       copy_self = p2
$       batch = p3
$       if copy_self .eqs. "" then ask modl_ b "_Copy Self?" -
                                                'modl_copy_self
$       if copy_self .eqs. "" then copy_self = modl_
$       if batch .eqs. "" then ask modl_ b "_Send in Batch?" -
                                                'modl_batch
$       if batch .eqs. "" then batch = modl_
$       modl_copy_self == copy_self
$       modl_batch == batch
```

```
$       exit modl__success
$
$! Module:      Process the SET Command
$!
$! Synopsis:    This module processes the SET command, which is
$!              used to specify various parameters for MODL.
$!
$!              The SET AGENT command specifies the mailing agent
$!              for future SEND commands.  The agent is stored in
$!              the MODL distribution file.  The SET NOAGENT command
$!              specifies that no mailing agent is used.
$!
$!              The SET SEND command specifies various things about
$!              how mail messages are sent.  These things are
$!              specific to the current user and are only remembered
$!              for the remainder of the terminal session.
$!
$! Format:      SET AGENT    "string"
$!              SET NOAGENT
$!
$! Parameters:  string:    The string which identifies the mailing
$!                         agent (e.g., "ma%").  This string is
$!                         prefixed on each mailing address before
$!                         mail is sent to it.
$!
$! Format:      SET SEND copy-self? batch?
$!
$! Parameters:  copy-self?:     A boolean specifying whether an
$!                              additional copy of a message should
$!                              be mailed to the sender.
$!              batch?:         A boolean specifying whether mailing
$!                              should be done with a batch job.
```

F.4.15 File MODL_SHOW.COM

```
$       on control_y then exit modl__ctrly
$       on warning then exit $status .or. %x10000000
$       check_open_file
$
$       what = p1
$       if what .eqs. "" then ask modl_ s -
                                "_What (FILE, KEYWORD, SEND, USER):"
$       if what .eqs. "" then what = modl_
$
$       libcall lookup_keyword modl_ "''what'" -
                                FILE,KEYWORD,SEND,USER
$       if modl_ .eqs. "" then signal e unkwhat -
                        "The item ''what is unknown or ambiguous."
$       goto 'modl_
$
$FILE:
$       read_nolock_header hdr
$       doer  = f$edit(f$extract(mf_t_doer,mf_s_doer,hdr),"TRIM")
$       time  = f$edit(f$extract(mf_t_time,mf_s_time,hdr),"TRIM")
$       title = f$edit(f$extract(mf_t_title,mf_s_title,hdr),"TRIM")
$       agent = f$edit(f$extract(mf_t_agent,mf_s_agent,hdr),"TRIM")
$       if agent .eqs. "" then agent = "(none)"
$       display ""
$       display "MODL file:    ", f$trnlnm("modl_opened_file")
$       display "Title:        ", title
$       display "Agent:        ", agent
$       display "(Created by: ", doer, ", on: ", time, ")"
$       display ""
$       exit modl__success
$
$
$KEYWORD:
$       keyword = p2
$       if keyword .eqs. "" then ask modl_ s "_Keyword or *:"
$       if keyword .eqs. "" then keyword = modl_
$       keyword = f$edit(keyword,"TRIM,UPCASE")
$       if keyword .eqs. "*"
$       then
$         count = 0
$         read_nolock /key="#"/match=ge rec /end_of_file=19
$10:      if f$extract(mf_t_key,1,rec) .nes. "#" then goto 19
$         gosub display_keyword
$         count = count + 1
```

```
$              read_nolock rec /end_of_file=19
$              goto 10
$19:
$          display f$fao("!/Keywords displayed: !UL!/", count)
$        else
$          key = f$fao("!#<#!AS!>", mf_s_key, keyword)
$          read_nolock /key="''key'" rec /error=25
$          gosub display_keyword
$          display ""
$          goto 29
$25:       signal e keynotdef "Keyword ''keyword is not defined." -
                               '$status
$29:
$        endif
$        exit modl__success
$
$display_keyword:
$        keyword = f$extract(mf_t_key,mf_s_key,rec) - "#"
$        doer = f$edit(f$extract(mf_t_doer,mf_s_doer,rec),"TRIM")
$        time = f$edit(f$extract(mf_t_time,mf_s_time,rec),"TRIM")
$        title = f$edit(f$extract(mf_t_title,mf_s_title,rec),"TRIM")
$        display ""
$        display "Keyword:     ", keyword
$        display "Title:       ", title
$        display "(Defined by: ", doer, ", on: ", time, ")"
$        return
$
$
$SEND:
$        read_nolock_header hdr
$        agent = f$edit(f$extract(mf_t_agent,mf_s_agent,hdr),"TRIM")
$        if agent .eqs. "" then agent = "(none)"
$        display ""
$        display "Agent:       ", agent
$        display "Copy Self: ", -
                f$element(modl_copy_self,"|","NO|YES")
$        display "In Batch:  ", f$element(modl_batch,"|","NO|YES")
$        display ""
$        exit modl__success
$
$
$USER:
$        user = p2
$        if user .eqs. "" then ask modl_ s "_User Name or *:" -
                                          'this_user
```

```
$          if user .eqs. "" then user = modl_
$          user = f$edit(user,"TRIM,UPCASE")
$          if user .eqs. "*"
$          then
$            count = 0
$            read_nolock /key="$"/match=ge rec /end_of_file=39
$30:          gosub display_user
$             count = count + 1
$             read_nolock rec /end_of_file=39
$             goto 30
$39:
$            display f$fao("!/Users displayed: !UL!/", count)
$          else
$            if user .eqs. "SELF" then user = this_user
$            key = f$fao("!#AS", mf_s_key, user)
$            read_nolock /key="''key'" rec /error=45
$            gosub display_user
$            display ""
$            goto 49
$45:         signal e usernotreg "User ''user is not registered." -
                                 '$status
$49:
$          endif
$          exit modl__success
$
$display_user:
$          user = f$extract(mf_t_key,mf_s_key,rec)
$          doer = f$edit(f$extract(mf_t_doer,mf_s_doer,rec),"TRIM")
$          time = f$edit(f$extract(mf_t_time,mf_s_time,rec),"TRIM")
$          title = f$edit(f$extract(mf_t_title,mf_s_title,rec),"TRIM")
$          full_name = f$edit(f$extract(mf_t_name,mf_s_name,rec),-
                      "TRIM")
$          address = f$edit(f$extract(mf_t_address,mf_s_address,rec),-
                      "TRIM")
$          keylist = f$edit(f$extract(mf_t_keylist,mf_s_keylist,rec),-
                      "TRIM")
$          display ""
$          display "User:              ", user
$          display "Full name:         ", full_name
$          display "Title:             ", title
$          display "Mailing address:   ", address
$          if keylist .nes. "" then -
           display "Keyword list:      ", keylist
$          display "(Registered by:    ", doer, ", on: ", time, ")"
$          return
```

```
$
$!  Module:        Process the SHOW Command
$!
$!  Synopsis:      This module processes the SHOW command, which is
$!                 used to display the contents of a MODL distribution
$!                 file and various other environmental items.
$!
$!                 The SHOW FILE command is used to display information
$!                 about the current MODL distribution file.  The
$!                 information includes the full file spec, title, and
$!                 mailing agent.
$!
$!                 The SHOW KEYWORD and SHOW USER commands are used to
$!                 display information about registered keywords and
$!                 users. The information includes the title in both
$!                 cases, and the full name, mailing address, and
$!                 keyword list for a user.
$!
$!                 The SHOW SEND command is used to display the mailing
$!                 parameters established with the SET SEND command.
$!                 The information includes the send-self and batch
$!                 parameters.
$!
$!  Format:        SHOW FILE
$!
$!  Format:        SHOW USER user | *
$!
$!  Parameters:    user:    The name of a registered user, or an
$!                          asterisk (*) to display all users.
$!
$!  Format:        SHOW KEYWORD keyword | *
$!
$!  Parameters:    keyword: The name of a registered keyword, or an
$!                          asterisk to display all keywords.
$!
$!  Format:        SHOW SEND
```

F.4.16 File MODL_SUBROUTINES.COM

```
$       on control_y then exit modl__ctrly
$       on warning then exit $status .or. %x10000000
$
$       goto 'p1
$
$! Title:        Parse a Selection Expression
$!
$! Synopsis:     This subroutine parses a selection expression and
$!               builds the corresponding DCL boolean expression.
$!               Each keyword in the expression turns into:
$!                  (F$LOC(",keyword,",KL) .NE. F$LEN(KL))
$!               under the assumption that the list of keywords for a
$!               particular user is stored in the symbol KL.
$!               Each boolean operator in the keyword is converted to
$!               a DCL operator by surrounding it with dots.
$!               Parentheses are simply copied to the DCL expression.
$!
$! Parameters:   P2:  The symbol to receive the resulting DCL
$!                    expression.
$!               P3:  The selection expression to be parsed.
$!
$! Returns:      The DCL expression representing the selection
$!               expression.
$
$PARSE_SELECTION:
$
$       selection = f$edit(p3,"COMPRESS,TRIM,UPCASE") + "~"
$       if selection .eqs. "*~"
$       then
$         'p2 == "true"
$         exit modl__success
$       endif
$
$       result = ""
$       i = 0
$ps10:  char = f$extract(i,1,selection)
$       if f$locate(char," ()~") .ne. 4
$       then
$         if char .eqs. "~" then goto ps19
$         result = result + char
$         i = i + 1
$       else
$         keyword = ""
```

```
$ps20:          keyword = keyword + char
$               i = i + 1
$               char = f$extract(i,1,selection)
$               if f$locate(char," ()~") .eq. 4 then goto ps20
$             if keyword .eqs. "AND" .or. keyword .eqs. "OR" .or. -
                  keyword .eqs. "NOT"
$             then
$               result = f$fao("!AS.!AS.", result, keyword)
$             else
$               gosub check_keyword
$               result = -
                    f$fao("!AS(f$loc("",!AS,"",kl) .ne. f$len(kl))",-
                        result, keyword)
$             endif
$           endif
$         goto ps10
$ps19:
$
$       'p2 == result
$       exit mod1__success
$
$check_keyword:
$       key = f$fao("!#<#!AS!>", mf_s_key, keyword)
$       read_nolock /key="''key'" rec /error=ps95
$       return mod1__success
$ps95:  signal e undefkey "Keyword ''keyword is not defined."
```

F.4 Listings

```
$! Title:        Remove Keywords from a List
$!
$! Synopsis:     This subroutine removes one or more keywords from an
$!               original list of keywords.
$!
$! Parameters:   P2:  The symbol to receive the resulting list.
$!               P3:  The original comma-separated list of keywords.
$!               P4:  The list of keywords to be removed.
$!
$! Returns:      The original list with specified keywords removed.
$
$REMOVE_KEYWORDS:
$
$       original = "," + p3 + ","
$       k = -1
$rk10:  k = k + 1
$          keyword = f$element(k, ",", p4)
$          if keyword .eqs. "," then goto rk19
$          l = f$locate(","+keyword+",", original)
$          if l .ne. f$length(original) then -
$             original = f$extract(0, l, original) + -
$                    f$extract(l+f$length(keyword)+1,9999,original)
$       goto rk10
$rk19:
$       if f$extract(0,1,original) .eqs. "," then -
$          original = original - ","
$       'p2 == f$extract(0,f$length(original)-1, original)
$       return modl__success
```

F.4.17 File MODL_FILE.FDL

```
TITLE       "MODL File Description"

IDENT       "18-APR-1988 12:36:23    OpenVMS FDL Editor"

SYSTEM
            SOURCE                      OpenVMS

FILE
            ORGANIZATION                indexed

RECORD
            CARRIAGE_CONTROL            carriage_return
            FORMAT                      variable
            SIZE                        400

AREA 0
            ALLOCATION                  35
            BEST_TRY_CONTIGUOUS         yes
            BUCKET_SIZE                 2
            EXTENSION                   8

AREA 1
            ALLOCATION                  4
            BEST_TRY_CONTIGUOUS         yes
            BUCKET_SIZE                 2
            EXTENSION                   2

KEY 0
            CHANGES                     no
            DATA_AREA                   0
            DATA_FILL                   100
            DATA_KEY_COMPRESSION        yes
            DATA_RECORD_COMPRESSION     yes
            DUPLICATES                  no
            INDEX_AREA                  1
            INDEX_COMPRESSION           no
            INDEX_FILL                  100
            LEVEL1_INDEX_AREA           1
            NAME                        "Record Key"
            PROLOG                      3
            SEG0_LENGTH                 16
            SEG0_POSITION               0
            TYPE                        string
```

Glossary

Absolute time   A string representing an exact point in time. The full OpenVMS format is *dd-mon-yyyy hh:mm:ss.cc*.

Access category   A level at which a process accesses a file or other object. The four levels are system, owner, group, and world.

Access control entry (ACE)   An individual entry in an access control list.

Access control list (ACL)   A list of access control entries that specify detailed protection information for OpenVMS objects.

Access mode   The VAX hardware or Alpha PALcode privilege mode at which a process runs or makes requests. The four access modes are user, supervisor, executive, and kernel.

Allocation   See Device allocation.

Alternate key   A secondary key field in an indexed file.

Ampersand substitution   An explicit form of substitution in a DCL command, which is specified by the ampersand (&).

Apostrophe substitution   An explicit form of substitution in a DCL command, which is specified by the apostrophe (').

Append   See Open for append.

Argument   A value that serves as input data for a particular operation. For example, a lexical function may require one or more arguments to specify the operation it is to perform. See also Optional argument.

Arity The number of operands required by an operator.

Array A collection of data items stored together under one name. Associated with each item is an index by which the item is identified from among all other items.

Array index A number or character string identifying a particular element of an array.

ASCII character set The character set used by the OpenVMS operating system. ASCII stands for American Standard Code for Information Interchange. OpenVMS uses both seven- and eight-bit ASCII characters, depending on the particular devices involved.

Assignment command A DCL command that assigns data to a symbol.

Authorized privilege A privilege that a user is allowed to enable. The system manager determines the authorized privilege for each user. Most users are authorized for the NETMBX and TMPMBX privileges.

Automatic login facility The automatic login facility (ALF) permits a user to log into an OpenVMS system from specified terminals, without having to specify a user name or password.

Automatic substitution See Personal command substitution.

Batch job A detached process created by OpenVMS to run a procedure submitted to a batch queue. A batch job runs without an interactive user at a terminal.

Batch process A process created by OpenVMS to run programs in a batch job. See also Interactive process, Network process.

Batch queue A batch or print queue maintained by the queue manager. Jobs are submitted to a batch queue with the SUBMIT command. Files are submitted to a print queue with the PRINT command.

Bidirectional communications Communications that can occur in two directions are refered to as bidirectional. DECnet task-to-task communications permit messages to be read and written over the network channel; they are bidirectional.

Binary operator An operator that requires two operands (its arity is 2).

Bit Short for "binary digit." A single digit of binary information, representing a 0 or 1.

Boolean A data type that represents the two logical values true and false.

Call See Invoke.

Captive user An OpenVMS user account that "captures" users as they log in. A user is forced to execute the LOGIN.COM procedure and cannot interrupt it with CTRL/Y. Once the login procedure is complete, the user is automatically logged out.

Carriage return carriage-control A file attribute specifying that each record in the file is assumed to have a carriage return/line feed pair at the end. This attribute affects how records are displayed and printed.

Case statement A flow-of-control construct that chooses one of several possible execution paths based on the value of a symbol. There is no case statement in DCL, but it can be simulated using the GOTO command and substitution.

CGI script A program or a command procedure used to dynamically generate the information displayed on a web page. This program or command procedure operates in conjunction with a web server.

Character set The collection of printable and control characters used by a computer or other device. The OpenVMS operating system uses the ASCII character set.

Character string A data type that represents a sequence of characters in some character set. In DCL, the character set is ASCII. A character string may contain zero, one, or more characters.

Child process A subprocess owned by some other process, which is called the parent process.

Cleanup See Procedure cleanup.

Combination time A string representing the combination of an absolute time and a delta time. A combination time represents a particular point some time before or after another point in time. The full OpenVMS format is *dd-mon-yyyy hh:mm:ss.cc+dddd-hh:mm:ss.cc*.

Command See Assignment command, DCL command, Flow-of-control command, Personal command.

Command language interpreter A system program that can analyze and perform commands entered by the user. The standard command language interpreter for OpenVMS is the Digital Command Language (DCL).

Command parameter An item of information included in a command, which specifies an object that the command should manipulate. Command parameters are separated from the command verb and from one another by spaces.

Command procedure See DCL command procedure.

Command qualifier   A keyword included in a DCL command to specify an option or modify the standard behavior of the command. Qualifiers can be interpreted as global or as local. Global qualifiers apply to the entire command, while local qualifiers apply to a particular parameter. Qualifiers can be positional: a particular qualifier can be interpreted as global or as local, depending on where it is positioned in the command. Qualifier keywords are preceded by a slash (/).

Command syntax   The form of a command. Command syntax includes the verb, parameter order, qualifiers, and the punctuation used to connect them.

Command verb   A word identifying a particular command to be performed. DCL includes verbs such as `COPY` and `WRITE`.

Comment   A phrase or sentence included in a program to make it more readable by human beings. Comments are completely ignored by the computer. In DCL, comments begin with an exclamation point (!) and extend to the end of the line.

Common Gateway Interface (CGI)   This is the mechanism by which an application procedure can communicate with a web server.

Comparison time   An absolute time that has been reformatted so that two times can be compared as if they were character strings. The full OpenVMS format is *yyyy-mm-dd hh:mm:ss.cc*.

Condition   The Boolean expression in an `IF` statement, which determines whether the "then" statements or the "else" statements are executed.

Context symbol   A DCL symbol that keeps track of the state of an ongoing request such as that performed with the `F$PID` lexical function. The `F$PID` function obtains the process identifiers of the system processes, one on each call. The context symbol keeps track of the last process examined between each call to the function.

Control character   A character used to control the terminal or other device to which it is sent. For example, the line-feed character causes the cursor on a terminal to move down to the next line. Contrast with Printable character.

Control sequence   A sequence of characters sent to a terminal in order to perform a control or formatting action other than displaying a character. For example, most terminals accept a control sequence that clears the screen.

Control string   The character string that specifies how data is to be formatted by the `F$FAO` lexical function.

Current directory See Working directory.

Data The collection of information created and manipulated by a program.

Data item An individual item of information, such as an integer or a character string.

Data type The class of information to which a data item belongs. DCL supports integer and character string types.

Date See Time.

DCL code The DCL commands that make up a DCL procedure.

DCL command A sequence of words and punctuation marks that instructs DCL to perform some operation. A command consists of a verb, parameters, and qualifiers.

DCL command procedure A file containing DCL commands, which can be executed by DCL in place of commands entered at the terminal.

DCL environment A collection of information that affects the way DCL operates. Environment items include the working directory and the state of procedure verification. This information can be inspected and altered by the DCL user.

DCL procedure See DCL command procedure.

DCL prompt A character string displayed at the terminal to signal that the user may enter a new command. The DCL prompt is the dollar sign ($) unless the user changes it.

DECnet A communications network package used on many OpenVMS systems.

Default answer The answer to a question, which is automatically provided when the user does not enter any other answer. It is an OpenVMS convention to include the default answer in square brackets ([]) after the question.

Default directory The official OpenVMS term for working directory.

Default value A value used by a program when no value is explicitly specified.

Delta time A string representing a certain amount of time, or the difference between two absolute times. The full OpenVMS format is *dddd-hh:mm:ss.cc*.

Detached process A main process that is not owned by any other process. OpenVMS creates a detached process for an interactive user, a batch job, or a remote network request.

Device A hardware component, attached to a computer, which provides input or output capability. Examples are terminals, disk drives, tape drives, and communications controllers.

Device allocation The act of reserving a device for exclusive use by a process. This is accomplished with the `ALLOCATE` command.

Device name A character string that uniquely identifies a particular device from among all devices accessible to a system. The device name includes components identifying the system to which the device is connected, the type of device, its controller letter, and its device number.

Directory An OpenVMS file that acts as a catalog for other files. A directory contains a list of data files and other directories, which are considered to reside in that directory. Using directories, a hierarchical structure is imposed on all the files on a device. See also Login directory, Master file directory, Root directory, Working directory.

Disk quota An OpenVMS system manager can enable a mechanism that controls the amount of disk storage available to a user on a particular disk volume, or that tracks the amount of disk storage occuped by each user who owns files on a disk volume.

Distribution list A text file containing a list of user names. Distribution lists are used by the `MAIL` utility to send messages to groups of users.

End-of-file The state of an input file in which all records have been read. In the case of a disk file, the next read operation will return a "no more records" status.

Equivalence string The value associated with a logical name.

Error handler The portion of a DCL procedure that deals with errors detected during the execution of the procedure.

Escape character A specific ASCII character used to introduce a control sequence, a sequence also sometimes called an escape sequence. The ASCII value of the escape character is 27.

Escape sequence See Control sequence.

Evaluate To determine the final value of an expression. The expression's operators and operands are combined in a predefined order to produce a new value.

Execute A term often applied to programs, including DCL procedures. A program is executed when a computer interprets the statements (commands) in the program and carries out the actions specified by those statements.

Expression   A combination of operators and operands that specifies a new value to be computed. For example, A + B produces a new integer by adding the values of the symbols A and B.

Field   An individual data item in a record or structure. The fields in a structure can be manipulated as separate items.

File   A collection of data arranged in the form of records. Each record contains a related portion of the data, and all the records taken together make up the entire file. See also Log file, Process-permanent file, Sequential file, Temporary file, Text file.

File attributes   A collection of information associated with a file, which identifies the file, describes its internal format, and specifies its file protection.

File prologue   The portion of an indexed file that contains descriptions of the record keys and other aspects of the file.

File protection   The scheme used by OpenVMS to safeguard files against unauthorized access or modification.

File sharing   An RMS facility, which allows multiple processes to access and modify the same file at the same time.

File spec   Short for "file specification."

File specification   A character string identifying a particular file or a group of files.

File Transfer Protocol (FTP)   A network protocol commonly used for transfering files in IP networks. FTP supports the transfer of both text files and image files and is available on a variety of computer systems.

Fixed-length record   A record in a sequential or indexed file whose design stipulates that every record in the file be the same size. Such records are usually formatted according to one or more predetermined record structures.

Flow-of-control command   A DCL command that enables a procedure to alter its flow of execution. Such commands include IF and GOTO. Flow-of-control commands provide the power required to make DCL a general-purpose programming language.

Generic match   An indexed file key lookup based on a partial key rather than on the whole key. For example, the generic key "K" will match any record whose key begins with the letter K.

GET data   CGI scripts have two means of receiving data or passing state information from one web page to the next: GET data and POST data. GET data is encoded and passed in as part of the URL specification, while

POST data is passed in via the input stream. GET data is simpler and is useful with fairly limited quantities of data, while POST data is somewhat harder to process but is better suited for larger data transfers.

Glossary   A list of terms and their definitions.

Group number   The portion of a UIC that identifies a related group of users. See also Member number.

Home directory   See Login directory.

Hyperlink   Within the World Wide Web, a document can contain references to other sections of the current document, to other documents or applications on the local system, or to documents and applications on other host systems. These references are called hyperlinks. Users and automated web tools can easily follow the hyperlinks that interest them, allowing quick and easy access to information related to the current document. Hyperlinks are embedded in web documents using Hypertext Markup Language (HTML) tags.

Hypertext Transport Protocol (HTTP)   The basic protocol used to access web pages and applications. HTTP allows a web browser or other similar tool to communicate with a web server and transfer the information on the web page from the web server to the web browser.

Hypertext Markup Language (HTML)   Web documents and web applications use a simple language for communications. HTML keywords control the images, hyperlinks, and format of the text on a web page. Web pages can be simple files containing a document with text and embedded HTML keywords, the files can be created using other tools and then converted into files containing the text and HTML keywords, or the HTML and the text can be dynamically generated by applications known as CGI scripts.

Images   Four general classes of executable programs exist on OpenVMS: executable images, shareable images, user-written system services (also called privileged shareable images), and system images. Unlike an interpreted DCL command procedure, images are built using tools known as assemblers or compilers and using the OpenVMS LINKER utility.

Image data   Lines in a command procedure that do not contain DCL commands but rather contain input data for a program (image). This input data is used in lieu of data read from the terminal. Any procedure lines not beginning with a dollar sign ($) are considered image data.

Index   In DCL, an identifier used to select an individual character in a character string or to identify an item in an array. See also Array index, String index.

Infinite loop A loop in the flow of control of a program that, once initiated, can never be terminated. Infinite loops are caused by loops with no termination checks or faulty checks. For additional details, see Infinite loop.

Initialization See Volume initialization.

Integer A data type that represents whole numbers—negative, zero, or positive. In DCL, an integer is represented as a 32-bit (longword) quantity, allowing the integer to range from $-2,147,483,648$ to $+2,147,483,647$.

Interactive process An OpenVMS process created to perform work for an interactive user logged in at a terminal. See also Batch process, Network process.

Interrupt A break in execution caused by a system event, which requires immediate attention when it occurs. If a program is executing when an interrupt takes place, program execution must be suspended so that the interrupt can be handled as soon as possible. The only interrupt handled by a DCL procedure is the one caused by the CTRL/Y key.

Invoke To begin the execution of a command procedure or other sequence of command.

Iteration A single execution of a loop body; one cycle through a loop.

Iterative translation The process by which a logical name is successively translated until a final equivalence string is produced.

Job A detached process and all its subprocesses. The term *job* is also used to refer to a batch job.

Job logical name table A logical name table associated with a job. All the processes in the job can access the table.

Key field In an indexed file record, a field whose values are to be indexed for fast lookup. Every indexed file has a primary key field and may have additional alternate keys. Key fields are usually referred to simply as keys.

Keyword A character string chosen from among a fixed set of valid strings, used to represent a particular function or option. Keywords are used in some lexical functions to define the exact action taken by the function.

Label A name given to a command in a DCL procedure. The name allows the GOTO command to alter the sequential flow of execution by specifying the named command as the next one to execute.

Latin-1 A character set used by various OpenVMS applications. Latin-1 is a superset of the Multinational (MCS) and ASCII character sets.

Length See String length.

Lexical function A built-in DCL subroutine that can be used as an operand in an expression. Lexical functions compute all kinds of values, from the current time to the name of the local DECnet node.

List A sequence of items separated by some delimiter character, often a comma (,).

Literal A sequence of characters that represents a constant data value, such as 0, -42, or `"my name"`). A literal specifies a constant value, while a variable stands for a changing value.

Loading See Volume loading.

Log file A file created by a batch job to contain the output of the job. Because there is no terminal on which to display results, the results are sent to the log file.

Logical name A named entity that stands for all or part of a file specification or other value. Logical names are maintained in logical name tables.

Logical name table A table of logical names and their values. Each process has its own logical name table. There are also logical name tables available to more than one process.

Logical name table directory A system data structure that specifies a set of logical name tables. There is one directory for each process and one for the system as a whole.

Logical name translation The process by which a logical name is replaced with its equivalence string.

Login directory The directory established as the working directory when a user first logs in. The login directory is usually the root of all the user's directories.

Longword The VAX and Alpha term for a collection of 32 bits. A longword is the amount of memory occupied by a standard VAX or Alpha integer.

Loop A sequence of commands that is executed repeatedly until some termination condition occurs. The sequence of commands is called the loop body. See also Infinite loop.

Loop body The sequence of commands that is repeatedly executed in a loop.

Main procedure The command procedure in a DCL application where execution begins when the application is invoked. The main procedure is the first procedure to be executed; it may invoke other subprocedures in turn.

Master file directory The top-level directory on a disk volume. All system and user directories are accessed through the master file directory.

Member number The portion of a UIC that identifies a particular member within a user group. See also Group number.

Message file A special kind of image file, which contains the codes and text for OpenVMS messages.

Metalinguistic symbol A symbolic name that stands for some information to be included in a command or other instruction to a computer. For example, in DELETE *file*, the word *file* is a metalinguistic symbol standing for any valid file specification.

Mounting See Volume mounting.

Network channel DECnet interprocess communications occur using a set of opaque DECnet data structures collectively referred to as a DECnet network I/O channel, or more commonly as a network channel. Each DECnet network channel has two ends, typically with a process operating on each. With DCL, a particular network channel is specified by a logical name included on the OPEN, READ, CLOSE and other related commands..

Network process A process created by OpenVMS to perform a task for a remote network node. See also Batch process, Interactive process.

Node A computer system in a DECnet network. A DECnet node can be a host system running OpenVMS or other software, a DECnet router, or another dedicated DECnet network device.

Null device A nonphysical device that serves as a "black hole" for data. All output to the null device is discarded. An attempt to read from the null device results in an immediate end-of-file condition. The null device on OpenVMS is named NLA0:.

Null string A character string composed of no characters. It has a length of zero.

Null value A special value stored in an alternate key field of an indexed file. The value specifies that the field is empty and should not be indexed.

Open a file To identify and prepare a specific file for input/output operations. A file must be opened before it can be read or written.

Open for append To open a sequential file so that new records can be added to the end of the file.

Operand A literal, symbol, or other data value used in an expression.

Operator A character or character sequence that specifies a particular kind of data manipulation in an expression (e.g., + for addition).

Operator precedence A number that determines the order in which operators are applied to operands. An operator with a higher precedence is evaluated before one with a lower precedence.

Optional argument A lexical function argument that may be included in the function call, but need not be. If an optional argument is omitted, the function provides a common default value.

Optional parameter A command or procedure parameter that may be included in the command line but need not be. If an optional parameter is omitted, a common default is provided.

Owner UIC The user identification code (UIC) of the person who owns a particular object such as a file. The owner UIC is used to determine whether a particular user has access to the object.

P0 space The region of process memory in which OpenVMS utilities and application programs are executed.

P1 space The region of process memory in which the DCL program is executed.

Parameter See Command parameter, Optional parameter, Procedure parameter, Product parameter, Required parameter.

Parent process A process that owns one or more subprocesses, which are called the child processes.

Parsing a file spec The process through which a partial file spec entered by the user is transformed into a complete file spec with all elements filled in. A file spec must be parsed, either explicitly by a program or implicitly by OpenVMS, before it can be used to access files.

Pattern A character string that acts as a template or example for some kind of matching operation. For example, the SEARCH command requires one or more patterns to tell it which records are to be matched.

Personal command A symbol set to a particular combination of DCL command verb, parameters, and qualifiers. When used as the initial symbol in a command, DCL performs personal command substitution to replace the symbol with its value.

Personal command substitution An implicit form of substitution in which DCL automatically replaces the initial symbol in a command with its value.

PID See Process identifier.

Pipe A software construct that allows the output from one DCL command or application image to be routed into the input of another. See the DCL PIPE command.

POST data CGI scripts have two means of receiving data or passing state information from one web page to the next: GET data and POST data. GET data is encoded and passed in as part of the URL specification, while POST data is passed in via the input stream. GET data is simpler and is useful with fairly limited quantities of data, while POST data is somewhat harder to process but is better suited for larger data transfers.

Precedence See Operator precedence.

Primary key The main key in an indexed file record. Every indexed file has a primary key.

Printable character A character that can be displayed on a terminal or printed on a printer. Each printable character has a glyph, which represents it visually. Contrast with Control character.

Privilege A visible indication of the assignment of additional responsibilities to a particular user that is made by the system manager. Privileges allow access to security-relevant components of the OpenVMS operating system, as well as potentially allowing access to the information stored on the OpenVMS system by other users.

Procedure See DCL command procedure, Main procedure.

Procedure call unwind The mechanism by which a subprocedure unwinds all active procedure calls so that the main procedure is terminated. During the unwind, the cleanup code of all active procedures is executed.

Procedure cleanup The procedure termination code executed to close open files, delete temporary files, or otherwise restore the DCL environment to its normal state.

Procedure exit The termination of a procedure, which occurs when there are no more commands to execute or when an EXIT command is encountered.

Procedure level A level at which DCL reads and executes commands from a procedure. The procedure invoked at prompt level runs at procedure level 1. A subprocedure invoked by that procedure runs at procedure level 2, and so on.

Procedure parameter A value received by a procedure, used to control the procedure or provide data for it to operate upon. A DCL subprocedure or CALL subroutine can receive up to eight parameters.

Process The OpenVMS environment in which programs are run for users. See also Batch process, Detached process, Interactive process, Network process.

Process identifier (PID) An integer that uniquely identifies a process on a single OpenVMS system or OpenVMS Cluster. A process identifier is often called a PID.

Process mode A keyword identifying the type of a process: interactive, batch, network, or subprocess.

Process-permanent file A file opened by DCL, which remains open until it is explicitly closed. Examples include `SYS$INPUT`, `SYS$OUTPUT`, `SYS$ERROR`, and the `PIPE` command's `SYS$PIPE`.

Process privilege A privilege that a particular process has enabled. A process can only enable privileges listed in the user's authorized privileges.

Processor mode OpenVMS memory management supports a series of four concentric rings of protections, called processor modes. The four modes, from least to most privileged, are user, supervisor, executive, and kernel. Enhanced privileges are required for user-mode code to alter inner-mode memory, and privileges can be required to even view inner-mode data. The processor mode design is the central core of OpenVMS security, and all application and system security is based on this model. DCL procedures typically only see processor modes in conjunction with logical names and logical name tables, with the inner-mode logical names requiring privileges to create or alter.

Product parameter An item of information required by a software product for its normal operation. Product parameters are often specified with logical names.

Prompt level The level at which DCL accepts commands from the terminal by issuing a prompt and waiting for user input.

Protection mask The 16 indicators that determine which of the four access categories (system, owner, group, world) are allowed which types of access to a file (read, write, execute, delete). See System privilege, User identification code, and Privilege.

Proxy DECnet security permits the system manager to configure a transparent association of a remote node and user name to a local user name. This association allows a user to avoid having to include an explicit user name when communicating with a remote DECnet host node, and avoids any need to include a password.

Qualifier See Command qualifier.

Queue Manager The OpenVMS program that maintains the batch and print queues.

Record A group of related data fields, which a program treats as a unit. A file is composed of a collection of records: individual records are read from and written to a file. This term is often used interchangeably with Structure. See also Fixed-length record, Variable-length record.

Record locking The mechanism by which RMS implements file sharing. In simple terms, a record is locked when it is read and remains locked until it is updated or until another record is read.

Record management system (RMS) The subsystem of OpenVMS that handles data files, both sequential and indexed.

Record structure The format of the records in a file; the layout of the fields in the record.

Required parameter A command or procedure parameter that must be specified when the command is entered.

Resource identifier An identifier to which authorized users can charge disk storage.

Restartable batch job A batch job that can be restarted if the system fails during its execution. A restarted job can determine that it was in fact restarted and change its behavior accordingly.

Restricted user An OpenVMS user account that "captures" users as they log in. A user is forced to execute the LOGIN.COM procedure and cannot interrupt it with CTRL/Y.

Resultant file spec The expanded file spec returned by the F$PARSE lexical function.

Return point The command in a procedure at which execution continues after a subroutine is invoked and returns. When a subroutine is invoked, DCL remembers the position of the next command in the procedure, the return point. When the subroutine completes, DCL continues execution at the return point.

Return value The data item that is the result of a lexical function.

Rights identifier A name identifying a particular user, category of user, or application. Rights identifiers are associated with users and are needed to determine whether a user has access to a system object, such as a file or application.

Root directory A directory whose fundamental purpose is to act as the parent for a related set of subdirectories and the files contained in them.

Run See Execute.

S0 space   The region of system virtual memory that contains the core of the OpenVMS operating system.

Scheduler   The OpenVMS facility that periodically selects a process to execute on the VAX or Alpha hardware. The scheduler guarantees that all processes get a chance to run.

Search list   A logical name that has more than one equivalence string. The strings specify directories to be searched, in order, for specified files.

Search operation   A file operation in which a parsed file spec is used to locate one or more files. The search succeeds if at least one file matches the file spec; it fails otherwise.

Sequential execution   The default method of command procedure execution, in which DCL executes commands sequentially from beginning to end. Sequential execution can be altered with flow-of-control commands.

Sequential file   A file composed of a sequence of individual records. The records can only be written or read in sequential order.

Signal an error   The means by which a program or procedure notifies the user that an error has occurred. A signaled error often results in a message being displayed at the terminal.

Spawning   The creation of a new subprocess in the job tree. The process issuing the `SPAWN` command will be the parent process of the new subprocess.

Statement   A command or instruction in a programming language. In DCL programming, "statement" is often used in place of the more common "command."

Status code   The means by which OpenVMS returns an indication of the success or failure of a subroutine, program, or entire application.

Stream ID   An integer that identifies a file search operation performed by the `F$SEARCH` lexical function. Multiple stream IDs are needed if more than one search operation takes place simultaneously.

String   See Character string.

String index   The number assigned to each character in a string. The first character is index 0, the second 1, and so forth. The string index allows a character string to be treated as an array of characters.

String length   The number of characters in a character string.

Structure   A data aggregate that consists of multiple fields organized into one collective data item. The entire structure can be manipulated as one data item, and the fields can be accessed individually. The fields need not all be of the same data type.

Subdirectory   A file directory subordinate to another directory. A subdirectory is an ordinary directory, but the prefix "sub" clarifies its relationship to the parent directory.

Subprocedure   A command procedure invoked by another procedure as a subroutine.

Subprocess   A process created and owned by another OpenVMS process. The `SPAWN` command can be used to create a subprocess from DCL.

Subroutine   A portion of a program that stands by itself and can be called by other parts of the program. In DCL, there are three kinds of subroutines: subprocedures invoked with an at-sign (`@`) command, `CALL` subroutines, and `GOSUB` subroutines.

Subscript (array)   See Array index.

Substitution   The alteration of a DCL command by replacing a symbol or lexical function with its value. See also Ampersand substitution, Apostrophe substitution, Personal command substitution.

Substring   A portion of an existing character string. For example, `"OO BA"` is a substring of `"FOO BAR"`.

Symbol   A named entity used as a variable in a DCL procedure. A symbol is created and assigned a value with an assignment command.

Symbol level   The command level at which a symbol is created. The levels are global level, DCL prompt level, procedure level 1, procedure level 2, and so on.

Symbol name   The sequence of characters that names a DCL symbol.

Symbol table   The data structure in which DCL stores symbols and their values. The overall symbol table is organized into levels, each with its own symbols.

Symbol value   The integer or character string value of a symbol.

Symbolic array   An array whose data items are identified by a character string index (as opposed to a numeric index).

System group   A user group with system privilege. System groups are usually the groups with numbers 0–10 (octal, since UICs are specified in octal).

System privilege   A process can access an object such as a file using the system portion of a protection mask if the process UIC is in the system group, or if the process has the SYSPRV privilege. Without system privilege, access is made via the owner, group, or world portion of the protection mask.

Task-to-task communications DECnet communications between applications. Applications can be DCL command procedures, user-written application images, or various OpenVMS components.

Tee When working with pipes, it is often desirable to duplicate the output, allowing a copy to be written to a file and another copy of the output to be written to the next application participating in the pipe. This mechanism, directly analogous to the plumbing fixture of the same name, is called a tee.

Temporary command level The command level created by DCL's default interrupt handler when CTRL/Y is pressed during execution of a command procedure.

Temporary file A file created for the purpose of storing temporary information for a relatively short time. A program that creates a temporary file is responsible for deleting the file before it exits.

Terminal characteristics A set of values that determines the appearance and behavior of a terminal. These values can be displayed with the SHOW TERMINAL command and altered with the SET TERMINAL command.

Text file A sequential file whose records contain arbitrary text. Most of the time such files have variable-length records with the carriage return carriage-control attribute.

Time A general OpenVMS term used to refer to a date, a time, or some combination of the two. See also Absolute time, Combination time, Comparison time, and Delta time.

Translation See Iterative translation, Logical name translation.

Unary operator An operator that requires one operand (its arity is 1).

Universal Resource Locator (URL) A character string that specifies the access protocol, address, and name of a specific resource on the World Wide Web. An example is `http://www.openvms.digital.com/index.html`

URL encoding Various applications within the World Wide Web can have problems displaying specific characters, and applications that parse URL specifications can have trouble with URL specifications that include these characters. Further, certain characters are used within the specification of URLs, and these characters cannot appear within other fields of the URL. For instance, the question mark (?) has a specific meaning within the syntax of a URL, and any other occurence of the question mark within a URL must be encoded to prevent confusion.

Update a record To perform a file operation that modifies the contents of an existing record.

User address A string that identifies a user on an OpenVMS system. The user address consists of a node name and a user name.

User identification code (UIC) A number that identifies the owner of an OpenVMS object. The UIC is divided into two fields, the group number and the member number.

User name The symbolic name assigned to an OpenVMS user's account. User names are typically last names, initials, or nicknames.

Variable-length record A record in a sequential or indexed file whose design allows each record in the file to be of a different size. The text files on OpenVMS contain variable-length records.

Variable with fixed control (VFC) A type of record format in which each record has a variable length and includes a fixed-size control area at the beginning. This control area might contain a line number or some other control information common to all records. The DCL OPEN command creates VFC records.

Verification A method of debugging a command procedure by tracing its commands as they are executed by DCL. Verification is enabled with the SET VERIFY command.

Virtual device A facility provided by OpenVMS software, which acts like a hardware device and is therefore used by a program as if it were a hardware device. Examples are mailboxes, virtual terminals, and DECwindows windows.

Volume The medium used on a disk or tape drive to store permanent information.

Volume initialization The act of formatting a disk or tape volume so that it can accept and store data.

Volume label The character string that names a particular disk or tape volume.

Volume loading The action taken when a human being places a data volume on a disk or tape drive. Once the volume is loaded, it can be mounted to make it available to the system.

Volume mounting The process by which OpenVMS recognizes a data volume loaded on a disk or tape drive. Data transfers cannot be performed until the volume is mounted.

Web browser A software application that presents documents and applications made available for viewing on the World Wide Web. Various web browsers are available for OpenVMS.

Web page A page of information made visible through the use of a web server and a web browser. This information can be generated from a static source such as a file, or from a dynamic source such as a CGI script.

Web server A software application that makes documents and applications available for remote viewing on the World Wide Web. Various web servers are available for OpenVMS.

Whitespace A sequence of spaces or tabs in a command or character string.

Wildcard spec A file spec containing one or more of the wildcard matching characters (asterisk, percent sign, or ellipsis).

Working directory The directory in which a user is currently working, as established with the SET DEFAULT command. Files are located in the working directory if no other device and directory is specified.

World Wide Web (WWW) A loose collection of computer systems that participate in serving documents and applications to users, primarily involving communications between software packages known as web servers and packages known as web browsers.

Index

Command qualifiers are sorted under slash (/). A reference to a table is indicated by an italic "*t*" after the page number.

' (apostrophe)
   explicit use of
      symbol or lexical function values, 65
      text in DCL command, glossary entry, 403
   interpretation when input to INQUIRE, 126
   trailing, when required in apostrophe substitution, 66
' ' (double apostrophe)
   use inside string literals to cause substitution, 66
− (minus)
   integer operator, arity, result type, and value, 34*t*
   line continuation symbol in DCL, 14
   string operator, arity, result type, and value, 35*t*
/ (slash)
   integer operator, arity, result type, and value, 34*t*
   use in DCL command qualifiers, 13
! (exclamation point)
   comment, glossary entry, 406
   DCL command procedures, use for comments in, 20
   use in F$FAO directives, 78
!!! (triple exclamation point)
   flag to help locate temporary debugging commands, 141

" (double quote)
   DCL command parameter use, 14
   DCL command qualifier syntax use, 14
   rules for use in parameters, 60
" " (paired double quotes)
   default answer trigger for READ, 129
   INQUIRE, removes quotes but leaves whitespace and lowercase, 126
   matched double quotes used to denote string literal, 26
   used inside double quotes to represent one double quote, 26
$ (dollar sign)
   alone on line ignored in DCL command procedures, 19
   DCL command procedure, use to indicate command, 19
   DCL prompt character, use by DCL command interpreter, 12
   device name segment divider, 246
$RESTART
   batch jobs, controlling restart entry point, 283
$SEVERITY
   reserved symbol for recording success of command, 92
% (percent)
   wildcard for one character in a file spec component, 155

& (ampersand)
    explicit substitution of text in DCL command, glossary entry, 403
    used in concert with apostrophe substitution, 72

* (asterisk)
    integer operator, arity, result type, and value, 34t
    wildcard
        for characters in file spec components, 155
        use in logical names blocks iterative translation, 171

\+ (plus)
    integer operator, arity, result type, and value, 34t
    string operator, arity, result type, and value, 35t

, (comma)
    DCL command
        parameter syntax use, 14
        qualifier syntax use, 14
    use as placeholder for optional arguments, 39

. (period)
    separator for subdirectories in file specification, 150
    separator for version number in file specification, 152
    type component of DCL file specification syntax use, 15

... (ellipsis)
    wildcard for directory subtree, 155

.COM
    type given file containing DCL command procedure, 19

.EQ.
    integer operator, arity, result type, and value, 34t

.EQS.
    example of use with .OR., description of precedence, 57
    string operator, arity, result type, and value, 35t

.EXE
    file type for executable file produced by linker, 150

.FOR
    file type for FORTRAN source file, 150

.GE.
    integer operator, arity, result type, and value, 34t

.GES.
    string operator, arity result type, and value, 35t

.GT.
    integer operator, arity, result type, and value, 34t

.GTS.
    integer operator, arity, result type, and value, 35t

.LE.
    integer operator, arity, result type, and value, 34t

.LES.
    string operator, arity, result type, and value, 35t

.LIS
    file type for listing produced by Fortran compiler, 150

.LT.
    integer operator, arity, result type, and value, 34t

.LTS.
    string operator, arity, result type, and value, 35t

.MAP
    file type for image map produced by linker, 150

.NE.
    integer operator, arity, result type, and value, 34t

.NES.
    string operator, arity, result type, and value, 35t

.OBJ
    file type for object file produced by FORTRAN compiler, 150

: (colon)
    appended to prompt by INQUIRE, 126
    device component of DCL file specification syntax use, 15
    label for GOTO command destination used, 50

:: (double colon)
    distinguishing DECnet or IP node name, 148
    node component, DCL file specification syntax, 15

:= (colon equal)
    substring assignment character for procedure level, 43

:== (colon double equal)
    substring assignment character for global symbols, 45

; (semicolon)
    separator for version number in file specification, 151

version component of DCL file specification
    syntax, 15
< > (angle brackets)
    alternate characters for delimiting directory
        name, 150
= (equal)
    assignment command described and discussed,
        27
    assignment command for creating symbols, 24
    assignment statement meaning different from
        equality comparison, 28
    bit-field assignment operator for current
        procedure level, 46
    DCL command qualifier syntax use, 14
    use in setting value to DCL command qualifiers,
        13
== (double equal)
    assignment command for symbols at global
        level, 31
    bit-field assignment operator for global level,
        46
@ (at-sign)
    command, compared with CALL command, 61
    procedure invocation by @ creates procedure
        level symbols, 29
    summarized, 63*t*
    use to invoke a DCL command procedure, 19
        detailed description, 58
/BACKUP
    file selection qualifier, one line description,
        163*t*
/BEFORE
    example of use of DCL command qualifiers, 13
    file selection qualifier, one line description,
        163*t*
/BY_OWNER
    file selection qualifier, one line description,
        163*t*
/CONFIRM
    example of use of DCL command qualifiers, 13
/CREATED
    file selection qualifier, one line description,
        163*t*
/END_OF_FILE
    qualifier specifies end-of-file handler for READ,
        191
/ERROR
    OPEN qualifier specifies handler for open errors,
        190

READ qualifier specifies handler for read errors,
    190, 219
/EXCLUDE
    file selection qualifier, one line description,
        163*t*
/EXPIRED
    file selection qualifier, one line description,
        163*t*
/KEY
    qualifier for READ access to indexed file, 218
/LOG
    capturing terminal session output with, 145
    example of use of DCL command qualifiers, 13
/MATCH
    qualifier for READ access to indexed file, 219
    qualifier for SEARCH patterns, 200*t*
/MODIFIED
    file selection qualifier, one line description,
        163*t*
/NOLOG
    DEFINE qualifier to turn off message concerning
        previous existence, 169
/OUTPUT
    capturing procedure output with, 145
    utilities qualifier for redirecting output to files,
        80
/SINCE
    file selection qualifier, one line description,
        163*t*
/SYMBOL
    qualifier for WRITE to allow larger record size,
        224
/TRANSLATION_ATTRIBUTES
    concealing root directory logical name values
        with, 175
/USER_MODE
    qualifier to define logical name for duration of
        image, 172
    temporary redirection of input, 136
    temporary redirection of output, 80
[.DATA]
    example of subdirectory under working
        directory, 149
[000000]
    master file directory, root of entire directory
        tree, 149
[ ] (empty brackets)
    stands for working directory, 149

[ ] (square brackets)
    bit-field assignment statement syntax, 46
    directory component of DCL file specification syntax, 15
    substring assignment statement syntax, 43

[-]
    parent directory of default working directory, 150

( ) (parentheses)
    DCL command qualifier syntax use, 14
    lexical functions format requirement, 38
    modifying operator precedence with, 36

0::
    DECnet local node is named zero, 148

1 Jan 1970
    Unix base date, 340

17 Nov 1858
    OpenVMS base date, 340

1B
    hexadecimal value of ESC character, control sequence initiator for seven-bit terminals, 76

2000
    leap year, 342

2038
    date-related problems, 339

9B
    hexadecimal value of CSI character, control sequence initiator for eight-bit terminals, 76

abbreviations
    caution about using in command procedures, 20
    DCL verbs
        allowed abbreviation of, 14
        rules for, 12
    keywords, building so that they may be abbreviated, 206
    personal commands as, 70
    terminal input, using F$LOCATE to allow, 132

absolute time. *See also* combination time; delta time; time.
    glossary entry, 403
    represents specific points in time, 207

access. *See also* captive accounts; protection; security.
    /READ access when opening file, 190
    algorithm, used for UIC- and ACL- based protection checking, 242
    blocking access by route of entry, 236
    category
        based on relation of owner to user, 230
        glossary entry, 403
    control entry (ACE)
        glossary entry, 403
        identifier, format and description of components, 236
        setting working directory protection using an ACE, 238
        use in file protection, 234
    control list (ACL)
        ACE assigned creator when not owner of file, 242
        compared with user identification codes (UIC), 229
        default ACL for new file, steps determining, 242
        default identifier entry for directories, 237
        default, for directories, 241
        default, for files, 242
        file protection use of ACL, 229
        format of identifier entries, description of components, 236
        glossary entry, 403
        kinds of rights identifiers, 235
        matching process when a file has an ACL, 235
        modifying ACLs with editor or SET., 238
        NOPROPAGATE used to control default ACL, 242
        potential outcomes of matching process, 235
        SET SECURITY command qualifiers, 239*t*
        use in file protection, 234
        warning, order of entries is critical, 237
    flags for each access category, 231
    modes
        defining logical names in different modes, 173*t*
        glossary entry, 403
        logical names, OpenVMS use of each mode, 172
        privileges assigned to processes, 172

privilege scheme description, 17
requirements for directory operations, 232*t*
requirements for file operations, 232*t*
rights identifier
    glossary entry, 417
    maintained with `AUTHORIZE`, 235

accessing
    files in personal directories before those in public directories, using search lists, 177

ACE. *See* access, control entry.
ACL. *See* access, control list.

addition (+)
    integer operator, arity, result type, and value, 34*t*

address, user
    glossary entry, 421
    identifies location and name of user, 176

ALF
    automatic login facility, 316
    glossary entry, 404

ALLOCATE
    command to request exclusive use of device, 251

allocating
    devices, 251

altering. *See* modifying.

alternate key
    glossary entry, 403
    in indexed file, 215

ampersand substitution. *See also* apostrophe substitution; substitution.
    description, 72
    explicit substitution of text in DCL command, glossary entry, 403
    used in concert with apostrophe substitution, 72

ANALYZE/RMS_FILE
    file utility, one line description, 162*t*

AND (.AND.)
    Boolean operator, arity, result type, and value, 35*t*
    integer operator, arity, result type, and value, 34*t*

annotation. *See also* documentation.
    separator, use of $ alone on line in DCL command procedures, 19
    use of comments to clarify complex procedures, 20

answer, default. *See* default answer.

apostrophe substitution. *See also* ampersand substitution; substitution.
    creating DCL arrays, techniques and problems, 292
    explicit substitution of symbol or lexical function values, 65
    explicit substitution of text in DCL command, glossary entry, 403
    interpretation when input to `INQUIRE`, 126
    trailing, when required in apostrophe substitution, 66

APPEND
    file utility, one line description, 162*t*
    protection mask setting, 233

appending. *See also* creating; modifying.
    files, OPEN/APPEND allows records to be added to file, 195
    open for append, glossary entry, 413

applications
    appropriate for DCL, 3
    passing commands to applications from DCL, 135
    sample, description, and listing. *See* MODL.
    structure, overview of application design, 113

archiving
    files, possible application for DCL, 5

arguments. *See also* parameters.
    allowing for prompts or batch, 133
    input for an operation, glossary entry, 403
    lexical function
        characteristics, 39
        in format of lexical functions, 38
    optional, glossary entry, 414

arithmetic
    techniques built up from rudimentary operations, 201

arity
    defined as number of operands required by an operator, 33
    glossary entry, 404

arrays. *See also* lists.
    glossary entry, 404
    handling
        procedure parameters as an eight element array, 294
        substitution of array element names, 293
    index, glossary entry, 404
    integer, arrays with integer indexes, 291
    simulation

arrays *(continued)*
   simulation *(continued)*
      in DCL, 291
      double substitution used for simulating arrays, 72
   symbolic
      array, glossary entry, 419
      creating, 295
      warning, arrays may require symbol table expansion, 298
   symbolic problems connected with symbolic arrays, 296
ASCII (American Standard Code for Information Interchange)
   character set, 335
      glossary entry, 404
      used by VAX and Alpha architectures, 26
   output, formatting, 78
ASK
   features of complex input routine, 133
   listing in subroutine library, 349
   personal command created using READ, 127
ASSIGN
   logical name definition, parameters reversed from DEFINE, 169
assignment. *See also* symbols; values.
   bit-fields in character strings, 46
   command
      description of use, 27
      expression use by, 27
      glossary entry, 404
      s ubstring, 43
      summary of assignment command, 48t
      symbols are assigned a value with, 24
attributes
   complete list returned by DIRECTORY/FULL, 161
   file
      attributes, glossary entry, 409
      descriptive information, 160t
AUTHORIZE. *See also* access; protection; security.
   access control rights identifiers defined with AUTHORIZE, 235
   command, accessing with DCL, 4
   DECnet proxy commands, 306
authorized privileges
   description, 18
   glossary entry, 404

automatic login facility
   glossary entry, 404

background execution
   SPAWN/NOWAIT allows simultaneous execution of processes, 267
BACKUP
   file utility, one line description, 162t
   message file handling, 102
   protection mask setting, 233
backups
   example of use for DCL, 4
base
   numeric, use of octal, decimal, and hexadecimal, 25
batch. *See also* interactive.
   breaking batch procedures into steps for possible restart, 284
   controlling restart entry point, 283
   environment described, 277
   jobs
      application for DCL, 3
      concepts and facilities, 277
      duplicate jobs, preventing occurrence of duplicate jobs, 288
      glossary entry, 404
      invoking with SUBMIT command, 278
      manager responsible for job queue maintenance, 277
      periodic batch jobs resubmit themselves on schedule, 286
      restartable batch jobs, restarting after STOP/REQUEUE, 283
      status report can be tailored and mailed to user, 281
   LOGIN.COM procedure invoked, 278
   process
      description, 258
      glossary entry, 404
      versus interactive, 278
   queues
      glossary entry, 404
      queues for running batch jobs, 277
BATCH system identifier
   description, 235
BATCH$RESTART
   controlling restart entry point, 283
BB_WATCH
   Alpha hardware register, 340

beginning DCL command procedures
    detailed description, 58
    using @ command, 19
binary operators. *See also* unary operators.
    notation, description in relation to hexadecimal, 333
    operators
        description and examples, 33
    operators glossary entry, 404
bit
    glossary entry, 404
    numbering of bits in character string, 46
bit bucket. *See* null device.
bit-field assignment
    altering sequence of bits in value of symbol, 45
    control characters can be created in DCL command, 47
Boolean
    description and use, 26
    FALSE, even integers and certain character strings are used to represent FALSE, 27
    field type, definition symbol and characteristics, 212
    fields in record structures, created with bit-field assignment, 213
    glossary entry, 404
    operators, arity, result type, and value, 35t
    responses, limiting to yes or no, 132
    TRUE, odd integers and certain character strings are used to represent TRUE, 27
Buffett, Jimmy, quotation, xx
building
    software systems from components, use for DCL, 6
BYPASS
    bypass privilege, 243
    privileges that affects protection-checking scheme, 232

calendar
    possible use for DCL, 4
CALL
    compared with
        @ command, 61
        GOSUB command, 63
    description and use, 61
    new to OpenVMS Version 5.0, 61
    summarized, 63t

calling. *See also* subroutines.
    command procedures, using @ command, 19
    command procedures, using @ command, detailed description, 58
    DCL applications methodology for, 114
    subroutines, 122
canceling
    a procedure from temporary command level, 106
captive account. *See also* access; protection; security.
    controlling CTRL/Y interrupt processing, 110
captive login, 312
captive user
    glossary entry, 405
    prohibitions for, 312t
card reader
    specified as device name, 148
carriage return carriage control
    glossary entry, 405
    standard, but not guaranteed, record format, 194
case
    characters must be same case before comparison, 129
    DCL converts all symbols to uppercase, 24
    statement
        glossary entry, 405
        how to emulate case statement in DCL, 207
catalog
    directory as a catalog of files, 149
cautions. *See* warnings.
CGI (Common Gateway Interface)
    file types, 324
        description of common, 325t
    form, 329
    glossary entry, 406
    purpose, 323
    script, 323
        glossary entry, 405
    symbols, 324
        created by web server, 324t
changes attribute. *See also* file, indexed.
    required if alternate key fields are to be updated, 225
changing. *See* modifying.
characteristic
    terminal, description, 250
    terminal, glossary entry, 420

characters
    control
        character, glossary entry, 406
        component of DCL character set, 26
        creating control characters in DCL command, 47
        not representable in string literals, 26
    glossary entry, 405
    printable
        component of DCL character set, 26
        glossary entry, 415
    set of
        ASCII character set used by VAX and Alpha architectures, 26
        defined as complete collection of characters and code numbers, 26
        ISO Latin 1 character set used by VAX and Alpha architectures, 26
        special, sending special characters to terminal, 76
    strings. See strings, character.
checking. See also cleanup; debugging; errors; status, code.
    existence of file with F$SEARCH, 156
    file specification validity with F$PARSE, 157
    status code
        methods for, 92
        with ON command, 95
    terminal input, character strings, 131
    type of symbol values with F$TYPE, 40
    validity of integer in input string, 130
child. See also parent; process.
    directory, parsing requires special treatment, 154
    process, glossary entry, 405
choosing
    DCL, reasons to choose DCL as programming language, 2
cleanup. See also checking; debugging; errors; status.
    closing open files as part of cleanup code, 192
    code
        example of use in main procedure, 118
        use in subprocedures, example structure, 119
    keyword checking in cleanup code, 206
    procedure
        example of use of EXIT, 61
        glossary entry, 415

terminating procedures after errors, techniques for, 97
client
    network task, 300
CLISYMTBL
    effect on symbol table size, 298
CLOSE
    necessary for closing open files, 190
    open files must be explicitly closed, 192
    use in DECnet communications, 302
closing. See also opening.
    files, as part of cleanup code, 192
Cluster
    device names are segmented, 246
CLUSTER_CONFIG.COM
    procedure for configuring OpenVMS Cluster systems, 5
code. See DCL, code; status, code.
combination time. See also absolute time; delta time; time.
    format using absolute and delta times, 209
    OpenVMS format, glossary entry, 405
command
    DCL command, glossary entry, 407
    description of format and use for DCL commands, 12
    execution, controlling in subprocesses, 266
    file location of error messages for status code interpretation, 103
    flow-of-control, glossary entry, 409
    interpreter, guided by information concerning DCL environment, 83
    language interpreter, glossary entry, 405
    level
        temporary following interrupt, 106
        temporary, canceling a procedure from, 106
    modifying, using the substitution facilities for, 65
    parameter. glossary entry, 405
    personal
        application invocation use of, 115
        command substitution , glossary entry, 414
        glossary entry, 414
    procedures. See procedures, command.
    protection mask, commands that can set the protection mask, 233
    qualifier, glossary entry, 406
    sequence, stored in text file as command procedure, 18

430   Index

syntax, glossary entry, 406
temporary command level, glossary entry, 420
verbs
    description and use in DCL, 12
    glossary entry, 406
comments. *See also* documentation.
    description and use in DCL command procedure, 20
    glossary entry, 406
    move to end of procedure to avoid slow down, 347
Common Gateway Interface. *See* CGI.
comparison. *See also* Boolean.
    time
        format to represent times to be compared, 208
        OpenVMS format, glossary entry, 406
    times using DCL commands, 208
computer-supported cooperative work
    DCL as a tool for, 6
concatenation (+)
    string operator, arity, result type and value, 35*t*
concealing
    root directory logical name values, 175
condition
    glossary entry, 406
    IF command test, 52
conditional execution
    IF command as control structure for, 52
constant. *See also* symbols.
    literal, glossary entry, 412
context symbol
    glossary entry, 406
    use with F$PID lexical function, 262
continuation lines. *See also* documentation.
    use of hyphen to allow multiple lines in DCL command, 14
`CONTINUE`
    returning to program after interrupt, 106
control
    characters
        component of DCL character set, 26
        creating in DCL command with bit-field assignment, 47
        glossary entry, 406
        not representable in string literals, 26
    flow. *See* control, structures; flow-of-control.
    keys
        CTRL/Y, program interrupt handling, 105

sequences
    glossary entry, 406
    terminals, sending special characters to terminal, 76
    uses for, 77
string, to specify format for `F$FAO`, glossary entry, 406
structures. *See also* flow-of-control.
    concepts and commands, 49
    conditional execution, `IF`, 52
    iteration, 55
    sequential execution, 49
    unconditional goto, `GOTO`, 50
control sequences
SYS$SYSTEM:SMGTERMS.TXT, 78
conventions
    typographic, 7
conversion
    data, using `F$STRING` and `F$INTEGER` lexical functions, 41
    noninteger strings converted to integers become zero, 37
    rules for matching operators and operand types, 37
    time formats converted using `F$CVTIME`, 209
`CONVERT`
    file utility, one line description, 162*t*
Coordinated Universal Time. *See* UTC.
`COPY`
    file utility, one line description, 162*t*
    protection mask setting, 233
`CREATE`
    file utility, one line description, 162*t*
    protection mask setting, 233
    use in creating indexed file using FDL file, 221
    use to build normal text file, 194
`CREATE/DIRECTORY`
    file utility, one line description, 162*t*
`CREATE/FDL`
    file utility, one line description, 162*t*
creating. *See also* appending; modifying.
    arrays
        with integer indexes, 291
        with symbolic indexes, 295
    Boolean fields in record structures, created with bit-field assignment, 213
    control characters in DCL command with bit-field assignment, 47

creating *(continued)*
    data fields in record structures, created with substring assignment, 212
    files
        impact of search lists on, 177
        using CREATE, 194
        using OPEN, 193
        using WRITE, 194
    global symbols, prevented by NOGLOBAL keyword, 85
    indexed files, 221
    integer fields in record structures, created with bit-field assignment, 213
    lists, 203
    procedure status codes, 94
    record structures by storing values in character string, 212
    string
        with 1 character using bit-field assignment, 46
    strings
        with multiple characters using bit- field assignment, 47
    subprocesses, 264
    symbols
        global, 31
        procedure level, 29
        prompt level, 28
        using assignment command for, 24, 27
    text fields in record structures, created with substring assignment, 212
CSI (control sequence initiator)
    eight-bit terminal use of hexadecimal 9B as, 76
CTRL/C
    procedure interrupt handling, 105
CTRL/Y
    program interrupt handling, 105
    use SPAWN to execute commands without terminating interrupted process, 266
CTRL/Z
    end-of-file when read from terminal, 128
current directory. *See also* directories.
    defined as default file directory, 88
customer. *See also* status, code.
    facility member, required by procedure status codes., 94

data. *See also* symbols.
    entry, interactive, obtaining, 125

    glossary entry, 407
    image
        data, input to applications called form DCL, 135
        input data for program, glossary entry, 410
    internal and external representation of data, 25
    item, glossary entry, 407
    manipulation techniques in DCL, 201
    structuring, nonexistent in DCL, 2
    types
        associated with value not symbol, 28
        Boolean, representation and use, 26
        description, 24
        integer, representation and use, 25
    types, character, representation and use, 25
    types, glossary entry, 407
    volumes, UIC protection available, 229
date. *See also* time.
    field type, definition symbol and characteristics, 211
    fields in record structures, created with substring assignments, 212
    manipulating using DCL commands, 207
DCL (Digital Command Language). *See also* command.
    application domain, 3
    caution about viruses, 6
    code
        glossary entry, 407
        name for commands in DCL command procedure, 19
    commands
        description and use, 13
        format description, 12
        glossary entry, 407
        interpreter, description of program that carries out instructions, 12
        qualifiers, description and use, 13
        syntax, description and use, 14
    commands procedure, glossary entry, 407
    debugging. *See* debugging.
    defined, 1
    environment, glossary entry, 407
    as a programming language, 2
    prompt
        character, dollar sign ($) as prompt, 12
        glossary entry, 407
    software development, 5
    strong points, 2

system management, 4
used in
    environmental extension, 3
uses in
    complex file manipulation, 5
weak points, 2
deaccess locking
    contrasting with OpenVMS file locking, 161
`DEALLOCATE`
    command to release an allocated device, 253
deallocating
    devices, 253
`DEASSIGN`
    logical name deletion command, 181
debugging. *See also* checking; cleanup; errors; status, code.
    ! ! ! (triple exclamation point)
        flag to help locate temporary debugging commands, 141
    capturing
        output with `/LOG`, 145
        procedure output with `/OUTPUT`, 145
    concepts and techniques, 139
    DCL advantages and disadvantages compared with conventional languages, 139
    enabling verification
        from inside procedure, 140
        from outside procedure, 140
    permanent debug lines
        activated with flag, 143
        cost execution time, 144
    `SHOW`, displaying values of symbols, 143
    temporary debug lines marked with ! ! ! (triple exclamation point), 143
    tracing procedures using `SET VERIFY`, 84
    using `SET PREFIX` to annotate verification output, 142
    verification, glossary entry, 421
decimal base (base 10)
    representation and use, 25
decisions. *See also* control, structures.
    flow-of-control commands discussed, 49
    IF commands discussed, 51
DECnet
    access control, 314
    DCL task-to-task communications, 301
    default user name and password, 306
    glossary entry, 407
    `NETSERVER.LOG` log file, 300

node, file specification component, full description, 147
non-default proxy, 306
objects, 307
path specification for reaching nodes, 148
permanent database, 315
proxy, 306
proxy access, 314
second log session created to record debug output, 145
task object, 307
task-to-task, 300
volatile database, 315
DECnet network control program
    NCP, 314
DECnet Phase IV
    communications protocol, 299
DECnet-Plus
    communications protocol, 299
DEC/shell, 1
default
    answer
        glossary entry, 407
        for `READ` command, 128
    directory
        component of DCL environment, characteristics, 88
        do not change in a procedure, 88
        glossary entry, 407
        importance to OpenVMS user, 16
    error handler. *See* errors.
    interrupt handler described, 106
    protection ACE, use in setting protection of new files in a directory, 238
    question responses should not contain dangerous material, 128
    value
        glossary entry, 407
        lexical functions with optional arguments provide a default value, 39
    working directory, glossary entry, 422
`DEFINE`
    defining logical names with, 169
    logical name
        creation and value assignment, 16
        definition with, 166
    redirecting
        program input using, 136
        screen output to file, 80

DEFINE *(continued)*
    temporary definition of symbol using /USER_MODE, 80
defining. *See also* undefining.
    logical names
        with DEFINE command, 166
        in different access modes, 173*t*
    symbols, with assignment command, 27
DELETE
    example of DCL command parameters and qualifiers, 13
    file utility, one line description, 162*t*
DELETE access
    description, 231
deleting
    duplicates from lists with DCL commands, 203
    files
        temporary, 197
    indexed file records, avoid use of generic matching, 225
    logical names using DEASSIGN command, 181
    records in an indexed file, 225
    symbols using DELETE/SYMBOL command, 48
    temporary files, procedure for, 59
DELQA
    Ethernet controller, 303
delta time. *See also* absolute time; combination time; time.
    format for showing differences between two times, 208
    glossary entry, 407
DEQNA
    Ethernet controller, 303
detached process. *See also* process.
    description, 258
    glossary entry, 407
devices
    ALLOCATE command to request exclusive use, 251
    allocating specific devices with /GENERIC qualifier, 252
    characteristics and operations, 245
    DEALLOCATE, command to release an allocated device, 253
    device class, integer useful for verification, 247
    existence checking with EXISTS keyword to F$GETDVI, 247
    file specification component
        full description, 148
    overview, 15
    glossary entry, 408
    information available with F$GETDVI, 246
    list potential devices, 245
    logical name use with, 166
    messages about allocation using /LOG, 252
    MOUNT qualifiers, 255*t*
    mount, steps performed in mounting a volume, 255
    names
        characteristics, 245
        format has changed with advent of new technology, 246
    null device, glossary entry, 413
    specifying with logical names, advantages, 148
    system, listing with SHOW DEVICE, 249
    terminal server is single device that appears as many, 246
    UIC protection available, 229
    virtual
        description and examples, 245
        glossary entry, 421
    volume initialization, description of parameters and use, 253
DIALUP **system identifier**
    description, 235
DIFFERENCE
    using $SEVERITY to analyze its status code, 96
differences
    integer subtraction operator, arity, result type, and value, 34*t*
    time, how to calculate and represent differences between times, 208
DIFFERENCES
    file utility, one line description, 162*t*
Digital Command Language. *See* DCL.
directories. *See also* file.
    <> is alternate symbol for demarcating directory name, 150
    access protection categories, 232*t*
    accessing public and private directories with search lists, 177
    as catalog of files, 149
    child, parsing requires special treatment, 154
    concepts
        and facilities, 147
        introduced, 15
    default
        do not change in a procedure, 88

glossary entry, 407
importance to OpenVMS user, 16
protection, how to determine default
   protection, 241
determining parent of arbitrary directory
   difficult, 154
facility code use for naming compatibility, 114
file specification
   component, full description, 149
   component, overview, 15
glossary entry, 408
home
   glossary entry, 410
   importance to OpenVMS user, 15
logical name
   descriptions of, 186
   table directory, glossary entry, 412
   use with, 166
login
   glossary entry, 412
   importance to OpenVMS user, 15
manipulation involving rooted directory
   difficult, 154
master file directory, glossary entry, 412
operations, required access categories, 232t
parent, parsing requires special treatment, 154
protection, setting default protection using an
   ACE, 238
root
   defining with logical names, 175
   glossary entry, 417
searching for files, 155
searching multiple, method, 159
subdirectory, glossary entry, 419
system directory organization, overview, 181
UIC protection available, 229
wildcards for parts of directory name, 155
working directory, glossary entry, 422
DIRECTORY
   command useful in search, 155
   file utility, one line description, 162t
DIRECTORY/FULL
   file attributes display by, 161
DIRECTORY/PROTECTION
   displaying values in protection mask, 233
DIRECTORY/SECURITY
   displaying security attributes, 233
disabling
   automatic checking of status codes, 97

predefined personal commands inside of
   procedures, 71
discarding output
   device NLA0, 149
   form a SEARCH command, 200
   used for, 149
disk
   specified as device name, 148
disk quota
   glossary entry, 408
DISK$*volumelabel*
   disk logical name, 173
DISPLAY **suggested personal command for writing
   to screen**, 76
displaying. *See also* output; terminal.
   commands and data during program execution,
      140
   default process protection mask, 241
   logical name values, 170
   output during procedure execution, 75
   protection mask, 233
   sequential files
      record at a time is slow but allows more
         control, 198
      TYPE/PAGE displays text a screenful at a
         time, 198
   suppressing error message display on terminal,
      80
   text, using TYPE command, 136
   values of symbols for debugging purposes, 143
distributed applications
   using DCL with distributed applications, 5
distribution list
   glossary entry, 408
   managed by sample application MODL, 355
division
   integer operator, arity, result type, and value,
      34t
documentation. *See also* annotation; comments.
   OpenVMS documentation important for DCL
      programmer, list of, 8
   separator, use of $ alone on line in DCL
      command procedures, 19
   use of comments to clarify complex procedures,
      20
DUMP
   file utility, one line description, 162t
duplicate jobs. *See also* jobs.
   preventing occurrences of duplicate jobs, 288

EDIT
    file utility, one line description, 162t
EDIT/FDL
    file utility, one line description, 162t
editing
    terminal input, READ input string editing with F$EDIT, 129
ELSE
    use with IF for listing alternative commands, 53
end-of-file
    CTRL/Z signal from terminal, 128
    glossary entry, 408
    handler can be provided for READ, 191
    indexed files, signaled by key match failure, 220
ENDSUBROUTINE
    use with CALL command, 62
environment
    batch jobs, 277
    DCL
        concepts and facilities, 83
        environment, glossary entry, 407
        main procedure use in establishing DCL environment, 116
    process
        commands to establish, 264t
        some information available only for current process, 263
        steps in establishing DCL environment for a procedure, 118
    subprocesses, list of inherited and not-inherited environment properties, 264
environmental extension
    application for DCL, 3
equals (.EQ., .EQS.)
    integer operator, arity, result type, and value, 34t
    string operator, arity, result type, and value, 35t
equivalence string
    glossary entry, 408
    value of logical name, 166
errors. *See also* checking; cleanup; debugging; interrupts.
    captive account handling of, 314
    cleanup before termination of procedure, 97
    creating procedure status codes, 94
    default error handler
        characteristics, 95
        modifying, 95
        problems, 95
    disabling automatic checking with SET NOON, 97
    handler, glossary entry, 408
    handling
        with cleanup code, example of use in subprocedures, 119
        concepts and facilities, 91
        custom, example of use in main procedure, 116
        integrating with interrupt handling, 107
        without cleanup code, example of use in subprocedures, 119
    ignoring error codes using SET NOON, 101
    nested procedures require unwinding to handle errors, 99
    SIGNAL
        listing in subroutine library, 352
        message and error handling subroutine, characteristics and use, 123
    signal on error, glossary entry, 418
    suppression of error message display on terminal, 80
ESC (escape character)
    seven-bit terminal use with [, 76
escape character
    glossary entry, 408
escape sequence
    glossary entry, 408
    terminals, sending characters to older terminals, 76
evaluate. *See also* evaluation.
    glossary entry, 408
evaluation. *See also* substitution.
    environments for automatic substitution of expression, 69
    expressions, how processed by DCL, 33
    precedence rules for expression evaluation, 36t, 36
        modifying with parentheses, 36
    symbols, using apostrophe substitution, 65
EXECUTE access
    description, 231
execute, execution. *See also* control, structure; flow-of-control; invoke; run.
    glossary entry, 408
    invoking procedures, 58
    overview, 19
    parallel processes, using SPAWN, 267

sequential glossary entry, 418
sequential, description, 49
executive
    access mode in which a process may run, 172
existence
    symbols, checking using F$TYPE, 40
exit. *See also* EXIT.
    procedure, description, 60
    procedure, glossary entry, 415
EXIT
    command to force termination of procedure, 61
    convention to use explicitly for ease of understanding, 62
    GOSUB requires use of EXIT to avoid dropping into subroutine, 63
    status code parameter for reporting procedure outcome, 93
expiration date
    setting using combination time, 209
expressions
    arbitrary, substituting the value of, 67
    assignment command use of, 27
    evaluation precedence rules, 36t, 36
        modifying with parentheses, 36
    glossary entry, 409
    using, 33
    where legal, 68
    WRITE command use of expression, 76
extracting
    fields from a structure, 213
    list items, 204
    substrings, using F$EXTRACT, 42

F$
    used to begin name of lexical function, 38
F$CVSI
    extracts fields from a structure, 213
F$CVTIME
    converts between time formats, 208
F$CVUI
    reason not used in this book, 214
F$EDIT
    edits character strings, 129
    trims trailing spaces from a line, 199
F$ELEMENT
    extracts items from a list, 204
    file specs, do not use to extract components, 205

F$ENVIRONMENT
    item descriptions, 261t
    obtains process environment information, 260
    process message settings, 86
    process verification settings, 142
F$EXTRACT
    extracts fields from a structure, 213
    extracts substrings from a string, 42
F$FAO
    directive description, 79t
    formats strings with text and data, 78
F$FILE_ATTRIBUTES
    item descriptions, 160t
    obtains file information, 160
    obtains protection mask values, 234
F$GETDVI
    item descriptions, 247t
    obtains device information, 246
F$GETJPI
    item descriptions, 259t
    obtains process information, 258
    retrieving the process index, 297
F$GETSYI
    obtains system information, 39
F$INTEGER
    avoids operators with mixed operand types, 37
    converts string to integer, 41
    substitutes value of arbitrary expression on command, 68
F$LENGTH
    returns length of character string, 38, 42
    validates length of input string, 131
F$LOCATE
    searches string for pattern, 42
    validates Boolean input, 132
F$LOGICAL
    replaced by F$TRNLNM in OpenVMS Version 5, 180
F$MESSAGE
    obtaining message for status code, 101
F$MODE
    use F$GETJPI instead to obtain process mode, 260
F$PARSE
    checks validity of file specification, 157
    parses and expands file specs, 152
    preferred function to extract file spec component, 205

F$PID
    obtains process ID's of system processes, 262
    privileges determine which other processes will be located, 262
    used to display CPU time of all users, 295
F$PROCESS
    use F$GETJPI instead to obtain process name, 260
F$SEARCH
    searches for files that match a given spec, 156
F$SETPRV
    enables or disables privileges, 86
F$STRING
    avoids operator with mixed operand types, 37
    converts integer to string, 41
    substitutes value of arbitrary expression command, 68
F$TIME
    returns current absolute time, 208
    returns current system time, 38
F$TRNLNM
    item descriptions, 180*t*
    replaces F$LOGICAL in OpenVMS Version 5, 180
    translates logical name, 178
F$TYPE
    determines whether symbol exists, 40
    returns type of symbol value, 40
    validates integer in input string, 130
F$USER
    use F$GETJPI instead to obtain UIC, 260
F$VERIFY
    enables and disables procedure verification, 140
    work-arounds for inconsistent behavior, 142
facility
    code, naming compatibility use of, 114
    number, required by procedure status codes, 94
FALSE **Boolean value**
    even integers and certain strings used to represent, 27
    literal must be established with assignment command, 27
FDL (File Definition Language)
    editor, creating indexed files using FDL editor, 221
    use in creating indexed files, 221
field. *See also* record.
    extracting fields from a structure, 213
    glossary entry, 409

key, glossary entry, 411
structured records are formatted into fields, 210
types, records, definition symbols, and characteristics, 211
file. *See also* directories.
    /READ access requested when opening a file, 190
    access
        categories, based on relation of owner to user, 230
        protection categories, 231
    aliases for system directories, 184
    appending, OPEN/APPEND allows WRITE to add records to text file, 195
    attributes
        complete list displayed with DIRECTORY/FULL, 161
        file descriptive information, 160*t*
        glossary entry, 409
    blocks, free paging, testing with IF command, 52
    carriage return carriage-control attribute set in normal text file, 194
    changing file type with F$PARSE, 155
    checking
        existence of file with F$SEARCH, 156
        validity of file spec with F$PARSE, 157
    CLOSE necessary to close open files, 190
    close open files in two places in a procedure, 192
    command
        procedure given type COM, 19
        procedure, defined, 1
    concepts and facilities, 147
    counting files of a given type using F$SEARCH, 157
    create
        impact of search lists on, 177
        using CREATE, 194
        using OPEN, 193
        using WRITE, 194
    CREATE not WRITE builds normal text file, 194
    default protection, steps to determine default protection, 241
    deleting temporary files, 197
    directory, file specification component, full description, 149
    displaying sequential files

    record at a time is slow but allows more control, 198
    TYPE/PAGE displaying text a screenful at a time, 198
expiration date, setting using combination time, 209
F$SEARCH, existence checking with, 156
facility code use for naming compatibility, 114
glossary entry, 409
indexed
    alternate key, glossary entry, 403
    attributes of primary and alternate keys, 215
    creating alternate key fields using changes attribute for later updating, 225
    creating indexed files using FDL, 221
    file operations, 215
    file prologue contains information describing keys, 215
    file prologue, glossary entry, 409
    generic match using /MATCH qualifier, 219
    key fields indexed for fast lookup, 215
    key lookup for exact match, 218
    limitation on number of alternate keys, 215
    opening an existing indexed file for reading, 217
    opening for writing with /READ/WRITE qualifier, 223
    operations, concepts and operations, 215
    reading duplicate records from a file, 218
    reading randomly by key, 218
    reading sequentially, 217
    updating, 224
    updating a file using WRITE command, 224
    warning to avoid generic matching when deleting records, 225
    writing, 223
information, file attributes, 160
locked records, ways to unlock records, 227
log, glossary entry, 412
manipulation
    complex, using DCL for complex file manipulation, 5
    DCL usefulness for, xvii
master file directory
    glossary entry, 412
    root of entire directory tree, 149
message, glossary entry, 413
multiple: copies of same file distinguished by version number, 151

opening
    for append, glossary entry, 413
    existing files, 190
    a file, glossary entry, 413
OpenVMS utility names and purposes, 162t
operations
    for manipulating files, 162t
    required access categories, 232t
output of WRITE may not be normal text file, 194
overview, 14
owner identification UIC described, 16
parsing file spec
    glossary entry, 414
    without existence, 153
permanent files, differences from temporary files, 195
process-permanent
    file or video, 75
    file, glossary entry, 416
    standard files and uses, 269
prologue, glossary entry, 409
protection
    concepts and facilities, 229
    displaying values in protection mask, 233
    glossary entry, 409
    mask, access flags for each access category, 231
    obtaining values of mask in a procedure, 234
    setting flags in protection mask, 233
reading
    existing file, 190
    sequential, 189
record format
    free-format text versus record structures, 189
redirecting output from screen to file, 80
resultant file spec, glossary entry, 417
searching file contents, 199
searching multiple directories, method, 159
sequential
    concepts and operations, 189
    file operations, 189
    file, glossary entry, 418
    files with structured records, 210
sharing
    files over multiple processes, 226
    glossary entry, 409

file *(continued)*
- specifications
  - annotated list of components of DCL file specification, 15
  - complete parsing algorithm, 169
  - full description of each component, 147
  - glossary entry, 409
  - logical names in, 166
  - parsing and completing missing component, 152
  - search list for parsing, 186
  - warning, do not use F$ELEMENT to extract components, 205
- structured records, introduction and description, 210
- superseding in personal over public directories using search lists, 177
- SYS$COMMAND, process-permanent file for input from procedure or keyboard, 125
- SYS$INPUT, process-permanent file for input from procedure or keyboard, 125
- temporary files
  - deleting temporary files, 197
  - description and differences from permanent files, 195
  - glossary entry, 420
- text, glossary entry, 420
- transfer over network at night is good use for DCL, 5
- type changing, 155
- UIC protection available, 435
- utilities, 162*t*
- variable-length versus fixed-length records, 190
- warning, protection mask does not include all information about file protection, 234
- writing
  - sequential, 189
  - to, 193

File Definition Language. *See* FDL.
File Transfer Protocol. *See* FTP.
fixed-length records. *See also* records.
- glossary entry, 409
- uncharacteristic of text files, 190

flag. *See also* checking; cleanup; debugging; errors.
- global debug flag, allows permanent debug lines, 143

floating-point numbers
- nonexistent in DCL, 2, 202

flow-of-control. *See also* control, structures.
- commands, glossary entry, 409
- concepts and commands, 49

FOR loops. *See also* loops.
- DCL is missing FOR loops, 3

form feed
- bit-field assignment to create, 46

formats
- DCL command format described, 12
- disks, standard is Files-11 Structure Level 2, 253
- tapes, standard is Level 3 ANSI, 253

formatting
- input prompt lines, using READ and F$FAO, 127
- output to terminal using F$FAO directives, 79*t*

FTP (File Transfer Protocol)
- copying files via IP, 325
- glossary entry, 409

functions, lexical. *See* lexical functions.

generic match
- glossary entry, 409
- reading records in an indexed file, 220

GET data
- glossary entry, 410

global
- level, symbol creation and properties, 31
- sections, UIC protection available, 229
- symbol
  - assigning the value, 31
  - creation prevented by NOGLOBAL keyword, 85
  - deleting, 48
  - distinguishing from prompt-level symbols, 31
  - examples of use, 31
  - existence limited to login period, 32
  - facility code use for naming compatibility, 114
  - flag use to activate permanent debug lines, 143
  - level, creation and properties, 31
  - name for symbols created at global level, 31
  - obtaining the value, 31
  - substring assignment on, 45

glossary
- glossary entry, 410

glyphs
- printable characters in DCL character strings, 26

goals in writing book, xviii
GOSUB. *See also* calling.
    command, compared with `CALL` command, 63
    description of DCL command, 63
    `EXIT`, importance of `EXIT` to avoid dropping into subroutine, 63
    limited to 16 `GOSUB` levels, 64
    summarized, 63*t*
graphics
    DCL has no graphics capabilities, 3
greater than (.GT., .GTS.)
    integer operator, arity, result type, and value, 34*t*
    string operator, arity, result type, and value, 35*t*
greater than or equal (.GE., .GES.)
    integer operator, arity, result type, and value, 34*t*
    string operator, arity, result type, and value, 35*t*
group
    access category, who can access, 230
    logical name
        table described, 168
        table, detailed description, 185
    number
        component of UIC, 17
        glossary entry, 410
    system group, glossary entry, 419
GRPPRV
    group privilege, 243
    privilege that affects protection- checking scheme, 232

handler. *See also* error handling; interrupt handling.
    error handler, glossary entry, 408
HELP/MESSAGE
    displaying complete text for status code, 103
hexadecimal
    base 16, used in DCL, 25
    notation, appendix, 333
hiding, symbols, 29
hints. *See also* warnings.
    `.COM` file type may be omitted after `@`, 19
    allowed abbreviation of DCL verb, 14
    components of DCL file specification may be omitted, 15
    directory specifications, 150
    how to use this book, 6

    logical name can include nonadjacent file spec components, 167
    master file directory name may be omitted, 149
    rules of abbreviation in DCL command verb, 12
    time functions allow omission of certain fields, 209
    times can be specified with fields omitted, 209
    using implicit substitution to write personal commands, 70
    versions, access new and old files, 151
    wildcards for parts of file spec components, 155
hits
    web page accesses, 327
home directory. *See also* directories.
    glossary entry, 410
    importance to OpenVMS user, 15
hosts
    network nodes, 299
HTML (Hypertext Markup Language)
    defined, 320
    design considerations, 332
    example, 320
    form, 329
    glossary entry, 410
    tag summary, 322*t*
    tags, 320
HTTP (Hypertext Transport Protocol)
    defined, 320
    glossary entry, 410
hyperlink
    glossary entry, 410
Hypertext Markup Language. *See* HTML.
Hypertext Transport Protocol. *See* HTTP.

identifier
    `BATCH` system identifier, 235
    `DIALUP` system identifier, 235
    `INTERACTIVE` system identifier, 235
    `LOCAL` system identifier, 235
    `NETWORK` system identifier, 235
    `REMOTE` system identifier, 235
    resource, glossary entry, 417
    `SYS$NODE_nodename` system identifier, 235
identifiers
    ACE, format and description of components, 236
    process identifier, glossary entry, 416
    resource identifier, 316

identifiers *(continued)*
    rights identifier, glossary entry, 417
    stream ID, glossary entry, 418
    types of identifiers assigned when user logs in, 235
    UIC, description of components, 17
IF. *See also* control, structures.
    flow-of-control command discussed, 51
    lacking compound form prior to OpenVMS 5.0, work-around discussed, 54
    simple versus compound forms, 52
IF_DEBUG
    conditional versus debugging with, 144
image data. *See also* data.
    for applications called from DCL, 135
    input data for a program, glossary entry, 410
images
    glossary entry, 410
inclusive OR (.OR.)
    Boolean operator, arity, result type, and value, 35*t*
index, 423; *See also* arrays.
    arrays can be simulated in DCL, 291
    identifier for selecting item form string or array, glossary entry, 410
    string index, glossary entry, 418
    substring assignment format, 44
INDEX
    qualifier for READ access to indexed file, 218
indexed files. *See* file, indexed.
infinite loop. *See also* control, structures; infinite loop.
    glossary entry, 411
    preventing in file searching, 158
infinite loops. *See also* loops.
    example using GOTO command, 51
inheritance. *See also* process.
    symbols and logical names by subprocesses, 268
initialization
    code for setting DCL environment in a procedure, 89
    how to block interrupts during initialization, 109
    volume
        initialization, glossary entry, 421
        parameters and use, 253
input
    ASK, listing in subroutine library, 349
    checking validity, 130
    program, redirecting using DEFINE, 136
    spawned processes accept command string or procedure file, 266
    terminal, features of complex ASK routine discussed, 133
    user
        converted to uppercase by INQUIRE unless quoted, 126
        obtaining for an interactive program, 125
        READ, preferred input command, 127
INQUIRE
    description and warnings about using, 126
INQUIRE command
    considerations in secure environments, 318
integer
    checking for valid integer in input string, 130
    even integers used as Boolean FALSE, 27
    field type, definition symbol and characteristics, 211
    fields in record structures, created with bit-field assignment, 213
    glossary entry, 411
    indexes, arrays in DCL, 291
    network node name specified by integer, 148
    noninteger strings converted to integers become zero, 37
    odd integers used as Boolean TRUE, 27
integers
    operators, arity, result type, and value, 34*t*
    representation and use, 25
    restricted in size to 32 bits in DCL, 25
interactive. *See also* batch.
    process
        description, 258
    processes
        description, 11
        glossary entry, 411
        versus batch, 278
    programs, obtaining user input, 125
    session, description, 11
INTERACTIVE system identifier
    description, 235
interpreter
    command language interpreter glossary entry, 405
    DCL command interpreter, description of program that carries out instructions, 12

interrupting
    processes, SPAWN used to execute commands
        without terminating interrupted process,
        266
interrupts. *See also* errors.
    captive account ignores CTRL/Y, 313
    custom interrupt handler, how to establish, 107
    default
        interrupt handler described, 106
        interrupt handler, problems discussed, 107
        error handling should also handle interrupts,
            107
    glossary entry, 411
    handling
        with cleanup code, example of use in
            subprocedures, 119
        CTRL/Y, concepts and facilities, 105
        custom, example of use in main procedure,
            116
        integrating with error handling, 107
        without cleanup code, example of use in
            subprocedures, 109
    how to block during initialization, 109
    other uses not necessarily terminating program,
        110
    subroutine interrupt handler, potential
        problems, 106
    temporary command level, characteristics, 106
    warning about using SET NOCONTROL, 109
invoke, invoking. *See also* control, structures;
        execute; flow-of-control; run.
    batch jobs, 278
    command procedures, 19, 58
    DCL applications, directory and personal
        command conventions for, 114
    subroutines with @, 58
    subroutines with CALL, 61
    subroutines with GOSUB, 62
    use of system logical name and personal
        command to invoke an application, 115
IP
    Internet Protocol, 299
    node, file specification component, full
        description, 147
    path specification for reaching nodes, 148
ISAM. *See* file, indexed.
ISO Latin 1
    character set
        used by VAX and Alpha architectures, 26

item
    data item, glossary entry, 407
iteration. *See also* control, structures.
    execution of commands in loop, 55
    glossary entry, 411
iterative translation
    blocked by * wildcard in logical names, 171
    glossary entry, 411
    logical names look up described, 167

Jennings, Will, quotation, xx
jobs
    batch
        concepts and facilities, 277
        glossary entry, 404
        restartable, glossary entry, 417
        restarting, 283
    description of uses, 270
    detached process or batch, glossary entry, 411
    duplicate, preventing occurrence of duplicate
        jobs, 288
    invoking batch job using SUBMIT command,
        278
    logical name table
        described, 168
        description of uses, 271
        detailed description, 185
        glossary entry, 411
    queues
        for running batch jobs, 277
    status, sending mail about batch job status, 281

kernal. *See also* access; protection; security.
    access mode in which a process may run, 172
keyboard
    logical names for keyboard input, 125
keys. *See also* file, indexed.
    alternate key in indexed file, glossary entry, 403
    attributes of primary and alternate keys, 215
    field, glossary entry, 411
    indexed file
        fields to be indexed for fast lookup, 215
        matching, 219
    primary, glossary entry, 415
keywords
    abbreviation, how to recognize keywords that
        may be abbreviated, 206
    arguments, character strings used in many
        lexical functions, 40

keywords *(continued)*
    description and suggestions for use, 206
    glossary entry, 411
    `LOOKUP_KEYWORD`, listing in subroutine library, 351

labels
    destination for `GOTO`, 50
    duplicate, second label replaces first, 51
    glossary entry, 411
    volumes
        can be labeled during initialization, 253
        label, glossary entry, 421

languages
    command language interpreter, glossary entry, 405
    debugging, DCL advantages and disadvantages compared with conventional languages, 139

Latin-1
    character set, 335
    glossary entry, 411

length
    character string length has upper limit of about 900 characters, 26
    file specification name component, maximum length, 150
    string
        glossary entry, 411
        length, glossary entry, 418
    substring assignment format, 44
    terminal input strings, checking, 131

less than (.LT., .LTS.)
    integer operator, arity result type, and value, 34*t*
    string operator, arity result type, and value, 35*t*

less than or equal (.LE., .LES.)
    integer operator, arity result type, and value, 34*t*
    string operator, arity result type, and value, 35*t*

letters. *See* glyphs; strings, characters; substrings.

level
    global, symbol creation and properties, 31
    procedure
        creation and properties of symbols at procedure level, 29
    procedures
        glossary entry, 415
        levels of source of DCL commands, 58
    nesting depth limit for calls is 32, 58
    prompt
        creation and properties of symbols at prompt level, 28
        level, glossary entry, 416
        levels as source of DCL commands, 58
    subroutine at same procedure level using `GOSUB`, 63
    symbol
        determination and use, 28
        level, glossary entry, 419
        level, indicates defining context, 23
    temporary command level
        following interrupt, characteristics, 106
        glossary entry, 420

lexical functions. *See also* individual names.
    argument characteristics, 39
    description and use, 38
    explicit substitution using apostrophe, 66
    glossary entry, 412

LIBCALL
    personal command
        to call library of subroutines, 122
        definition, 347

library, subroutine
    example of use, 121
    library, complete listings, 347
    use of large procedure as, 121

limitations
    `GOSUB`, limited to 16 `GOSUB` levels, 64
    procedure calls may only reach depth up to 32, 58
    procedures may only accept up to eight parameters, 59

lists. *See also* arrays; Manager for Organized Distribution Lists, sample application, MODL.
    creating and manipulating lists with DCL commands, 203
    distribution list, glossary entry, 408
    extracting list items with `F$ELEMENT`, 204
    file types, constructing list from a directory, 203
    glossary entry, 412
    removing duplicates from lists with DCL commands, 203
    splitting apart, 204

literals. *See also* symbols.
    character string literal represented by use of double quotes, 26
    external representations of data within programs, 25
    glossary entry, 412
LNM$DCL_LOGICAL
    search list used by SHOW LOGICAL command, description, 186
LNM$DIRECTORIES
    search list of the two logical name table directories, description, 186
LNM$FILE_DEV
    search list for file specification parsing description, 186
LNM$GROUP_TABLE
    group logical table description, 185
LNM$PROCESS_DIRECTORY
    l ogical name table directory, description, 186
LNM$PROCESS_TABLE
    process logical table description, 185
LNM$SYSTEM_DIRECTORY
    log ical name table directory, description, 186
LNM$SYSTEM_TABLE
    system logical table description, 185
LNMJOB_TABLE
    group logical table description, 185
loading
    glossary entry, 412
    volume loading, glossary entry, 421
LOCAL system identifier
    description, 235
local symbols. *See* procedure level.
localhost
    IP local node is named localhost, 148
locking records. *See also* records.
    glossary entry, 417
    sharing files over multiple processes, 226
log file. *See also* debugging; errors.
    glossary entry, 412
logical data. *See* Boolean.
logical names. *See also* names.
    access modes, use by OpenVMS of each mode, 172
    characters allowed in logical name, 166
    concepts and facilities, 165
    defining
        logical names in different access modes, 173*t*

        root directories with, 175
        and using, 166
    deleting with DEASSIGN command, 181
    device specification with, 148
    differences between logical names symbols, 165
    directories of logical name tables, 185
    DISK$*volumelabel* disk logical name, 173
    displaying values using SHOW LOGICAL, 170
    facility codes use for naming compatibility, 114
    glossary entry, 412
    inheritance by subprocesses, 268
    iterative translation
        blocked by * wildcard, 171
        described, 167
    for keyboarding input, 125
    names of logical name tables, 185
    nonadjacent file spec components, 167
    overview, 16
    privileges required to access each table, 169
    purposes in replacement of device and directory names, 166
    search lists replacement of device and directory names, 177
    standard process and job logical names, 174*t*
    SYS$DISK working directory device name, 149
    system logical names, 183*t*
    tables
        description of four types, 168
        detailed description, 185
        directory , glossary entry, 412
        glossary entry, 412
        job, description of use, 271
        job, glossary entry, 411
        relationship to processes, 165
        UIC protection available, 229
    TAPE$*volumelabel* tape logical name, 174
    translating using F$TRNLNM, 178
    translation, glossary entry, 412
    user address, identifies location and name of user, 176
    using for product parameters, 178
    wildcard * use with logical names, 171
login
    automatic login, 316
    automatic login facility (ALF), 316
    directory
        glossary entry, 412
        importance to OpenVMS user, 15

login *(continued)*
    procedure, description and use of `LOGIN.COM`, 21
`LOGIN.COM`
    description and use of login procedure, 21
    user login command procedure, 312
    user login procedure, 308
`LOGOUT` command
    replacing with a DCL procedure, 3
longword
    glossary entry, 412
    hexadecimal notation, 333
    restriction of size of integers to 32 bits, 25
`LOOKUP_KEYWORD`
    library routine for manipulating keywords, 206
    listing in subroutine library, 351
loops. *See also* control, structures; `GOTO`; infinite loops.
    body
        component of loop, characteristics, 56
        glossary entry, 412
        preventing in file searches, 158
    glossary entry, 412
    terminating
        multiple termination tests, 57
        techniques for, 56
lowercase. *See also* strings.
    input to `INQUIRE` must be inside double quotes to remain lowercase, 126

mail
    batch job status report can be tailored and mailed to user, 281
    Manager for Organized Distribution Lists, sample application, 355
    user address, glossary entry, 421
`MAIL`
    executing commands in mail utility from DCL, 135
mailbox
    virtual device example, 245
main procedure
    example of establishing DCL environment, 116
    glossary entry, 412
management
    system management applications for DCL, 4
manager
    queue, supports batch processing facility, 277

Manager for Organized Distribution Lists. *See also* MODL.
manipulating
    data in DCL, techniques and tricks, 201
    files, DCL usefulness for
    , xvii
masks, protection
    access flags for each access category, 231
    default
        for directories, 241
        for files, 241
    glossary entry, 416
master file directory
    glossary entry, 412
matching
    access control list, algorithm, 235
    generic
        glossary entry, 409
        match using /MATCH qualifier, 219
    indexed file keys, 219
    rules used by DCL to match operators and operand types, 37
maximum
    how to compute with DCL arithmetic commands, 201
`MAXSYSGROUP`
    SYSGEN parameter, 232
MCR (Monitor Console Routine), 1
member number
    component of UIC, 17
    glossary entry, 413
memory
    system, associated with OpenVMS processes, 257
`MERGE`
    file utility, one line description, 162*t*
messages
    conversion of status codes to messages with F$MESSAGE, 101
    customizing OpenVMS messages, 86
    enabling components and returning to entry settings, 86
    environment, establishing, example of use in main procedure, 116
    file
        containing error messages for status codes, 103*t*
        glossary entry, 413

four components of an OpenVMS message, 85
need to explicitly set file to search for status
    codes, 102
setting, saving, example of use in main
    procedure, 116
metalinguistic symbol
description and typography, 8
glossary entry, 413
minimum
how to compute with DCL arithmetic
    commands, 201
modifying. *See also* appending; creating.
access control list, 238
character strings, using bit-field assignment
    for, 46
commands, using the substitution facilities,
    65
default error handler, 95
file type, 155
symbol values
    using assignment command for, 24, 28
MODL (Manager for Organized Distribution
    Lists)
command descriptions, 357
file layout
    description, 362
    record structures, 363*t*
how to use, 356
introduction, 355
listing
    command procedures, 364
    file definition, 401
sample application, appendix, 355
selection criteria, how to specify, 358
modulus
how to compute with DCL arithmetic
    commands, 202
MOUNT
command to mount a volume, 254
qualifiers, 255*t*
mounting volumes. *See also* volume mounting.
Multinational Character Set
character set, 335
multiple commands
stored in text file as command procedure, 18
multiplication (*)
integer operator, arity, result type, and value,
    34*t*

names
component of DCL file specification, overview,
    15
device name, glossary entry, 408
file specification component
    characters allowed, 150
    full description, 150
    maximum length, 150
    overview, 15
global symbols, conventions for, 31
job logical name table, glossary entry, 411
logical
    inheritance of logical names by
        subprocesses, 268
    name table directory, glossary entry, 412
    name table, glossary entry, 412
    name, overview, 16
    names for keyboard input, 125
OpenVMS process, same as user name for first
    interactive process, 11
process, setting, 263
symbol
    description of use, 23
    name, glossary entry, 419
    rules for composition, 24
terminal name, item of information associated
    with OpenVMS process, 12
unique names must be created for temporary
    files, 196
UNIQUE_NAME, listing in subroutine library,
    353
user name
    glossary entry, 421
    item of information associated with
        OpenVMS process, 11
naming
conventions for compatibility with other
    OpenVMS applications, 113
NCP
DECnet network control program, 314
negation (-)
integer operator, arity, result type, and value,
    34*t*
NETSERVER.LOG
DECnet, 300
network
copying files over a network using DCL, 5
process
    description, 258

Index   **447**

network *(continued)*
   process *(continued)*
      glossary entry, 413
    service
      description of commands, 300*t*
NETWORK system identifier
   description, 235
network channel
   DECnet communications, 301
   glossary entry, 413
`NL:`
   null device, used for discarding output, 81
`NLA0:`
   null device, 200
node
   file specification component
      full description, 147
      overview, 15
`NOGLOBAL`
   keyword to hide global symbols in a procedure, 85
`NOLOCAL`
   keyword to hide predefined symbols in a procedure, 85
`NOON` **is not a time of day.** *See* `SET NOON`.
NOT (`.NOT.`)
   Boolean operator, arity, result type, and value, 35*t*
   integer operator, arity, result type, and value, 34*t*
not equal (`.NE.`, `.NES.`)
   integer operator, arity, result type, and value, 34*t*
   string operator, arity, result type, and value, 35*t*
null
   device
      glossary entry, 413
      mechanism for discarding SEARCH output, 200
      `NLA0:` used to discard output, 149
      used for discarding output, 81
   string
      character string with no characters, 26
      glossary entry, 413
   value glossary entry, 413
number. *See* integers.

obtaining
   protection mask values, 234

octal base
   base 8 used in DCL, 25
`ON CONTROL_Y`
   establish interrupt handler with, 107
`ON ERROR/SEVERE_ERROR/WARNING`
   establish error handler with, 95
`OPEN`
   danger of opening file twice, 192
   files must be opened before reading, 190
   use in DECnet communications, 302
open for append
   glossary entry, 413
   used to add records to end of sequential file, 195
opening files
   glossary entry, 413
   indexed files, 217
   sequential files, 190
`OPEN/READ`
   indexed files, preparation for reading, 217
`OPEN/READ/WRITE`
   indexed files, preparation for writing, 223
`OPEN/SHARE`
   sharing file over multiple processes, 226
OpenVMS
   designing compatible command procedure applications, 113
   documentation set listed, 8
   note about differences in versions, 7
   process
      items of information associated, 11
   review of basic concepts, 11
   versions
      CALL introduced in Version 5.0, 61
      compound `IF` introduced in Version 5.0, 54
      lack of compound `IF` command prior to Version 5.0, work-arounds, 54
      lexical function to obtain, 39
      replacement of `F$LOGICAL` by `F$TRNLNM` in Version 4, 180
`OPER`
   privilege that allows users to perform operator functions, 18
operands
   associated with operator to create new values, 33
   glossary entry, 413

operations
    file manipulation, summary of operations and qualifiers, 162*t*
    search operation, glossary entry, 418
operators. *See also* individual operators.
    arity, number of required operands, 33
    binary
        description and examples, 33
        glossary entry, 404
    Boolean, arity, result type, and value, 35*t*
    character string, arity, result type, and value, 35*t*
    evaluation precedence rules, 36*t*, 36
        modifying with parenthesis, 36
    glossary entry, 413
    integer, arity, result type, and value, 34*t*
    precedence, glossary entry, 414
    rules used by DCL to match operators and operand types, 37
    unary
        description and examples, 33
        glossary entry, 420
    using in expressions to create new values, 33
optional
    arguments
        glossary entry, 414
        lexical functions may accept optional arguments, 39
    parameters, glossary entry, 414
OR (.OR.)
    Boolean operator, arity, result type, and value, 35*t*
    example of use with .EQS., description of precedence, 57
    integer operator, arity, result type, and value, 34*t*
    returning status codes with, 96
order of evaluation
    precedence rules for expression, 36*t*, 36
        modifying with parentheses, 36
OSI
    Open System Interconnect, 299
other
    process, description, 258
output. *See also* displaying.
    debugging output using SHOW, 143
    discarding, from a SEARCH command, 200
    displaying during a procedure execution, concepts and commands, 75
    formatting terminal output, 78
    procedure
        captured with /OUTPUT, 145
    program, redirecting, 80
owner
    access category, who can access, 230
    identification through UICs, 16
    UIC
        associated with files and directories, 230
        glossary entry, 414

P0 space
    glossary entry, 414
    virtual memory in which program image is run, 257
P1 space
    glossary entry, 414
    virtual memory for processes controlled by DCL command interpreter, 257
P1-P8
    reserved symbols for parameters of a procedure, 59
padding
    blank spaces inserted during substring replacement, 44
paging file blocks
    free, testing with the IF command, 52
parallel execution
    among processes, 266
    of processes using SPAWN/NOWAIT, 267
parameters. *See also* arguments.
    allowing for prompts or batch, 133
    command parameter, glossary entry, 405
    DCL command parameters, description and use, 13
    glossary entry, 414
    handling as an eight element array, 294
    limited to eight for a procedure, 59
    optional, glossary entry, 414
    passing product parameters using logical names, 178
    procedure
        concepts and characteristics, 59
        parameter, glossary entry, 415
    product parameter, glossary entry, 416
    required, glossary entry, 417
    subroutines use of, 62

parent. *See also* child; process.
   directory, parsing requires special treatment, 154
   process, glossary entry, 414
parsing
   controlling default specs with F$PARSE, 152
   file specifications
      complete algorithm, 169
      completing missing components, 152
      glossary entry, 414
   protection masks, warning against, 234
   subdirectories requires special treatment, 154
   SYNTAX_ONLY allows skip of existence check, 153
path
   DECnet or IP specification for reaching nodes, 148
pattern
   glossary entry, 414
   matching
      character string, using F$LOCATE, 42
      file searching, 199
      wildcard use for searching directories, 155
percentage
   how to use DCL commands to calculate percentages, 202
periodic batch jobs
   resubmit themselves on schedule, 286
permission
   to access files. *See* access.
personal commands
   application invocation use of, 115
   calling subroutines with, 122
   evaluating with implicit substitution, 69
   glossary entry, 414
   predefined
      blocking example of use in main procedure, 116
      dangerous to procedure execution, 71
   protecting procedures
      from their effects, 84
      using SET SYMBOL, 85
   substitution, glossary entry, 414
PID (process identifier)
   glossary entry, 414
   used to specify a process, 261
pipe
   glossary entry, 414

PIPE
   &
      background execution, in a subshell, 275
   &&
      conditional execution, on success, 275
   (. . .)
      execute the enclosed commands within a subshell, 275
   ;
      sequential execution, 275
   <
      redirect SYS$INPUT, 275
   >
      redirect SYS$OUTPUT, 275
   |
      sequential command execution, 275
   ||
      conditional execution, on failure, 275
   2>
      redirect SYS$ERROR, 275
   redirecting output with, 145
   SYS$PIPE logical name, 274
   tee, 274
POSIX shell, 1
POST data
   glossary entry, 415
precedence
   glossary entry, 415
   operator, 36t
   operator, glossary entry, 414
   order in which operators are applied, 36
primary key
   description of indexed file, 215
   glossary entry, 415
print jobs
   application for DCL, 3
printable character
   character with a corresponding glyph, 26
   glossary entry, 415
privilege
   glossary entry, 415
privileges
   to access files. *See* access.
   access modes assigned to processes, 172
   authorized
      description and usefulness, 18
      glossary entry, 404
   description of OpenVMS privilege scheme, 17
   effect on protection-checking scheme, 231

environment, establishing, example of use in
    main procedure, 116
explicit enabling within procedures, 86
logical name tables, privileges required to
    access, 169
OPER, privilege that allows a user to perform
    operator functions, 18
pro cess
    setting, 263
process
    description and usefulness, 18
    glossary entry, 416
rights identifier for access, glossary entry,, 417
SETPRV, privilege that allows a user to enable
    privileges, 18
setting, saving, example of use in main
    procedure, 116
SPAWN requires TMPMBX or PRMMBX privilege,
    264
system group, glossary entry, 419
procedures, command. *See also* command.
    call unwind, glossary entry, 415
    calling with
        detailed description, 58
    calling with @, 19
    cleanup, glossary entry, 415
    complex, using comments to clarify, 20
    DCL command procedures, glossary entry, 407
    debugging using verification, 139
    default error handler, problems, 95
    disabling predefined personal commands
        inside of procedures, 71
    error handling, 91
        status code checking methods, 92
    example of DCL command procedure, 18
    exit, glossary entry, 415
    GOSUB allows subroutine at same procedure
        level, 63
    hiding predefined local or global symbols, 85
    input, obtaining user input for an interactive
        program, 125
    invoking with @, 19
        detailed description, 58
    level
        creation and properties of symbols at
            procedure level, 29
        glossary entry, 415
        as sources of DCL commands, 58
        symbols, substring assignment, 43

limitation in number of parameters is eight, 59
login procedure, description and use, 21
main
    example of use in establishing DCL
        environment, 116
    glossary entry, 412
mechanism to capture DCL command
    sequence, 18
message components must be enabled, 86
obtaining values of protection masks, 234
organization requirements, 120
parameters
    glossary entry, 415
    handling as arrays, 294
passing values, allow for prompts or batch, 133
personal commands, uses and dangers, 71
privileges may need to be enabled by procedure,
    86
protecting from effects of predefined personal
    commands, 84
redirecting a program's input from
    SYS$COMMAND, 135
setting DCL environment at beginning and
    end, 89
status code
    returned by EXIT command, 93
    use for reporting outcomes, 91
status must be checked after every command,
    92
steps in establishing DCL environment, 118
terminating
    automatically, 61
    effect on procedure-level symbols, 29
    with EXIT, 61
tracing, 21
unwinding nested procedure calls after errors,
    techniques, 99
verification as debugging tool for DCL, 139
verifying, 21, 84
process. *See also* child; parent.
    access modes, full description, 172
    batch
        glossary entry, 404
        pro cess described, 258
        versus interactive, 278
    child, glossary entry, 405
    components associated with OpenVMS
        processes, 257
    concepts and facilities, 257

Index   451

process *(continued)*
   creating subprocesses, 264
   current, obtaining information, 258
   default protection
      changing with SET PROTECTION, 242
      displaying with SHOW PROTECTION, 241
   detached process
      described, 258
      glossary entry, 407
   environment, cannot obtain information for other than current process, 263
   four sets of privileges associated, 18
   glossary entry, 415
   how to list all processes on the system, 262
   identifier
      glossary entry, 416
   identifier, PID is used to specify a process, 261
   information associated with OpenVMS process, 11
   interactive
      glossary entry, 411
      versus batch, 278
   interrupting, SPAWN to execute commands without terminating interrupted process, 266
   items of
      DCL information available using F$ENVIRONMENT, 261*t*
      information associated with a OpenVMS process, 11
      process information available using F$GETJPI, 259*t*
   kinds of processes described, 258
   logical name
      directory for, 186
      table described, 168
      tables accessible to, 168, 185
      tables relationship to, 165
   logical names, 174*t*
   mode
      glossary entry, 416
      obtaining to check if process in interactive, 259
   multiple, SPAWN/NOWAIT allows simultaneous execution of processes, 267
   name, setting, 263
   network
      glossary entry, 413
      process described, 258
   other
      described, 258
   owner identification UIC described, 17
   parallel execution, 266
   parent, glossary entry, 414
   privileges
      glossary entry, 416
      setting, 263
   process-permanent, files. *See* process-permanent files.
   scheduler chooses process to run, 257
   setting process environment, commands available, 264*t*
   SPAWN requires TMPMBX or PRMMBX privilege, 264
   spawned, characteristics, 266
   subprocess
      described, 258
      glossary entry, 419
      inheritance of symbols and logical names, 268
   in teractive
      description, 11
      process described, 258
processor mode
   glossary entry, 416
process-permanent
   files
      batch process, 271*t*
      glossary entry, 416
      interactive process, 270*t*
      standard files and uses, 269
      SYS$COMMAND, 125, 269
      SYS$ERROR, 269
      SYS$INPUT, 125, 269
      SYS$OUTPUT, 75, 269
      SYS$PIPE, 136, 269
      logical names, importance for command procedures, 173
product
   integer multiplication operator, arity, result type, and value, 34*t*
   parameters
      glossary entry, 416
      passing parameters using logical names, 178
program
   input, redirecting from SYS$COMMAND, 135
   interrupting, SPAWN to execute commands

without terminating interrupted process, 266
redirecting output, 80
prologue
   file prologue
      glossary entry, 409
      information describing an indexed file, 215
prompt
   character, DCL, dollar sign ($) as, 12
   DCL prompt, glossary entry, 407
   level
      creation and properties of symbols at prompt level, 28
      glossary entry, 416
      as source of DCL commands, 58
      symbols, deleting, 48
      symbols, distinguishing from global symbols, 31
   missing parameters can be requested, 133
   READ, controlling prompt display, 127
protection. *See also* access; captive accounts; security.
   access
      algorithm for UIC- and ACL-based protection checking, 242
      categories based on owner relation to user, 230
      control entries, format and description of components, 236
      glossary entry, 403
   blocking access by route of entry, 236
   default protection ACE, applies protection to new files in directory, 238
   dialup, access control list, use to deny dialup access, 236
   files, concepts and facilities, 229
   mandatory access controls, 244
   masks
      access flags for each access category, 231
      default, for directories, 241
      default, for files, 241
      format for specifying protection mask, 232
      glossary entry, 416
      obtaining values of mask in a procedure, 234
      setting during creation or with SET FILE, 233
   mechanism involving access control list, 229

UIC code, 229
networks, access control list, use to deny network access, 236
objects that can be protected, 229
privileges alter protection-checking scheme, 231
process default
   changing with SET PROTECTION, 242
   displaying with SHOW PROTECTION, 241
remote, access control list, use to deny remote access, 236
rights identifiers defined for access control with AUTHORIZE, 235
warning, default process protection may be overridden by ACE, 242
Proxy
   DECnet access control, 314
   glossary entry, 416
PURGE
   file utility, one line description, 162*t*
purging
   temporary files, procedure for, 59

qualifiers
   command qualifier, glossary entry, 406
   DCL commands, description and use, 13
queries, user
   ASK listing in subroutine library, 349
   features of complex ASK routine discussed, 133
   obtaining user input for an interactive program, 125
queue manager
   glossary entry, 416
   responsible for job queue maintenance, 277
queues
   batch queue, characteristics, 277
   batch, glossary entry, 404
   UIC protection available, 229
quitting
   procedures, 60
quotations
   technical folklore, 9
quotient
   integer division operator, arity, result type, and value, 34*t*

ratios
   how to use DCL commands to calculate percentages, 202

READ
    description, 127
    mismatched reads in network tasks, 308
    obtains records from open file and stores in symbol, 191
    preferred input command, reasons discussed, 127
    use in DECnet communications, 302
READ access
    description, 231
READALL
    privilege that affects protection-checking scheme, 232
    readall privilege, 243
READ/DELETE
    deleting records in an indexed file, 225
reading
    duplicate records from indexed files, 218
    files
        existing, 190
        sequential, 189
    indexed files, 217
Record Management System. *See* RMS.
records. *See also* fields.
    /SYMBOL, qualifier for WRITE to allow larger records size, 224
    components of sequential files, 189
    deleting, in an indexed file, 225
    file component, overview, 14
    fixed-length, glossary entry, 409
    glossary entry, 417
    indexed files may contain fixed- or variable-length records, 215
    locked
        overriding with READ/NOLOCK, 227
        ways to unlock locked records, 227
    locking
        glossary entry, 417
        for use with shared files, 226
    sample application records, description of fields, 363t
    size limit can be extended with /SYMBOL qualifier, 224
    structures
        field types, definition symbols and characteristics, 211
        file format alternative to free-format text, 189
        glossary entry, 417

    introduction, 210
    updating
        glossary entry, 421
        locked records, how to wait for them to be unlocked, 228
    variable
        with fixed control format, glossary entry, 421
        record, glossary entry, 421
        versus fixed-length records, 190
recursion
    DCL permits, 58
redirecting
    program input
        forcing input from SYS$COMMAND, 135
        using DEFINE, 136
    program output, 80
reduction (−)
    string operator, arity, result type, and value, 35t
regression test
    DCL good choice in software development, 6
remainder
    how to compute with DCL arithmetic commands, 202
REMOTE system identifier
    description, 235
removing. *See* deleting.
RENAME
    file utility, one line description, 162t
replacement. *See* substitution.
replacing
    symbol values using assignment command, 28
representation
    internal and external representation of data, 25
required parameter
    glossary entry, 417
resource identifier
    glossary entry, 417
responses
    obtaining user input for an interactive program, 125
restartable batch jobs
    $RESTART and BATCH$RESTART control restart entry, 283
    glossary entry, 417
restarting
    batch jobs, 283
restricted login, 312

restricted user
    glossary entry, 417
resubmitting
    batch jobs, 286
resultant file spec
    file spec returned by parsing operation, 152
    glossary entry, 417
return
    point
        glossary entry, 417
        place where DCL continues after returning from subroutine, 58
    value
        glossary entry, 417
        value used in place of lexical function in expressions, 38
RETURN
    use with GOSUB command, 63
rights identifiers
    glossary entry, 417
    maintained using AUTHORIZE, 235
    mnemonic identifiers for UICs, 17
RMS (Record Management System)
    facility for reading and writing files, 189
    glossary entry, 417
root
    directory
        defining with logical names, 175
        glossary entry, 417
    master file directory, root of entire directory tree, 149
rounding
    how to compute with DCL arithmetic commands, 202
RSX-11
    deaccess locking, 161
run, running. *See also* control, structures; execute; flow-of-control; invoke.
    batch jobs, 277
    command procedures, 19, 58
    DCL applications, directory and personal command conventions for, 114
    glossary entry, 417

S0 space
    glossary entry, 418
sample application
    appendix with listing and description of use. *See* MODL.

scheduler
    chooses process to run, 257
    glossary entry, 418
screens
    checking for ANSI control sequence acceptance before screen formatting, 251
script
    command procedure, defined, 1
SCS
    System Communications Services, 299
search
    lists
        glossary entry, 418
        logical names with more than one value, 177
    operation, glossary entry, 418
SEARCH
    file utility, one line description, 162*t*
    qualifiers and method of matching, 199
    using to search files, 199
searching
    directories
        F$SEARCH useful in checking for file existence, 156
        using wildcards to facilitate, 155
    files
        contents can be searched, 199
        loop to count files, precaution against infinite loop, 158
        string, using F$LOCATE, 42
    symbol value
        complete DCL algorithm for, 31
        partial DCL algorithm for, 30
security. *See also* access; captive accounts; protection.
    access modes give privileges to processes, 172
    concealing root directory logical name values, 175
    DECnet access control string, 305
    description of OpenVMS privilege scheme, 17
    disable verification to conceal contents of procedure, 141
    file protection, 229
    mandatory access controls, 244
    user name and password security, 305
selection
    file selection qualifiers, 163*t*

Index   455

separator lines
    use of $ alone on line in DCL command procedure, 19
sequential
    execution
        form of DCL flow of control, 49
        glossary entry, 418
    files
        concepts and operations, 189
        glossary entry, 418
server
    network task, 300
SET
    command to set process environment, 263
SET AUDIT
    using security auditing to debug access controls, 243
SET DEFAULT
    command to change working directory, 16
    extending with a DCL procedure, 4
    file utility, one line description, 162t
SET DIRECTORY
    file utility, one line description, 162t
SET FILE
    file utility, one line description, 162t
    protection mask setting, 233
SET FILE/ENTER
    entering alias entries, 184
SET FILE/REMOVE
    removing alias entries, 184
SET HOST
    second log session for recording debug output, 145
SET MESSAGE
    explicitly set file to check for status code interpretation, 103
    suppressing error message text, 86
SET NOCONTROL
    blocking interrupts during initialization with, 109
SET NOON
    used to disable status checking, 97
SET NOVERIFY
    disabling procedure verification, 140
SET ON
    used to enable status checking, 97
SET PREFIX
    used to annotate verification output, 142
SET SECURITY
    command qualifiers, 239t
    file utility, one line description, 162t
    protection mask setting, 233
SET SYMBOL
    keywords to hide symbol definitions, 85
SET UIC
    obsolete command, 88
SET VERIFY
    enabling procedure verification, 140
    tracing procedures for debugging, 84
SETPRV
    privilege that allows users to enable privileges, 18
setting
    default directory protection using access control entries, 238
    process
        environment, 263
        name, 263
        privileges, 263
    protection mask, 233
    status codes with ON or .OR. logical operator, 96
severity. *See* status code severity.
SEVMS
    security enhanced OpenVMS, 244
shadowing
    symbols, 29
sharable images
    calls from DCL procedures not supported, 3
sharing
    files over multiple processes, 226
shortcuts. *See* hints.
SHOW DEFAULT
    file utility, one line description, 162t
SHOW DEVICE
    listing system devices, 249
SHOW ERROR
    displaying system error counts, 301
SHOW LOGICAL
    logical names, displaying values, 170
SHOW SYMBOL
    use following interrupt, 106
SHOWERR.COM
    displays system error counts, 302
    network server task, 302
SIGNAL
    listing in subroutine library, 352

message and error handling subroutine,
  characteristics and use, 123
signal on error
  glossary entry, 418
simultaneous
  execution of process using SPAWN/NOWAIT, 267
Smithsonian Astrophysical Calendar
  OpenVMS base date, 340
software development
  DCL as appropriate management tool, 5
SORT
  file utility, one line description, 162*t*
spawn
  glossary entry, 418
SPAWN
  qualifiers, 265*t*
  temporary command level, use after interrupt, 106
  used to execute commands without terminating interrupted process, 266
SPAWN command
  use in captive procedures, 314
spawning a subprocess
  description, 264
  examples, 267
SPAWN/NOWAIT
  allows simultaneous execution of processes, 267
SPAWN/TRUSTED command
  use in captive procedures, 314
specification. *See* file, specification.
  parsing a file spec, glossary entry, 414
  resultant file spec, glossary entry, 417
  wildcard spec, glossary entry, 422
starting DCL command procedures
  using @ command, 19
    detailed description, 58
statements
  glossary entry, 418
  used to mean commands in most languages, 27
status. *See also* checking; cleanup; debugging; errors.
  batch job, sending mail about status, 281
  code
    checking with ON command, 95
    checking, methods for, 92
    conversion to text message with F$MESSAGE, 101

defining, example of use in main procedure, 116
disabling automatic checking with SET NOON, 97
displaying complete text using HELP/MESSAGE, 103
explicit checking, examples, 96
facility code use for naming compatibility, 114
format of fields described, 92*t*
glossary entry, 418
procedure, creating, 94
returned by program to indicate success or failure, 91
searching message files for status codes, 101
severities described, 93*t*
SIGNAL, listing in subroutine library, 352
SIGNAL, message and error handling subroutine, characteristics and use, 123
command outcome must be checked within procedures, 92
STATUS
  reserved symbol for recording status of command, 92
STOP
  canceling a procedure from temporary command level, 106
stopping
  procedure execution, 60
  programs, CTRL/Y, program interrupt handling, 105
STOP/REQUEUE
  batch restart option, 283
stream ID
  glossary entry, 418
  required when searching multiple directories, 159
string
  assignment of substrings, 43
  character
    altering bits in, 46
    control characters not representable in, 26
    glossary entry, 405
    length as number of individual characters, 26
    length has upper limit of about 900 characters, 26
    literal represented by use of double quotes, 26

string *(continued)*
   character *(continued)*
      manipulation of lexical functions, 42
      null string has no characters, 26
      operators, arity, result type, and value, 35t
      representation and use, 25
      terminal input validating, 131
   checking for valid integer in input string, 130
   concatenation operator (+), arity, result type, and value, 35t
   creating
      1-character strings using bit-field assignment, 46
      more than one character with bit-field assignment, 47
      strings with multiple characters using bit-field assignment, 47
   determining length with F$LENGTH, 38
   equivalence string, glossary entry, 408
   formatting output using F$FAO directives, 78
   glossary entry, 418
   hints
      about manipulating character strings, 43
      about substring assignment, 45
   indexes
      creating arrays with symbolic indexes, 295
      glossary entry, 418
   length, glossary entry, 418
   lexical functions to manipulate strings, 42
   noninteger strings converted to integers become zero, 37
   null, glossary entry, 413
   numbering of bits in character strings, 46
   operators, arity, result type, and value, 35t
   reduction operator (−), arity, result type, and value, 35t
   representation and use, 25
   searching, suing F$LOCATE, 42
   substitution of symbol values using apostrophe, 66
   terminal input, checking length, 131
   using loops to remove spaces in a string, 56
structures
   application, overview of complex design, 113
   extracting fields from, 213
   glossary entry, 419
   record
      creating structures by storing values in character string, 212
      displaying record structure may cause strange results, 213
   structure, glossary entry, 417
   structured records, introduction, 210
   symbols defining position, size, and type of field, 211t
   type symbols for fields, 211
subdirectories
   glossary entry, 419
   parsing requires special treatment, 154
   tree structure allowed in directory specifications, 149
SUBMIT
   command
      description of qualifiers, 279t
      for queueing batch jobs, 278
submitting
   batch jobs, 278
subprocedures
   with cleanup code, example of use in subprocedures, 119
   custom interrupt handling of, 109
   defined, 58
   glossary entry, 419
   interrupt handler behavior, potential problems, 106
   without cleanup code, example of use in subprocedures, 119
subprocess
   creating with SPAWN command, 264
   glossary entry, 419
   inheritance of symbols and logical names, 268
   input at spawn time from command string or procedure file, 266
   list of inherited and not-inherited environment properties, 264
   parent process execution controlled by /WAIT, 266
   process, description, 258
   termination, possible conditions, 269
SUBROUTINE
   use with CALL command, 62
SUBROUTINE-LIBRARY.COM
   complete listing, 348
subroutines. *See also* calling.
   characteristics and commands that invoke, 63t
   with cleanup code, example of use in subprocedures, 119
   de fined, 58

glossary entry, 419
GOSUB allows subroutine at same procedure
        level, 63
invoking with
    @, 58
    CALL, 61
    GOSUB, 62
library
    complete listings, 347
    example of use, 121
    use of large procedure as, 121
SUBROUTINE command use with CALL, 62
summary of facilities, 63t
without cleanup code, example of use in
        subprocedures, 119
subscript. *See also* arrays.
    array, glossary entry, 419
    arrays can be simulated in DCL, 291
substitution
    ampersand
        explicit substitution of text in DCL
                command, glossary entry, 403
        used in concert with apostrophe
                substitution, 72
    apostrophe
        creating DCL arrays, techniques and
                problems, 292
        description, 65
        explicit substitution of text in DCL
                command, glossary entry, 403
    bit-field assignment using integer values, 46
    concepts and operators, 65
    explicit, using apostrophe substitution for, 65
    glossary entry, 419
    implicit
        in evaluation of personal commands, 69
        requirements for, 69
    INQUIRE input apostrophe substitution, 126
    logical name values substituted, 165
    personal command substitution, glossary entry,
            414
    principle underlying, 65
    substring assignment to replace parts of strings,
            44
    textual, contrasted with assembler macros and
            C preprocessor, 65
    value of arbitrary expression, 67
wildcards
    file operations use of, 162t

logical names allow use of wildcard, 171
pattern matching templates for parts of file
        spec components, 155
spec, glossary entry, 422
using with F$SEARCH, 157
substrings
    assignment, 43
    extracting substring with F$EXTRACT, 42
    glossary entry, 419
subtraction (−)
    integer operator, arity, result type, and value,
            34t
suggestions. *See* hints.
sum
    integer addition operator, arity, result type, and
            value, 34t
superseding
    files in personal over public directories, using
            search lists for, 177
supervisor
    access mode in which a process may run, 172
suspending program execution
    program interrupt handling, 105
SYLOGIN.COM
    system wide login command procedure, 312
    system-wide login command procedure, 308
symbolic arrays
    creation and use, 295
    glossary entry, 419
symbols. *See also* assignment; literals; procedure
        level, local; values.
    case, DCL converts all symbols to uppercase, 24
    checking
        the type or existence with F$TYPE, 40
        validity, VERIFY_SYMBOL, listing in
                subroutine library, 354
    creating
        global, 31
        procedure level, 29
        prompt level, 28
        using assignment command for, 24, 27
    data type, associated with value not symbol, 28
    description and items of information
            associated, 23
    differences between logical names and symbols,
            165
    evaluating, using apostrophe substitution in,
            65
    explicit substitution using apostrophe, 66

Index   459

symbols *(continued)*
   facility code use for naming compatibility, 114
   global
      assigning the value, 31
      creation prevented by `NOGLOBAL` keyword, 85
      deleti ng, 48
      distinguishing from prompt-level symbols, 31
      examples of use, 31
      existence limited to login period, 32
      facility code use for naming compatibility, 114
      level, creation and properties, 31
      name for symbols created at global level, 31
      obtaining the value, 31
      substring assignment on, 45
   glossary entry, 419
   inheritance of symbols by subprocesses, 268
   keywords to hide symbol definitions, 85
   level, glossary entry, 419
   metalinguistic
      description and typography, 8
      glossary entry, 413
   name
      glossary entry, 419
      rules for composition, 24
   procedure-level
      creating and properties of symbols at procedure level, 29
      effect of terminating a procedure on, 29
      substring assignment, 43
   prompt-level
      creation and properties of symbols at prompt level, 28
      deleting, 48
      distinguishing from global symbols, 31
   reserved, P1–P8 procedure-level symbols for procedure parameters, 59
   shadowing, 29
   `SHOW SYMBOL`, use following interrupt, 106
   table
      arrays may require symbol table expansion, 298
      glossary entry, 419
   values
      assignment using assignment command, 24
      complete search algorithm for, 31
      glossary entry, 419
      modifying using assignment command, 24, 28
      partial search algorithm for, 30
      replacing using assignment command, 28
   variables, symbols are used as variables in DCL, 23
syntax
   command syntax, glossary entry, 406
   format and rules governing format of DCL commands, 14
`SYNTAX_ONLY`
   parsing without existence check, 153
`SYS$BATCH`
   name of system batch job queue, 278
`SYS$COMMAND`
   forcing program input to use, 135
   process logical name, brief description, 174*t*
   process-permanent file for input from procedure or keyboard, 125
   READ use of, 127
   sources for detached and subprocesses of batch procedure, 271*t*
   interactive procedure, 270*t*
`SYS$DISK`
   process logical name, brief description, 174*t*
   working directory device name, 149
`SYS$ERROR`
   destinations for detached and subprocesses of batch procedure, 271*t*
   interactive procedure, 270*t*
   process logical name, brief description, 174*t*
   redirection of screen output using, 80
`SYS$INPUT`
   process logical name, brief description, 174*t*
   process-permanent file for input from procedure or keyboard, 125
   sources for detached ad subprocesses of batch procedure, 271*t*
   interactive procedure, 270*t*
   work-around for input from procedure, 135
`SYS$LOGIN`
   job logical name, brief description, 174*t*
`SYS$LOGIN_DEVICE`
   job logical name, brief description, 174*t*
`SYS$MESSAGE`
   directory, status code messages stored in, 102
`SYS$NET`
   network channel logical name, 301

SYS$NODE_nodename system identifier
    description, 235
SYS$OUTPUT
    destinations for detached and subprocesses of, 271t
        interactive procedure, 270t
    process-permanent file for video output, 75
    redirecting with DEFINE command, 80
SYS$PIPE
    logical name for reading PIPE input, 274
    process logical name, brief description, 174t
    process-permanent file for input from a pipe, 136
SYS$SCRATCH
    job logical name, brief description, 174t
    temporary file logical name, 196
SYS$SYSTEM:SMGTERMS.TXT
    common control sequences, 78
SYSGEN
    system parameters, 298
SYSPRV
    privilege that affects protection-checking scheme, 232
    system privilege, 243
system
    access category, who can access, 230
    devices, listing with SHOW DEVICE, 249
    directory organization, overview, 181
    displaying CPU time for all users, use of an array, 295
    F$GETSYI lexical function to get system information, 39
    groups
        access privileges for certain UICs, 17
        glossary entry, 419
    identifiers, category of rights identifiers, 235
    logical names, 183t
        application naming convention use of, 114
        directory for, 186
        table described, 168
        table, detailed description, 185
    management, applications for DCL, 4
    satellites, adding new OpenVMS Cluster satellites, 4
system privilege
    glossary entry, 420

tables
    job logical name table, glossary entry, 411

logical name table
    described, 165
    directory, glossary entry, 412
    glossary entry, 412
    symbol table, glossary entry, 419
tape
    used as device, 148
TAPE$*volumelabel*
    tape logical name, 174
task-to-task
    DECnet communications, 301
task-to-task communications
    DECnet communications, 300
    glossary entry, 420
Technical Character Set
    character set, 335
techniques. *See* hints.
tee
    duplicating output within a PIPE, 274
    glossary entry, 420
    PIPE input via SYS$PIPE, 274
TEE.COM
    example of using a tee in a PIPE, 274
telephone directory
    possible use for DCL, 4
temporary. *See also* file.
    command level, glossary entry, 420
    file, glossary entry, 420
terminal
    characteristics can be determined with F$GETDVI, 251
    characteristics, glossary entry, 420
    checking for acceptance of ANSI control sequences, 250
    controlling the behavior, 251
    input
        obtaining with INQUIRE, 126
        READ, preferred input command, 127
    name, item of information associated with OpenVMS process, 12
    output, formatting, 78
    sending special characters to control a terminal, 76
    session output, capturing with LOG, 145
    specified as a device name, 148
    visual display methods during procedure execution, 75
terminating
    loops

terminating *(continued)*
   loops *(continued)*
      multiple termination tests, 57
      techniques for, 56
   procedures
      automatically, 61
      effect on procedure-level symbols, 29
      using EXIT, 61
   subprocesses, possible conditions, 269
test case library
   possible use for DCL in software development, 6
text. *See also* image data.
   DCL command procedure stored in text file, 18
   displaying
      contents of file, 198
      large amounts with TYPE command, 136
      text on video screen using WRITE command, 75
   field type, definition symbol and characteristics, 211
   fields in record structures, created with substring assignment, 212
   file, glossary entry, 420
   formatting output using F$FAO directives, 78
   free-format text, file format alternative to record structure, 189
   OPEN/APPEND allows WRITE to add records to text file, 195
THEN
   use with IF command, 52
time. *See also* date.
   absolute time
      format to represent specific points in time, 207
      glossary entry, 403
   combination time
      format using absolute and delta times, 209
      OpenVMS format glossary entry, 405
   comparison
      time, format to represent times to be compared, 208
      time, OpenVMS format, glossary entry, 406
      of two times, 208
   converting absolute time to comparison time, 208
   delta time
      format for showing difference between two times, 208

      OpenVMS format glossary entry, 407
   difference between times, how to calculate, 208
   displaying CPU time of all users, use of an array, 295
   F$CVTIME converts between time format, 208
      glossary entry, 420
   maintenance of UTC using UTC$CONFIGURE_TDF, 178
   manipulating using DCL commands, 207
   omission of certain time fields is permitted, 209
   READ prompt string can display current time, 127
   TODAY, absolute time in DCL, 207
   TOMORROW, absolute time in DCL, 207
   truncating current time to minutes filed, 212
   Universal Coordinated Time (UTC), 178
   YESTERDAY, absolute time in DCL, 207
TODAY, absolute time in DCL, 207
TOMORROW, absolute time in DCL, 207
TOY
   VAX hardware register, 340
tracing. *See also* debugging; errors.
   command procedures, using SET VERIFY, 21
   procedures using SET VERIFY for debugging, 84
translating, logical names
   using F$TRNLMN, 178
   value look up in, 167
translation
   iterative, glossary entry, 411
   logical name translation, glossary entry, 412
trash
   device NLA0: used to discard output, 149
tricks. *See* hints.
troubleshooting
   common DECnet problems, 307
TRUE Boolean value
   literal must be established with assignment command, 27
   odd integers and certain strings used to represent, 27
truncations
   allowed abbreviation of DCL verbs, 14
   rules of abbreviation in DCL command verbs, 12
TYPE
   /PAGE qualifier displays text screenful at a time, 198
   file utility, one line description, 162*t*

invoking network servers, 302
  text display using TYPE command, 136
types
  changing file type, 155
  data
    associated with value not symbol, 28
    Boolean, description and use, 26
    character string representation and use, 25
    integer representation and use, 25
    type, glossary entry, 407
    types in DCL, 24
  file specification component
    full description, 150
    overview, 15
  noninteger strings converted to integers become zero, 37
  rules used by DCL to match operators and operand types, 37
  standard file types for different file contents, 150, 211
  structures use codes for type of fields, 211
  symbols, checking using F$TYPE, 40
typographic conventions, 7

UIC (user identification code)
  glossary entry, 421
unary operators. *See also* binary operators.
  description and examples, 33
  glossary entry, 420
unconditional goto. *See also* control, structures.
  GOTO command as control structure, 50
UNDEFINE
  suggested personal command for deassigning logical names, 181
undefining. *See also* defining.
  logical names using personal command, 181
Unicode
  character set, 335
UNIQUE_NAME
  listing in subroutine library, 353
  subroutine for creating a name for temporary file, 196
Universal Coordinated Time. *See* UTC.
Universal Resource Locator. *See* URL.
unwinding. *See also* calling; cleanup; debugging; errors.
  nested procedure calls after errors, techniques for, 99
  procedure call unwind, glossary entry, 415

updating
  alternate key fields requires use of changes attribute at creation, 225
  indexed files, updating a file using WRITE/UPDATE command, 225
  locked records, how to wait for them to be unlocked, 228
  records, glossary entry, 421
URL
  encoding
    glossary entry, 421
URL (Universal Resource Locator)
  defined, 320
  encoding, needed for certain characters, 329
  examples, 320, 327
  glossary entry, 420
user
  access mode in which a process may run, 172
  address
    glossary entry, 421
    identifies location and name of user, 176
  identification code (UIC)
    avoid changing UIC with in a procedure, 88
    characteristics, 88
    compared with access control list (ACL), 229
    description of purpose, 16
    file protection use of UIC, 229
    glossary entry, 421
  name
    glossary entry, 421
    item of information associated with OpenVMS process, 11
    process name for first interactive process same as user name, 11
user identification code. *See* UIC subentries.
UTC (Universal Coordinated Time)
  maintenance using UTC$CONFIGURE_TDF, 178
utilities
  file manipulation, 162*t*
Utley, Michael, quotation, xx

validating. *See also* checking; errors; verification.
  checking validity of input, 130
  file specification with F$PARSE, 157
  terminal input
    Booleans, 132
    character strings, 131
    integers, 130

Index 463

values. *See also* assignment; symbols.
  default
    glossary entry, 407
    in lexical functions with optional arguments, 39
  global symbols
    assigning, 31
    obtaining, 31
  logical names
    displaying with SHOW LOGICAL, 170
    equivalence string as, 166
  null, glossary entry, 413
  prompting for procedure parameters in batch, 133
  return value, glossary entry, 417
  returned from lexical functions, use in expression, 38
  symbol
    assignment using assignment command, 24
    characteristics of, 24
    complete search algorithm for, 31
    modifying using assignment command, 24, 28
    partial search algorithm for, 30
    replacing using assignment command, 28
    value, glossary entry, 419
variable
  character matching, wildcard spec, glossary entry, 422
  with fixed control (VFC), record format, glossary entry, 421
variable-length record
  allowed in indexed file, 215
  characteristic of text files, 190
  glossary entry, 421
variables. *See* symbol.
verbs. *See also* command.
  command verb, glossary entry, 406
  description and use of DCL command, 12
verification. *See also* debugging; errors; validating.
  command procedures, using SET VERIFY for tracing, 21
  debugging
    method, glossary entry, 421
    tool for DCL, 139
  enabling
    before entering procedure, 140
    from inside procedure, 140
  image
    displaying image data lines, 140
    verification, setting from inside procedure, 141
  procedure
    displaying command lines, 139
    verification, setting from inside procedure, 141
verifying procedures. *See* verification.
VERIFY_SYMBOL
  listing in subroutine library, 354
versions
  32767 is the highest permissible version, 308
  file
    −0 gives lowest version, 152
    −1 gives next highest version, 151
    0 gives highest version, 151
    accessing highest and lowest versions, format, 151
    range of version numbers is 1–32767, 151
    specification component, description, 151
    specification component, overview, 15
  OpenVMS. *See* versions.
VFC (variable with fixed control)
  record format, glossary entry, 421
video screen output methods during procedure execution, 75
virtual devices
  description and examples, 245
  glossary entry, 421
viruses
  possible problem for DCL, caution, 6
VMSINSTAL
  choosing DCL for software installation, xvii
  file manipulation, example of DCL use, 5
  lack of second "L" in name, xvii
volume
  initialization, to format disk or tape, glossary entry, 421
  label, glossary entry, 421
  loading, glossary entry, 421
  magnetic medium on which information is stored, 245
  medium to store permanent information is stored, 421
  mounting
    to allow system to recognize a device, 254
    glossary entry, 422
  owner UIC described, 16
  steps performed in mounting, 255

warning messages
    SIGNAL subroutine treats as informational, 124
warnings. *See also* hints.
    "job" does not necessarily mean batch job, 270
    angle brackets (< > must be accepted as directory delimiters, 150
    arrays may require symbol table expansion, 298
    avoid
        ampersand substitution, list of problems, 72
        changing UIC within a procedure, 88
        SET NOCONTROL, 109
        SET NOVERIFY from inside a procedure, 141
        using abbreviations in command procedures, 20
        using operators with mixed operand types, 37
    characters must be same case before comparison, 129
    comments should be moved to end of procedure to avoid slowdown, 347
    common mistakes using apostrophe substitution, 68
    debug commands cost execution time even when inactive, 144
    default
        answers should not contain dangerous material, 128
        directory, do not change in a procedure, 88
        error handler does not always detect syntax errors, 95
        interrupt handler would be confusing naive user, 107
    DEFINE and ASSIGN have reverse order of parameters, 169
    deleting records from indexed file, avoid generic matching, 225
    determining parent of arbitrary directory difficulty, 154
    device names cannot be trusted to show class of device, 250
    displaying record structure on screen may cause strange results, 213
    F$ELEMENT should not be used to extract component from file spec, 205
    file
        spec manipulating involving rooted directory difficulty, 154
    global symbols, creation prevented by NOGLOBAL keyword, 85
    GOSUB requires EXIT to avoid dropping into subroutine, 63
    GOTO commands sunned, reasons discussed, 52
    indexed file, open for writing with /READ /WRITE qualifiers, 223
    INQUIRE is idiosyncratic and should be used sparingly, 126
    labels, avoid using duplicate labels, 51
    limit Boolean input to yes or no, 132
    P1-P8 reserved for names of procedure parameters, 59
    passing parameters using logical names, 178
    personal commands must be prevented from influencing a procedure, 84
    predefined personal commands may damage procedures, 71
    protection
        default process protection may be overridden by ACE, 242
        mask does not include all information about file protection, 234
    record size should always be extended with /SYMBOL qualifier, 224
    SPAWN requires TMPMBX or PRMMBX privilege, 264
    specifying local node on file spec has network overhead, 148
    status codes are not returned by all DCL commands, 93
    subprocesses should inherit symbols and logical names with caution, 268
    SYS$SCRATCH is not automatically deleted, 198
    updating indexed file alternate key fields requires use of changes attribute during creation, 225
    WRITE command does not create normal text file, 194
web. *See* WWW (World Wide Web).
web browser. *See also* WWW (World Wide Web).
    glossary entry, 422
web page
    displaying, 81
    glossary entry, 422
web server. *See also* WWW (World Wide Web).
    glossary entry, 422
WHILE loops. *See also* loops.
    DCL is missing WHILE loops, 3

whitespace
    F$EDIT can be used to remove, 129
    glossary entry, 422
    removed from input to INQUIRE unless double quotes, 126

wildcards. *See also* substitution.
    file operations use of, 161
    logical names allow use of * wildcard, 171
    pattern matching templates for parts of file spec components, 155
    spec, glossary entry, 422
    using with F$SEARCH, 157

windowing
    DCL has no windowing capabilities, 3

windows
    virtual device example, 245

working directory. *See also* directories.
    defined as default file directory, 88
    glossary entry, 422

world. *See also* access; protection; security.
    access category, who can access, 230

World Wide Web. *See* WWW.

worms
    possible problem for DCL, caution, 6

WRITE
    displaying text with, 75
    files, creating a new file, 194
    limitations on record size and expression values, 194
    mismatched writes in network tasks, 308
    output of WRITE is not normal text file, 194
    use in DECnet communications, 302

WRITE access
    description, 231

WRITE/UPDATE
    indexed files, using to update file, 225

writing
    files
        indexe d, 223
        sequential, 189

WWW (World Wide Web)
    displaying web pages, 81
    glossary entry, 422
    introduction, 319
    port 443 is secure web server port, 328
    port 80 is default web server port, 328
    web browser, 319
    web server, 319

XDA (eXample DCL Application)
    introduced as fictitious application for purposes of illustration, 7

XQTYPE.COM
    network task to recognize Ethernet controllers, 303

year
    2000
        date-related problems, 339
    2038
        date-related problems, 339

YESTERDAY
    absolute time in DCL, 207

zero
    local DECnet node is named zero, 148
    noninteger strings converted to integers become zero, 37
    version number giving highest version, 151

About this Book

THE TEXT OF THIS BOOK IS SET in Adobe Minion, while the headings are set in Adobe Rotis SemiSans and SemiSerif. The monospaced "typewriter" font is ZztexMono Regular. The bits of math here and there are set in MathTime by The TeXplorators Corporation.

The book was designed and composed by one of the authors, Paul, using the ZzTEX typesetting system. This system is based on Donald Knuth's TEX system, one of the great typesetting systems of the world. Paul developed ZzTEX and has been using it to compose technical books for 10 years, ever since he composed the first edition of this book.

All illustrations were created by Paul using CorelDRAW version 8.

The entire text was rekeyboarded from the first edition book by Cheryl Debankah. This was necessary because both archives, stored on floppy disks, were found to be corrupted. Floppy disks do not last 10 years.

The book was copyedited by Kristin Landon.

Dick Hannus designed the wonderful cover for this edition.

The folks at Butterworth-Heinnemann who managed this project include Elizabeth McCarthy, the acquisitions editor, Susan Prusak, the production editor, and Pam Chester, the assistant editor.

Thanks to everyone!

Page v   *Quietly Making Noise.* Coral Reefer Music © 1994, Written by Jimmy Buffett, Michael Tschudin. All rights reserved. Used by permission.

Page xx   *La Vie Dansante,* Jimmy Buffett / Michael Utley / Will Jennings © 1984 Coral Reefer Music BMI & Coconutley Music ASCAP & Time Warner Tamerlane Music & Blue Sky Rider Songs BMI.